RENEWALS 458-4574

DATE DUE

| | | | |
|---|---|---|---|
| | | | |
| | | | |
| | | | |
| | | | |
| | | | |
| | | | |
| | | | |
| | | | |
| | | | |
| | | | |
| | | | |
| | | | |
| | | | |
| | | | |
| | | | |
| | | | |

WITHDRAWN
UTSA Libraries

GAYLORD                                                         PRINTED IN U.S.A.

Philosophical Approaches to the Study of Literature

# Philosophical Approaches to the Study of Literature

Patrick Colm Hogan

University Press of Florida

Gainesville · Tallahassee · Tampa · Boca Raton
Pensacola · Orlando · Miami · Jacksonville

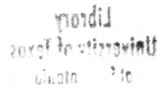

Library
University of Texas
of Austin

Copyright 2000 by the Board of Regents of the State of Florida
Printed in the United States of America on acid-free paper
All rights reserved

05  04  03  02  01  00   6  5  4  3  2  1

Library of Congress Cataloging-in-Publication Data
Hogan, Patrick Colm.
Philosophical approaches to the study of literature / Patrick Colm Hogan.
p.cm.
Includes bibliographical references and index.
ISBN 0-8130-1764-5 (alk. paper)
1. Criticism. 2. Literature—History and criticism—Theory, etc.
3. Literature—Philosophy. I. Title.
PN49.H625 2000
801'.95          00-021196

The University Press of Florida is the scholarly publishing agency for
the State University System of Florida, comprising Florida A&M
University, Florida Atlantic University, Florida International University,
Florida State University, University of Central Florida, University of
Florida, University of North Florida, University of South Florida, and
University of West Florida.

University Press of Florida
15 Northwest 15th Street
Gainesville, FL 32611-2079
http://www.upf.com

Library
University of Texas
at S     ntcuio

This book is dedicated to Rev. Walter J. Ong, S.J.

"Criticism is necessary because art implies something beyond itself."

# Contents

Acknowledgments  ix

Introduction: The Field of Literary Theory  1

**Part I: Classical and Early Modern Theories**

1. Classical Greece, the Arab World, and South Asia  13

2. Early Modern Europe: Philosophical Aesthetics,
Romanticism, Historical Materialism  43

**Part II: Modern and Contemporary Theories**

3. Philosophy of Mind and Experience: Phenomenology,
Existentialism, Hermeneutics, Pragmatism  107

4. Social and Political Philosophy: Ideological Critique,
Feminism, Theories of Culture and Power, Postmodernism  158

5. Philosophy of Language and Linguistic Autonomism:
Formalism, Bakhtinian Dialogism, Structuralism, Deconstruction  219

6. Philosophy of Language and Cognition: Analytic Philosophy,
Chomskyan Linguistics, Cognitive Science, Empirical Poetics  253

7. Literary Meta-Theory and the Philosophy of Science  313

Appendix: "I Dream It Is Afternoon When I Return To Delhi"
by Agha Shahid Ali  339

Bibliography  341

Index  355

# Acknowledgments

I tested both oral and written versions of the following chapters in graduate and undergraduate classes. I am grateful to my students for their comments. I should mention in particular Chris Amann, Marie Burman, Dan Connolly, Jeff DiCicco, Amy Dietz, Mike Flagge, Larry Foster, and Mark Jass.

The origins of the book extend back more than twenty years. As a junior in high school, I began reading Hegel and Marx (as well as Freud and Propp). Patrick Conley encouraged me in this, and helped me apply theory to literary texts. Just after high school, I met Rev. Walter Ong; over the next decade, he served as a mentor in philosophy and literary theory. After college, I was able to take graduate courses with a number of the theorists whose works I had read—Ong, Northrop Frye, Donald Davidson, Paul Ricoeur, and Norman Holland. The present volume was significantly shaped by these courses, as well as by more informal interactions with Elizabeth Anscombe, Jonathan Culler (whose outstanding *Structuralist Poetics* was one of the first works that drew me to literary theory), B. N. Pandit, and, above all, Noam Chomsky. For many years Mike Walsh urged me to undertake a project along these lines; without his urging, this book may not have been written. An earlier version of this manuscript benefited greatly from careful readings by Paul Hernadi and Brandy Kershner. I am very grateful to both of them. Finally, many thanks to my editor Sue Fernandez, who handled the manuscript with intelligence and care.

Parts of chapter 8 appeared previously as "What is feminism?" *Critical Survey* 5.1 (1993). Agha Shahid Ali's "I Dream It Is Afternoon When I Return to Delhi" from *The Half-Inch Himalayas* (copyright 1987 by Ali Agha Shahid, published by Wesleyan University Press) is reprinted by permission of the University Press of New England, Hanover, New Hampshire.

# Introduction

## The Field of Literary Theory

There is a sense in which literary theory is just one thing: the formulation of general principles concerning literary texts or the practices associated with these texts. Most of our attention in literary study is devoted to single works, sometimes to the works of a single author, sometimes to the works of a single period. When we do literary theory, we try to rethink these practices, to reunderstand what we are doing in examining single works, authors, periods, and to reunderstand the nature of works, authors, periods, in general. On the other hand, the way in which such rethinking and reunderstanding take place is highly varied. Thus, when we encounter literary theory concretely—in interpretations, theoretical polemics, and so on—we encounter it, not as a single project, but as a multiplicity of particular ideas and practices, goals and presuppositions. To make sense of this multiplicity, we need to identify some clear and readily applicable organizing principles.

Perhaps the most basic and obvious distinction is that between *descriptive* and *normative* theories. All literary theories have descriptive and normative elements. However, some theories set out to describe aspects of literature, while others set out to judge them. The former are concerned with what literature, in its various aspects, is; the latter are concerned with what literature, in its various aspects, should be. For each category, I should like to distinguish two primary subcategories: the *theory of interpretation* and the *theory of literature* for the descriptive category; *aesthetic theory* and *ethical/political theory* for the normative category.

A *theory of interpretation* does two things: (1) It defines the object of literary interpretation: literary meaning. And (2) it establishes a method of determining, in specific cases, what that meaning is. In other words, it says what meaning is in general (the verbal structure of the text, the author's intent, the response of "competent" readers), and it says what critics can do to find that meaning for specific texts (look at image patterns, read biographies, study histories). In short, a theory of interpretation, though a general theory, aims at isolating what is unique to individual literary works. A good theory of interpretation, when applied to *Othello*, will tell us something about what is particular to that play. A *theory of literature*, in contrast, focuses not on the unique, but on the common. It concerns the principles, structures, and so on, that are repeated across literary works.

Clearly, there are connections between the theory of interpretation and the theory of literature. Indeed, most theories of literature lead to at least partial theories of interpretation. For example, a psychoanalytic theory that explains literary creation by reference to Freud's account of dreams—a theory of literature that seeks to explain what all literature has in common—leads to the interpretation of particular literary works in terms of unconscious fantasy. On the other hand, it is important to emphasize the different goals of these undertakings, for if we do not keep this difference in mind, we may fail to recognize the value of one or the other undertaking and misjudge theories of that type. For example, if a theorist sets out to discover what all plots have in common, he/she is considering an important issue with ramifications for our broad understanding of literature, our knowledge of the human mind, and so on. However, the nature of the undertaking is such that it will probably not lead to terribly valuable or interesting interpretations of individual works. In consequence, if we judge such a theory by the criteria of a theory of interpretation, we are likely to undervalue it greatly. In other words, we risk a sort of literary theory version of the ugly duckling phenomenon—denigrating the theoretical swan because we insist on thinking of it as a duck.

Descriptive theories are meant to guide literary study, but not to guide literary creation or other sorts of literary decision. Evaluative theories, in contrast, are designed to guide literary creation, as well as our (evaluative) response to literature—including our practical decisions as to whether given works should be published, taught in schools, and so on. Again, there are two major subcategories of normative theory: *aesthetic theory*, which is concerned with what makes a literary work beautiful (sublime, aesthetically effective), and *ethical or political theory*, which is concerned with what makes a literary work ethically beneficial or politically admirable.

Literary theories are differentiable not only by reference to basic goals (interpretation, ethical evaluation, etc.), but also by reference to the primary objects of theoretical concern or focus. These too fall into a limited number of categories. Specifically, theorists tend to divide into one of three general groups, depending upon whether they conceive of literature as primarily a matter of language, mind, or society. Thus interpretive theories might focus on the text (language), authorial intent (mind), or historical context (society). Theories of literature may look for common textual structures, shared authorial propensities, patterns of social development in the genesis of literature. Ethical theories might be concerned with the author's views (for example, whether he/she was racist), the likely social effects of the work (for instance, whether it is likely to foster racism), or the linguistic implications of the work. Aesthetic theories may address an author's emotional expression or textual structure or social reception—and so on.

Each of these categories may be subdivided. Perhaps the most consequential divisions are among mentalistic theories. These may be roughly organized into three groups—cognitive, affective, and experiential. Cognitive theories concern reasoning, inference, understanding, general procedures of human judgment, and so forth. Affective theories concern human feeling, impulse, everything that falls under the names "instinct" and "emotion." Both cognitive and affective theories tend to have an "intrapsychic" focus. They tend to devote primary attention to the structure and operation of the individual mind. Experientially oriented theories, in contrast, concern the human mind in interaction with a material world and with other minds and focus on the physical and social relations into which the individual mind enters. Indeed, one could think of experiential theories as intermediate between psychological and social theories.

As this last point suggests, here as elsewhere, such approaches may or may not be mutually exclusive. Clearly, a theory of literature may be combined with an interpretive or aesthetic or ethical/political theory, even with all three. Moreover, a theory that focuses on language may or may not be at odds with a theory that focuses on cognition or society; it depends on the theories. Indeed, language-oriented theories are quite likely to be synthesized with mentalistic or social approaches. Some theorists conceive of language as autonomous, as relatively independent of individual mind or society. I shall refer to these more "pure" language theorists as "textualists" or "linguistic autonomists." But other theorists who focus on language see language as ultimately bound up with or even a function of cognition, affective impulse, human experience, or social structure. Clearly, then, these categories are not antithetical or mutually exclusive.

Nonetheless, there is a strong tendency for any given theorist to focus on one or another variety of object (social, mental, or linguistic). As a result, this provides a broad and useful, if to a degree loose, typology of literary theories as well.

In the following pages, I shall make repeated reference to these ways of organizing the field of literary theory. However, the volume as a whole is defined by yet a third principle, that of the disciplinary or subdisciplinary structures in which the theories in question are located. From the very beginning, most literary theories have not been simply literary. They have almost invariably involved the integration of literary concerns into the questions, and hypotheses, and methods of another discipline. For example, literary theory may be a type of anthropology, taking part in the study of foreign cultures. It may be subsumed under psychoanalysis, manifesting and extending the study of the unconscious mind. It may be understood as part of economics, or education theory, or neurophysiology. And there are literary theories of each sort. On the other hand, from Plato and Aristotle, through the Arabic and Indian theorists, to such contemporary figures as Jacques Derrida, literary theory has been developed most widely and most consistently as a part of philosophy. Indeed, it has frequently been integrated into technical philosophy and based on highly complex speculative or analytic systems, systems that are often unfamiliar and obscure to students of literature. The purpose of the present volume is to introduce the major literary theories that have their center or origin in technical or systematic philosophy, largely by explaining and clarifying that technical or systematic philosophy, both on its own and in relation to the study of literature.

Of course, it is not always an easy matter to determine what is to count as philosophical and what is not. I take it that I have included the literary theories everyone would agree are philosophical (Plato, Aristotle, Hume, Kant, Nietzsche, Marx, and so on), and excluded the literary theories that everyone would agree are not philosophical in the technical sense (Horace, Sidney, Corneille, Propp, Frye, and so on). However, a number of marginal cases remain (such as theories based in linguistics). Moreover, some nonphilosophical theories provide necessary background for some philosophical theories. In both types of case, I have tended toward inclusiveness. On the other hand, one has to stop somewhere. There will no doubt be theories and theorists that readers feel should have been included. I can only plead that the book is already long and simply could not include everyone. I do not intend it as a final and definitive listing of all philosophical literary theory. Rather, I intend it to be a representative treatment that draws from all of the central *schools* of philosophical literary theory (phenomenology, deconstruction, and so on)—but not every theory or theorist from these schools—and from a reasonable selection of more marginally philosophical schools (such as structuralism).

In organizing the following chapters, I have followed the standard practice of giving an historical rather than a conceptual structure to the treatment of philosophical theories formulated prior to the twentieth century. Thus the first chapter treats classical theories of Europe, the Arab world, and South Asia, while the second chapter takes up philosophical aesthetics, Romanticism, and historical materialism. All subsequent theories are organized conceptually, by reference to the area of philosophy in which they are located. In parallel with the preceding division of object in literary theory, I take the primary categories to be the following: social and political philosophy, parallel to the social category of literary theory; philosophy of language, parallel to the linguistic category; philosophy of mind, parallel to the mentalistic category. Finally, philosophy of science may be added to this list in parallel with literary meta-theory, which is to say, the formulation of general principles concerning literary *theories* or the practices associated with these theories (as opposed to the formulation of general principles concerning literary *texts* and the practices associated with these texts).

More exactly, the first chapter begins with Plato and Aristotle, the two earliest theorists of note in any tradition. Following this, I turn to the Arabic tradition and discuss the major commentators on Aristotle, particularly al-Fārābī, Ibn Sinā, and Ibn Rushd. In conclusion, I take up the Indian tradition, discussing the two major schools of classical Indian literary theory—*dhvani* and *rasa,* or suggestion and sentiment—and the ideas of such influential philosophers as Ānandavardhana and Abhinavagupta. Though little known in the West, both the Arabic and Sanskrit traditions of literary theory were highly developed and highly philosophically sophisticated, arguably far more so than anything to be found in the European tradition from Aristotle until the eighteenth century.

The second chapter returns to Europe, beginning with the philosophical aesthetics of Burke, Hume, and, most importantly, Kant. It then turns to Romanticism, focusing on a few of the great Idealist and post-Idealist philosophers (Fichte, Schelling, Hegel, Nietzsche) and some of their literary fellow travelers (Schiller, Coleridge, Shelley, de Stael). It is no accident that the historical overview places such an emphasis on Romanticism. One of the recurring motifs in the following pages is that Romanticism marks a distinctive break with previous literary theory and in effect maps out the major tendencies of virtually all subsequent continental philosophical theory—and even some Anglo-American theory—up to our own day. The final section of this chapter considers one of the most practically influential philosophical theories ever articulated—Marx's historical materialism, at once an extension and a thorough repudiation of Romantic Idealism.

The third chapter brings us into the twentieth century, taking up the main philosophical developments out of Idealism—phenomenology, existentialism, and hermeneutics—as well as the similar American movement of Pragmatism. This chapter focuses on the philosophy of mind and experience, considering Husserl, the literary extensions of Husserl by Ingarden and others, Heidegger, Sartre, Gadamer, Habermas, Dewey, and a few more minor figures related to phenomenology.

While philosophers of experience are most obviously indebted to Kant and the Romantics, the major social and political philosophers (or, rather, the social and political philosophers who have had the most significant impact on literary theory) have been more obviously writing in the tradition of Marx. In chapter 4, we take up these social and political philosophies. The first section returns to Marxism, considering not historical materialism, but the Marxist notions of ideology and ideological critique. These notions certainly figure in the writings of Marx and Engels. However, they have been developed thoroughly only by later theorists, and thus are more appropriately included here than in the historical chapter. Relatively little feminist theory derives from professional philosophy or is clearly associated with or derived from philosophical movements. Nonetheless, feminism is perhaps the most important and influential movement in cultural and political thought bearing on literary study today. It is also enormously diverse, and areas of feminist thought overlap ideological critique and culture study. In the second section, then, I sketch an outline of feminist positions as they occur in influential theoretical writings of the past several decades. The third section begins with Michel Foucault's theories of institutional structure, knowledge, and power. From here, the discussion turns to two important varieties of "culture study." The first, derived to a significant extent from Foucault's work, is New Historicism; the second is that of Pierre Bourdieu. The final section takes up a specific area of culture study, postmodern theory, considering the ideas of Jean Francois Lyotard, Jean Baudrillard, and Fredric Jameson.

Chapter 5 moves from the experientially and socially oriented theories to consider the main textualist currents in the philosophy of language and linguistics—Russian formalism and Bakhtin's response to Russian formalism, French structuralism, and Derridaean deconstruction. This chapter has an unusual amount of nonphilosophical material in the treatment of formalism and structuralism, especially in the treatment of de Saussure. This is due in part to the fact that formalism provides important background for Bakhtin, while structuralism provides necessary background for deconstruction. Moreover, it seemed appropriate to treat Jakobson and de Saussure in parallel with Chomsky, who is clearly a philosopher in the technical sense.

The last two chapters turn to Anglo-American philosophy. Chapter 6 extends the consideration of the philosophy of language (and linguistics), this time incorporating cognitive mentalism. It begins with logical positivism and logical atomism, continuing through more recent formally oriented analytic philosophers, such as Willard Quine and Donald Davidson. From here, it turns to the ordinary language philosophy of Austin, Grice, and Searle, and the related work of Wittgenstein and Elizabeth Anscombe. It also takes up extensions of this work by Mary Louise Pratt and others. The chapter continues with a consideration of recent linguistic work by Noam Chomsky and still more recent developments in cognitive science, concluding with a brief discussion of empirical poetics, an important adjunct to both Chomskyan and cognitive theories.

The final chapter turns to the issue of meta-theory and the philosophy of science, which forms the basis for most meta-theoretical discussion in literary study today. This chapter presents an overview of major trends in the philosophy of science, discussing not only Karl Popper and Thomas Kuhn—the theorists most widely cited by literary critics—but also Imre Lakatos, Roy Bhaskar, Paul Feyerabend, and others.

There are many reasons why one might study literary theory, and correspondingly many ways in which one might approach its evaluation. One might study literary theory in order to achieve a certain level of professional competence—in which case, one's concern is not with the validity of the theories in question, but with their standing or prestige. One might study theories as tools, heuristic devices for producing new interpretations of particular literary works. In that case too the validity of the theory is not a primary concern. Only the "fecundity" of the theory is significant. One might study literary theory as an incitement to reflection and as a challenge to otherwise unquestioned presuppositions. Here, a theory has merit insofar as it highlights and criticizes standard views. These are all common reasons for studying literary theory, and common methods for evaluating literary theories.

Perhaps the least common way of approaching literary theory—but, in my view, the most important way—is as a system of explanatory hypotheses regarding interpretation, literary structure, and so forth. Even the fecundity and intellectual challenge of a theory must in part rest on this. After all, one presumably wants new interpretations that are illuminating, not merely novel; challenges to dogma that are superior to the dogma, or that lead to ideas superior to the dogma. For this, one needs a theory that, in general, has greater evidential validity and explanatory reach than the alternatives. Or perhaps one needs a set of competing theories of comparable validity and reach. In any case, issues of explanatory force, empirical adequacy, and so forth, enter crucially. It is here that the philosophy of science has obvious relevance, for the systematic meta-theoretical study of science has been extremely valuable in examining precisely what it means to understand and evaluate a theory as a system of explanatory hypotheses. At the same time, philosophy of science has broader relevance as well, contributing significantly to our (meta-theoretical) understanding of the organization or structure of theories, the ordinary practices of theorists, the pervasiveness of interpretive bias, and so on.

My general stance in explicating these theories is certainly influenced by the philosophy of science. However, it is perhaps best characterized in terms of Paul Ricoeur's distinction between critical and revelatory hermeneutics. Simplifying somewhat, we could say that a critical hermeneutics sets out to show where a philosophical theory fails, where it is contradictory, or inadequate to the facts, or misleading. A revelatory hermeneutics, in contrast, sets out to show where such a theory succeeds, how it might yield new insights, more general comprehension, deeper aesthetic pleasures. (For a more technical definition of Ricoeur's distinction, in its philosophical context, see chapter 3 below.) I have tried to combine both modes with respect to each theory or type of theory. However, in some cases, I have relied more on one hermeneutic mode than the other. In part, this is the result of my own personal sense of which theories are the most valuable, which lend themselves most readily to revelatory interpretation, and which to critical interpretation. However, the primary reason for the difference has to do with the professional study of literary theory and the standard evaluative presumptions that pervade such study. As John

Stuart Mill wrote, "if either of . . . two opinions has a better claim than the other, not merely to be tolerated, but to be encouraged and countenanced, it is the one which happens at the particular time and place to be in a minority. That is the opinion which, for the time being, represents the neglected interests, the side of human well-being which is in danger of obtaining less than its share" (297). I have tried to follow the principle this analysis implies. In other words, I have leaned toward critical hermeneutics in those cases where the value of a theory is widely accepted, and leaned toward revelatory hermeneutics in those cases where the value of a theory is widely discounted (or simply ignored). My hope is that this will foster more balanced dialogue on literary theory than has been the case in recent years, and will encourage a broader, more inclusive understanding of literary theory, both among those who specialize in the field, pursuing theoretical reflection as an end in itself, and among those who draw on literary theory for its instrumental value in their own distinct areas of specialization.

Finally, even with theories that are not primarily interpretive, I have made a point of giving concrete examples of literary applications. In order to make the applications more accessible, and to make clear both the similarities and differences among the various theories, I have, when possible, focused on a single work, Shakespeare's *Othello*. When a lyric poem is more appropriate, I have most often turned to Agha Shahid Ali's "I Dream It Is Afternoon When I Return to Delhi," which is reprinted as an appendix.

# I

---

# Classical and
# Early Modern Theories

# 1

## Classical Greece, the Arab World, and South Asia

Like every historical treatment of philosophical literary theory, this chapter begins with Plato and Aristotle. Few treatments, however, go on to discuss the important Arabic commentators on those seminal Greek writers, commentators such as al-Fārābī, Ibn Sīnā, and Ibn Rushd—the topic of section 2. The third section takes up the other great tradition of Classical and medieval philosophical literary theory, that of India, which began with the ancient *Nāṭyaśāstra* and culminated in the work of Ānandavardhana and Abhinavagupta some ten centuries later.

### Plato and Aristotle

As in so much else, Plato and Aristotle initiated a debate in literary theory that has been replicated again and again in both the West and the East. Where Plato sees poetry as inspiration, Aristotle sees it as craft; where Plato stresses the instrumental, ethical function of literature, Aristotle emphasizes its intrinsic, aesthetical value; where Plato views literature as typically opposed to reason and philosophy, Aristotle argues that it is allied with both; where Plato analyzes literature to see how it might serve the state, Aristotle analyzes literature to see how it might move the heart; while both share a view of poetry as mimesis or imitation, Plato emphasizes that imitation is secondary to and representative of some real object, whereas Aristotle emphasizes that imitation is creative and thus not bound by realism.

Plato's two most widely read discussions of literature are the early dialogue "Ion" and various sections from the *Republic*. In "Ion," Plato presents his view that "all good poets, epic as well as lyric, compose their beautiful poems not by art, but because they are inspired or possessed";

moreover, when a poet is inspired, "reason is no longer in him" (14). This case is demonstrated by way of a hyperrealist argument, which tacitly relies on the view that the highest achievement of art is a reproduction of reality. Specifically, Socrates argues that the poet is lacking in art and reason by demonstrating two things: (1) In creating a work of art, the poet necessarily represents the objects of other arts (thus he/she may represent illness, the object of medicine, or war, the object of military science), and (2) he/she does not actually know those arts (that is, he/she is not a doctor or a general).

In "Ion," these arguments do not lead to any practical conclusions. However, they are taken up again in the *Republic* as part of an ethico-political evaluation of literary works and a defense of wide-ranging censorship. In the *Republic*, Plato is concerned to establish an outline of utopia, the perfect society. It is in this ethical/political context that he raises the issue of literature, immediately announcing: "the first thing will be to establish a censorship of the writers of fiction," so that "mothers and nurses tell their children the authorized [tales] only" (141). The problem with fiction is twofold. Fiction is "false"; and, even when true, it often serves "no good purpose" (142). Plato vacillates between these criteria. Frequently, he insists that the major problem is that poets misrepresent the world and are thus distant from reason. But equally often he denies the importance of realism and affirms only the prerogatives of the state, as when he says, "even if they were true, [certain tales] ought certainly not to be lightly told to young and thoughtless persons; if possible, they had better be buried in silence." Or later when he insists that "if anyone at all is to have the privilege of lying, the rulers of the state should be the persons; and they, in their dealings either with enemies or with their own citizens, may be allowed to lie for the public good" (154).

Plato implicitly reconciles these views by drawing on his theory of the Ideas. For Plato, the material world is an imperfect realization of the Ideal world. To take a simple example, any physical chair is an imperfect realization of Ideal "chairness." The Idea of a chair is perfect, while the physical object is necessarily a more or less flawed embodiment of that Idea. For Plato, then, the most fully real chair is the Idea, for it is perfect and eternal, while any material chair is imperfect and ephemeral. As Hegel pointed out, there is a certain common sense to this seemingly outrageous idea. Suppose we meet someone who does not know what a harpsichord is and asks us to explain. We do not describe a particular harpsichord—for example, the stringless, one-legged harpsichord lying on its side in the basement of the music building—but rather the "idea" of a harpsichord. The battered instrument in the basement, we might say, is not a "real" harpsi-chord. For Plato, the same holds for virtue as holds for chairs and harpsi-chords. Specifically, the good and the expedient, the just and the benefi-cial, are unified in the Idea of the Good, and usually in material reality as well, just as a harpsichord has strings in the Idea of a harpsichord and usually has them in material reality. There are, however, occasional excep-tions due to accident.

More exactly, Plato argues that "the good is advantageous" and "there-fore the cause of well-being" (144), for that is its essential or Ideal nature. Sometimes it does happen that the good is not advantageous, just as some-times it happens that harpsichords lack strings. But just as it would be a mistake to represent harpsichords as stringless, it is a mistake to represent the good as not advantageous, even though this is sometimes true in the imperfect, material world. Moreover, in the case of goodness, this mistaken representation might have dire social consequences. Thus the guardians of the state cannot permit art that does not illustrate the essen-tial connection between virtue and well-being. The poet must represent only the "wicked" as punished; he/she must not represent good people as suffering (145), for it is crucial to the proper functioning of the state that the populace believe that good actions (as defined by the state) are in their own best interest. Unfortunately, "poets and storytellers are guilty of mak-ing the gravest misstatements when they tell us that wicked men are often happy and the good miserable . . .—these things we shall forbid them to utter, and command them to sing and describe the opposite" (158).

Plato further develops the relation between the Ideal and the poetic by arguing that there are three levels of reality. The most real things are, again, the Ideas, which are made by God. Less real than these are the im-perfect realizations of the Ideas in material objects. Least real of all are the poet's representations of these material objects. Plato is explicit on this: the poet is not, in fact, a maker. He/she is merely a copier; indeed, he/she is the copier of a copy. Thus, God makes the Idea of a bed, and a craftsperson makes a material bed, but a poet merely makes a representation of a mate-rial bed (390–91). To make matters worse, the poet may focus on those aspects of the copy, the material world, that are imperfections with respect to the Ideal—the absence of strings in a particular harpsichord, or, more seriously, the suffering of a particular person who has behaved justly. This is why it is crucial that the poets be controlled by the state, so that in mat-ters of justice and happiness, they represent the material world insofar as it mirrors the Ideal, not insofar as it diverges from the Ideal.

Plato takes his attack upon poetic falsity beyond the object of imitation to what Aristotle will call the "manner" of imitation as well. Specifically, Plato points out that a poet may speak in his/her own voice or may assume the voice of a character. According to Plato, the latter sort of poetry—including, for example, all drama—is execrable on two counts. First of all, it is a lie, for by definition the poet is in these cases assuming a persona that is not his/her own. Secondly, it invariably involves the poet—a man, for Plato—in assuming the character of inferiors. How can we raise "good men" when we present the spectacle of a man "imitat[ing] a woman" or a slave, Plato asks—especially as these women and slaves are often presented in emotionally distraught conditions that it is unmanly and undignified to imitate (401). For this reason, Plato bans from his ideal state all poetry in which speakers assume voices that are not their own.

Plato does not confine his concern about literary emotion to the question of narrative voice. A central part of his criticism of literature is that it is overly emotional. The mind has a rational faculty that should always be in control of the passions. The task of philosophers—especially those who are guardians of the ideal state—is to articulate and enact reason themselves and to encourage in all others the complete domination of reason. In this sense, poetry is diametrically opposed to philosophy (403), for "the imitative poet who aims at being popular [that is, the poet who is not guided by the dictates of the leaders of state] is not by nature made, nor is his art intended, to please or to affect the rational principle in the soul; but he will appeal rather to the lachrymose and fitful temper, which is easily imitated"; this poet "awakens and nourishes" the "inferior part of the soul" or passion, "and by strengthening it impairs the reason" and makes men take "the part of a woman" in being hysterical and undignified (400–401). Thus, on the whole, "poetry . . . feeds and waters the passions instead of drying them up" (402–3). Plato has particular concern with the emotions of pity and fear. For in giving rise to pity for others, he insists, poetry encourages self-pity (402). And in giving rise to fear, it destroys the courage of men (150). Plato concludes that "hymns to the gods and praises of famous men are the only poetry which ought to be admitted into our state" (403).

Though the specific conclusions change considerably, it is easy to see that Plato's instrumental view of literature, his stringent evaluation of literature in terms of political function, is far from unique in history. It is a view that recurs in an extreme form in the Soviet Union or Iran or in the pronouncements of the Moral Majority. However, it also recurs, in a less extreme form, in debates over textbooks, anthologies, and canon revision. Seeing literature primarily as politics is a view to be found in all political and religious groups, right and left, ancient and modern. And it is almost always opposed to a view that strives to see literature both in its own terms and in a broader aesthetic context. This view also is to be found in all political and religious groups. Its first important exponent was Aristotle. For Aristotle did not deny the political or ethical responsibilities of the poet, or the critic. But he wanted to understand literature as a literary phenomenon, as aesthetic, and not confine it to a political function.

Indeed, Aristotle responded to Plato's views virtually point for point. Before going on to elaborate Aristotle's theory of poetry, it is worth going through and enumerating these responses. First of all, Aristotle's entire project in the *Poetics* is to isolate and articulate the rules of art, the principles that define a well-made play or poem, the very principles denied by Plato in his insistence that poetry is inspiration, not craft. Aristotle also responds to Plato's notion that the poet must have knowledge of the various arts he/she imitates (such as medicine). Specifically, Aristotle distinguishes between errors of representation that are due to a lack of poetic skill, and errors of representation that are due to a lack of technical knowledge (for example, medical knowledge); he then goes on to maintain that only the former are "essential to the poetry" (99), clearly indicating the relative unimportance of special knowledges of the sort emphasized by Plato.

While Plato claims that a poet may be forgiven misrepresentation only if this benefits the state, Aristotle responds that a poet may be forgiven even a representation of "the impossible" if the aesthetical effect of the work is thereby enhanced (99). To Plato's view that in poetry the good should succeed and the wicked suffer, for this is the most politically effective plot, Aristotle offers the alternative that tragedy must be the story "of a man who is not eminently good and just, yet whose misfortune is brought about not by vice or depravity, but by some error or frailty" (45), for this is the most aesthetically effective plot. In contrast with Plato's notion that the poet is not a maker, but a copier of a copy, Aristotle gives his essay a title that roughly means "On Making" (it certainly does not mean "On Copying"), urges the poet "to show invention," and stresses that poets may portray a wide range of real and unreal subjects, including "things as they were or are," "things as they ought to be," and "things as they are said or thought to be" (97). Indeed, for Aristotle, poetry is potentially superior to historical truth primarily due to this broad freedom of poetic imitation (35).

While Plato finds it objectionable for a poet to assume another voice, Aristotle maintains that the "poet should speak as little as possible in his own person" (93); and while Plato has particular scorn for drama, Aristotle views tragedy as the most excellent of poetic genres (111). In connection with this, Plato was particularly disturbed by the prospect of men imitating women and slaves, and poetry making men less manly and dignified. In a passage that sounds sexist and classist, Aristotle responds to this assertion of Plato in a way that, in context, is antisexist and anticlassist (if insufficiently so, from our point of view): "A woman may be good, and also a slave; though the woman may be said to be inferior, and the slave wholly vulgar [*phaulos,* perhaps as opposed to *sophos*—thus the woman is inferior in intellectual cultivation, the slave wholly lacking in it; or as opposed to *spoudaios,* thus less weighty or, perhaps, consequential—in, for example, social affairs]" (52, my translation; Butcher's here is very misleading).

And while Plato views poetry as opposed to philosophy, Aristotle sees the two as closely linked, because "poetry tends to express the universal" (35). Moreover, by "universal" here, Aristotle does not mean the Platonic Ideal (as defined by the state), but the empirical universal "according to the law of probability or necessity" (35). Perhaps most strikingly, Plato sees poetry as producing a politically dangerous excitement of the passions, especially the unmanly emotions of pity and fear. But Aristotle sees tragedy as achieving its highest aesthetic aim through the excitement and subsequent catharsis or purging of pity and fear (23).

But Aristotle's poetics is not primarily a response to Plato. It is a coherent theory of poetry, and is most importantly to be understood in that context. Aristotle sets himself the task of outlining the general nature and varieties of poetry, of devising a theory of literature in the above sense. He begins by noting that art is mimesis. This is a notoriously difficult and controversial notion. However, several things about the idea are fairly clear. First, an art is imitative, for Aristotle, in the sense that it is not the functional, real thing. Rather, it repeats aspects of the real thing, outside of a practical context, or at least outside of an intrinsically practical context. A painting of a chair is not itself a chair and does not function as a chair. Rather, a painting of a chair takes certain aspects of the chair and repeats them. Music too can be mimetic in this sense. Thus a sorrowful composition might abstract a steady, slow rhythm from a funeral procession; the loud volume of argument or battle may be imitated in a work of anger and conflict, and so on. The piece of music is not itself a funeral procession or argument or battle. However, it repeats certain aspects of these. Turning to poetry, the same point holds. A dramatist may represent a murder on stage, but it is not in fact a murder; it is an imitation of a murder. The second thing to note about imitation is that, as we have already indicated, for Aristotle imitation implies some degree of creativity. The painting, the music, the drama are not mere copies, but creative abstractions.

Having noted that mimesis is the common characteristic of all arts, Aristotle goes on to maintain that arts may be distinguished in several ways; he later organizes these under three categories: "the medium, the objects, and the manner" of imitation (13). He begins by discussing medium. Painting, for example, uses the media of color and form; music employs harmony and rhythm. Poetry, of course, makes primary use of language. But it also uses rhythm—meter, in particular—and, when it is sung, harmony. Aristotle stresses that metrical use of language alone does not qualify a work as poetry. An historical or scientific treatise may be written in verse, but it is not thereby poetry, for it is not imitation. Note that statements such as this stress the degree to which imitation is creative, a remaking of the world rather than a mirroring of it. Art is mimetic, but history and science are not, precisely because history and science seek to mirror the world, precisely because they seek to *copy* exactly; art does not.

In poetry, there are three manners of imitation. The poet may tell the tale in his/her own voice "unchanged," or he/she may adopt another voice or personality, or he/she "may present all . . . [the] characters as living and moving before us" (13). The first is, so to speak, pure narrative, in which the narrator speaks solely in his/her own voice, never taking up the voice of a character. The third is drama, in which actors speak only as characters and in which there is no narrator. The second is, in a sense, intermediate between the other two. Works of this sort are told by a narrator, and are thus a form of narrative. However, the poet imitates the voice of one or more characters (including the voices of women and slaves, as Plato complained), speaking as if he/she were those characters.

The objects of poetry are, Aristotle tells us, "people in action." Moreover, these people and their actions may be either weighty and serious (*spoudaious*) or slight and trifling (*phaulous*), and their character may be superior to us, equal to us, or inferior to us. Comedy concerns inferior characters in trifling situations; tragedy concerns superior characters in serious situations. In addition, Aristotle adds subsequently, both comic and tragic characters are marked by a flaw or error.

Aristotle discusses tragedy at length. He begins by maintaining that tragedy "is an imitation of an action that is serious, complete, and of a certain magnitude; in language embellished with each kind of artistic ornament . . . in the form of action, not of narrative; through pity and fear effecting the proper purgation of these emotions" (23). We should consider these elements in turn. The simplest is ornate language; this is language involving rhythm and harmony, which form the media of imitation. Aristotle argues that style should be unusual but still clear, "[f]or by deviating in exceptional cases from the normal idiom, the language will gain distinction; while, at the same time, the partial conformity with usage will give perspicuity" (83). Also relatively uncomplicated is what Aristotle refers to as spectacle—dramatization or staging—that is, everything resulting from the manner of presentation in which actors speak in the voices of characters.

The rest of the definition of tragedy concerns the object of imitation, and the effect of imitation. An action necessarily involves plot and character, a sequence of events and a number of agents. The agents or characters are defined by personal qualities that explain their actions. An action may also involve "thought" or sequences of reasoning. Plot, character, and thought are, then, the objects of imitation in tragedy. Of these, plot—namely, the "synthesis of incidents," their integration—is the most important. Character is second, and thought is the least important. Character and thought are subsidiary to plot for they are delineated in a drama only in order to explain the action. A playwright does not portray random character traits or random sequences of reasoning, however intrinsically interesting, but rather portrays those aspects of character and those sequences of thought that are relevant to the action.

Aristotle does allow for works that concentrate on character (see 65–66). His point is merely that these works are either not tragedies at all, or are inferior as tragedy—though they may be valuable in other ways. As he puts it: "if you string together a set of speeches expressive of character, and well finished in point of diction and thought, you will not produce the essential *tragic effect* nearly so well as with a play which, however deficient in these respects, yet has a plot and artistically constructed incidents" (27, emphasis added). This is due primarily to the fact that tragedy concerns happiness and unhappiness, and while "character determines men's qualities . . . it is by their actions that they are happy or the reverse" (27).

In keeping with this hierarchy, Aristotle discusses plot at some length. His opening characterization of tragedy as "serious, complete, and of a certain magnitude" is primarily a characterization of plot, and is worth examining in some detail. "Serious" is *"spoudaias,"* which includes the senses of "weighty" and "intense." Here, again, is the implicit contrast with the slight or trifling comedy. "Complete" is *"teleias,"* having achieved its *telos* or end or goal. The idea, then, is that a tragic plot is a serious action that reaches a resolution and that is of an appropriate length. As he explains subsequently, "in the plot, a certain length is necessary, and a length which can be easily embraced by the memory" (32–33). In other words, the work should be neither too short nor too long. If it is too short, it hardly counts as a plot at all. If it is too long, the dramatic intensity is dissipated; we may even have forgotten the beginning by the time we get to the end.

More exactly, for Aristotle, plot is a "synthesis" or integration of incidents into a coherent structure. It is "complete" or resolved (teleias) and "whole" ("holēs") only if it has a beginning, middle, and end. Aristotle defines these terms in a famous passage: "A beginning is that which does not itself necessarily follow anything but after which something naturally is or comes to be. An end, on the contrary, is that which itself naturally follows some other thing, either by necessity, or as a rule, but has nothing following it. A middle is that which follows something as some other thing follows it" (31, altered). While this definition hardly solves all the problems connected with understanding plot, it is not trivial, as it might at first seem. Specifically, Aristotle identifies plot as a coherent causal sequence. In other words, it is a sequence of events that leads to a result, and this result is explained by the preceding events. Plot involves all and only what is necessary to understand the outcome.

Perhaps if we go a bit beyond Aristotle, developing his idea, we will see its value. Specifically, if we place the definition in the context of everyday or normal events as understood by the audience—and, as we shall see, Aristotle is ultimately very concerned with the reaction of the audience—then this comes close to being an adequate definition of plot. Specifically, we all have some notion of normalcy, of what sorts of things happen in an ordinary day. These are things that do not need explanation. "This morning I ate breakfast" does not require explanation. "This morning I skipped breakfast" does, because it is not the norm. We may both extend and appreciate Aristotle's notion of beginning, middle, and end by redefining a plot as a nonnormal causal sequence such that before the beginning and after the end we can assume normalcy. "He got mad and hit me" is not a plot, because it does not tell us why he got mad or what happened afterwards. In contrast, consider the following: "I accidentally bumped into a fellow on the street and knocked him over. Evidently, he had just lost his job and was mad at the world, so he jumped up and socked me, then went away. Fortunately nothing was broken, though I was sore for a few days. I haven't seen him since." This is a complete causal sequence, at least with respect to the speaker. It is complete (that is, resolved and whole) because we can assume normal activities on the speaker's part both before and after the events related. In other words, there is no point in asking: "What happened then?" or "What happened before that?" The first question would only get an answer such as "I just went on with my life"; the second would get an answer such as "Nothing, I was just walking along" (compare Labov 366).

It is worth noting that, while this story has a beginning and an end, it has virtually no middle, and thus lacks proper magnitude. By Aristotle's criteria, it is simply too short to be a successful plot. Moreover, to be a genuine tragedy, the consequences must be more serious. In order to satisfy Aristotle on this score, we could make the man a sociopath who suppresses his anger, then follows the speaker, planning revenge, perhaps murder.

Returning to the structure of plot, Aristotle goes on to stress causal necessity yet again. In a famous passage, he contrasts poetry with both philosophy and history or historiography. Historiography concerns only what has actually happened, particular sequences of events that may be a matter of mere accident. Philosophy—which, of course, includes natural philosophy or what we would call "science"—isolates the universal, that is, the principles of probability and necessity, but removed from particulars. Poetry, Aristotle insists, concerns particular sequences of events structured according to the causal principles of probability and necessity. In other words, poetry takes the universals discussed in philosophy, primarily those of causal necessity, and manifests them in particular sequences of events of the sort examined in historiography; poetry combines the principled generality of philosophy with the concrete particularity of history, thereby avoiding the abstraction of the former and the contingency of the latter. This view of the relation between poetry, philosophy, and history had tremendous influence on later writers; however, it was most often changed to an opposition based on morality rather than causal coherence.

Despite all this discussion of causality, Aristotle does allow for certain sorts of plot that are not strictly causal, but rather achieve resolution by "design." He gives the following example: "We may instance the statue of Mitys at Argos, which fell upon his murderer while he was a spectator at a festival, and killed him." "Such events," he explains, "seem not to be due to mere chance" (39). This category of "design" includes what we would refer to as "poetic justice," but also a wide range of other noncausal sequences that viewers would nonetheless feel to be resolutions.

As this last point indicates, the structure of plot is, for Aristotle, always the experienced structure. A plot is successful only if we find it unified, not if it is unified in and of itself. This is why Aristotle says that the poet has no choice but to imitate one of three objects: "things as they were or are," "things as they ought to be," or "things as they are said or thought to be" (97). Indeed, if the poet "describes the impossible, he is guilty of an error; but the error may be justified, if the end [or goal] of the art be thereby attained . . . if, that is, the effect of this or any other part of the poem is thus rendered more striking" (99). Indeed, Aristotle goes so far as to insist that "the poet should prefer probable impossibilities to improbable possibilities" (95); he/she should prefer impossibilities that readers accept, impossibilities that are aesthetically effective, over possibilities that readers do not accept, possibilities that are not aesthetically effective. (The point is made clear by Aristotle's use of "'*apithana*"—translated by Butcher as "improbable," but perhaps more appropriately rendered "unconvincing" [see Liddell and Scott 82].)

In keeping with this emphasis on the spectator, Aristotle goes on to indicate that the tragic effect "is best produced when the events come on us by surprise; and the effect is heightened when, at they same time, they follow as cause and effect" (39). Aristotle is here isolating what has come to be called "retrospective necessity." The most effective causal sequence is one that does not allow us to infer what is going to happen, but does allow us to understand, retrospectively, how it did happen. In other words, the best plot is not one, after which we say, "Of course the butler did it; that was obvious by the third act." Nor is it one that causes us to say, "The butler did it? Why? I don't understand." Rather, the best plot is a plot after which we say, "My God! The butler did it! Now it makes sense!"

But surprise and necessity too are insufficient. The tragic events must inspire fear or pity in the spectators. For this to occur, the plot must involve a change in fortune for the main character. Plots presenting such a change may be either simple or complex. In a simple plot, the progression is steady from good fortune to ill. In a complex plot, however, there is a sudden reversal or a recognition, or both. "Reversal of the Situation is a change by which the action veers round to its opposite, subject always to our rule of probability or necessity," while recognition "is a change from ignorance to knowledge, producing love or hate between the persons destined by the poet for good or bad fortune" (41). Aristotle notes that these are particularly effective means for producing surprise in a causal sequence (43). They are followed by what he calls the "scene of suffering" or *pathos*. (There are a number of complications in Aristotle's account of "reversal of the situation" or *peripeteia*, especially as this is related to or differentiated from "change of fortune" or *metabasis*. For a discussion, see Butcher 329–31.)

We may illustrate by reference to *Othello*. Othello and Desdemona are initially happy and in love. By a (causally) plausible sequence of events, Othello is turned against Desdemona, until he falsely believes that he has caught her in adultery, that he has achieved a recognition of her true character, a recognition that, of course, produces "hate between the persons destined by the poet for . . . bad fortune." This leads directly to the moment of reversal when he murders her. Shortly after this follows his true recognition that she was innocent; this, then, leads to a scene of suffering in Othello's anguished final speech, ending in death. (Aristotle names the first part, up to the reversal, "tying-up" or "complication," and the second part "untying" or "denouement.") Some readers will disagree with my view that the development of Othello's jealousy is plausible as a causal sequence. However, this is likely to fit Aristotle's view equally well, for readers will probably find the play less effective insofar as they find it causally implausible.

Again, the purpose of the entire structure is to produce fear and pity in the spectators, and to lead to the purging or "catharsis" of these emotions; the point is to call up these tense and conflicted emotions, and then resolve them, leading to a feeling of emotional release or calm.

More exactly, in Aristotle's view, a successful tragedy should move us, arouse our feelings, but it should integrate those feelings into a structure—a causally coherent sequence of events—that resolves them. A tragedy will arouse our feelings by presenting us with a hero whose character and situation inspire empathy. Thus the hero cannot be so degraded that we would neither fear for him/her nor pity him/her. On the other hand, the hero also cannot be faultless, for then, in Aristotle's view, his/her suffering would shock our sensibility. Seeing the completely innocent subjected to cruelty makes life appear senseless—not necessary, but random, and thus unresolvably painful. In consequence, the ideal tragic hero is a person "who is not eminently good and just, yet whose misfortune is brought about not by vice or depravity, but by some error or frailty" (45). We most pity and most fear for a character who is good, but flawed.

The point is closely related to Aristotle's distinction among degrees of culpability in the *Nicomachean Ethics*. In that work, Aristotle distinguishes purely accidental events, for which the agent bears no moral responsibility; intentionally chosen acts, for which the agent bears full responsibility and which result finally a morally depraved character; and finally those intermediate cases that are neither accidents nor the result of full knowledge or full choice. In these intermediate cases, the agent is indeed morally responsible. However, the wrongful act does not result from an immoral character; rather, it results from some more local or specific ethical failing, such as culpable misunderstanding or rashness in the particular case at hand (see 415, 1135b). Indeed, in the *Ethics,* Aristotle notes that it is these intermediate cases that inspire "pity" (350, 1110b–1111a).

Othello provides a good example here as well. One standard interpretation of Othello's character is that he is a noble soul who suffers from excessive jealousy, which thus becomes his tragic flaw. It is important to note, however, that this is not the only way in which one can apply Aristotle to the play. Indeed, in my view, it is not a particularly good way. There seems little evidence that Othello is prone to excessive jealousy, or that he cannot control his violent impulses. Within the play itself, we find Iago convinced of his wife's infidelity on virtually no grounds whatsoever, and Cassio brawling at the least provocation. Othello is, in fact, calm, reflective, prone to reason rather than passion (see, for example, his equanimity in the face of Brabantio's verbal and physical attack upon him in 1.2.55–91). He is not only a general, a military strategist, but a surgeon (2.3.252); he is a man of intellect and learning.

Why, then, does he believe Iago, murder Desdemona, and kill himself? Because he is in a society pervaded by racialist beliefs and race hatred and his tacit sense of this has warped his perception—not only of others, but ultimately of himself as well. The racialist views of Iago and Roderigo are made clear in the opening scene; those of Brabantio are aired in the second scene (see, for example, his reference to "the sooty bosom/Of such a thing as thou—to fear, not to delight" [1.2.69–70]). Even Desdemona proves herself part of this society when she repeatedly refers to her new husband, not as "Othello," but as "the Moor" (see, for example, 1.3.248) and when she explains that she loved him for his bravery, *despite his blackness* (1.3.252). The narrowing of Othello's perception until it includes nothing but race, and indeed his internalization of the Venetians' racialist view, is most clear in his final monologue. Here he compares his crime to the crime of "a malignant and a turban'd Turk" who "Beat a Venetian" and sees himself as a "circumcised dog" who deserves to die. He can only think of his act as the act of an African killing a European—and for this he kills himself. Othello is a man greater than ourselves, more excellent and substantial, who falls from bliss to misery due not to depravity or broad degeneration of character, but to a single flaw: His understanding of others and of himself was perverted by the view of his inferiors, that he is of a lesser race.

This is a particularly good example, because it is widely thought that Aristotelian analyses are necessarily conservative and unable to accommodate contemporary political or other concerns (such as racism). But this is simply untrue. Another common misconception about Aristotle is that he claims all tragedies have a character with a tragic flaw. In fact, his claim is rather different: that the most successful tragedies will be understood by spectators in this way. For me, *Othello* is a great play in part because I believe Othello's character is as I have described him. And this is all that is relevant to Aristotle's thesis. It does not really matter whether or not my interpretation of the play is correct. All that matters is that I find the play more effective to the degree that I believe the main character is superior, but tragically flawed.

As already mentioned, according to Aristotle, comic characters too suffer a flaw. However, in this case, it is laughable and "not painful or destructive" (21); it is exemplified by the comic mask, which is "ugly and distorted, but does not imply pain" (21). If we consider Greek comedy of Aristotle's time, we can form some plausible conjectures as to what Aristotle had in mind in speaking of the comic flaw. For example, if one thinks of a work such as Aristophanes' *The Clouds,* one can see how Socrates' inability to think practically, his goofy abstractness, is a ludicrous flaw—light or trifling, and quite different from cognitive distortion due to racism. Of course, in Aristophanes' play, Socrates' abstractness has rather more serious consequences than many of us find compatible with comedy. But here too, my reaction, at least—shock and repulsion at the final lynching—fits perfectly, for I do not find the ending to be slight or trifling, and thus do not find the play comic in this respect.

Unfortunately, the portion of the *Poetics* examining comedy has been lost, thus we know relatively little about Aristotle's views on this topic—only what can be gleaned from extant parts of the work, along with other, related works. (For a controversial attempt to reconstruct Aristotle's discussion of comedy from later treatises, see Janko.)

In what remains of the *Poetics*, Aristotle goes on to discuss epic poetry, noting its use of both kinds of narration, multiple plots, and so on. Like tragedy, it may be simple or complex, may focus on plot or on character or scenes of suffering. However, he concludes, it is inferior to tragedy for its aesthetic effect is lesser. Aristotle also pays considerable attention to matters of linguistic ornamentation. However, his most lasting contributions are no doubt to be found in his analysis of tragedy, especially of tragic plot.

## The Middle East and North Africa

Literary theorists and aestheticians in the Arabic tradition, which is to say Muslim writers of Arabic poetics from the Middle East, North Africa, and the Iberian peninsula, have dealt with many of the same issues and have engaged in many of the same debates as writers in the West. Indeed, the development of Arabic poetic theory had a profound and lasting influence on the poetic theories of Europeans from the Middle Ages onward. The Western emphasis on the ethical value of literature has been in some degree the result of the influence of such writers as al-Fārābī (870–950 C.E.), Ibn Sinā (980–1037 C.E.), and especially Ibn Rushd (1126–1198 C.E.), for these writers stressed the ethical component in Aristotle's work and thus helped to guide subsequent interpretations in that direction. The current Western view of the humanities, which is strongly ethico-political in focus, is in part the legacy of these authors. In addition to their great intrinsic value, the writings of the Arab theorists are important to any historical understanding of the development of Western poetics.

One of the recurrent debates in literary theory in the West and elsewhere concerns the differences between a purely formal conception of literature and an emotive conception. This debate is implicit in Aristotle's advocacy of mimesis and catharsis over meter as distinguishing characteristics of poetry; it is explicit in the conflicts between the alaṃkāra and dhvani/rasa theories of the Sanskrit writers, as we shall see in the next section. It was also a concern of Arabic writers.

The study of ornamentation was extensive in the Arabic tradition, as it was elsewhere, and it led to catalogues of tropes, much like those found in Greek, Roman, Sanskrit, and other writings (see, for example, Cantarino 54). Ornamentation was not, however, the sole topic of concern in traditional Arabic poetics. The perennial issue of the deceitfulness of poets—an issue of importance in the West since at least the time of Plato, and a topic of serious concern in China—was hotly debated as well. In the case of Arabic writers, this issue arose at the time of Muḥammad, when the poetic eloquence of non-Muslim Arab leaders appeared to be a particular threat to the nascent Islamic religion and politics (for a discussion of this issue, see Cantarino 28).

Indeed, there is a chapter of the Qurʾān devoted to the condemnation of "The Poets." In the course of the chapter, poets are linked with necromancy, idolatry, homosexuality, commercial fraudulence, and a variety of other abominations. Indeed, they are characterized as the direct opposite of "true believers, who . . . remember God," for "Poets are followed by erring men" (264). With their false eloquence, poets are the antithesis of the Prophet who "warn[s] mankind in plain Arabic speech" (263). And, yet, the Qurʾān was considered not plain speech, but the inimitable perfection of language and style, that is, the ideal of literary art. These two doctrines—of the reprehensible deceitfulness of poets and the literary perfection of the Qur'ān—left Muslim literary theorists in a double quandary. First of all, in studying poetry, they were studying a body of work that God had seemingly condemned. Secondly, the word of God appeared itself to be an instance—indeed, the ultimate instance—of poetry. This tension is most evident in the writings of Ibn Rushd, for he is particularly intent upon condemning the poetry of the Arabs on moral grounds, but at the same time his aim in writing his commentary is to establish the potential moral excellence of literary art and to make this consistent with the Qur'ānic view of poets.

It was primarily the translation and study of Aristotle's writings that spurred Arabic theorists to develop an affective or more generally a nonformal theory of literary art, and that simultaneously allowed them a way of overcoming their dilemmas surrounding the deceitfulness of poets. This is not because the Arabic writers understood Aristotle particularly well. As any reader familiar with Aristotle will recognize, they frequently did not. In some specific cases, their interpretations are wildly inaccurate—which, of course, says nothing about their intrinsic value as poetic theory. There are two reasons for these misunderstandings. First of all, the major commentators were working from unreliable translations (on the available Arabic translations—themselves based on Syriac translations, not on the original Greek—see Dahiyat 3–9). Secondly, they misidentified the genres discussed by Aristotle (for instance, Ibn Sīnā defines tragedy as "the praise meant for a living or dead person" [73]).

Beyond these two factors that misled the Arabic commentators, there are other factors that narrowed their interpretations, leading them to highlight and develop certain aspects of Aristotle's work, while ignoring or downplaying others, factors that, in short, led them to interpret in precisely the same way everyone always interprets—selectively. More exactly, the interpretations put forth by the Arabic commentators were guided not only by Aristotle's (badly translated) text, but also by the context in which the commentators were writing. This includes not only the narrowly literary context (in which the lyric was dominant and drama virtually absent [see chapter 1 of Badawi], leading to the mistakes about genre already mentioned), but also, and more significantly, the broader cultural context. Arabic commentators—like commentators elsewhere—were concerned to understand Aristotle in relation to the central religious, philosophical, and other debates of their own society, in this case most particularly the debates over the deceitfulness of poets and the possibility of reconciling poetry with the teachings of the Qur'ān.

As to the philosophical context, the Arabic commentators interpreted Aristotle's *Poetics* in relation to Plato's didacticism and in relation to the theories of other writers, such as Themistius, who saw poetry as closely allied with rhetoric, and thus as having a pragmatic and moral function (see Dahiyat 25–26 n). Arabic writers were always careful to distinguish the methods of rhetoric from those of poetry, but this presumed philosophical context, along with the strongly moral concerns of Islam and the nature of the Islamic debate over poetry, inclined them to identify the aims of these two verbal arts. Thus the Arabic commentators tended to assume that poetry, like rhetoric, sets out to guide people's thought and action, but seeks to achieve this end by different means. For example, in his commentary on Plato's *Republic*, Ibn Rushd says that "there are two ways of establishing virtues in the souls of citizens" (117). The inferior way is coercion (118). The superior way "is to establish the [right] convictions in their souls through rhetorical and poetical statements" (117), which is to say "persuasive and emotive statements, which will move them towards the virtues" (118).

For these and other reasons, the central notion of the Arabic Aristotelians is not catharsis, or reversal, unity, or any other purely aesthetic property. It is not even imitation per se. Rather, the crucial concept for the Arabic Aristotelians is moral imitation toward moral ends. More exactly, in the view of these writers, the poet need not tell the literal truth. However, any poetic representation must present an image of possible moral or immoral action, and it must do so in such a way as to encourage people to emulate the former and avoid the latter. The problem with the poetry condemned in the Qur'ān is not so much that it lies about facts as that it lies about morals—or, rather, that it fails to foster (Islamic) virtue and to diminish vice.

In this context, a number of otherwise obscure claims become clear, most importantly the claim that there are only two major varieties of poetry, eulogy and satire (see, for example, Ibn Rushd's commentary on Aristotle, 59), and the related claims that in poetry "only praise and blame are sought" and that all poetry seeks "to represent . . . either virtues or vices" (Ibn Rushd on Aristotle, 66). When one tries to understand these in relation to their distant Aristotelian precursors (eulogy and satire derive from Aristotle's tragedy and comedy), the claims make relatively little sense. They appear at best idiosyncratic, perhaps applicable to Arabic writing, but hardly generalizable. Thus they seem to run counter to the whole point of poetic theory in every tradition, including the Arabic tradition: the isolation of universal features of literary art. As Ibn Rushd says at the outset of his middle commentary on Aristotle, "The purpose of this discussion is to comment upon those universal rules . . . that are common to all or most nations" (59). However, when one understands these claims in the context of the Arabic view of the aims of poetry—encouraging virtuous action and discouraging vicious action—they become clear, and their claims of universality make sense.

Specifically, the Arabic writers almost uniformly follow Aristotle in distinguishing moral levels of agents: those who are better than we are, those who are worse, and those who are the same. Incorporating this into their own framework, they conclude that the proper function of poetry is to praise the first and condemn the second, eulogize goodness and satirize evil. Thus, in his commentary on Plato's *Republic*, Ibn Rushd wrote that "those who make representations and comparisons seek thereby to encourage the performance of some voluntary actions and discourage others" (66), subsequently explaining that the representation of "virtuous people . . . is necessary so that children and youths, as they listen to good narratives, may also see beautiful things, until good actions entrench themselves in them in every form" (133). Later theorists adopted the same view. For example, al-Qarṭajannī (1211–85 c.e.) wrote that poetry "has the function of making [actions] attractive or repugnant to the human spirit" (214).

The relation between poetry and rhetoric in this scheme should be clear. Indeed, the limitation of poetry to praise and blame makes it parallel certain forms of oratory. However, the Arabic writers emphasize differences as well. Specifically, rhetoric appeals to thought. An orator makes a case for a certain course of action, encouraging its pursuit through the conscious inculcation of beliefs. Poetry, in contrast, operates on feeling. It does not in the first place present an argument for virtue and against vice. Rather it inspires feelings conducive toward virtue and away from vice, primarily the feelings of mercy and piety (distant derivatives of Aristotle's pity and fear; see, for example, Ibn Sīnā 88–89).

More exactly, the writer inspires virtuous feelings through an imitative, but imaginative creation. This creation is structured around implicit or explicit approbation or derogation, sometimes called "embellishment" and "defacement." As Ibn Sīnā put it, "The aim of every imitation is either amelioration or depreciation" (74). In other words, to praise a person or action, the author must elevate or purify that person or action; to blame a person or action, the author must highlight the flaws of that person or action. Finally, this imitative and imaginative creation must engage the audience members, absorb them, immerse them, for it is in that engagement, absorption, immersion, that audience members begin to feel attraction to virtue or aversion to vice (first by feeling mercy and piety in relation to the particular persons, actions, and situations of the poem).

Thus al-Fārābī wrote that a reader "is aroused by imaginative creation (*takhyīl*) to the action requested from him in such a way that the imaginative creation takes . . . the place of reflection" (117). The crucial Arabic term here is "takhyīl." Takhyīl is a mimetic imaginative creation (a notion that is far more in keeping with the spirit of Aristotle's theories than are most European conceptions of mimesis; in this respect, the Arabs were more faithful to Aristotle, despite the problematic translations). Takhyīl functions to capture the audience so that they forget reality and accept the creation, granting it what is sometimes called "imaginative assent," *takhayyul*. Al-Jurjānī defines takhyīl as "that process in which the poet presents as existing an object which actually does not exist, and makes a statement for which there is no possibility of a scientific presentation, and uses an expression which he himself makes up, and shows himself as seeing what he does not see" (167–68). But, again, this is important because of its effects. As Ibn Sinā wrote: "The imaginative is the speech to which the soul yields, accepting and rejecting matters without pondering, reasoning or choice" (61–62). Indeed, "human beings are more amenable to imaginative representation than to [rational or reflective] conviction" (62)—which is precisely what makes it so valuable, but also what makes it so dangerous, and thus open to Qurʾānic condemnation when immoral.

It is important to emphasize that this view is broader than the usual ethical view of the pre-Romantic Western writers. It is not a matter of inculcating particular ethical precepts—teaching a moral lesson through literature. Rather, it is a matter of training our moral sensibility, defining our character, forming the ways we feel. And this too is why poetry is more efficacious than rhetoric. Rhetoric convinces our mind that one act is right and another wrong, so that when faced with a dilemma, we will know (reflectively) what decision is proper. Poetry, on the other hand, makes us feel a certain way, so that we are in a sense not faced with a decision at all. If our sensibility is correct, then if we encounter a moral dilemma, we will not have to think and choose, for we will automatically follow the right path. Put differently, for Plato, as well as for such later European writers as Sidney, the ethical effect of literature is primarily a matter of showing that the good are rewarded and the evil punished, either in this life or in the afterlife. In other words, it is a matter of encouraging people to believe that it is in their best interest to do good. The Arab writers, in contrast, maintained that literature should operate to make us feel mercy and piety.

This difference has practical consequences for literary creation and evaluation that make the point clearer. Consider the parable of the Good Samaritan. A man is beaten by robbers and left by the side of the road to die. A Samaritan comes along, helps the man, bandages his wounds, and so on. According to Sidney's theory, the best version of this story would end with some reward for the Samaritan. Perhaps it would turn out that the man he helps is a millionaire and therefore gives him a huge amount of money; or perhaps we find out that the Samaritan goes to heaven, whereas those who did not stop to help, end up suffering agony in hell. If such a story is successful, we will help someone who has been hurt because we will tacitly expect (temporal or eternal) reward for doing so. The Arab theory in contrast does not imply that there should be some reward. Rather, it implies that the beaten man's suffering should be presented in such a way that it makes us feel mercy for him. If such a story is successful, we will help someone who has been hurt because we will automatically feel mercy for him/her, not because we anticipate reward.

### India

Literary theory in South Asia began several centuries before the common era and continued to develop in important ways until the Mughal invasions some 1,500 years later. Indeed, the history of Sanskrit poetics is remarkable for its almost continuously progressive development of a few basic principles established relatively early on. In this way, it is more reminiscent of the systematic development of natural sciences than of humanistic speculation, and is perhaps unique in the history of literary theory. Specifically, in the Indian tradition, as elsewhere, we may draw a broad distinction between theories focusing on ornamentation or *alaṃkāra* and theories focusing on nonformal features. The latter may be divided into two subgroups, eventually fused: "*dhvani*" theory, or the theory of suggestion, and "*rasa*" theory, or the theory of sentiment.

The alaṃkāra tradition tended to focus on the "*mahākāvya*" or long poem, and over several centuries developed into a formalistic/rhetorical poetics which was sometimes tediously over-categorizing, but which was sometimes highly sophisticated. Alaṃkāra theorists isolated not only the specific forms and figures of speech that characterize poetry, but distinguished qualities and faults as well, formulated literary typologies, and so on. The faults are particularly interesting because they are precisely the sorts of things that are considered faults everywhere—for example, excessive ornamentation, obscurity, and, despite the supposed irrationalism of the East, logical errors such as implicit contradiction (a fault discussed at particular length by Bhāmaha in the early eighth century [see Gerow 230–33]).

Alaṃkāra theory involved elements that pointed toward both the rasa and dhvani theories and thus helped contribute to their eventual integration. In the ninth century, writers such as Vamana began to speak of the aesthetic effect of poetry and of the "*ātman*" or soul of the poem (see Gerow 236; this is a common metaphor cross-culturally). He also distinguished figures of speech based on meaning (such as synecdoche) from figures based on sound (such as alliteration) and sought to present a general theory of semantic figures by deriving them all from simile (Gerow 238). Later in the same century, Rudraṭa emphasized the importance of simile as well. In a related way, he pointed to linguistic ambiguity and punning as crucial features of literary language, thus extending alaṃkāra theory further into semantics (see Gerow 238ff.).

One of the most interesting theorists in this tradition is the late tenth century Kashmiri writer, Kuntaka. Kuntaka isolated *vakrokti*—the striking, unexpected twist—as the definitive feature of poetry. For him, it was a certain sort of linguistic novelty, at the level of sound, word, sentence, and so on, which was most important in distinguishing literary art from mundane discursive speech. On the other hand, Kuntaka emphasized that novelty alone is inadequate. Like writers on novelty in all cultures, he stressed that the entire work must be unified and that incoherent innovation is a flaw. Moreover, like Flaubert many centuries later, Kuntaka emphasized the importance of choosing the one correct phrasing, *le mot juste*. Indeed, the striking turn of phrase is striking precisely because it is the one perfectly fitting phrase. It is "The unique expression which alone can fully convey the poet's intended meaning out of a hundred alternatives before him" (1.9). Its novelty derives not from innovation alone, but from the artistic refusal to say what is expected or common when the expected or common phrasing is not the perfectly correct phrasing.

The rasa tradition is of as great antiquity as the alaṃkāra tradition. It stretches back at least to the *Nāṭyaśāstra* (or treatise on dramaturgy), attributed to Bharata-muni but composed by various hands between the second century B.C.E. and the sixth century C.E. "Rasa" initially meant flavor. In poetic theory, it came to refer to a sentiment felt by a spectator when experiencing a work of art. However, it retained its sense of "flavor" as well, for rasa theorists repeatedly stated that aesthetic experience involves a "savoring" of the sentiment evoked by a work, just as the enjoyment of a good meal involves savoring the complex flavor of well-prepared foods. (The metaphor of aesthetic "taste" is also common cross-culturally.)

More exactly, rasa theorists maintained that any given work of literary art, if it is to be successful, must be dominated by a single sentiment. Other sentiments can, indeed must enter in the course of the work, but these subsidiary sentiments must always contribute to the overall sentiment. To use a common Western example, one might say that moments of comic relief are permissible or even necessary in a tragedy, but extended periods of giddiness ruin the tragic effect.

Bharata-muni listed eight sentiments: the erotic, comic, pathetic, furious, terrible, odious, marvelous, and heroic. These sentiments, savored by the spectator, correspond with eight emotions ("*bhāvas*") experienced by characters in the literary work: romantic love, mirth, sorrow, anger, terror, disgust, astonishment, and energy (or confidence in one's own powers, leading to "enterprise, bravery, charity, or forgiveness," according to Lal [xvi]). (As Monier-Williams notes in his entry on "rasa," some theorists add to each list an appropriate version of "*vātsalya*," affection or tenderness, especially toward one's children.) It is important to emphasize that the sentiments are related to, but not identical with, the corresponding emotions. According to rasa theorists, we experience emotions in life, but in viewing art we experience sentiment. Thus, when we watch a play in which two characters are in love, we savor a sentiment related to love, the erotic sentiment, but we do not ourselves experience love; we savor the furious sentiment when watching conflict, but we are not ourselves angry. Indeed, if we experience the emotion rather than the sentiment, the aesthetic experience will be lost. For example, if we experience anger, rather than the furious sentiment, we may rush on stage to batter the villain, rather than enjoying the play.

Just as there are ancillary sentiments, there are ancillary emotions. Thus, a lover may temporarily experience anger in connection with his or her love, just as we may briefly savor the furious sentiment in the context of an overall erotic sentiment. In addition, each emotion is associated with a series of "transitory feelings." For example, a lover may temporarily experience hopelessness in connection with his or her love. Perhaps more importantly, all such emotions are made clear to the spectator by way of the "*vibhāvas*" or "determinants" and "*anubhāvas*" or "consequents." The determinants include every factor that gives rise to a given emotion. Thus the existence of the two lovers, the events that join them together, their personal circumstances, are all determinants of their love. The consequents are all the things that result from the emotion. Thus the affectionate play of the lovers, their lack of interest in anything other than amorous activities, their physical decline during separation, and so on, are all consequents of their emotion of love. It is through an appreciation of these determinants and consequents, and the emotions and transitory feelings which they allow us (tacitly) to infer, that we may savor the main and subsidiary sentiments of a work of art.

Rasa theory was given its most philosophically and psychologically significant development in the ninth and tenth centuries by the Kashmiri writers Ānandavardhana and Abhinavagupta, who understood rasa in relation to dhvani, or suggestion. Specifically, Ānandavardhana distinguished three types of meaning: (1) the literal, denotative, or "expressed" meaning; (2) the directly implied or "indicated" or "secondary" meaning; (3) the suggested meaning (*dhvani*). Moreover, within the third category, he distinguished three varieties: (1) *vastudhvani*, the suggestion of conditions or things; (2) *alaṃkāradhvani*, the suggestion of figures of speech; and (3) *rasadhvani* or dhvani proper, the suggestion of sentiment.

Denotation is the direct, literal meaning of an utterance. "Secondary" meaning is the indirect but literally paraphraseable meaning that we may derive from the words of an utterance, once their primary sense is blocked. Suppose someone says, "Hugo used to be a blimp, but now he's a stick." The primary meanings are clearly false, and thus blocked—Hugo never was actually an aircraft and is not now a bit of foliage. Thus we have to shift to other, "secondary" meanings: huge, with enormous girth, for "blimp," and small, narrow, fleshless for "stick." (Ānandavardhana distinguishes two varieties of secondary meaning, roughly equivalent to metaphor and metonymy [see Ingalls 48 n].)

Vastudhvani is a suggestion of a meaning that is not available from the individual words themselves—as "huge" is available from "blimp"—but rather only from the context. Thus, if your spouse says, "We don't need to do anything special on my birthday," there is nothing that blocks the primary sense, and there is no secondary meaning available through the inspection of the words—for example, there are no secondary meanings for "birthday" that would yield an appropriately different sense. But this utterance may suggest a range of things, from "We do need to do something special on my birthday" to "I suppose you've forgotten that my birthday is approaching." These suggestions are cases of vastudhvani.

Alaṃkāradhvani is the suggestion of a figure of speech. The figure of speech is suggested in that it is rendered inexplicit by the mention of only one term of comparison. In ordinary conversation, this sort of suggestion is usually not terribly interesting, for the unstated term of the comparison is most often directly evident. If someone exits a lecture and says, "No light, but darkness visible," it is fairly clear that he or she is referring to the lecture. However, the use of alaṃkāradhvani in a poem is different. For here the missing term of the comparison is often far from obvious.

Take Faiz's poem, "Spring Comes." It begins by addressing someone in terms that are fairly common in love poetry, referring to "youthful" memories that return each spring, when the roses blossom. But it includes unusual, disturbing references to death. These references accumulate, as the roses of spring become the "blood" of the addressee's "lovers." In connection with this, Faiz refers not simply to the pain of unrequited love, but to "the heart's oppression." From the beginning of the poem, then, the addressee is not entirely clear. It seems to be a woman, the poet's stereotypically cruel beloved. But as one reads the poem, one begins to suspect that Faiz is speaking of Pakistan. The reader gradually comes to understand the poem as treating the love that Faiz and other dissidents have had for Pakistan, and the cruelty of the Pakistani government in its treatment of these "lovers"—a cruelty that, in some cases, did involve "oppression" and "blood." Thus the center of the poem is a complex, three-way comparison between Pakistan, a woman the poet once loved, and spring. But this metaphor is never explicit; it is only suggested.

It is clear that both vastudhvani and alaṃkāradhvani, as well as primary and secondary meaning, are important to literary art. Moreover, it is important for critics to be aware of these and to be able to recognize and interpret each appropriately. Indeed, based in part on these distinctions, the Sanskrit critics practiced a form of painstaking textual explication that was uncommon in the West prior to New Criticism. But Ānandavardhana and Abhinavagupta emphasize that rasadhvani is the soul or ātman of poetry. Unlike other sorts of suggestion, rasadhvani or dhvani proper is, first of all, never completely paraphraseable. One can never state all of the suggestions of a work in this sense. (Hereafter, I shall use "suggestion" to refer to rasadhvani alone, in keeping with Ānandavardhana's conception of rasadhvani as true dhvani.)

For example, Faiz's poem is not reducible to a paraphrase; it cannot be encompassed by primary meaning, secondary meaning, vastudhvani, and alaṃkāradhvani. Put differently, it can never be translated into primary meaning. Even one image—for example, that of roses as the blood of lovers—cannot be encompassed in restatement. We can list any number of its suggested meanings. But this list can never be final or definitive. Nor can it fully specify the relations among the various meanings and images. We can note that the rose suggests beauty, passion, romantic love, that it has both religious and secular, literary and popular resonances in several traditions. We can note connections between all this, on one hand, and the suggestions of "blood," on the other. We can examine the relations of both to patriotism and political dissidence. But none of this will bring our task to an end.

Even more important than being unparaphraseable, suggestion or rasadhvani operates to evoke rasa or sentiment in the spectator or reader. It involves affect as well as meaning, or as part of meaning—a part of meaning that is itself unparaphraseable, because it is an experience ("*rasa* is something that one cannot dream of expressing by the literal sense," Abhinavagupta writes in the *Locana* [81]). Faiz's poem is redolent of a continuing love made painful by the beloved's cruelty and rejection. And those who are moved by the poem savor the sentiment associated with such love. In relation to this, Ānandavardhana emphasizes the literary importance of showing rather than saying (a cross-cultural commonplace of normative poetics). What is crucial about Faiz's poem is that it evokes the sentiment of unrequited love in us rather than explicitly informing us (or leading us self-consciously to infer) that Faiz loves Pakistan despite the brutality of its leaders. The suggestive statement has an emotional effect in the way that a direct statement of this feeling ("I love my country despite the government") or simple implication ("I hold my country in my heart, though the government is cruel") would not.

The Sanskrit writers make the experience of rasa more comprehensible by allowing suggestion to involve a broader range of associations than do other sorts of meaning. It is not merely that Faiz's poem generates an indefinite number of paraphrases; even more importantly it calls to our minds a wide range of images, ideas, and so on. From a modern critic's point of view, this is one of the most fascinating things about the Sanskrit conception of dhvani. We have various ways of talking about what a given word or sentence or image means. But there is much that a word, for example, calls to mind beyond what it means—beyond its primary meaning, secondary meaning, and so on. Consider, for example, the reunion of Othello and Desdemona after the tempest. Othello greets Desdemona with the phrase "O my fair warrior!" This phrase calls to the mind many things that are crucial to our experience of the play, but which can hardly be said to be part of the meaning of that phrase. For example, the word "fair"—meaning "beautiful," but also "white"—calls to mind the racial difference between Othello and Desdemona; it calls to mind as well the fact that, at their last meeting, she repeatedly referred to him, not as "Othello," but as "the Moor," and said that she ignored the ugliness of his black face because of the beauty of his soul (1.3.247). This is reinforced by the next word, "warrior," for it was precisely Othello's deeds as a warrior that made Desdemona love him, despite his color. None of this is part of the "meaning" of the phrase, at least as we usually understand "meaning." Nor is any of this consciously considered by a spectator, except upon subsequent critical reflection. However, it makes an enormous difference to our experience of the scene. Those who have these associations to the scene are likely to find the following exchange very sad, evocative of *karuṇarasa*, the sentiment of pathos. Those who do not have these associations may find well find the dialogue cheerful, or tediously hyperbolic, or something else, but probably not sad. In any event, the notion of rasadhvani allows us to isolate, discuss, and (at least in part) understand these crucial associations, which are not, again, a matter of meaning in the usual sense.

As this discussion indicates, the emotional effect of suggestion is not in and of itself universal. Not everyone experiences the pathos of Othello's reunion with Desdemona or savors Faiz's love of Pakistan. In order to experience the latter, we must, for example, know quite a bit, for without various sorts of knowledge, we simply will have no associations, or our associations will be inappropriate. Thus we must have a sense of the history of Pakistan, a knowledge of Faiz's early enthusiasm for independence and of his various experiences of disillusion—or, rather, a knowledge of the common postcolonial experience of enthusiasm for independence and subsequent disillusionment—an understanding of Faiz's dissident stance in Pakistan, his arrests, and so forth, and it helps to have some familiarity with the conventions of Urdu love poetry so that we can share the literary associations of the imagery. Moreover, we must be so familiar with all this that it is part of our unself-conscious associations with the work, not part of an elaborated series of self-conscious inferences. Ideally, we must have read and understood widely, and assimilated the tradition in which a work is written.

In addition to having the relevant associations, we should not have irrelevant associations. We should be able to filter out those personal, idiosyncratic, or other associations that are not germane. As Ānandavardhana emphasizes, suggestion cannot be identical with association, for association can lead anywhere. Chains of association extend in all directions, and thus through a wide range of contradictory and idiosyncratic memories and feelings. In experiencing literary art, we must be able to bring an appropriately structured set of associations to our reading.

The state of full associative expertise, in which the reader's associations are both extensive and appropriate, is the state of the "*sahṛdaya*," the connoisseur or, literally, the one "with heart," for it is only when our heart is sensitive to the suggestions of a work that we may experience and savor the appropriate sentiments. In Sanskrit poetic theory, aesthetic effect is always first and foremost aesthetic effect on the sahṛdaya.

Abhinavagupta wrote commentaries on both Bharata-muni and Ānandavardhana. In doing so, he sought to explain aesthetic experience, not simply to describe it. First of all, Abhinavagupta stressed that aesthetic experience is not merely a matter of the nature of the work or of one's training or taste; it is also a matter of how one approaches the work. For Abhinavagupta, the suggestions of a given word, sentence, and so on, are in part the product of "the imagination of the listener," specifically the sahṛdaya (*Locana* 88). For this reason, even the trained reader or observer must approach a work of literary art with a specific attitude, a nonordinary or "super-normal" attitude—what Anand Amaladass has called the "dhvani attitude"—ready to savor the suggestions and associated sentiments, and not merely glean the (paraphraseable) semantic message.

For example, someone does not have a full aesthetic experience of a drama if his or her sole interest is in finding out what happens at the end. The outcome of the plot is not irrelevant to aesthetic experience. However, suggestion involves a wide range of particular thoughts and feelings woven throughout the fabric of the work and cannot be reduced to any one of these, not even those that occur at the end. Abhinavagupta repeatedly compares the experience of a play or poem to eating. The aesthetic experience of a literary work is like the savoring of food and is to be contrasted with swift consumption to satisfy hunger. The satisfaction of hunger is, of course, not irrelevant to one's aesthetic enjoyment of food. But one's aesthetic enjoyment of food involves a wide range of experiences—seeing the food, smelling it, tasting it, and so on—that cannot be reduced to the satisfaction of hunger.

In order to formulate a fuller explanation of the emotional experience of the sahṛdaya who approaches a literary work in the dhvani attitude or "with heart," Abhinavagupta introduces the notion of memory traces. Again, when we savor a sentiment, we do not experience the emotion of the character. But what, then, do we experience—what is rasa? And how does it come about? Abhinavagupta argues that, if we are sensitive and trained viewers, the portrayal of an emotion in literature activates—through a series of associations—the traces of memories of times when we ourselves experienced those emotions. This "activation" does not actually cause us to remember those earlier experiences. Rather, it brings to us a hint of the feeling associated with them, so that we might reexperience that feeling in connection with the work we are reading or observing. In cognitive psychological terms, we might say that the relevant memories are "primed" but not "accessed" (that is, made readily available to direct recollection, but not directly recalled).

This is a phenomenon that is familiar to all of us from everyday life. I might enter a building and suddenly feel sad, but not know why, realizing only upon reflection that it is because my last visit to that building was very unhappy. Clearly, when I entered the building initially, the memory of my last visit was "primed." Though it was not directly accessed or made conscious, its associated feeling "bled" into my consciousness experience—divorced from its cause. Abhinavagupta brilliantly connected this phenomenon with aesthetic experience, arguing that aesthetic feeling or rasa is nothing other than this.

There is, however, one partially implicit qualification, already indicated in the work of Ānandavardhana. Specifically, the trained reader or specta-tor—the sahṛdaya—must be to some degree capable of disciplining his/her associative thought so that he/she is able to avoid or minimize idio-syncratic associations that are contradictory to the rasa of the work. To take a simple example, if I have idiosyncratically sorrowful associations with flower shops, these may interfere with my experience of a comedy concerning a flower shop. While it is difficult if not impossible to give necessary and sufficient conditions for what would count as relevant in this context, it is in general true that relevant memory traces concern the sorts of events or objects that define the emotion within the literary work itself. Thus if, in a given work, sorrow is the result of the separation of lovers, then sorrowful memories of love in separation are relevant; if anger is generated by racial injustice, then angry memories of racial injustice—or other forms of injustice based on group bias—are relevant. There are also various circumstances that typically suggest particular sentiments, with varying degrees of universality or cultural/historical specificity. For ex-ample, a dark, unpredictable environment gives rise to fear in life and thus suggests the terrible sentiment in art. The sahṛdaya is able to have his/her "heart with" others as regards these typical situations, not responding id-iosyncratically, but unreflectively filtering out atypical memories that might disrupt the dominant rasa with an irrelevant, or indeed contradic-tory rasa—for example, the comic disturbed by the pathetic, the terrible by the comic, the erotic by the odious, and so forth.

*Othello* provides a good example here. In the passage we examined above, "O my fair warrior!", we noted that readers may or may not "prime" Desdemona's references to Othello as "the Moor," along with her use of other racial characterizations, and stressed that whether they do or do not makes a great difference to their feeling about the passage. However, this was inadequate. The association alone does not make us feel karuṇarasa (the pathetic sentiment). Rather, the association must call up relevant memories—for example, memories of loving someone whose love involved an unself-conscious strain of condescension, or who (unself-consciously) said hurtful things due to that condescension. It must call up recollections of dehumanization, of not being recognized as a human being even, and most cruelly, by those whom we love and who think they love us. It might also call up memories of racism or related sorts of prejudice to which we or people we care about have been subjected. Without these memories, without these feelings about real life and the ability to have our *heart with* Othello so as to associate these memories with the play, we will feel little sorrow in reading this passage.

Abhinavagupta stresses that different sorts of people will have different preferences with respect to rasa. Other writers have emphasized that our experiences change with age, as well as history and culture. While Abhinavagupta is firm in his commitment to a universal poetics, he acknowledges certain sorts of variation. And this (universal) schema explains those variations. For at different ages, we will have different experiences, different memories, and different feelings associated with those experiences and memories. What carries great sorrow in adolescence might appear trivial in middle age; and what is sorrowful in later life may be nothing but an unexperienced idea in youth. This is something we have known for a long time. But Abhinavagupta is one of the few aestheticians to have provided a plausible explanation for the operation of these differences in literary response.

Abhinavagupta's theory, then, allows us to understand aesthetic experience in a way that is not "distanced" to the point of being inhuman, not uniform beyond anything that is empirically plausible, and not subjective to the point of pure idiosyncratic individualism. Though there are still issues to sort out here, he presents a theory of aesthetic experience arguably more subtle and more plausible than any of the well-known parallel discussions in the Western tradition. Moreover, he uses this reformulation to contribute to a fuller understanding of the sense of affective resolution achieved by art, what Aristotle referred to as "catharsis."

Specifically, aesthetic experience, for Abhinavagupta, is not and cannot be merely the savoring of the eight sentiments, for these involve us in uncertainty, in attachment to the changeable world and to changeable others, and even in emotional pain. In the Hindu view, all attachment to the world is painful. One does not have to adopt the entire Hindu metaphysics of karma, rebirth, and so forth, to recognize the truth in this—that sorrow, anger, fear, and disgust are painful in themselves, that love makes our well-being contingent on changeable circumstances and thus contains within itself the (often realized) possibility of pain, and that mirth and astonishment are necessarily short-lived, inspired as they are by necessarily unusual circumstances (when an occurrence becomes habitual, it ceases to inspire joy or astonishment). Thus, for Abhinavagupta, any truly satisfying experience must in the end lead beyond these feelings, beyond uncertainties and attachments, to *śānti,* peace. In consequence, for Abhinavagupta, peace is the final and ultimate rasa, the rasa that subsumes all others. This peace, Abhinavagupta tells us, is analogous to spiritual enlightenment, when we have fully withdrawn our emotional attachment from all memory traces and become absorbed entirely in Godhead. The implication, then, is that the peace which resolves an aesthetic experience is produced by the partial, temporary withdrawal of emotional attachment from those memory traces linked with the literary work. Further extrapolating, we might say that the work of art, by activating the feelings associated with certain complexes of memory traces, for a time reduces those feelings—catharts them.

This does not entirely explain catharsis. For one thing, it fails to distinguish works that stimulate emotions in a noncathartic or nonresolving manner. I, at least, find that some works move me and lead to a feeling of peace, while others move me, then leave me overwrought (for example, Kavanagh's poem "Memory of My Father" falls into the former category; Kodak commercials about Father's Day, which "prime" many of the same associations, fall into the latter category). Thus, it seems, simply calling forth the associations is not enough. There may be some sort of structural resolution required—in the case of plot, the sort of structural resolution discussed by Aristotle. This structural resolution could be a matter of moving, via "probability or necessity," from the dhvani of painful rasas (such as *karuṇa*) to a conclusion in which the dhvani of the work primes peaceful memories and thus leads to an experience of *śāntarasa.* In any event, whatever we decide, Abhinavagupta's work gives us the ability to consider these issues far more adequately.

# 2

---

# Early Modern Europe:
## Philosophical Aesthetics,
## Romanticism, Historical Materialism

One could argue that, for over two thousand years, European literary theory involved little philosophical advancement beyond the writings of Plato and Aristotle. This situation changed radically with Immanuel Kant, who transformed the terms in which literature and art are discussed, in part by transforming the terms in which epistemology, the study of knowledge, is discussed. The first section focuses on Kant and two immediate precursors, Burke and Hume.

The intellectual changes initiated by Kant were carried further by the German Idealist philosophers Fichte, Schelling, and Hegel. Though little understood by literary theorists, their work provides many of the underpinnings for modern and contemporary philosophical literary theory. Moreover, that work is bound up with Romanticism, a movement that continues to pervade our approach to literature and literary theory. The second section isolates some general principles of Romanticism and examines the work of the major German Idealists, along with related literary figures (Schiller, Coleridge, Shelley, de Stael) and one philosopher who radically and influentially revised Idealist and Romantic principles—Nietzsche.

The final section takes up the most influential repudiation of Idealism—Marx's historical materialism, which is also deeply bound up with Romanticism.

## Philosophical Aesthetics: Burke, Hume, Kant

After Plato and Aristotle, much if not most European critical theory prior to the eighteenth century was written by poets or men of letters. Leaving aside a few medieval and Renaissance Platonists and Aristotelians, it was only in the late 1700s that European philosophers systematically ad-dressed the problems of poetics and began the rigorous theoretical inquiry that had been pursued centuries earlier in Greece, the Middle East, and South Asia. In this section, I shall consider three such writers: Edmund Burke, who took up the notion of the sublime and developed an extended, empirical theory of aesthetic feeling; David Hume, whose "Of the Stan-dard of Taste" summarizes and addresses many of the major philosophi-cal issues surrounding beauty; and, finally, Immanuel Kant, perhaps the most influential post-Classical writer on aesthetics, a wide-ranging phi-losopher whose work marks a watershed in intellectual history. All three writers were concerned with the issue of aesthetic value, and most par-ticularly with how we might validly judge one work aesthetically superior to another. Kant's radical response provided a considerable part of the intellectual impetus for Romanticism, and thus for the bulk of modern critical theory.

In *A Philosophical Enquiry into the Origin of Our Ideas of the Sublime and Beautiful*, Edmund Burke set out to explicate and defend the following thesis: "On a superficial view we may seem to differ very widely from each other in our reasonings, and no less in our pleasures; but, notwith-standing this difference, which I think to be rather apparent than real, it is probable that the standard both of reason and taste is the same in all hu-man creatures" (11). In other words, it was Burke's view that we all oper-ate by the same principles in judging beauty. However, we come to differ-ent conclusions about what is beautiful. Burke's dilemma was to explain the latter without sacrificing the former.

Burke begins by arguing that we all naturally delight in both imitation and imagination—seeing likeness, and seeing change in likeness, alter-ation made by the human mind. In this, he provides one link between the Classical emphasis on mimesis and the later, Romantic focus on imagina-tion. On the other hand, Burke's notion of imagination is very limited, and does not extend beyond the creative element present in Aristotle's notion of mimesis. Indeed, it does not go nearly so far as the Arabic concept of takhyīl. However, in setting up the terms of discussion in this way, he helps prepare for the subsequent, Romantic elaboration of the concept of imagination.

From here, Burke goes on to maintain that taste is not a simple experi-ence of pleasure or pain. Rather, it is a combination of three distinct types of pleasure or pain—that of the senses, that of the imagination, and that of judgment. As to the first, all human sensibility follows the same prin-ciples, Burke tells us. However, we can nonetheless differ in our sense of pleasure or pain (and thus in our taste) for two reasons. The first is that, in addition to our natural sensibility, we *acquire* various propensities for enjoyment due to *association*. The taste of tobacco is naturally displeasing, but the feeling produced by the nicotine is pleasing, and this leads a smoker to enjoy the taste of tobacco: "The effect of the drug has made us use it frequently; and frequent use, combined with the agreeable effect, has made the Taste itself at last agreeable" (16). One might further support Burke's point by adding that repulsion too can be the result of association; naturally attractive objects can be made repulsive by association just as naturally repulsive objects can be made attractive.

But association is not the only source of differences in our sensible experiences of pleasure and pain. In addition, while our natural sensibilities are, again, all naturally attracted or repulsed by the same sort of object, they are not all naturally attracted or repulsed in the same degree. In short, our sensibilities vary in sensitivity; we differ in the degree, though not in the kind, of our natural endowments. This is true both in terms of how "sensitive" we are emotionally and simply in terms of how well we hear or see.

Burke defines the imagination as a "creative power" employed "either in representing at pleasure the images of things in the order and manner in which they were received by the senses, or in combining those images in a new manner, and according to a different order" (16; as we shall see, this is roughly equivalent to the Romantic notion of a limited and mechanical "fancy"—not the powerfully creative Romantic "imagination"—since this Burkean imagination "is incapable of producing any thing absolutely new" [17]). By presenting us with images, the imagination allows us to experience the pleasures of sense. At the same time, it gives us pleasure through creating resemblance between this image and some original—much in the manner of Aristotelian mimesis.

While imagination, like sensibility, is common to all humans, and while its principles are identical in all, it too gives rise to differences in taste because our pleasure in imitation is in part a function of knowledge, knowledge of the individual work of art, knowledge of the object portrayed, and knowledge of related works of art. Burke's notion of "knowledge" here is not a matter of recalling factual information. It is more properly conceived of as a matter of experiential acquaintance or familiarity, on one hand, and careful attention to details, on the other. Burke illustrates his point with the following example: if I have never seen a sculpture before, then I am likely to be pleased by even the crudest piece of work. However, as I become more fully acquainted with sculpture, my response becomes more discriminating. Note that Burke's point about knowledge holds independently of his views on mimesis; whether we are judging the sculpture by internal structural properties or by accuracy of representation, we are likely to notice more about the sculpture, and thus judge it differently, when we have seen many works of sculpture than when we have seen few. On the other hand, this is not to say that we should bypass Burke's statements about representation as passe. Indeed, his claims in this regard are quite plausible. Suppose I read a novel about Yoruba village life without knowing anything about Yoruba culture. I may admire and enjoy the novel. But someone else, endowed with the same broadly human sensibility and imagination, but familiar with Yoruba culture, may find the novel inaccurate and stereotypical, and thus neither admirable nor enjoyable.

Judgment, for Burke, is a self-conscious procedure of evaluation. Its primary function in aesthetic experience is negative; it serves to articulate the faults of works, thereby "dissipating" our "enchantment." In other words, it serves to alter our familiarity with a range of works or our attention to a single work by providing us with information. Consider again mimesis: I say that I like a given painting. Smith responds by pointing out several errors in perspective. This draws my attention to those flaws, thus changing my acquaintance with the work, thus (perhaps) altering my response to the work.

There are two problems with Burke's claims about judgment. First of all, judgment does not appear to be part of aesthetic experience, at least not in the way sense and imagination are part of that experience. Rather, judgment (in Burke's usage) seems to be a sort of external, cognitive operation. It does serve to alter our knowledge, and thereby to affect our pleasure in imaginative imitation. But it is this (altered) knowledge that enters into aesthetic experience, not the judgment per se. In this respect, judgment is similar to the operations, such as smoking, that alter our enjoyment of sense. Our altered sense is part of our aesthetic experience, but the operation that leads to the alteration is not part of that experience—it merely accounts for the alteration of sense.

Secondly, he seems to be mistaken in claiming that judgment is necessarily more negative than positive. At least if we move outside the realm of mimesis, judgment can serve a positive function—as should be clear from the study of literature. A student comes into class and insists that a particular sonnet makes no sense; after discussion—namely, after the articulation of many judgments concerning the meaning of the poem ("Look at the first line. It begins by asserting that . . . .")—the student comes to see that the sonnet does indeed make sense. In this process, he/she may come to experience pleasure in reading the sonnet, in which case, judgment has helped create, rather than dissipate, the enchantment.

In any event, the main point of Burke's argument here is quite plausible: Differences in aesthetic responses to particular works in no way indicate that people do not follow the same tacit principles in responding to literature. Indeed, starting with the same general principles, it seems very likely that we would have different responses, for reasons of sensitivity, familiarity, and attention, precisely as discussed by Burke.

Before going on, we might consider an example of the sort of difference in taste that Burke is concerned to explain. Suppose that I am moved by *Othello* (as I am), but Jane is not. Burke could account for this difference either by saying that Jane and I understand the work or its object differently or that I am more emotional than Jane or that one of us has had his/ her natural response altered by associations. In short, we naturally delight in the same sorts of things, but do not see the same things in this particular work, or we have different conceptions of some actuality depicted in the work, or we require different degrees of aesthetic intensity to experience aesthetic delight, or one of us has, through experience, built up positive or negative associations with this work. While things are probably not as simple as this, Burke's point is well taken. Suppose Jane sees Othello as an impassioned lunatic who brutally murders his wife on the hint of infidelity and I see Othello as a man brutalized by racism who murders his wife when he thinks that she has betrayed him because she finds him black and ugly, because even she hates him for his race. This would no doubt go at least some way toward explaining the differences in our responses. Similarly, Jane and I might both see the play as dealing with racism, but Jane might find Shakespeare's treatment of the internalization of racism to be inaccurate (and thus itself racist), while I find it plausible. Our divergent responses are equally explained if I am a weepy sap who starts blubbering during Hallmark card commercials while Jane is calm, unemotional, prone neither to tears nor laughter. Finally, if my first experience of the play was a very enjoyable seminar, while Jane's was a dreadful class, this too could account for the difference.

The other important and influential part of Burke's essay is his delimitation of the sublime as a category complementary to that of beauty, the two falling under an enlarged notion of the aesthetic. For Burke (as for Freud a century and a half later), there are two primary sets of "passions" that guide human action: the social or reproductive passions relating to sexuality and the individual passions relating to self-preservation. The emotion most closely related to reproduction is love; that most closely related to self-preservation is fear. Beauty, for Burke, is a function of love (42), while sublimity is a function of fear ("Whatever is fitted in any sort to excite the ideas of pain, and danger, that is to say, whatever is in any sort terrible," he tells us, "is a source of the sublime" [39]). Thus both primary aesthetic feelings may be derived from the universally human nature of the passions.

It is worth noting that there is a certain parallel between the beautiful and the sublime, on one hand, and the central Platonic/Aristotelian emotions of pity and fear, on the other. Indeed, Burke emphasizes that sympathy is another social (though not specifically reproductive) passion and that it is only due to sympathy that "poetry, painting, and other affecting arts, transfuse their passions from one breast to another" (44). In this way, beauty becomes a function of sympathy and love, a combination that is broader than pity, but includes it centrally. Sublimity is more directly and obviously a function of Aristotelian *phobos* (fear). As we shall see below, the opposition between the beautiful and the sublime will have far-reaching consequences in the development of Romanticism. It is striking to what an extent this important and influential opposition derives from Plato's casual selection of pity and fear as unmanly and unmilitary—especially striking when one recalls the much broader Indian catalogue of aesthetic feelings.

It is also worth noting that Burke is one of the first theorists to have been influenced by Asian aesthetics. And I think it is no accident that this influence coincides with what is in effect the birth of serious poetic theory in Europe. Most obviously, Burke sees the Orient as a place of purer and more direct communication of feeling, a place where languages "have a great force and energy of expression" (176). The West, in his view, is more highly critical, more focused on judgment than on sensibility or imagination. Needless to say, this view of East and West is not only mistaken, but perniciously so, for it takes part in the ideological infantilization of non-Europeans, their assimilation to children who are "not critical" but "natural," who are "unpolished" and "Uncultivated" (176). Nonetheless, this highly ideological view of the East provided Western theorists with a vision of an alternative to then-standard ways of thinking about literature—a liberating alternative, filled with emotion and sense and imagination. In this way, it provided a significant part of the impetus that turned mainstream European theory away from Neoclassical formalism as well as Platonistic (and, to some degree, Arab) moralism, leading eventually to Romanticism.

In addition to explicit references, such as those just cited, there are also some hints of connections to Indian thought in Burke's theory of association. Primarily, Burke explains the arousal of feeling by reference to memories of which we are not consciously aware (130). However, this may not be a matter of influence. Burke may simply be rediscovering—in an intuitive and underdeveloped form—what Abhinavagupta discovered, specified, and elaborated eight centuries earlier.

David Hume's "Of the Standard of Taste" was published in the same year as Burke's *Philosophical Enquiry* and covers some of the same issues. Hume begins his essay by noting the vacuousness of evaluative terms. We seem to agree on what makes a work of art beautiful—for example, unity and innovation—and on what mars a work—for example, affectation and vulgarity. However, all we are really agreeing on is that "innovative" is a term of praise and "affected" a term of blame. For once we try to specify precisely what works are unified or innovative or affected or vulgar, we find that we differ. In other words, while we were assigning these terms the same normative value (good or bad), we were giving them different descriptive meanings.

Hume then asks, once we have admitted this, does it follow that there is no right or wrong in matters of taste, that a judgment of beauty is purely subjective? Keeping to the empiricist premises of his entire philosophy, he asserts, "It is evident that none of the rules of composition are fixed by reasoning *a priori*" (309). Thus for Hume there is no possibility of isolating prescriptive rules of taste on the basis of, for example, a supposed essence of beauty. We cannot define "the beautiful" by intuition or logical analysis. However, there are works that have consistently been held in high esteem and these provide an empirical basis for the study of taste. There is, then, the possibility of isolating empirical rules "concerning what has been universally found to please in all countries and in all ages" (309). These rules would be part of a general psychology, explained in terms of human psychological structure, and so on. While they would not have normative force, they would systematize our judgments and render them comprehensible.

However, Hume does not try to isolate these rules. Rather, he assumes that they exist, then goes on to discuss the problem of how one can reconcile the (putative) existence of universal aesthetic principles with the fact that there are so many disagreements in matters of taste. Like Burke, Hume states that differences in aesthetic judgment are in part the result of differences in knowledge and sensitivity. Again like Burke, he specifies knowledge as not only knowledge of the particular work in question, but knowledge of the competition, knowledge of the body of literature in which a given work is situated. Hume also notes differences in momentary moods and various idiosyncrasies of personal situation, as well as some larger social variables, such as strong moral and religious beliefs. The woman who has just lost her job may not be in the proper frame of mind to judge a concert; the man who is friends with the composer may allow personal interest to interfere with his aesthetic assessment. As to the social variables, men from a country where women are veiled may be offended by any drama in which women appear unveiled, and thus think ill of it.

This issue of moral and religious beliefs is somewhat more complicated than the others, as Hume recognizes. It is quite plausible to claim that my mood on a given day or even my familiarity with a given body of work is a superficial and corrigible matter, with no real bearing on the general principles of my aesthetic feeling. However, it might seem that moral and religious beliefs, which are often not superficial or corrigible, are so intimately a part of my aesthetic feeling as to be inseparable from it. Hume's view of the issue is that we can and should set aside our religious beliefs in judging beauty, but that we should retain our moral beliefs. This is consistent with his general claims if he believes that ethics, purged of religion, would be as universal as aesthetics and thus would not interfere with aesthetic universality—a currently unpopular view, but not, I believe, absurd or indefensible (for a recent version of this view, see Nussbaum 10–11 and 11 n). However, it is not clear that Hume believes this (see 315).

In any event, Hume concludes that "A perfect serenity of mind, a recollection of thought, a due attention to the object; if any of these circumstances be wanting . . . we shall be unable to judge of the catholic and universal beauty." And subsequently, "Thus, though the principles of taste be universal, and, nearly, if not entirely the same in all men; yet few are qualified to give judgment on any work of art, or establish their own sentiment as the standard of beauty," because "strong sense, united to delicate sentiment, improved by practice, perfected by comparison, and cleared of all prejudice, can alone entitle critics to this valuable character" (313). It is important to note that Hume does not believe it to be obvious who such critics might be: "Whether any particular person be endowed with good sense and a delicate imagination, free from prejudice, may often be the subject of dispute, and be liable to great discussion and inquiry: But that such a character is valuable and estimable will be agreed in by all mankind" (313). Thus Hume's theory does not by any means lead to a stifling and oppressive elitism—as many people assume when they hear that he believes some readers are better critics than others—for Hume does not define who those readers are, and he explicitly acknowledges that their identity is not obvious.

While Hume's discussion is sensitive and sensible, it hardly lays the problem to rest. He has done a good job of explaining how there might be universal, empirical rules of taste, how it is possible that we all follow the same principles, even though we often differ in our literary evaluations. But he doesn't give us any examples of such rules. Again, he never undertakes the empirical investigation to which his argument points. In consequence, we are left only with the vague terms of praise ("unified," "innovative") that he has criticized so convincingly, and perhaps the lingering, rigid, implausible rules of Neoclassicism (such as the three unities, according to which all dramatic action should take place within twenty-four hours, etc.). It was in the context of this dilemma, along with the disintegration of Neoclassicism as a literary force, and in relation to his own revolutionary epistemology, that Immanuel Kant took up the problem of aesthetics in *The Critique of Judgement*.

Kant is simply the greatest modern European philosopher. Virtually all subsequent epistemology, ethics, and aesthetics is formulated to some degree in relation to his work. His major ideas are presented in three volumes: *The Critique of Pure Reason* develops his epistemology; *The Critique of Practical Reason* sets out his ethical theory; and *The Critique of Judgement* presents his theory of the beautiful and the sublime.

In order to understand Kant's notions of beauty and sublimity, it is important to understand something about Kant's epistemology. According to Kant, the human mind is constituted by three faculties: knowledge, desire, and pleasure/pain. These faculties are governed by the understanding, reason, and judgment respectively. Kant devoted one *Critique* to each faculty. The first, *Pure Reason,* concerned the understanding and set out the conditions for the possibility of knowledge; the second, *Practical Reason,* concerned the reason and set out the conditions for ethical decision (which should govern desire); the third, *Judgement,* concerned judgment and set out, among other things, the conditions for aesthetics (one important aspect of the experience of pleasure and pain).

Kant's view of our experience is what might be called "radically constructive." Kant believed that our understanding of the world is primarily the result of our mind's formative activity. Specifically, sensations are a disordered whirl, a mere "sensible manifold" without shape or meaning. Our mind automatically organizes this sensible manifold in space and time and shapes the fragments of sensation into objects. In other words, our sensibility puts sensations into temporal order and spatial relations, and links certain elements together to form objects. These organized sensations are subsumed under concepts—including such empirical concepts as "lamp," "desk," and so on—and under the broader categories of the understanding, which define causal relations, and so forth.

Thus, I look at my desk and see a book, a computer, some pens. I push a button and the monitor lights up. According to Kant, what is happening here is that I have synthesized a scattered array of perceptions. What I am faced with when looking at my desk is, so to speak, a patch of this, a glint of that, a line here, and a fuzzy bit there. Moreover, as far as I am concerned, these are purely internal phenomena (that is, they are indistinguishable from a hallucination). My sensibility places them in space—outside of me—and orders them in time. It also links this patch of white and this glint, and these lines, into one object, these patches of brown into another object, these patches of red and black into a third object, and so on. These objects, which have been synthesized out of the disorganized manifold of sensibility by the *imagination* (*"Einbildungskraft,"* roughly "one-formation-power" or "one-image-power"), are subsumed under and filled out by various concepts: the first is bodied forth by the concept of a computer; the second is rendered comprehensible by "desk"; the third is understood by "lamp." Moreover, these concepts are themselves organized under various categories of the understanding; for example, having comprehended "switch" and "monitor" and the changes in the state of the switch (off/on) and the monitor (dark/lit), I subsume these under the category of cause and effect, thereby understanding the relation between the first event (my pressing the switch) and the second event (the monitor lighting up) as a matter of causal sequence.

Thus, for Kant, we do not in any way directly perceive the world. We do not directly perceive a switch or a monitor, or directly apprehend a causal relation. Rather, the structure of the human mind forms our (otherwise chaotic) experience into the switch, the monitor, and the causal relation. But for Kant this does not lead to subjectivism or idealism. (Here and below, I use "idealism" to refer to a doctrine that denies the existence of material objects independent of mind; I should note that Kant often uses the term "idealism" in this way, but not always.) Kant's theories do not lead to subjectivism because the structure of the human mind is universal (except for certain empirical concepts). They are not idealist for two reasons. First of all, for Kant, there is a *thing-in-itself* or "noumenon," a reality independent of our sensation and construction. Secondly, according to

Kant, reason provides us with a set of principles that necessarily lead us to conceive of the world and of ourselves in a realist manner.

Positing a noumenon is, of course, crucial in keeping Kant from becoming a subjectivist or an idealist. But this abstract conjecture of a thing-in-itself does not alone guarantee that our universal construction of the world is in any way accurate—that there really is a lamp, a computer, a causal connection between pressing the button and the monitor lighting up, or that there is anything at all corresponding to these notions. As we shall discuss below, German Idealist philosophers after Kant eliminated the noumenon entirely, and thus were led to a conception of the world as nothing but idea, the mind thinking itself. But even *with* the noumenon, Kant might have been left in this position—for our construction of the world could be completely imaginary. Indeed, this was one of the earliest and most important criticisms of Kant, one of the criticisms that inaugurated German Idealism: If causal connections are our own construction, in what sense can we say that our constructed world derives from (is caused by) the thing-in-itself; if our picture of the world is constructed by our categories and concepts without causal connection with a thing-in-itself, in what sense can we claim that this picture accurately represents a real world? The noumenon, it would seem, is a mere phantom, a meaningless assertion of realism in the midst of a system that pushes inexorably toward idealism (compare Fichte 54–55).

But Kant had a solution to this dilemma. And it is worth considering this solution in the context of more recent trends in criticism. Much current theoretical debate is framed in terms of an opposition between "foundationalists" and "antifoundationalists." Foundationalists wish to supply absolutely certain grounds upon which to base notions of truth, moral good, and so on. Antifoundationalists claim that this is a pointless project. Kant is neither a foundationalist nor an antifoundationalist, and that is why his position is so often misunderstood. Kant maintained that, through reason and judgment, we may infer what he called "regulative" and "transcendental" principles and ideas, that is, principles and ideas that we in effect have no choice but to accept, principles and ideas without which we cannot act or think. However, we cannot show these principles and ideas to be true; we can only argue that they are necessary to our thought. "A transcendental principle," Kant tells us, "is one by means of which is represented, *a priori*, the universal condition under which alone things can be in general objects of our cognition" (*Judgement* 17). Along the same lines, he writes in *The Critique of Pure Reason* that ideas of reason or transcendental ideas "are imposed by the very nature of reason itself, and therefore stand in necessary relation to the whole employment of understanding" (319).

We could consider the laws of logic as falling under this category. We simply cannot think without the principle of noncontradiction (the principle that a sentence cannot be both true and false in the same sense at the same time). But we cannot prove the validity of this principle without presupposing its validity in the course of the "proof." Thus, it is something we must simply assume; we have no choice in the matter. For our purposes, the most important of Kant's transcendental principles is that nature is "subjectively purposive," in other words, that the world is structured in such a way as to conform to our understanding. We do indeed construct the world. But we assume that the world is amenable to such construction. And we do this because we *must* assume that the world is subjectively purposive. As Kant puts it, "we say that nature specifies its universal laws according to the principles of purposiveness for our cognitive faculty, i.e., in accordance with the necessary business of the human understanding of finding the universal for the particular which perception offers it." However, in doing this we "neither prescribe to nature a law, nor do we learn one from it by observation." Rather, we prescribe to ourselves "a law for . . . reflection upon nature" (*Judgement* 22); we articulate a principle that we necessarily presuppose in undertaking any consideration of nature. This principle is not only important to Kant's anti-Idealism, it also forms the basis of his aesthetics, to which we may now turn.

Specifically, according to Kant, we experience pleasure whenever we experience the conformity of nature with the understanding, the purposiveness of the world with respect to our faculties. This feeling of pleasure is universal, and depends solely on universal faculties (sometimes referred to as "common sense," or perhaps less misleadingly "common sensibility"). On the other hand, Kant does note that pleasure in specific sorts of conformity becomes dulled with experience (see *Judgement* 79–81). This latter point becomes important to those strains of Romantic theory that urge art to "make things strange" and overcome habituation, but its basis is less elite and esoteric: Children delight in recognizing ordinary objects and ordinary causal relations or object "syntheses" and continuities (for instance, they take pleasure in recognizing that the ball that went under one end of the sofa is the same ball that came out from the other end). This is not true of adults, due, presumably, to the sort of habituation mentioned by Kant. The pleasure of beauty is a subtype of our general pleasure in the conformity of nature with understanding and imagination. Specifically, it is that part (of pleasure deriving from conformity) that is *independent of any particular concept under which an object is subsumed*. As Kant put it, the judgment of beauty is a judgment of "purposiveness without a purpose," the general conformity of an object to our sensibility without reference to a specific concept (with its corresponding functions, values, and so on). The imagination synthesizes or unifies the object and brings it into harmony with the understanding. This harmony is judged beautiful, Kant insists, only in respect of its formal conformity with the structure of the understanding, and not due to any particular concept or definition.

This view may make more intuitive sense if one thinks of music. We experience pleasure in music insofar as we synthesize it into a unity, hearing melodic and harmonic patterns and not random noises. This synthesis allows us to experience pleasure in the conformity of the sound with imagination and understanding, for it is patterned, unified, structured through these faculties, and thus pleasing to them. Or, rather, it is pleasing to these faculties because it can be synthesized, but has not been synthesized so easily or automatically that we are habituated and thus dulled to its conformity with our faculties. For example, Jones may experience pleasure in Mozart, but not in Barry Manilow or in the avant-garde composer Karlheinz Stockhausen. The problem with Manilow would be that his tunes are too readily synthesized and thus immediately become banal (compare Kant's assertion that we soon "weary" of "a song . . . produced in accordance with . . . rules" [*Judgement* 80]). As to Stockhausen, Jones might find his works random, unsynthesizable. Of the three, Jones would find Mozart alone conformable to the faculties (unlike Stockhausen), but not habitually so (unlike Manilow). Finally, consider the relation of all this to concepts. Ordinarily, we synthesize sounds and subsume them under concepts. We hear a sequence of beeps, synthesize them into a pattern, and subsume them under a concept—something like "car horn"; this, in turn, leads to practical action, such as checking to see if the traffic light has changed from stop to go. Our pleasure in music is removed from any such conceptual subsumption, with its practical consequences.

It is worth remarking on some implications of this view, most of them developed by Kant himself. First of all, all judgments of beauty—or judgments of taste, in Kant's terminology—must be "singular"; they must apply only to particular objects (a particular rose, a particular poem, a particular person), which may be appropriately synthesized and brought into harmonious "play" with the imagination and understanding. In other words, judgments of beauty do not apply to classes of objects (to, say, roses as a group), for in that case such judgments would be tied to concepts—

specifically, the concepts defining the classes (for instance, "rose"). Related to this, there can be no normative rules governing taste—no "principles of taste," Kant calls them—for all judgments of taste are unique and conceptless.

Kant's insistence on the irrelevance of concepts would seem to imply that judgments of taste should have the form "That is beautiful" rather than "That is a beautiful x" ("That is a beautiful rose" or poem or whatever). As we shall see, however, Kant did not take it to mean this. In any case, it necessarily entails that each judgment of beauty is a judgment of a pure experience, and thus it is not open to conceptual evaluation as valid or invalid. It is not open to norms or to dispute. As Kant puts it, there is no *"ground of proof* which would force a judgment of taste upon anyone" (126). And later: "The judgment of taste is distinguished from a logical judgment in this that the latter subsumes a representation under the concept of the object, while the former does not subsume it under any concept"; if it did, "the necessary universal agreement [in these judgments] would be capable of being compelled by proofs," which it is not (128–29). The Kantian view also implies that there are no empirical rules of beauty— no "laws of taste," in Kant's phrase—such as those posited by Hume.

This purely individual conception of beauty is clearly at odds with Neoclassical doctrine, which lingered in the writings of Hume and Burke. At least prima facie, Kant's view seems entirely anti-Aristotelian also. It would seem that Kant's conception of art is not only nonmimetic, but antimimetic. Again, precisely what an object is—whether it is a chair or a dog or a cloud—would seem to be irrelevant to the judgment of taste. As we have just noted, Kant opposed the judgment of taste, which does not involve "any concept," to the logical judgment, which "subsumes a representation under the concept of the object." Or, as Kant put it elsewhere, "That which in the representation of an object is merely subjective, i.e., which decides its reference to the subject, not to the object, is its aesthetical character" (25).

On the other hand, Kant did offer some qualifications of this general view, at one point going so far as to insist that in art (as opposed to nature), mimetic accuracy must be taken into account (154). One could explain this by saying that our experience of beauty is nonconceptual merely in that we do not have a concept of the "beautiful" under which we subsume objects. Perhaps Kant would allow the subsumption of objects under *some* concepts in judgments of taste. Perhaps, despite his statement, just quoted, that "The judgment of taste . . . does not subsume [a representation] under any concept" (128–29), he only rigorously excludes normative aesthetic concepts, such as "beautiful." In other words, something is a dog if it falls under our concept of *dog*. Indeed, something is a sonnet if it falls under our concept of *sonnet*. In other words, the object has certain properties that go to constitute what we count as a dog or a sonnet. However, there is no such concept by which we judge things that are beautiful. A poem is a sonnet if it has a certain number of lines, a certain type of rhyme scheme, and so on. But we cannot define objective properties that, if present, make the object beautiful—or, more generally, pleasurable (we shall return to this presently). In this view, the thrust of Kant's non-conceptualism would not be, in the first place, antimimetic. But, ultimately, this does not solve the problem. For even this minimal nonconceptualism would seem to exclude mimetic criteria of beauty along with all other criteria; indeed, Kant appears to indicate just this, in the passages quoted above, and elsewhere. In short, to say that mimetic accuracy is relevant to judging beauty not only involves subsuming the representation under some concept ("horse," in a particular equestrian painting). It also involves establishing mimetic accuracy as part of a concept of beauty relevant to the determination of whether or not an object is beautiful—and thus it involves defining a concept of beauty of precisely the sort Kant sets out to deny.

Perhaps, then, Kant's view would be something along the following lines. Harmony between intuition and understanding does not make any necessary reference to concepts. However, in certain cases, one cannot avoid linking intuitions with concepts. For example, in representative painting, certain images trigger certain concepts (of people, animals, landscapes, or whatever). Certainly, Kant must say that concepts do, as a matter of contingent fact, enter into the experience of art and are thus part of aesthetic experience in many cases. He claims that *judgments* of taste cannot subsume the object under a concept. This is not to say that concepts do not enter into the *understanding* of the work and thus the experience of the harmony between imagination and understanding. Of course, in many cases—including most music and decorative art—concepts do not enter. But once concepts have entered (in, say, representational painting) there cannot be a harmonious interplay between intuition and understanding if the discrepancy between the concept and the intuition is inharmonious— if, say, a portrait is inaccurate or perspective is marred. This makes a certain amount of sense, but still seems inconsistent with Kant's general principles. This inconsistency is most obvious if Kant intends realism to operate normatively (that is, to provide grounds for judging a work good or bad). But suppose this is merely a descriptive claim—in such-and-such circumstances, we just don't experience the harmonious interplay of image and understanding. This too is inconsistent with Kant's principles in that it implies an empirical law of taste that Kant equally denies (not to mention the fact that such an empirical claim would be false, as demonstrated by a wide range of modernist, non-European, and other art). Moreover, none of this really accounts for Kant's sharp distinction between natural beauty and artistic beauty. After all, if the crucial issue concerns the relation between the object and some concept, it should not really matter whether the object in question is, for example, a real person or a portrait of a person. Indeed, if it does matter, then harmony with the concept should be more important in the case of the real person—think of our reaction to a Picasso painting, then to a real person with three eyes, and a nose on the side of his/her face. (Kant in effect acknowledges this point but maintains that such considerations are "no longer purely aesthetical" in the case of natural beauty [154].)

Perhaps the most plausible explanation of all this is that, living prior to the development of modern and postmodern avant-garde art, Kant could not accept the radically antimimetic consequences of his own theory. In other words, Kant does contradict himself, because he continues tacitly to believe in and operate on many of the traditional aesthetic principles in which he was educated, but with which his theory is inconsistent. (This sort of discrepancy between a theorist's implicit beliefs and the implications of his/her theory is fairly common.)

Another possible problem with Kant's theory arises from the fact that, for Kant, *all* judgments of pleasure—not just aesthetic judgments—are nonconceptual in the most relevant sense. We do not have an adjudicative concept for "fun" or even "pleasurable" any more than we have one for "beautiful." What, then, distinguishes beauty from fun, or an experience of beauty from having fun? This is a question that Kant addresses directly. To be a pure judgment of taste, thus a judgment involving beauty, Kant tells us, our evaluation of an object must be disinterested: "when the question is if a thing is beautiful," we are indifferent to anything having to do with its practical nature; specifically, "we do not want to know whether anything depends or can depend on the existence of the thing" (38). According to Kant, this is what distinguishes the beautiful from the merely pleasant (which involves our self-interest), and one thing that distinguishes it from the good. Unfortunately, we frequently confuse the beautiful and the pleasant and "thus lay down an erroneous judgment of taste" (51). This is one principle that Kant takes over from earlier philosophers of aesthetics—for example, the case of the playgoer who is friends with the playwright fits here, as does mere sensuous pleasure (such as sexual pleasure).

Kant accepts other concepts from philosophical aesthetics as well. Some of these too are difficult to reconcile with his general principles. For example, Kant allows for differences in sensibility resulting from history and culture, but history and culture would seem to have a place only in the determination of concepts, which, again, should be irrelevant to aesthetic experience. Indeed, it is not easy to see how Kant can account for the fact that, unlike Jones, some people never find Barry Manilow habitual or banal, and others come to find Stockhausen pleasurably synthesizable—or why some people appreciate Japanese classical music, but not Indian classical music, or Indian, but not European, or European, but not Japanese.

Perhaps in each case we could assume that our synthetic capacities can be trained or developed in experience; thus individually, historically, or culturally different experiences would lead to different imaginative/synthetic abilities and/or propensities. (For the intercultural case, think of a European first hearing Japanese classical music and finding it an unsynthesizable chaos.) While Kant does not really develop such a notion (beyond mentioning habituation to everyday synthesis), this sort of "education of sensibility" does become central to subsequent Romantic theory, as we shall see. This still seems at odds with Kant's insistence on the universality of common sensibility. But perhaps the tension is with Kant's specific articulation of his theory, rather than with the theory itself in its basic principles; perhaps this is merely the result of Kant's focus on straightforward and simple examples (decorative arts, birdsong) where these issues do not arise. Given that some syntheses can become habitual, it may be reasonable to think that further, more complex syntheses could develop, that the synthetic faculty of imagination could grow in its capacities. On the other hand, precisely how this would occur, or even what it means for synthesis to develop, is highly obscure. The most obvious way of accounting for this would be to say that we achieve a fuller representation of the thing-in-itself. But, given Kant's general principles, it is not clear how—or even if—this can occur.

In any event, whatever he may draw from past theorists, and however consistent or inconsistent he may be in these respects, Kant breaks with those earlier writers who emphasized the craft of writing (for example, adherence to the three unities), maintaining in contrast that great art is produced by natural genius: "beautiful art is only possible as a product of genius." And genius involves "a *talent* [thus, not a skill] for producing that for which no definite rule can be given." Moreover, genius "cannot describe or indicate scientifically how it brings about its products" (150–51)—for this description would amount to a set of adjudicative criteria for beauty. (Note that this too seems to exclude any concern with mimetic accuracy, indicating again that Kant's statements on accuracy of representation are simply inconsistent with the rest of his theory.) Great art is, then, inspired and sui generis. It is marked by *"originality"* and "is entirely opposed to the *spirit of imitation"* (that is, imitation of other artists; 150). Genius is a matter of *"audacity* in expression" (162)—specifically "expression of thoughts and of intuitions [thus perceptions, in Kant's terminology]" (165; "thoughts" finding their proper outlet in the verbal arts, "intuitions"/perceptions in the plastic arts and music)—as well as spirited or creative imagination (163).

Thus, rather than a craftsperson engaging in imitation through the employment of universal rules (the standard Neoclassical idea), we have a genius engaging in expression through creative imagination. This view is a necessary outcome of two of Kant's general epistemological conclusions: (1) that aesthetic experience is conceptless, thus singular and not determined by general rules; and (2) that aesthetic pleasure is likely to become dulled by habit, thus necessitating novelty (as opposed to imitation). As we shall see, variations on this view are central to Romanticism and later movements.

Continuing with Kant's more specific views, we find that he is consistent with earlier writers (in every tradition) in insisting that the judgment of taste is not a matter of mere ornamental charms; however, he shows his distance from earlier writers by insisting that emotions too are irrelevant to judgments of taste (58), for they are bound up with interest (62). Kant's point is most succinctly put in connection with the sublime: "we can regard an object as *fearful* without being afraid *of* it . . . . He who fears can form no judgment about the sublime in nature" (100). In connection with this, Kant makes a somewhat obscure distinction between affections and emotions (see 113); unlike emotions, affections are aesthetically relevant. Readers will immediately recall the similar, but more lucid and better developed, distinction in Sanskrit aesthetics between emotion (*bhāva*) and sentiment (*rasa*). This seems to be quite close to what Kant had vaguely in mind. Indeed, a number of points in Kant read like an obscure version of Sanskrit aesthetics. It is hard to say to what extent this is a matter of influence. Later Romantic theorists were certainly influenced by (a highly selective version of) South and East Asian philosophies (metaphysical theology and literature itself more than aesthetic theory). At the very least, Kant developed some parallel ideas, which later theorists could more readily combine with Indian and other non-Western views.

In any event, the mention of fear and fearfulness takes us from the beautiful to the sublime. At a purely descriptive level, the sublime is, for Kant as for his precursors, a painful pleasure involving a sense of the terrible. However, Kant goes on from this to give a systematic account of the sublime. While the beautiful is the result of the conformity of intuition with the faculty of understanding due to form alone (without subsumption under a concept), the sublime is the result of an indication of formlessness connected with the faculty of reason. Specifically, reason produces *ideas* that cannot be subsumed under the understanding—the idea of God, the idea of the noumenon, the idea of freedom. The sublime is what gives rise to the sense of infinitude, the unconceptualizability that characterizes the "objects" of these ideas (that is, God Him/Herself, the noumenon itself, freedom itself, and so on). Thus it is associated with a sense of fearfulness that is more akin to respect than to dread; indeed, it is most similar to what the Arab theorists referred to as "piety," their version of Aristotle's "fear."

Note that, given this explanation of sublimity, no object of experience can itself be sublime—for such an object is necessarily finite and conceptualizable. Rather, an experiential object can inspire a feeling of sublimity in us. Kant does cite some experiential properties that tend to contribute to this—for example, unencompassable enormity in size (see 94). However, even these are of limited importance, for objects inspire a feeling of sublimity through their suggestion of ideas—specifically, through what Kant calls "aesthetical ideas."

Aesthetical ideas are a sort of variation on the ideas of reason. The ideas of reason *proper* are purely intellectual and reflective. Their milieu is philosophy or theology. Aesthetical ideas, in contrast, are linked with some sensible content, some image, which cannot by any means encompass the idea, but which serves to give us a feeling of it, an intimation of, for example, the awesome grandeur of God, not merely an intellectual formulation of the necessity of the idea of God. Aesthetical ideas are to art what the ideas of reason are to philosophy.

Aesthetical ideas, Kant tells us, "do not, like *logical attributes,* represent what lies in our concepts of the sublimity and majesty of creation, but something different, which gives occasion to the imagination to spread itself over a number of kindred representations that arouse more thought than can be expressed in a concept determined by words" (158). Kant cites as an example the inscription on the Temple of Isis: "I am all that is and that was and that shall be, and no mortal hath lifted my veil." He comments: "Perhaps nothing more sublime was ever said" (160 n). This is a particularly good example for Kant, for the inscription makes reference not only to those ultimate, nonconceptual realities that we strive to think in terms of the ideas of reason (the thing-in-itself, freedom, God), but also to our inability to conceptualize them.

In keeping with this analysis, Kant links the feeling of the sublime in particular with morality—not with specific moral precepts, but with moral feeling. For Kant, it is precisely in the development of the moral faculty of reason that judgments of sublimity achieve their universality. This is not to say that everyone develops appropriately. There are some who cannot fully experience the sublime because their moral cultivation has been inadequate. But, again, this is not a matter of a lack of familiarity with specific moral principles. Rather, it is a matter of moral feeling or sensibility. Thus Kant tells us that someone "who remains unmoved in the presence of that which we judge to be sublime" is someone we judge to have "no *feeling*" (105). For the sublime does not incline us to specific moral acts, but rather it "prepares us to esteem something highly even in opposition to our own (sensible) interest" (108). Though this involves a moral conception of art, it marks a radical change from previous European moralism. In this view—which is, again, closer to the Arabic view of takhyil and piety than to earlier European ideas—art does not teach us what is moral, but trains us to feel the moral sentiment. Though, here too, it is not entirely clear how such training might occur within Kant's general framework.

Kant's theories are open to criticism on the grounds of inconsistency and pernicious vagueness. (Does it really explain anything to say that the feeling of beauty results from the "conformity" of nature with the understanding? Doesn't this merely change the question from "What is beauty?" to "In what sense does a beautiful object 'conform' to my understanding in a way that an ugly object does not?") However, in terms of breadth of philosophical thought and extent of influence, Kant is unparalleled in modern philosophy. While it is no doubt true that ideas alone do not determine even intellectual history, Kant's ideas, along with the similar non-European ideas brought to Europe through colonialism, did have a profound impact on the way later writers conceived of literature, criticism, and the world, first of all through their pervasive presence in Romanticism. Kant's work is part of a turning point in Western thought and helped to initiate a way of thinking that, for better or for worse, continues to dominate humanistic reflection in the West, and to a degree elsewhere as well.

## Romanticism

Romanticism is frequently said to constitute a radical break with the past, the beginning of a new form of literary and philosophical thought. Like many broad generalizations regarding history, this is not entirely true. There are many continuities between Romanticism and earlier European theories—for instance, a recurring moralism. Moreover, many of the distinguishing features of Romanticism are to be found in Classical texts—for example, in the expressivism of Plato's "Ion" and Longinus' "On the Sublime." And yet, Romanticism is different. In many ways, it does define a new, or newly dominant, way of thinking, not only about literature, but about the world—a way of thinking that has in effect defined all subsequent literary thought. Despite the putative anti-Romanticism of modernism and postmodernism, prominent twentieth-century theories of literature, from New Criticism to deconstruction, remain firmly rooted in Romantic presuppositions.

As we have already noted, Kant marks the crucial break with Classicism and Neoclassicism. In some ways, his *Critique of Judgement* contains both the earlier and the later tendencies within it, most obviously in the division between the beautiful and the sublime, the one focusing on form, the other on formlessness, the one on conformity to understanding, the other on inconceivability. However, in Kant's case, the beautiful is already nonconceptual, nonmimetic, unregulated. In other thinkers, the division between the two primarily aesthetical properties—beauty and sublimity—more directly parallels that between the Neoclassical and the Romantic. Indeed, marking out a division of this sort is itself characteristic of Romantic thought. We shall repeatedly come upon examples of a dichotomy parallel to that between the beautiful and the sublime: Schiller's opposition between the formal and the sensuous, Coleridge's pairing of the mechanical and the organic, Nietzsche's separation of the Apollonian and the Dionysian, Bakhtin's contrast of the monologic/epical and the dialogic/novelistic. Even Freud's opposition between Eros and the death instinct and Derrida's between the logocentric and the deconstructive participate in this Romantic dualism. More exactly, one of the recurrent features that marks Romantic thought is the opposition between a systematic, rule-governed structure, which is abstract, static, uninvolved, and a violent, unruly force of nature which sweeps one along in movement. The systematic may be compared to Milton's God, far distant, all-knowing, imperturbable; the unruly to Milton's Satan, close by, deluded, weeping and cursing his fate. For the Romantics, a great poem requires both the systematic and the unruly, both God and Satan—but they are still of the devil's party.

This dichotomy is bound up with the Romantic understanding of what it means to be human. Most earlier European (and non-European) thinkers defined humans by their difference from animals. In this view, what makes one human is reason, in opposition to instinct. With the Romantics, humans came to be defined primarily by their difference from machines. In consequence, emotion, sensitivity, even brute instinct, came to be seen as essentially human, in opposition to any sort of mechanism, including mechanical reason.

In keeping with their Manichean view of both art and human life, Romantics proper as well as romantics (that is, the modern and postmodern progeny of the Romantic movement) tend to shift away from the traditional triadic opposition between poetry, history, and philosophy, to a diadic opposition between poetry (literature, the humanities) and science, with business or industry/technology (science as business) sometimes added as a third term. The nature of the contrast is correspondingly altered. Earlier writers, such as Sidney, had tended to elevate poetry for its potential didactic value, its power of teaching what is morally good. Poetry accomplished this by imitating reality—not simply repeating it, as did history, but reforming it according to moral and other principles derived from philosophy. Thus poetry was related to history, in being particular, but also to philosophy, in involving ethical precepts. The Romantic contrast with science is not entirely different from this earlier contrast with history, for science too was seen as merely repeating reality. More exactly, science was conceived of (inaccurately) as a distanced, frequently mechanical, transcription of reality. However, in previous European theories, poetry was conceived of as a *more* rule-governed activity than history—for history too often lacked moral principle. In the Romantic view, however, poetry was conceived of as *less* rule-governed than science. In opposition to a distanced, mechanical transcription of reality, an inhuman duplication made by a self-possessed observer, poetry was the organic, creative, fully human expression of a possessed—not self-possessed—experiencer. Along the same lines, when added, business was in effect a second form of mechanism, parallel with science, in this case an amoral adherence to the mechanics of the marketplace, the reduction of human aspiration and feeling to the rationalized, machine-dominated production and accumulation of wealth.

Thus, Romantic theory came to stress two elements of poetry as definitive: expression and creation. From imitation of external reality transformed by rules, poetry became the creation of a new reality out of the expression of inner emotion. Because of this, it was superior to science and to business.

First of all, poetry was thought to be humanizing. A standard romantic doctrine—common down to our own day—is that poetry trains the sensibility. Science and industry turn us into machines for recording facts or generating gain; poetry develops us into men and women. We read poetry in order to learn how to feel, how to empathize, how to experience the world, how to live. Science can at best help us to achieve the goals we forge in the smithy of poetry, smooth the path of a life made by poetry.

Again, this view is not unrelated to the didactic view of literature found in Sidney and others, but it is nonetheless different, closer, in fact, to the Arabic view, as we have already noted. Training the sensibility is a larger, and a more inward or subjective task than exemplifying moral precepts, and it is closely related to creative expression (itself more akin to the Arabic takhyīl than to the standard European conception of mimesis, or even to Burke's notion of imagination).

Indeed, in referring to "creative expression," it is important to emphasize not only the expressiveness of the Romantic poet, but his/her creativity as well. For the Romantic poet not only expresses a feeling, but re-creates the world. Romanticism partakes of Idealism, the post-Kantian movement in German philosophy that did away with the noumenon and did away with Kant's transcendental and regulative principles, leaving nothing but mind—mind as subject encountering itself as object, creating and re-creating itself. While it has had only limited effects in the natural sciences and in Anglo-American philosophy, German Idealist philosophy has been central to the humanities and to Continental social sciences and is to be found in such aspects of humanistic thought as the commonplace that we not only observe the world, but actively make it. All contemporary schools of philosophical and critical thought agree that the human mind is active in construing—understanding, interpreting—the world. But those derived from Romanticism tend to see this activity as at least in part formative as well. For Kant, the human mind structured sensations into objects, relations, and so on. However, the notion of the noumenon and the transcendental principle of subjective purposiveness make this activity a matter of knowing rather than making. The removal of the noumenon, the transcendental principle, or both, makes the structuring activity of mind partially or wholly creative, more a matter of making than of knowing.

In training our very sensibility, then, the poet becomes the ultimate creator. He/she shapes the very way we think—conceive, conceptualize, experience, indeed *make* the world—and thereby shapes the world itself. He/she does this through imagination, Kant's faculty of synthesis, now elevated to a faculty of new creation. The poet is thus more important, more necessary, more valuable for the Romantics than he/she—or anyone else—had been for earlier theorists. The poet is, in effect, second only to God.

But, of course, not all Romantic theorists are the same. I should like to take a few major examples, briefly outlining the thought of each. In part to give the reader a rest from German philosophy, I first discuss the theories put forth by three philosophically oriented literary artists—Schiller, Coleridge, and Shelley. I then turn to the great German Idealists Fichte, Schelling, and Hegel, with an intervening discussion of de Stael and Romantic historicism. I conclude with a brief discussion of Nietzsche.

Like a number of Romantic writers, Friedrich von Schiller drew extensively from Kant's *Critique of Judgement* in formulating his own aesthetic principles. In his extremely influential *Letters on the Aesthetic Education of Man,* he presents a number of arguments that typify Romantic attitudes. Unfortunately, Schiller does not develop his ideas entirely consistently, and they are difficult if not impossible to puzzle out in their details. However, the general structure of his theoretical views is clear enough.

Schiller begins, like many Romantic writers, with a basic opposition—that between sense and intellect. Sense—roughly, Kant's sensible intuition—is associated with matter, life, concreteness, and multiplicity. In contrast, intellect—roughly, Kant's faculties of understanding and reason—is associated with form, law, abstraction, and unity. For Schiller, neither is good or bad, per se. Or, rather, each is bad when separated from the other. Each is good when correctly combined with the other. Beyond being linked with an aspect of the human mind, each category represents a broad tendency of human behavior. We are governed by a sense drive and a form drive. To be human is to combine both sense and form. Sense alone is animal. Form alone is mere inhuman abstraction. It is only through sense combined with form that we are human. To be human is to fuse the concrete and the abstract into the aesthetic, the unified and the multiple into a unity of multiplicity, life and form into living form, matter and law into beauty, the sense drive and the form drive into a third drive, the "play drive."

More exactly, when either the individual or society operates solely on the basis of sense, then there is nothing but strife of natural impulses, anarchy, and struggle of power. When the individual or society operates solely on the basis of form, then there is despotism, rigid classification, mere mechanism. When sense and form combine, society becomes a unified community that still allows for diverse abilities and experiences, and the individual becomes fully human—not basely animal nor insensibly mechanical, but truly humanly alive and living a truly humanly moral life (for instance, he/she replaces animal lust and mechanical self-denial with full, human, sexual love).

Unfortunately, civilization—especially in the development of science, business, and the various technologies that connect them—has split the formal from the sensual, the intellect from feeling, leaving people divided, alienated, and dehumanized (compare T. S. Eliot's notion of "the dissociation of sensibility" ["The Metaphysical Poets" 247]). Indeed, when reason is linked to sense today, Schiller tells us, it is done wrongly. This linkage does not operate to elevate the individual from animal desire or to free him/her from the despotic mechanisms of law. Rather, it serves to make animal passions mechanical and despotic—for example, by systematizing or "rationalizing" greed in capitalist industry.

As this last example indicates, the mere concatenation of form and sense is not adequate to produce a fully human person in a true human community. More exactly, sense and form may be conjoined mechanically or synthesized organically and humanly. In capitalism, form and sense are either divorced from one another or are linked mechanically. But how is one to avoid a false, mechanical conjunction, which brings together what is worst in both drives, and achieve in its place a truly human and organic synthesis, which fuses what is best in them, especially in an age that pushes inexorably toward mere mechanistic conjunction?

Schiller's solution to this dilemma is aesthetic education, the training of sensibility. For Schiller, to achieve full humanity, one must be trained to experience beauty; one must become a person of aesthetic sensibility. Since beauty is the perfect reconciliation of form and sense, to cultivate an appreciation of beauty is to cultivate a sensitivity to such a human and organic reconciliation—a sensitivity that presumably extends to all other areas of personal and social life, allowing the pervasive reconciliation of form and sense in these areas as well. More exactly, it allows one to break away from animalistic attachments through aesthetic disinterest, as emphasized by Kant (note that this disinterest is crucially missing in mechanical pseudo-reconciliations of form and sense). At the same time, it anchors the formal—including pure morality and abstract intellect—in sense experience and feeling, thereby keeping it vital.

Samuel Taylor Coleridge too took up many of the standard Romantic themes—including the opposition between the formal or mechanical and the vital or living—and developed them in a philosophical manner. Perhaps most importantly, Coleridge drew an influential distinction between fancy and imagination. Beauty, he maintained, must exhibit "multeity in unity" (*Principles* 472). But how is the synthesis proper to such unified multiplicity achieved? Not by fancy, he tells us, but by imagination. The former is mechanical and involves "fixities and definites"; it is "no other than a mode of memory emancipated from the order of time and space." In contrast, the imagination is genuinely creative. It does not merely stitch together prefabricated materials, but fashions the world. Drawing on the Idealist epistemology of Fichte and Schelling, Coleridge goes on from here to distinguish primary from secondary imagination: "The primary imagination I hold to be the living power and prime agent of all human perception, and as a repetition in the finite mind of the eternal act of creation in the infinite *I am* [God]. The secondary imagination I consider as an echo of the former, coexisting with the conscious will, yet still as identical with the primary in the *kind* of its agency and differing only in *degree*, and in the *mode* of its operation" (*Biographia* 263). The primary imagination, as Coleridge has it, is the imagination that creates the world in experience; the secondary imagination is the imagination that re-creates the world in art.

As this implies, in Coleridge's view, the world is ultimately coextensive with mind. "During the act of knowledge itself, the objective and the subjective are so instantly united," he tells us, that they are "coninstantaneous and one" (242). Knowledge, in other words, is not merely a matter of recognizing something about an object. It is a matter of joining in cognitive unity with that object. Moreover, this unity is possible only because there is ultimately no thing-in-itself distinct from mind, no object distinct from subject, and thus "the spirit in all the objects which it views, views only itself" (250). The goal of all philosophy, Coleridge avers, is nothing other than the explication and demonstration of this coincidence of the subject who knows and the world that is known: "The theory of natural philosophy would then be completed, when all nature was demonstrated to be identical in essence with that, which in its highest known power exists in man as intelligence and self-consciousness" (243). Again, this is German Idealism—in effect, Coleridge's summary of Fichte and Schelling.

Percy Bysshe Shelley too takes up many of the standard Romantic themes in his "A Defense of Poetry," one of the most extreme statements of the humanizing function of the poet. Like Coleridge, Shelley was not a philosopher; however, he developed his poetic theory in a philosophical mode continuous with that of the German Idealists. He begins his essay, in typical Romantic fashion, by contrasting reason/analysis and imagination/synthesis. Reason, he argues, must be a mere instrument for the higher faculty of imagination. And, since poetry is "the expression of the imagination" (516), reason must be subordinated especially to poetry. But why precisely does (poetic) imagination deserve pride of place? For the usual Romantic reasons: It is through the synthetic activity of imagination that we experience life and it is through the activity of the poet that imagination itself is both uttered and developed. In contrast, reason merely orders and manipulates experiences and ideas already made. Though not quite as Idealist as Coleridge, Shelley sees the poet as forging new unities, new relations, new concepts through his/her re-creation of language. One could see this in Kantian terms: the poet can refashion the concepts of the understanding—which are, indeed, roughly linguistic—and thus alter many of the formative principles through which we organize the world. At the same time, Shelley here anticipates the emphasis on language as determinative of the world, an emphasis that, though important in Hegel, comes into the mainstream of humanistic study only much later, in, for example, various forms of structuralism and poststructuralism. This specifically *linguistic* idealism/romanticism has proven enormously influential in recent years.

Shelley develops his (moderate) idealist views by maintaining that "All things exist as they are perceived; at least in relation to the percipient" (527). He goes on to maintain that our everyday (mechanical) existence dulls our perceptions until we hardly even experience the world. Poetry makes us see again, and in doing so creates the world for us; it "creates anew the universe after it has been annihilated in our minds by the recurrence of impressions blunted by reiteration" (528). Here Shelley develops a view that we have already seen in Kant (see also Coleridge, *Biographia* 264) and that we will later find reiterated by a range of authors in a variety of modern and postmodern movements. For example, his claim is substantially identical with the Russian formalist view that poetry makes the world "strange." It is even to be found in the view of Adorno and Horkheimer that the function of art is to shock us into thought and remove us from the mechanical mindlessness of the culture industry. In any event, this function of the poet in creating or re-creating experience leads Shelley to assert, in a famous phrase, that "Poets are the unacknowledged legislators of the world" (529).

Unsurprisingly, the poet cannot create by rules—after all, he/she is fashioning the very concepts that allow rules to exist. To be guided by rules would be to have imagination serve reason, whereas reason should only operate on the basis of imagination. Thus, the poet must create by inspiration. Inspiration is, for Shelley as it was for Wordsworth, a reliving of intense emotion—a secondary rather than a primary imagination, in Coleridge's terms. But, for Shelley, this second moment is always a loss, always a decline: "the mind in creation is as a fading coal, which some invisible influence, like an inconstant wind, awakens to transitory brightness," though the fire itself does not return. "[W]hen composition begins, inspiration is already on the decline, and the most glorious poetry that has ever been communicated to the world is probably a feeble shadow of the original conceptions of the poet" (257).

Beyond idealism, Shelley took up a number of other typical romantic motifs. For example, like Schiller, Keats, and others, he emphasized the empathic function of poetry and its humanizing effect, an effect far more important than the mere teaching of moral doctrine. Thus, he tells us that in listening to a poem, "auditors must have been refined and enlarged by sympathy with such great and lovely impersonations" (519). Directly addressing the moral issue, he notes (echoing Plato) that some of the characters with whom we sympathize are immoral. But he insists, in striking contrast with pre-Romantic writers, that this is irrelevant because this immorality is superficial. Indeed, he argues that Milton is great precisely because he neglected "direct moral purpose" (524). Poetry does not teach ethical precepts, but "awakens and enlarges the mind itself by rendering it the receptacle of a thousand unapprehended combinations of thought" (519). Again, poetry is valuable not because it teaches us to act virtuously, but because it makes us sensible of the world and of others, makes us human, creates for us a human experience in a mechanical world. Moreover, the "great secret of morals is love . . . an identification of ourselves with the beautiful which exists in thought, action, or person, not our own" (519). Thus "The great instrument of moral good is the imagination" (520; contrast standard pre-Romantic view that reason is the instrument of good), especially insofar as this is manifest in poetry, for poetry "strengthens and purifies the affections, enlarges the imagination, and adds spirit to sense" (525).

As we have already noted, much of the theoretical work we have been considering derives more or less directly from the great works of German Idealism. In 1794, the *Wissenschaftslehre* or *Science of Knowledge,* by Johann Gottlieb Fichte, in effect inaugurated German Idealism, a philosophical movement that dominated its own time and that continues to exert a powerful influence on contemporary literary and philosophical thought, especially on the Continent. Fichte begins with Kant's critical philosophy, setting out, in effect, to be more Kantian than Kant himself. Specifically, Fichte sees Kant as remaining attached to certain aspects of traditional, pre-Kantian philosophy that are not consistent with Kant's own revolutionary insights. It is, then, Fichte's task to redevelop the Kantian system so that it is fully consistent with those revolutionary insights and is no longer bound by "precritical" views (which is to say, by those views that dominated philosophy prior to Kant's critiques).

More exactly, Fichte begins from the principle that any philosophy must explain experience, for a "finite rational being has nothing beyond experience" (8). In order to account for experience, Fichte tells us, a philosopher has two choices. He/she may see experience as "determined independently of our freedom" by a thing-in-itself or he/she may see experience as defined by the pure freedom of a self-in-itself without a noumenon (8). The former view, he calls "dogmatism," the latter, "idealism" (9). Needless to say, Fichte argues in favor of the latter alternative. He does so in part for reasons of realism. For Fichte, the most realistic view of experience is the view that fully allows experience to be accurate or true. If the knowing self and the known object are one and the same—as is the case in the Idealist view—then true experience is clearly possible. However, if the known object is a necessarily inaccessible noumenon, then it is not clear how experience can be true or accurate, for the object that determines truth and accuracy is defined precisely by its inaccessibility to experience.

Alternatively, one might say that, even if we posit a noumenon, it cannot be considered to provide any criterion for truth. Even if we posit a noumenon, our experience, in all of its richness and detail, necessarily defines truth and accuracy *for us.* And that leaves the noumenon with no experiential or other role. Consider a simple perception. Kant shows us that our mental faculties synthesize an object, its causal relations, and so forth. One way of thinking about this is to say that the mental faculties provide the form, while the noumenon is the content. But, Fichte points out (23), our experience is, in that case, solely one of form. There is nothing in our experience of, say, a lamp or a dog or a book which can legitimately be separated off as the content, opposed to the form. Take away everything contributed by the forms of sensible intuition, the understanding, and so on—take away the color, the shape, the other sensible properties, the temporal and spatial relations—and nothing is left. Indeed, we cannot even separate off the putative noumenal content as that which *causes* the experience, for causality itself is part of our mental synthesis. In sum, "Form and matter are not separate items; the totality of form is the matter."

For Fichte, then, the synthetic capacity of the mind is necessarily not at all mimetic. It does not represent or reproduce or even organize a reality. Rather, in making all that we know or can know, it makes reality, for it makes form, and form is reality. This creative synthetic capacity is, precisely, the *imagination,* and, according to Fichte, "the thing . . . is nothing else but the *totality of . . . relations unified by the imagination*" (23).

As this conception of creative imagination indicates, the self, for Fichte, is not itself a thing. It is, rather, an act, specifically an act that forms things. Moreover, it is an act that is both free and necessary, an act that is "autonomous" in the root sense of following its own internal rules (*auto* = self, *nomos* = law). As Fichte puts it, "The intellect, for idealism, is an *act,* and absolutely nothing more; we should not even call it an *active* something, for this expression refers to something subsistent in which activity inheres." Fichte goes on to say that "the intellect acts, but owing to its nature, it can act only in a certain fashion" in that "there are necessary laws of the intellect." It is these laws that define the limits that intellect experiences as reality. The "feeling of necessity that accompanies specific presentations" in experience (for example, our sense that, at a given moment, we can see one thing but not another, that we can move in one way, but not in another) is not due to "some external impression." In other words, it is not that there is a real, external wall out there blocking our vision and motion. Rather, our sense of all this is the result of the intellect feeling "the limits of its own being"—its auto-nomy (self-law)—in a specific action (21).

More exactly, the self has two drives, one an infinite striving outward in action, the other an imposition of finitude through reflection (see 231, 237, 241). As a result of these drives, the self acts to *posit itself* (or, what is roughly the same, the self expresses itself) as an object. As self alone exists, not only the subject, but the object too must be self; however, the object is, again, self as posited by self. This act of positing or *thesis* sets up an *antithesis* between the subjective self and the objective self and this antithesis must be overcome in a *synthesis.* Without such a synthesis, there would be no experience; subject and object would split apart, irreconcilable. Experience is precisely the synthesis of subject and object, their joining together in unity. This synthesis—and indeed the entire "interplay of the self, in and with itself, whereby it posits itself" in antithesis and in synthesis—is all the result of "the power of *imagination*" (193). Imagination, then, is what allows all experience. Indeed, it creates experience, as it "wavers," Fichte tells us, between subject/object antithesis and synthesis.

Here we have one source not only of subsequent aesthetic theories that give pride of place to the imagination, but of the Romantic concern with the contradictory, with "negative capability," in Keats's term (the capacity "of being in uncertainties, Mysteries, doubts, without any irritable reaching after fact & reason" [320]); we have a parallel (or perhaps predecessor) for Schiller's drives of sense and form, his play drive mimicking the wavering of imagination; we have an early formulation of the Romantic motif of the fluttering nature of experience, experience being both direct and distant, both immediate and inaccessible (a fluttering obvious, for example, in Wordsworth's poetic longings for lost immediacy).

These relations come out strikingly in passages such as that in which Fichte maintains that "It is the office of the synthesizing faculty to unite opposites, to *think* of them as one." However, "this it cannot do . . . and hence there arises a conflict." To resolve the conflict, the "mind . . . wavers between the requirement [to unify] and the impossibility of carrying it out." Through this wavering, "it lays hold on both at once" and "in touching them, and being repulsed, and touching them again, it gives them, in the *relation to itself*, a certain content and a certain extension." Fichte explains that this "condition is called the state of *intuition*" and the "power active therein" is called "the productive imagination" (201). As a result of all this, "all reality . . . is brought forth solely by the imagination" (202).

It is important to note that this is not the end of the process. Understanding serves to "arrest" and "settle" the transiency and wavering of productive imagination, giving the sense of a fixed objectivity, structured into stable categories and relations. In later theories, such arrest and settling is of a piece with the habituation induced by the mechanical activities of ordinary life, an habituation that must be disrupted by creative ("secondary") imagination in art.

Before going on it is important to point out that Fichtean Idealism, like that of Schelling and that of Hegel, seems likely to have derived in part from Hindu and other Asian philosophies. The Bhagavad Gita, which presents a broadly similar view, had appeared in English translation (by Charles Wilkins) a decade earlier. It had also been treated in various secondary sources (as had other relevant Hindu texts; for instance, a suggestive excerpt from the Ṛg Veda appeared in Halhed's 1776 preface to *A Code* of *Gentoo Laws* [156–57]). Schwab stresses "The *Bhagavad Gita's* impact on Europe." Quoting a French author from the early nineteenth century, he notes in particular the importance of its "completely spiritual pantheism, and . . . the vision of all-in-God" (161). Consider, for example, a passage translated in Jones's "On the Gods." It begins with an assertion about God as first cause that could equally be Christian: "I was . . . at first, not any other thing." But it then admonishes the reader that, except for this "I," "whatever may appear, and may not appear, in the mind, know that to be the mind's MA'YA' (or *Delusion*)." The passage goes on to assert a sort of wavering, cognitive monism, "As the great elements are in various beings, entering, yet not entering . . . thus am I in them, yet not in them . . . the principle of mind, in union and separation" (354). More exactly, Fichte's ideas recall specific doctrines of Śaivism, according to which all reality is the result of the divine "play" of Śiva in his self-manifestation, self-forgetting, and self-recognition (positing, antithesis, and synthesis, to use Fichte's terms). Indeed, in Śaivite philosophy, the movement of consciousness between the inward and the outward, between the subject and the self-positing is called *spanda*, which is to say "vibration" or—"wavering." The greatest philosopher of Śaivism was Abhinavagupta—the same Abhinavagupta whose work culminated in the theory of rasadhvani. At the pinnacle of a tradition of Hindu theology that had developed for millennia, he theorized the playful expressive positing of the self and the wavering imagination centuries before Fichte. (For a discussion of Abhinavagupta's metaphysics and theology, and a translation of one of his metaphysical works, see B. N. Pandit.) This parallelism is probably not a matter of direct influence, but there may have been indirect influence, as Abhinavagupta's ideas had become part of Hindu thought more generally. Moreover, there were common sources in the older Hindu texts.

In his *System of Transcendental Idealism* (1800), Friedrich Wilhelm Joseph von Schelling developed Idealist philosophy in such a way as to place art at the very center of both philosophy and human life. For this reason, his system was particularly influential in later literary and aesthetic thought. Schelling begins this work with the Fichtean idea that "All knowledge is founded upon the coincidence of an objective with a subjective" (5). Again, to genuinely know something is to have one's thought identical with the thing; the knower and the object known must "coincide." Here, as in Fichte, this poses a problem if there is a noumenon or thing-in-itself with which our consciousness cannot be united. As we have just discussed, Fichte solved this problem by explaining the world as the self-positing of a self, a self that is itself not a thing, but an act. Schelling took over this aspect of Fichte also, though he more greatly emphasized the freedom and willfulness of the self as act. Specifically, Schelling distinguished intellect, or knowing subjectivity, from nature, which is to say, the object known. He then maintained that both intellect and nature are the free products of will (see, for example, 12).

As with Fichte's theory of self-positing, Schelling's theory of will faces a problem here: we clearly do not experience nature as a free act of will. Rather, we experience it as objective, necessary, and as opposed to will. Schelling solves this problem through an important and influential innovation. Specifically, Schelling maintains that the intellect is the *conscious* act of will, whereas nature is a *nonconscious* or *unconscious* act of will. Our feeling that nature is "necessary" and opposed to our will, then, is due not to some sort of separate noumenal existence, but to our unconsciousness of the free will of which nature is in fact the expression. Note that this is in effect an extension of Kant's view. For Kant, the synthesis and categorization of the manifold of intuition, its formation into phenomena (objects of experience) is an unconscious process by which a self forms a world. Moreover, that self, in turn, consciously experiences that world as separate, objective, necessary, even though it is the product of the self's own formative activity. Schelling alters Kant only in construing that formative activity as an expression of will, rather than a synthesis presumptively in accord with a noumenal world.

Readers of Schelling often wonder how we can have an objective, common world, given this theory. If the world is made by will, that would seem to imply that it is made differently by different wills. And as Schelling himself says, "intelligences who [willed and thus] intuited utterly different worlds would have absolutely nothing in common, and no point of contact at which they could come together" (164). In order to explain the common world, then, Schelling posits "a preestablished harmony" of all "intelligences" or willing/intuiting minds: "if the intelligence brings forth everything objective out of itself, and there is no common archetype for the presentations that we intuit outside us [that is, no noumenon], the consilience among the presentations of different intelligences . . . is explicable no otherwise than from our common nature" (164). Indeed, it is such consilience, based on common nature, that makes the world objective: "The sole objectivity which the world can possess for the individual is the fact of its having been intuited by intelligences outside the self" (174).

Needless to say, this does not entirely solve the problem. Note, for example, that Schelling in effect assumes that human intelligences (which is to say, people) exist noumenally—and even with inherent properties, structures, divisions, and so on. This is not necessarily an incoherent position. However, once one allows for the existence of noumenal intelligences, and once one posits a wide range of inherent properties for those noumenal intelligences, Idealist arguments against noumenal nature seem almost entirely pointless.

Another question that arises in this context, and that leads more directly to Schelling's views on art and literature, is—how can we know that nature is unconsciously willed? Doesn't the positing of an unconscious will in effect land us with the problem of a noumenon in that such an unconscious will is an unknowable ultimate reality? Equivalently, how can "this simultaneously conscious and nonconscious activity . . . be exhibited in the subjective, *in consciousness itself*," as Schelling himself puts it (12)? How can we come to know this activity in the Fichtean/Schellingian sense of knowledge—achieving coincidence of subject and object?

Schelling's answer here has great importance for subsequent literary theory, for he believes that the possibility of such knowledge is located only in art. As Schelling puts it, "[t]here is but one activity" that exhibits conscious and unconscious will, makes both accessible to consciousness, and it is "*aesthetic*." Indeed, "every work of art can be conceived only as the product of such activity." In other words, the world is a creation of will in the manner of a work of art, and the work of art is a creation of will in the manner of the world. Shakespeare creates Othello, and experiences him (just as we experience him)—for example, on stage—as a distinct person, as an element of nature. The difference between the work of art and the world of life is merely that art is known in both its aspects, in creation and in experience, whereas life is known only in one: "The ideal world of art and the real world of objects are therefore products of one and the same activity; the concurrence of the two (the conscious and the nonconscious) *without* consciousness yields the real, and *with* consciousness the aesthetic world" (12).

It is important to point out that, even though we know both aspects of artistic creation, productive intuition in art is not entirely the result of conscious effort, and thus craft. Indeed, art necessarily manifests the unconscious and is necessarily an "identity of the conscious and the unconscious" (219). Again, this is what makes art parallel with the world. Art, then, involves an unlearnable, innate, "incomprehensible agency," Schelling tells us, an agency he calls "*genius*" (222). This unconscious genius, combined with conscious craft, leads to the production of the work of art, which leaves the artist with a feeling of *"infinite* harmony" (223), due to the reconciliation of the conscious and the unconscious.

Needless to say, such free and creative activity—whether that of ordinary perception or that of artistic genius—cannot be placed in, for example, the understanding, for that faculty organizes representations only; it does not produce anything. The activity that gives rise to nature and intellect—whether that of art or that of life—must be "productive intuition" and not mere representational or passive intuition. This "productive intuition," Schelling calls, unsurprisingly, "imagination" (230). Of course, this tight parallel between art and life is important not only for our understanding of art, but also, and more importantly, for our knowledge of metaphysics. It is precisely our ability to recognize the reconciliation of the conscious and the unconscious in art that allows us to conceive of such reconciliation in life as well. The philosophy of transcendental idealism is possible, Schelling tells us, solely because artistic creation provides a microcosm of life, allowing us to understand the operation of the conscious and the unconscious by attending to imaginative creation. Thus the making and experiencing of art become the most central and exemplary acts for the philosophical understanding of life, for life, like artistic creation, is necessarily nothing other than imaginative creation and experience. (It is worth comparing here William Jones's summary of Hindu metaphysics, from the 1792 essay "On the Mystical Poetry of the Persians and the Hindus": "nothing has a pure absolute existence but *mind* or *spirit*" and thus *"material substances,* as the ignorant call them, are no more than gay pictures presented continually to our *minds* by the sempiternal Artist" [220].) Here we see not only the philosophical source for Coleridge's notions of the primary and secondary imagination, but an early Romantic elevation of art to a privileged place of insight within philosophy—a position it will retain with Romantic and post-Romantic philosophers from Hegel and Nietzsche through Heidegger. Art, Schelling tells us, is "the only true and eternal organ and document of philosophy" (231).

It is also worth noting that Schelling's "imagination," like Fichte's, allows us "to think and to couple together even what is contradictory" (230), an important task for it is a "contradiction" that "sets the artistic urge in motion." This last claim puts Schelling even closer than Fichte to Keats and other writers who stressed "negative capability" and related notions. In addition, Schelling's account of art as, largely, the product of unconscious creative will, leads him to the view that a true work of art has "unfathomable depth" (224) and is thus "capable of being expounded *ad in-*

*finitum"* (225). In other words, such a work is infinitely interpretable and cannot be paraphrased, a standard post-Romantic view.

One central Romantic preoccupation that we have not yet considered is history. A number of Romantic writers developed a historicist and teleological view of art quite different from the occasional chronologies and narrow generic histories found in some earlier criticism (such as Aristotle's brief overview of the development of tragedy, which recounts its derivation from earlier poetic genres, the increases in the number of actors from one to two then to three, and so forth). The Romantic historicists saw literature as part of an historical process, altering by time and place—especially by nation—but usually developing toward some ultimate perfection. This is important for our purposes as philosophical Romanticism merged with historicism, most influentially in the writings of Hegel, and historicism became a major element in later social philosophy, via Hegel and Marx.

One of the earliest writers to adopt this approach was Mme. de Stael. In 1800, she published *On Literature Considered in Its Relation to Social Institutions,* in many ways a remarkable book for its time. Earlier historical narratives treating literature and culture had tended to be very abstract. For example, Schiller paints a picture of literary and cultural history in broad strokes, where the Greeks have a unified sensibility that is subsequently lost. The loss leads to alienation and social stratification, but also to progress. However, modern revolutions show that this situation is no longer adequate and a new society is needed—based on aesthetic education. Mme. de Stael's work is much more historically and culturally specific. For example, she isolates and seeks to explain various aspects of the emotional quality of Shakespeare's work by reference to historical/cultural circumstances, often focusing on national character. (An emphasis on nationalism was another common feature of Romantic writing.) In one case, she treats his originality in communicating "the terror of death" (195), relating this originality to the "national spirit of England," a nation whose "passions were strongly agitated by the horrors of civil wars" (194). In a related vein, she sees Shakespeare's tragic heroes as ordinary human beings whom we pity—unlike many French tragic heroes whom we admire. This too she understands in terms of national character, in this case a contrast between the English "jealous love of liberty" (196) and "the chivalric spirit of the French monarchy" (197). Today, after Marx and others, we may find these historical analyses somewhat overly simple (though many contemporary analyses are no more complex). But de Stael was one of the first to undertake this sort of historicist literary analysis. It was in part because of her efforts that subsequent writers, for example, those in the Marxist tradition, were able to develop historicist analysis of literature in more complex and illuminating ways.

Moreover, one part of Mme. de Stael's social analysis was particularly unusual in Romantic historiography and literary theory, and more advanced than subsequent Marxist analyses: her emphasis on the role of women. De Stael stresses the historical importance of women in forming taste since the Renaissance, and often focuses on the role of women in the works and societies she is discussing. Moreover, she defends the right of women to develop their aesthetic capacities in the practice of art, arguing that men oppress women in large part by dissuading them from pursuing excellence and encouraging mediocrity. This analysis is quite plausible even today. Indeed, few contemporary theorists recognize, as did de Stael, that oppression can be manifest not only in stifling the aspirations of subordinated groups, but in channeling those aspirations so as to assure that members of such groups do not achieve anything extraordinary.

Of course, de Stael was not the only important Romantic historicist to have dealt with literature. Perhaps the most influential was G. W. F. Hegel, who, in his *Philosophy of Fine Art*, developed Romantic and historicist views within the context of Idealist philosophy. In a sense, Hegel took up the views of Fichte and Schelling and historicized them. He took the broad Idealist conception of the world as an unconscious self-objectification—or expression—of subjectivity and developed it into a complex, detailed system of the temporal unfolding of "Spirit." In connection with this, and in keeping with Schelling's transcendental Idealism in particular, he established a system in which art is central to the historical self-realization of this all-encompassing, absolute Spirit. This historical development works itself out in a Fichtean manner, through a repeated, tripartite dialectical progression from an initial condition, through its negation or opposite (antithesis), and finally into a synthesis of the preceding elements or "moments" (see, for example, *Aesthetics* 97). More exactly, Hegel views history as a series of (antithetical) stages in Spirit's developing (synthetic) recognition that the world is nothing other than Spirit itself.

"Spirit" is a somewhat obscure concept in Hegel. A helpful, if inaccurate, way of understanding Spirit might be: God as manifest in the historically developing consciousness of humanity, which is always progressing to higher and higher levels of spirituality. For example, for Hegel, the development of Judaism was an historical advancement of Spirit from the stage of polytheism, and the development of Christianity was a further advance from Judaism. Each was an advance over a preceding stage in that each furthered Spirit's self-manifestation and self-recognition. This example is somewhat misleading, however, for the historical development of Spirit is not by any means purely religious, at least in the usual, narrow sense. Rather, this development concerns all forms of knowledge, which is to say, all forms of the coincidence of subject and object, for these are all forms of Spirit's self-manifestation and self-recognition.

The development of Spirit, in this view, is a strict result of the inner necessity guiding Spirit's self-manifestation and self-recognition (much as in Fichte). As already indicated, this development follows a strict pattern of three "moments." Each moment comes to an end due to some inadequacy in the self-manifestation of spirit, some lack of fit between subject and object, self and nature, concept and intuition. It is this inadequacy that causes the dialectical shift from an initial moment to its negation. By way of illustration, suppose we are considering the mind-body problem. We begin by assuming that the mind is entirely distinct from the body, that its existence and operation are entirely separate. However, we then recognize that this leaves us with some problems: if the mind and body are entirely separate, how can a mental decision lead to bodily action (as when I mentally set out to type this sentence and my body's fingers comply and do the typing)? And how can brain injuries affect mental capacities? Given this "inadequacy," we will shift to some opposing view, a view that negates the separation of mind and body. For example, we might decide that the mind is merely a part of the body—perhaps the brain. This too will lead to problems (for example, how can our subjective experience of self and of world be identified with an observable thing encased in the hard shell of the skull?). And these problems will indicate that this solution too is inadequate. From here, we will "negate the negation" and move to a third, "synthetic" moment that preserves both prior moments, but transcends them—for example, we might posit mind/brain interactionism, making the mind and brain partially autonomous, but causally interconnected and thus partially interdependent. Other problems will arise (for instance, if the mind is not physical, how can it interact causally with a physical organism?). These will lead to the beginning of a new dialectical sequence, and so on.

Note that the synthetic moment is, for Hegel, always a "raising" of the two prior, antithetical moments into the self-consciousness of spirit— "what was implicit at the previous stage . . . is raised from an *immediate* to a *known* unity" (*Aesthetics* 80). In other words, the synthetic moment is always a partial self-recognition of Spirit. But it is not a complete self-recognition until there is a complete identity between subject and object, cognition and nature. This occurs at the end or *telos* of this entire development and is called "Absolute Knowing," a total self-recognition that synthesizes Subjective Spirit (including all its conceptual structure and unity) with Objective Spirit (in all its manifest particularity)—a self-recognition that is Absolute, and fully and definitively real, as there is, again, no noumenon distinct from self-cognizing/self-cognized, self-recognizing/self-recognized Spirit. As Hegel puts it, "the universal infinite and *absolute* spirit . . . out of itself determines what is genuinely the true" (*Aesthetics* 92) and "spirit is alone the *true,* comprehending everything in itself" (*Aesthetics* 2).

Spirit manifests its self-recognition most fully in religion and philosophy. But art too is one moment of the final stage of Spirit's self-manifestation. In the *Phenomenology of Spirit,* a relatively early and an unusually literary work (in tone and style), Hegel actually includes art in the category of religion. In the final volume of his *Encyclopaedia of the Philosophical Sciences,* published twenty-three years later, Hegel distinguishes art from religion, but still connects the two, making art the first moment (thesis) of Absolute Knowing, followed by religion (antithesis), and, finally, philosophy (synthesis). The later view is the clearer of the two, and underlies Hegel's posthumously published *Aesthetics.* For the moment, I will confine my discussion to the later works.

Hegel's concern throughout these later works is with the manner of presentation of the universal to consciousness. In art, this presentation is always sensuous. In other words, art presents the absolute to consciousness as an experiential object. In "Revealed Religion," the moment following that of art, the absolute is pure subjectivity. In both art and religion, then, consciousness comes to think the absolute (and here the absolute is very close to ordinary conceptions of God), but it thinks the absolute one-sidedly, as an object (art) or as mere subjectivity (revealed religion). Only in the culminating moment of philosophy is consciousness faced with the absolute absolutely, that is, both objectively and subjectively.

More exactly, in the *Aesthetics,* Hegel sees art as having the task of presenting "the highest" reality "sensuously," that is, "bringing it thereby nearer to the senses" and "to feeling" (7–8). In other words, art sets out to manifest the universal in the particular, to exemplify the abstract principles of religion and philosophy. In this way, Hegel's conception of art is related to Kant's conception of aesthetical ideas. Art, in this view, does not function primarily to name or communicate a conceptual content—that is the province of philosophy. Rather, art functions to intimate or suggest the "higher" reality of the absolute and to communicate a feeling about that reality (say, a religious feeling) through a concrete image.

On the other hand, it is necessary to recall that this higher reality is not distinct from Spirit and subjectivity. The manifestation of the absolute in the dialectical development of art is precisely the dialectical *self*-manifestation of Spirit through art. Moreover, the production of the individual work of art is the self-manifestation of Spirit writ small. Regarding this individual self-manifestation, Hegel writes that an individual person is Spirit "only on the strength of [the] active placing himself before himself" or self-positing. This occurs *inwardly* when a person brings him/herself into consciousness, conceives of him/herself as "me," thereby achieving self-consciousness. It also occurs outwardly—in "*practical* activity," in action, which is, for Hegel, a concrete form of self-positing. In Hegel's view, this practical or objective self-positing reaches its highest form in art.

In the *Encyclopaedia* and, more thoroughly, the *Aesthetics*, Hegel isolates three dialectical moments in the broad development of art. In the first moment, "symbolic" art, the idea is inadequately concretized; the relation between thing and thought is arbitrary. The absolute is only suggested. This art is the realm of Kant's aesthetical ideas. It is "the art of sublimity" (*Philosophy of Mind* 295). Hegel ethnocentrically identifies this stage with non-Western art, though in this act of partial denigration, he simultaneously indicates the importance of non-Western art to his entire analysis—for, once again, the final dialectical synthesis will necessarily incorporate this initial moment, and thus will include non-Western art as an essential component.

The second type of art isolated by Hegel is "classical," the art of "beauty" (295). It suffers from precisely the opposite flaw: it is overly concretized, and thus it is the complete negation of "symbolic" art. For Hegel, classical art is superior to symbolic art in that it imitates reality, but elevates it, perfects it—as when it portrays the human body in flawless form. Yet perfected form appears to confine Spirit to finitude, and thus to deny its universality and infinitude. Hegel sees this moment as manifest most fully in classical Greece.

In his conception of the final and perfected stage of art—the "Romantic"—Hegel returns to Kant's conception of the sublime. ("Romantic" art is a broad category for Hegel; while including the work of his contemporaries, it encompasses a range of other appropriate works—for example, much of Shakespeare.) For Hegel, Romantic art connects with precisely that Spiritual infinitude that Kant saw as the province of sublimity, an infinitude that it takes up from "Symbolic," which is to say, from non-Western art. In other words, Romantic art combines the abstract signifi-cance of symbolic art with the nonarbitrary concreteness of classical art: "at this third stage the subject-matter of art is *free concrete spirituality*, which is to be manifested as *spirituality* to the spiritually inward" (*Aesthet-ics* 80). It is neither symbolic nor mimetic, but self-manifesting and "pro-ductive" (in Fichte's or Schelling's sense): "it can jumble the shapes of the external world . . . . For this external medium has its essence and meaning no longer, as in classical art, in itself and its own sphere, but in the heart which finds its manifestation in itself instead of in the external world" (81). Only in Romantic art, does art become what it should be—the lifting of "the inner and outer world into [man's] spiritual consciousness as an object in which he recognizes again his own self" (*Aesthetics* 31). Indeed, in this stage, "what was implicit in the previous stage, the unity of divine and human nature, is raised from an *immediate* to a *known* unity" (*Aesthetics* 80), most obviously "in the story of Christ," but "also of all others in whom the Holy Spirit is effective and the entire Godhead is present" (521), stories that are central to Romantic art, in Hegel's conception.

Of course, this too is inadequate. In the continuing dialectic, Romantic art begins as we have just described it—as "*religious* inwardness" (553). But this concern with "bliss in the Absolute" remains "abstract . . . sepa-rated from life, and removed from the concrete reality of human exist-ence" (552). In consequence, Romantic art turns to "inwardness . . . of a *worldly* kind" (553), taking up themes of honor, romantic love, and so on. This dialectic makes more sense if one connects it with historical proto-types. The first phase of Romantic art may be thought of as the Christian art of the Middle Ages—deeply religious, but isolated in churches. The unity of the symbolic and the classical, the divine and the human, is clear in Jesus on the crucifix above the altar, but this image is removed from the experience of ordinary people. The second phase of Romantic art—roughly, Romantic art in the ordinary sense—is "inward" and "worldly" in taking up the real experience of lived human emotion. But, in doing so, it tends to lose sight of "the entire Godhead." Thus the inward turn of Romantic art ultimately leads us away from art to the next phase of the encompassing dialectic—the inwardness of Revealed Religion. As Hegel puts it, in the Romantic phase, art ultimately "annuls itself and brings home to our minds that we must acquire higher forms for the apprehension of truth than those which art is in a position to supply" (*Aesthetics* 529).

Before going on, it is worth looking briefly at some major elements from the rather different dialectic outlined by Hegel in the *Phenomenology of Spirit*. Again, in the *Phenomenology*, Hegel includes art under the category of religion. Thus he combines what we would consider purely artistic with more narrowly religious moments. At the outset, we find the statue, a static beauty through which an artist seeks to express or manifest him/herself. But this self-manifestation is a "Thing which lacks self-consciousness" (430). Abridging Hegel's discussion somewhat, we may say that out of this inadequacy, art develops into the Cult, a communal expression that is marred by one-sided subjectivity (just as the statue is marred one-sided objectivity). The Cult expresses itself in "untamed revelry" of "the mystery of bread and wine, of Ceres and of Bacchus," a "festival which man celebrates in his own honour," a "perfectly free *movement*, just as the statue is perfectly free *repose*" (438), a "Bacchic enthusiasm" (439).

In the Cult, there is a relation between the divine and the human, but it is merely implicit or subjective. As it turns out, literature is required to advance this dialectic. Specifically, the next stage must raise this implicit divine/human relation to self-consciousness, to objectify it. That task, for Hegel, is accomplished by the Epic, in which the static "spiritual essence" of the statue (439) is combined with the "tumultuous life" of the Cult (437). This occurs by way of the objectification of "the relation of the divine to the human" (441) in language, specifically "the earliest language" defined by and in "a collective nation" (440), a true language that transcends the "wild stammering utterance" of the cult (439).

From here, Hegel continues on to tragedy, which supersedes the episodic Epic through the synthesis of events into Necessity. Here, Hegel takes the standard Aristotelian view that tragedy, unlike epic, follows strict principles of necessitation, and gives it a larger, social/religious significance. Unfortunately, tragedy leaves us with loss and alienation rather than spiritual unification. This, in turn, leads to comedy, which resolves into a state of repose—not the repose of the statue, but rather repose as "a state of spiritual well-being" (453). It does so in part through an undermining of the rigid moral precepts announced by the chorus in tragedy (see 451). In comedy, the "power of dialectic knowledge puts specific laws and maxims of conduct at the mercy of the pleasure and frivolity of youth . . . and provides weapons for deceiving old age with its fears and apprehensions" (452; Hegel here alludes to the standard New Comedy plot of lovers hoodwinking their parents so that they can be married and thus renew society on the basis of youth and love, rather than old age and prudence).

Of course, there are contradictions in comedy too, for in this self-repose or self-certainty, which results from overturning "laws and maxims of conduct" (as in the elopement of lovers), "the *reality* of the ethical Spirit is lost" (454): "Trust in the eternal laws of the gods has vanished and the Oracles . . . are dumb." Indeed, "The works of the Muse now lack the power of the Spirit, for the Spirit has gained its certainty of itself from the crushing of gods and men." Thus, this repose is equally a sort of "grief which expresses itself in the hard saying that 'God is dead'" (455); it is easy to see a parallel with the second phase of Romantic art, in Hegel's later theory. These contradictions lead finally to the supersession of Religion in the Form of Art by Revealed Religion, which itself yields finally to Absolute Knowing.

A final, and particularly influential variation on some of the central Romantic themes may be found in Friederich Nietzsche. For our purposes, Nietzsche's most relevant work is *The Birth of Tragedy,* in which he set out to explain the development and decline of Greek tragedy. In order to do this, he drew two sets of distinctions. The first is between the Apollonian and the Dionysian strains in art. The Apollonian impulse is a striving toward individual form, distinctness, proportion, contemplative calm, restraint, and realistic representation. It is closely parallel to the beautiful, to the mature Hegel's classical/mimetic, and especially to the young Hegel's notion of statuary—as well as Schiller's form drive, Fichte's reflective drive, and so on. Nietzsche further specified the notion of the Apollonian as visual, specifically as linked with the visual arts (particularly sculpture—thus strengthening the link with Hegel), and as associated with dreams.

The Dionysian, in contrast, is everything opposed to the Apollonian. It is the destruction of any sense of individuality; it is indistinctness, exuberance, indulgence, ecstasy, even pain, terror, and ugliness. In addition, Nietzsche associates the Dionysian with symbolism, particularly with symbolism of the body (40), and connects it with music and intoxication. The Dionysian impulse, then, is parallel to the sublime, to the older Hegel's symbolic, and especially to the young Hegel's notion of the Bacchic frenzy of the Cult which supersedes reposeful statuary—as well as Schiller's sense drive, Fichte's drive toward infinitude, and so forth. (Nietzsche, like Hegel, associates this tendency with the Orient [see, for example, 124]. On the other hand, Nietzsche explains both the Apollonian and the Dionysian in relation to such Hindu notions as *māyā* or illusion, seeing the former as "beautiful illusion . . . wrapped in the veil of *maya*" [35] and the latter as "the annihilation of the veil of *maya*" [40].)

Greek tragedy, Nietzsche maintains, is a blending of these two tendencies—much as the Romantic is, for Hegel, a synthesis of the symbolic and the classical/mimetic. Nietzsche particularly stresses the Dionysian/Eastern/Symbolic strain rather than the Apollonian/Greek/Classical strain, in keeping with common Romantic trends. Tragedy, for Nietzsche, is the (Dionysian) music of "primal unity" taken up into an (Apollonian) "*dream image*" which is now (Dionysianly) "*symbolic*" (49). Greek tragedy is great, and virtually unique in history, due precisely to this powerful synthesis. In connection with this, Nietzsche does insist that Greek Dionysianism was distinct from and superior to Eastern Dionysianism (see, for example, 39); however, this does not affect the point that Greek tragedy was, for Nietzsche, ideal precisely because it synthesized a formal tendency associated with Greece (and thus, implicitly, with the West) and a disruptive tendency associated with the East.

But, Nietzsche argues, this synthesis was unstable. Almost as soon as it arose, Greek tragedy began to decline. And here a second opposition comes into play: that between the Dionysian and the Socratic. According to Nietzsche, Socrates was the beginning of rationalism and the scientific attitude, aimed at intelligibility (see 84, 93). The Apollonian is opposed to the Dionysian as one form of art to another, as beauty to sublimity; they are capable of unifying and elevating synthesis. The Socratic, however, is the annihilation of the Dionysian. They cannot be synthesized. The Socratic/Dionysian opposition, then, is Nietzsche's version of the common romantic distinction between science and art, reason and imagination, dead mechanism and organic human life. One thing that is unusual about Nietzsche, however, is that he does not identify this opposition with that between form and impulse. Rather, he distinguishes the latter from the former, thus maintaining two fundamental oppositions, which are themselves opposed in turn.

While Nietzsche stressed the broad synthesis of the Apollonian and Dionysian in Greek tragedy, and the opposition of the Socratic to both, it is possible to employ his theory to isolate distinct manifestations of these three impulses in a single work. Consider Othello. Like the tragedy of Aeschylus, he embodies both the Apollonian and the Dionysian—constraint and proportion, but seething impulse as well. Until the end of the play, the Apollonian dominates, giving form and purposeful orientation to a submerged chaos of feeling. But in the end, the Dionysian emerges in a violent burst of destruction and self-destruction. In the intensity of his momentary ecstasy and more enduring pain, this Dionysian Othello is—just as Nietzsche would have it—the primary source of what is tragic in our experience of the play. Shakespeare is rather un-Nietzschean in valuing Apollonian restraint above Dionysian frenzy—indeed, a large part of the tragic feeling of the play derives from the murder of the Apollonian Desdemona and the overwhelming of the Apollonian part of Othello. On the other hand, both strains are important and to a degree elevated in Shakespeare's play, and both are opposed to a degraded third tendency. Shakespeare almost seems to anticipate Nietzsche in making the Socratic Iago into the agent of all this destruction, a destruction of both the Apollonian and the Dionysian. Iago is the plotting, deceitful, scientific temper, an evil Socrates. He analyzes circumstances, seeks intelligibility (for the sake of deception), reasons out his manipulations, and, in a manner perfectly in keeping with romantic ideas, separates beauty (in the form of Desdemona) and sublimity (in the form of Othello), distorting and finally destroying both, slaying both Apollo and Dionysus.

Such a reading of the play is not necessarily allegorical. These characters do not represent, but embody or manifest these impulses. Nietzsche—as well as Schiller, Hegel, and others—saw themselves as isolating genuine social and psychological tendencies, forces that shape society and art. Indeed, in this view, it is the Apollonian and Dionysian impulses in ourselves—the sense of beauty and the sense of sublimity—that are engaged during the creation and experience of tragedy; they make the tragic experience. They are, in short, part of the literary work at many levels.

As we have already noted, the common themes of Romanticism recur, with variations, in almost all modern and contemporary literary theories. Whatever one may think of it, we are still living in a Romantic age, and are likely to remain so for some time. This is not to say that all subsequent theories are somehow determined by Romantic premises, that there are no non-Romantic influences on such theories, or that all thinking in the field is thoroughly Romantic. However, it is to say that there is a strong and continuous pressure on our thought from Romantic presuppositions. Many such presuppositions are entirely unconscious to us, thus unquestioned and unquestionable. And even when they are not unconscious, even when we reverse them or qualify them, they have often determined the general principles according to which we examine and theorize literature, and the world.

However, before going on to the philosophical theories of our own century that have developed out of or in response to Romanticism, we need to consider the towering figure of nineteenth-century political philosophy:

Karl Marx. Marx took up some of the central Romantic and Idealist concerns—their focus on history, their use of dialectic—but entirely repudiated their fundamental idealism. For this idealism, he substituted his own historical *materialism*, a philosophical theory perhaps unparalleled in its practical influence (and, in my view, in its explanatory value for social phenomena) down to our own day.

## Marx and Historical Materialism

Historical materialism is an empirical and theoretical approach to the study of social phenomena, which places explanatory emphasis on political economy as it has developed in particular historical circumstances. It is in the first place a direct response to idealism—especially, but not only German Idealism. For Marx, idealism is any doctrine that sees reality as determined or guided by mental or spiritual entities. The great Romantic Idealists—Fichte, Schelling, Hegel—may be said to have absolutized idealism in this sense for they eliminate the material world entirely and replace it with the idea alone. But there are many less extreme forms of idealism as well. For example, the view that human society is guided by divine providence is an idealist view, by this definition. So is the view that history is molded by the ideas of great thinkers, or that reality is formed by Platonic Ideas or by language. In each case, the material world is explained by reference to an ideal world. For Marx, this sort of explanation gets everything upside down. In Marx's view, the material world explains the ideal world, not vice versa.

But Marxism is not materialism of any sort. It is a specifically *historical* materialism. Various forms of biologism are materialist as well. These would include Feuerbach's famous theory that "Man is what he eats" (actually Moleschott's theory, which Feuerbach reaffirmed and made famous—see Wartofsky 413, 416), as well as various more contemporary theories that stress human neurophysiology. Marx rejected "physicalism"—the view that all reality is physical (for instance, biological)—as vehemently as he rejected idealism (see, for example, Wartofsky 413). First of all, Marx maintained that it is social circumstances and particularly economic relations that explain our philosophical, literary, religious, and other ideas. Secondly, he maintained that such social/economic relations change systematically, moving through a comprehensible pattern of development. Thus any understanding of human ideas and their associated practices must be based on an understanding of the development of social/economic relations, that is, an understanding of the history of these material conditions.

In recent years, Marxist literary critics have stressed history far more than materialism. Indeed, Marxism today is often conceived of as equivalent with historicism—historicism being the view that human ideas, relations, and so forth, can be understood only as products of history. Historicists typically reject any search for human universals, and typically maintain that nonhistorical approaches lack even partial validity. (Indeed, they frequently dismiss nonhistorical approaches as "idealist," a misuse of the term that results in such oddities as neurophysiological linguistics being classed not as physicalist, but as idealist.) In keeping with this, many current theorists—especially "post-Marxists," such as Tony Bennett—adhere to the linguistic idealist premises of poststructuralism. In effect, they return to a form of Hegelianism, an historicism that privileges language over material conditions.

This "post-Marxist" linguistic idealism is pretty straightforwardly inconsistent with Marx's views—whether one agrees with the post-Marxists or with Marx. But even the ordinary varieties of historicism, commonly identified with Marxism, are not clearly coherent with Marx's ideas. Marx termed his method "historical materialism," not "historicism" or even "material historicism." And this was no accident. Marx himself believed in human universals. For example, he believed in "laws of beauty" (see *Economic* 114), though he maintained that the implementation of these laws varied historically and in relation to the material conditions of any given society in which art is being produced. Moreover, as far as I am aware, he did not deny the partial validity of nonhistorical studies. Thus, it is important to distinguish historical materialism from the range of historicisms with which it is frequently identified.

Historical materialism is equally *dialectical* materialism. We have already discussed dialectic briefly in connection with Fichte and Hegel. Marx takes over the Hegelian notion of dialectical progression as the developmental principle of history, but he grounds this progression in material conditions rather than in ideas. Dialectic is, again, a process whereby the tension between two opposing forces, conditions, ideas, is resolved in the production of a third force, condition, idea, which itself is taken up into a further oppositional tension, and so on. For Marx, this dialectal tension operates at all levels. Indeed, we have just, so to speak, passed through a conceptual example in the opposition that pits Hegelianism (which is historical and dialectical, but idealist) against physicalism (which is materialist, but neither historical nor dialectical). These form a pair of irreconcilable opposites, their tension or antithesis resolvable only through the formulation or synthesis of dialectical and historical materialism as a third "moment."

It is worth noting that the opposition between idealism and physicalism is recapitulated within dialectical materialism itself (that is, the dialectic does not stop, but is repeated on another level). Thus some Marxists have tended to view individual human action as fully determined by mechanical rules of political economy. This extreme, mechanical determinism, sometimes referred to as "economism," denies the dialectical tensions underlying individual action. This is clearly akin to physicalism. The antithesis of economism is "voluntarism," the view that, through the use of Marxist theory or through adherence to the correct political line of the Communist Party, human beings become free to change the world as they see fit, independent of the specific material conditions in which they are operating. This is clearly related to idealism. Genuine dialectical materialism, then, resolves the contradiction between economism and voluntarism much as it resolves that between physicalism and idealism.

The most important dialectical relations, however, are not conceptual, but material. Indeed, it is these material dialectics that give rise to and allow us to account for the conceptual oppositions. More exactly, for Marx, economy is the determinative aspect of social relations and historical development. Within the economic sphere itself, there are numerous dialectical oppositions, the most crucial of which is that between economic classes. It is the dialectical opposition between classes, or "class struggle," that is the driving force of history; it is the repeated, partial resolution and regeneration of class struggle, within changing forms of economy, that defines the basic forms of historical dialectic. Moreover, this material dialectic grounds any conceptual dialectic in the sense that it is only under certain material conditions that particular ideas can arise or take hold.

To take a literary example, according to Georg Lukács, such oppositions as that between naturalism and modernist experimentalism are the product of the specific conditions of capitalist production. Industrial capitalism reduced human beings to mere elements in a mechanical process of manufacture, factory machines more than people. (In some respects, Marxists too are Romantics.) This mechanization of human work gives rise to a mechanistic conception of human life, human motivation, human actions, and so on. This manifests itself in the mechanical aspects of naturalism—including its tendencies toward biological determinism in, for example, some works of Émile Zola. Modernist experimentalism, Lukács argues, reacts against this mechanization by taking us inside the minds of characters, making them completely subjective and nonmechanical, as in interior monologue and stream of consciousness works by Joyce, Woolf, or Faulkner. This is the result of a sort of "collapsing in" on oneself, a loss of real social relations and human interaction and identification. This "collapsing in" is itself the product of the complete mechanization of social relations, their reduction to industrial and monetary relations. In short, industrial capitalism consumes all human social life, so that people feel themselves to be human only in inner, isolated subjectivity—when they should feel themselves to be human most fully in social relations. This economically determined split of human life into the external/mechanical and internal/subjective is, according to Lukács, what is manifest in naturalism and modernism, respectively.

In a similar way, the opposition between idealism and physicalism is based upon material conditions of capitalist society. Even the Marxist overcoming of this opposition with the formulation of dialectical materialism is possible only because of the development of an organized and active working class that allows for the possibility of overcoming the capitalist system. For example, in England, trade unions significantly developed after 1824 and "took deep root . . . in the 1840's and 1850's" (Garraty and Gay 831), in keeping with which, the *Communist Manifesto* was published in 1848. The International Working Men's Association was formed in 1864 and the first volume of *Capital* appeared three years later. Of course, the first (politico-economic) event did not cause the second (theoretical) event in these cases. However, the first events indicate that the appropriate politico-economic conditions existed for the theoretical work to develop and have impact. Marx indicates that his theory could not have arisen and taken hold if the relations of material production had not reached a specific point. Marx's theory is in part a theory of the end of capitalism; it could arise only in circumstances where that end is historically and materially possible.

In classical Marxist theory, any given society has a dominant mode of production—for example, manufacture for profit through the exploitation of labor, in the case of industrial capitalism. This dominant mode of production forms the "base" for the political and ideological "superstructure"; it determines the political and ideological structure of the society. However, none of this is as monolithic or stable as the metaphor of base and superstructure seems to imply. Societies are, again, historical; they are changing, developing due to internal dialectic. Thus they contain within themselves traces of former stages and of future possibilities. In Raymond

Williams's terms, they include not only *dominant,* but also *residual* and *emergent* modes of production. For example, in capitalist society, the dominant mode of production may be manufacture for profit, but there will be residual feudal modes and emergent communist modes—in different proportions at different periods. For example, early in the bourgeois period, feudal modes of production are widespread; later, they diminish in importance and extent.

Classical Marxist theory in addition distinguishes three spheres of economic relation for each mode of production. These are: (1) relations of production, (2) relations of ownership, and (3) relations of distribution. Each centrally involves class conflict. Within capitalist society, relations of production are defined by the opposition between mental and manual laborers (more commonly referred to as management and labor). Relations of ownership are defined by the opposition between capitalists and workers—or, in feudalism, landlords and tenants—those who own the means of production and those who operate the means of production (work the assembly line, farm the land). Relations of distribution are defined by the opposition between rich and poor. Liberal theorists and humanists tend to see the opposition between rich and poor as the most crucial. For them, social action is and should be guided by the desire to ameliorate the condition of the poor, through charity or through government programs such as social security. Marxists certainly support aiding the poor. However, in their view, poverty is a result of the discrepancy between relations of ownership and relations of production. In every noncommunist society, those who produce wealth do not own the products of their labor and this is so precisely because they do not own the means of producing those products (the machinery, the land, and so on). For example, in capitalist society, the workers produce the commodities, but these commodities are owned by the capitalists who, in turn, sell them for profit—sometimes to the workers themselves. Thus for Marxists, the goal of political activism is not, ultimately, to get poor people some more money, but to eliminate the general necessity for this redistribution of wealth by putting an end to the class structure of society. One puts an end to class structure by revolutionizing the relations of ownership and production so that the workers are in control of their own products, so that there is no longer a contradiction between relations of ownership and relations of production. Hence the central importance to Marxism of the slogan: "Put the means of production into the hands of the workers."

There are two ways in which such a revolution is typically conceived. The first is the "statist" version—the standard Marxist view from at least the time of Lenin, and arguably from the time of Marx himself. In this view, the revolution in relations of ownership is effected by establishing a centralized state apparatus that is the representative of the entire working class. This state apparatus takes over ownership of all products in the name of the workers and determines hierarchies in the relations of production as well, also in the name of the workers. The alternative view is that of "left-wing" Marxists such as Rosa Luxemburg and Anton Pannekoek, as well as anarchists and anarcho-syndicalists, such as Emma Goldman, Peter Kropotkin, and Diego Abad de Santillan (for an overview of anarchism, see Guérin). According to these theorists—whose work was suppressed by mainstream Marxists and whose followers were often imprisoned or killed—the statists are not changing exploitative relations of production, but intensifying them. The state cannot be a mere representative of the workers. A state that owns the products of the workers' labor and that reestablishes hierarchies of mental and manual labor in production establishes nothing other than a centralized, oligarchic capitalism. Ownership should instead be given directly to workers and all production should be reorganized along democratic lines. Thus the workers in a factory should themselves own the factory directly (not through the supposed mediatory agency of the state) and they should have complete, democratic control of the operation of the factory through workers' councils. Moreover, everyone should engage in both mental and manual labor. Statist communists most often accept this as an ultimate goal, but maintain that statism is a necessary "transitional" phase (see, for example, Lenin's *The State and Revolution*). Left-wing communists and anarchists vehemently reject this view, arguing that the establishment of a strong centralized state apparatus will never be merely transitional. In addition to being brutal and exploitative, it will be unscrupulously self-perpetuating and self-extending.

In and of itself, this debate has little direct bearing on literary theory. However, it does introduce the issue of state power as a problem distinct from ideology and political economy. And, as examined by Foucault and the New Historicists, power has become an important concern in recent literary theory. Moreover, it is important to recognize that Marxist analysis does not inevitably lead the Stalinist Gulag—as both the Stalinist and Western liberal histories of Marxism imply, suppressing as they do the nonstatist alternatives of left-wing communism and anarchism.

As we have noted, classical Marxism isolates several main types of economic and social organization based on modes of production. These are systematized in the so-called five-stage theory according to which societies proceed from primitive communism through a slave economy to a feudal economy, then a capitalist economy, and finally a true communist society. Movement from one stage to another is the result of development of the productive forces and the dialectic of the class struggle. The rigidity of this scheme has been widely criticized. For example, a number of writers have taken issue with the notion that industrial capitalism is a necessary precursor to communism, arguing in favor of a transition directly from feudalism. Others have argued that this scheme fits Europe alone, that it is invalid for the rest of the world. Indeed, Marx himself thought that there was an "Asiatic" mode of production distinct from any of these. And, even in Europe the stages do not appear quite as neatly as this scheme implies. Capitalism operates as an "emergent" mode of production from the time of the earliest money economies. Its relative importance increases and decreases over millennia before it becomes the dominant mode of production. Moreover, there is considerable variation within each category, variation which is important and yet which this scheme might seem to obscure.

Nonetheless, an abridged version of this scheme, dividing societies into "preaccumulative" communist, feudal or "tributary" (in Samir Amin's term), capitalist, and communist modes of production seems valuable, if not conceived too rigidly. Each of the noncommunist modes of production is marked by particular class conflicts, particular political structures, and particular cultural forms, including literary tendencies.

Preaccumulative communism is the earliest communal stage of humanity, according to classical Marxist theory. At this stage, production does not exceed consumption. The goods that are necessary for the survival of the group—animals (wild or domesticated), basic tools, and so on—are held communally. Thus there is no accumulation of surplus, and there is no economic hierarchy, or class struggle, within the society. There cannot be, for there is in effect no wealth. For this reason, there is also no political hierarchy, and no division of labor. Art and "literature" (or "orature") are communal experiences—executed, perhaps, by individuals, but shared by the entire community. Certain literary genres would be likely to arise in such circumstances: proverbs and moral tales, ritual songs, mythological tales, and so forth.

Preaccumulative communism, however, is unstable, due to both internal and external factors. First of all, development of the means of production—for example, the improvement of farming techniques—will eventually create a surplus product, which is to say, wealth. As soon as there is wealth, there is a basis for economic hierarchization. Secondly, there is always the possibility of conquest and subjugation by societies that have more fully developed modes of production. In both cases, political hierarchization and the division of labor will develop concurrently with the economic hierarchization. This is the beginning of the tributary mode of production.

Tributary societies are organized into economic/political hierarchies with strict division of labor, such that producers at the lower levels owe tribute to owners at the higher levels. The political form of such a society is a hereditary aristocracy. Culturally, these societies most often develop a hierarchized religion (a religion involving a hierarchy of spiritual beings) administered by a hierarchized priesthood. In the aesthetic realm, a distinction develops between "high" art and popular or folk culture. The former is produced under patronage for an elite; thus it comes under the control of class interests. Tributary societies provide a ground for the development of heroic epics and drama, though not all tributary societies produce these genres. More generally, the patronized arts of tributary societies tend to promulgate the interests and attitudes of their aristocratic patrons.

Tributary societies are perhaps less unstable than primitive communist societies. First of all, mere accumulation of surplus is inadequate to lead such a society to capitalism. Secondly, even conquest by a capitalist society by no means guarantees that the capitalist mode of production will become dominant in the conquered country. Indeed, quite the contrary. The European conquest of Asian and African societies involved the systematic destruction of proto-capitalist elements in those societies. Specifically, accumulation of surplus in tributary societies fosters trade, first locally, in small markets, then in larger areas. As trade expands, a class of "merchant capitalists" arises. A capitalist is anyone who buys a product, not in order to consume or use it, but in order to sell it at a profit. A merchant capitalist is a capitalist who merely transports goods for this purpose. (Fully fledged capitalism is centered around industrial production of goods, as we shall see.)

The development of the merchant class is associated with a further division of labor throughout society and the development of another capitalist or proto-capitalist class. Increasingly, objects formerly produced privately for individual or familial use—for example, clothing—come to be produced by tradespeople and purchased at markets through trade of surplus (that is, unneeded) goods, perhaps abstracted into the form of money. Markets eventually become more permanent, developing into towns, where artisans—the "petit bourgeoisie" or "small bourgeoisie"—are able to live and engage in small-scale manufacture and where merchant capitalists are able to travel with their wares.

The degree of proto-capitalist development varies historically in any given society. Thus a particular society may at one point have a highly developed proto-capitalism, which subsequently declines, due to internal political instability, conquest, natural conditions such as drought, and so on. For fully fledged capitalism to develop, proto-capitalism must not only be sustained, but organized and expanded. Specifically, surplus produced by trade and manufacture, especially manufacture, must be reinvested in adequate quantities to expand enterprise. This must give rise to greater division of labor and must be associated with appropriate technological innovations. For example, a tailor turns a certain profit on a suit. He/she will necessarily reinvest some of that profit in materials for his/her next project. And he/she will certainly consume some of the profit in necessities. If there is surplus beyond all this—beyond what it takes to "reproduce" the initial conditions of production—he/she may either consume that in luxuries or reinvest it in his/her trade. For example, he/she may hire an assistant, subsequently several assistants, each employed to do part of the tailoring job (sleeves, buttons, and so on). As this occurs, the petit bourgeoisie slowly develops into an industrial bourgeoisie.

In Europe, the transition from a dominant feudal mode of production to a dominant capitalist mode of production was facilitated by technological innovation and, even more so, colonial conquest. Conquerors inevitably appropriate the goods of subject peoples and impoverish the subject society. Europe, however, proceeded more systematically to destroy colonized economies for the benefit of the capitalist class of the home economy. Specifically, merchant capitalists plundered the colonies for salable goods, both those with direct use value and, more importantly, those which could contribute to the manufacture of other commodities. This depleted the resources of the colonized countries and destroyed their merchant capitalism, while advancing industrial production in the colonizing country by providing inexpensive raw materials. Simultaneously, Europeans crushed virtually all petit bourgeois manufactury that produced a significant surplus, sometimes going so far as to crush even that which produced no surplus. Frequently they did this by brutal means, including "physical torture" (see Iftikhar-Ul-Awwal 297; according to one story, retold movingly in Agha Shahid Ali's poem "The Dacca Gauzes," they amputated the thumbs of highly skilled Dacca weavers). The colonized people were left with little choice but to retreat from the division of labor and try to produce necessities (utensils, furniture, clothing, and so on) at home, or to use what little surplus they had to buy imports from Europe—goods often manufactured using raw materials taken from the colonies initially. This artificial creation of a market for European goods served to further advance European industry and merchant capital.

In the early development of capitalism, in Europe, Asia, or elsewhere, a central division of labor develops between the city and the country. The country is strictly tributary and agricultural; the city is proto-capitalist and combines trade and manufactury. According to Marxist critics such as Arnold Hauser, this proto-capitalist urban culture has profound effects on the arts. Tributary cultures tend to be highly conservative and traditional, for they are based on hereditary hierarchy. For this reason, Hauser argues, such societies tend to give rise to a very manneristic, even formulaic art, an art based on rigid, inherited principles—and patronized by the (hereditary) aristocracy. In contrast, bourgeois societies tend to be more empirical and innovative, for knowledge and flexibility are necessary to success in a capital venture. In keeping with this, he maintains, art becomes more realistic and less stereotyped to the degree that the society becomes more capitalist. Even in largely tributary societies, a highly developed urban merchant capitalism will push art in this direction, at least that art produced in the city or as part of the mercantile economy.

Capitalism becomes the dominant mode of production after a transition period in which it is an increasingly strong emergent mode. This transition is frequently marked by a revolutionary change in political structure. Feudalism requires a fairly rigid aristocratic hierarchy, with vassals strictly bound to lords. Industrial capitalism, however, requires a free labor force. Specifically, the market for commodities is not constant. It expands and contracts. Thus capitalists need to produce more or less, in accordance with the demands of the market (while always working to expand the market). Thus they need to be able to hire or fire workers as necessitated by the market. Moreover, in order to maximize their profits, they need to minimize pay to the workers. However, if the labor pool, the group of workers from which they can draw, is too limited (if, for example, too many potential workers are bound to their feudal lords), the available workers will have greater collective strength, and thus a greater ability to force increases in wages. Capitalism also requires continual expansion, including expansion into the agricultural sector of the economy, a sector closed to them in a largely tributary economy. Finally, capitalism is based on domination through competition, and not through heredity. As a result of all this, rule by a hereditary aristocracy is a political form incoherent with capitalist procedures.

More exactly, for a brief time after the development of full-fledged capitalism, the politically dominant class is no longer the economically dominant class. Moreover, the political system as a whole is at odds with the interests of that economically dominant class. Through a democratic revolution, the political system is altered in such a way as to give political power to the economically dominant class (the bourgeoisie) and to facilitate further capitalist development. At the same time, such a revolution extends capitalist competition to government. (Needless to say, this competition is highly constrained in politics and in the economy—and it is greatly influenced by inheritance—but it is not directly a matter of hereditary right.) In short, the beginning of the capitalist era is often marked by a bourgeois revolution in which the aristocratic hierarchy is abolished, and a system of competitive democracy is established. Initially, this democracy is limited to men with property—the bourgeoisie, petit bourgeoisie, and former aristocracy. It is gradually extended, due to the struggles of oppressed people, and due to the internal contradictions of capitalism, to which we shall turn below.

From the very earliest texts, Marxists have maintained that, despite its advances, which are necessary to the ultimate achievement of communism, capitalism is the most brutally oppressive form of economy. It appropriates all surplus from the worker and in addition renders all of human life alienated and mechanical (as the Romantics insisted). Specifically, Marx argues that in capitalist society commodities—objects sold in the market for a profit—are "fetishized" such that human relations become subordinate to and defined by relations between commodities (see *Capital* 72). Indeed, in capitalist society, our human lives are completely commodified; everything in our lives is turned into an object salable for profit. As Lukács puts it, all human relations and properties are "reified"—that is, reduced to fetishized commodities (see, for example, "Reification" 92). Moreover, Lukács emphasizes, this reification involves the transformation of the historical processes of human relationships into the static timelessness of things. This, in turn, makes the historically determined conditions of capitalism—including the historical contingency of fetishism or reification itself—appear eternal, necessary, inevitable, an unchangeable part of the human condition that it is pointless to oppose (see *Essays* 53–54).

More exactly, the logic of the capitalist system dictates that individuals' self-interest is necessarily bound up with profit. Everyone in the system—from the capitalist to the worker—is subordinate to return on investment, for without return on investment, the capitalist will lose money and the worker will lose his/her job. The cycle of investment, production, sale, profit, reinvestment—the "circuit of capital"—must continue without stop or the economy will collapse. Thus, the lives of all people become mere functions of the circuit of capital. Moreover, the system of production structures our actions, desires, and so forth, in such a way that we can hardly conceive of ourselves outside of this circuit. Our most intimate relations come to be defined by commodity fetishism—as when the highest expression of romantic love becomes the purchase of the most expensive and indeed the most useless commodity, a commodity such as jewelry, which is the purest expression of *exchange* value rather than *use* value, thus, in Marxist terms, the purest expression of the exploitation of the working classes.

It is worth pausing for a moment over Marx's influential analysis of value (developed most importantly in *Capital*). Exchange value is the amount a given object is worth relative to another object (say, 1 chair = 3 shirts) or relative to some "universal" monetary standard (1 chair = $42.00). It is clearly the most important value in capitalism, for the circuit of capital relies solely on exchange value. All noncapitalist systems view exchange value as a mere means to the goal of use value, the practical usefulness of an object (for instance, the use value of a shirt is covering oneself, keeping oneself warm, and so on). Only in capitalism is use value a mere means to exchange value, a means of procuring exchange and thus sustaining the circuit of capital. Moreover, in capitalism, exchange value must not merely be preserved, it must be continually increased. And it must be increased in such a way as to lead to a profit. And it must lead to a profit that provides the capitalist with a surplus over his/her needs, a surplus that may then be reinvested. In other words, every commodity must have a *surplus* (exchange) *value*.

According to Marx, the exchange value of a commodity is the sum of the exchange values of the raw materials and of the various labors that transformed those raw materials (including labors of transportation, and so on). In this scheme, surplus value is that value which accrues to the commodity beyond what is used to replace the raw materials and "reproduce" the laborers—that is, beyond what is used to keep alive the laborers and continue the cycle of production. Simplifying somewhat, the exchange value of the raw materials may be considered a constant (if the raw materials for a shirt cost $3, then $3 of the final sale of the shirt will cancel out the cost of the raw materials; the raw materials thus are not the source of profit or loss). As a result, surplus value is the difference between the exchange value of the laborers' work and what the laborers are paid for that work. Suppose that the exchange value of the laborers' work is $10 for making a chair, but the capitalist pays them $4 for that work; the surplus value of that chair would then be $6. Surplus value is, therefore, a value created by workers. However, in capitalist society, this value is appropriated not by workers, but by the capitalist. In order to turn a profit, the capitalist systematically underpays the workers for their labor. Indeed, the capitalist pays the workers only what he/she needs to keep them working, only what he/she needs to "reproduce the relations of production." The remaining, surplus value he/she consumes or reinvests.

This is, in fact, a highly debatable theory. I myself do not believe that there is any such thing as exchange value distinct from price. But price is determined by supply and demand rather than by labor. On the other hand, the main thrust of the argument would seem indisputable: The capitalist's profit results from the difference between the price of the raw materials and labor on one hand and the price of the final commodity on the other; in consequence, as the price of the materials is presumably more or less constant, profit varies directly with the underpayment of workers.

In any case, according to Marx, the circuit of capital makes capitalism an inherently contradictory, and thus inherently unstable, system. Specifically, capitalism polarizes society into a very large group that produces surplus value, and a very small group that appropriates that surplus value for both consumption and reinvestment. This system is contradictory insofar as the impoverishment of the majority of the people is at the same time the impoverishment of the majority of consumers. In other words, the needs of capitalists as individuals are in direct contradiction with the needs of capitalists as a class. As individuals, capitalists need to pay their workers as little as possible in order to minimize costs. However, as a class, they need a large body of consumers in order to maximize sales—something they can achieve only by increasing workers' wages (on this and related contradictions, see Wallerstein 108 in Balibar and Wallerstein). This contradiction leads to periodic crises in capitalism, which will lead ultimately to the destruction of the system as a whole.

This final crisis may be delayed by several means. One is systematic state intervention, which operates to regularize relations among individual capitalists, to mediate between the class of capitalists and the class of workers, and to respond to the periodic crises of capitalism (through, for example, state spending). Another is imperialism, which allows the creation of a large "middle class" body of consumers in the home society through the hyper-exploitation of third world peoples. However, these and other strategies can never resolve the fundamental contradictions of capitalism as a system, contradictions which, in the Marxist view, will eventually lead to the end of capitalism.

Culturally, capitalism involves a movement away from aristocratic forms toward market interactions, from hierarchy and toward "individualism" (the pursuit of self-interest within the structure of the market), and so on. For example, in keeping with these general trends, we find the Reformation challenging the aristocratic/tributary structure of the Catholic church in the early period of capitalist development. This correlation is, of course, complex. For example, many feudal aristocrats made use of Protestantism toward their own ends (for an overview, see Garraty and Gay 530–39; for a broadly Marxist treatment, linking the Reformation to art and literature, see Hauser, vol. 2, 112ff.). Nonetheless, the broad historical result of the Reformation was to partially dissolve the feudal form of religion and to institute a form of religion with the structure and practices of capitalism.

Various cultural practices such as marriage change as well. Here too there was a movement away from hierarchical decision, in which marriage is arranged by parents who dominate their children much as lords dominate their vassals. In its place, we find the bourgeois idea of marriage as a sort of marketplace competition among free individuals.

In the arts, we witness a fairly direct correlation marked by a decline in patronage and an increasing reliance on the market. Literature is less and less produced for a noble patron; it is, rather, increasingly produced for a larger, paying readership or audience. This change affects both the content and the form of that literature. The heroic epic, celebrating aristocratic ideals in an erudite and allusive (or manneristic and formulaic) language, falls into decline. In its place, the novel arises—a vernacular literature accessible to the bourgeoisie (grand and petit) and consistent with their interest in the successful, but ordinary individual who encounters practical difficulties in the real world.

A number of Shakespeare's plays could be interpreted in terms of the transition from a tributary to a capitalist economy. Writing less than fifty years before the bourgeois revolution, Shakespeare found himself in a society where the bourgeoisie was in the process of transforming the political economy, but where the aristocracy was still powerful. His art was both patronized by the aristocracy and funded by sales in the marketplace of the theater. And the contents of his work involve both aristocratic and bourgeois themes (for instance, both nobility in battle and marriage by free choice), both aristocrats and ordinary people, mannerism (in, for example, the verse) and realism (in, for example, the vulgar diction).

Indeed, our reading of *Othello* can be extended by thinking of the work in these terms. The Venetian society of Shakespeare's play is clearly tributary and aristocratic. And there is virtually no mention of any aspect of capitalism. Thus the surface of the play is entirely precapitalist. However, the structure and presuppositions of the play are more complex, more conflicted, more in keeping with the transitional nature of Shakespeare's own society. First of all, Venice was the center of merchant capitalism in Europe, and Shakespeare himself makes it the site of a drama dealing directly with that topic, *The Merchant of Venice*. Historically, Venice was in continual conflict with the Ottoman empire over control of Cyprus because of its importance for Venetian merchants; in other words, control of Cyprus was important for the developing proto-capitalism of Venice. The plot of *Othello* is played out against the background of Othello's mission to save Cyprus from a Turkish invasion. Thus, while the foreground of the play is aristocratic, the background of the play is mercantile bourgeois.

As to the plot itself, like many of Shakespeare's comedies, *Othello* begins with a conflict over marriage. Desdemona chooses Othello as her husband in the bourgeois manner. Her father objects, insisting on his tributary right to decide on her behalf. But, of course, *Othello* is not a comedy, and complications enter immediately. Bourgeois society pretends to a sort of universalism, an affirmation of the rights of the individual to freedom, including freedom of choice in marriage. However, at the same time, it requires the subjugation of entire societies, even entire races. This is most obviously true in colonialism and the slave trade. In connection with these, the bourgeoisie must generate an antiuniversalist ideology as well, an ideology that functions to justify and thus preserve the exploitation of colonized countries (compare Wallerstein 34ff. in Balibar and Wallerstein). (Unsurprisingly, bourgeois ideology is as deeply self-contradictory as capitalist economy.) The historical facts of colonialism and the slave trade are only alluded to in *Othello*, but are nonetheless important. Othello explains that he himself was sold into slavery (1.3.136–37), and his reference to himself as formerly an aristocrat in his native (tributary) state (1.2.20–21) hints at the degradation of African social orders through colonial conflict—which was still in its very earliest stages when Shakespeare was writing. More importantly, the ideology that arose to justify the slave trade and colonialism, the antiuniversalist ideology of racism, is manifest abundantly in the play through the comparisons of Othello with black animals (1.1.85 and 1.1.108–11), Satan (1.1.87), and so on.

In this way, Othello's and Desdemona's marriage is quite different from the marriages desired by the protagonists of Shakespeare's comedies. For in this case, there is not only a conflict between the tributary hierarchy and bourgeois individual freedom. There is also a conflict between the putative universalism of bourgeois democracy, and the racist and colonialist antiuniversalisms which arise from the economic interests and practices of capitalism and which limit that putative universalism. The racism of Venetian society is, then, itself explicable by reference to a larger economic structure. And for this reason, the marriage of Othello and Desdemona reproduces in microcosm the tensions between universalism and antiuniversalism inherent in colonialist capitalism.

There are many other approaches that an historical materialist might adopt in studying literature. For example, some Marxist writers have sought to examine the economics of publishing in detail, scrutinizing such phenomena as the relation between marketing and editorial decisions. To take a rather small example, Gary Taylor has pointed out that Shakespeare's early reputation derived in part from the fact that a complete edition of his plays was printed quite early and thus made available both to readers and actors. This early publication was not so much the result of Shakespeare's unique quality as of the fact that copyright to all Shakespeare's plays was held by the Globe Theater company. Other early English dramatists (Taylor's example is Middleton) had written plays for a number of different companies; thus copyright to their plays was divided and a complete edition of their works was far more difficult to compile.

This sort of analysis of the political economics underlying such phenomena as literary reputation functions not only to explain but to "demystify." Much of the force of dominant ideology derives from "mystification." (Dominant ideology is the complex of ideas that fosters a general acquiescence in an exploitative or discriminatory system; see below, chapter 4.) Ideologically functional beliefs and practices seem entirely mysterious to us, something like divine dicta that we cannot question; appearing from nowhere, they seem absolute and unquestionable. For example, the canon of great authors or the reputation of a single author appears to be incontrovertible because its origins are unknown. Careful economic/historical explanation can reveal these origins, and thus allow us to question canonicity and reputation. When Shakespeare's reputation appears as a mere fact of existence, it also appears eternal and indisputable. Once one understands the economics behind the development of Shakespeare's reputation, it is easier to consider that reputation rationally. (Of course, this is not to say that we will decide Shakespeare's reputation is undeserved—I, for one, believe it is fully deserved.)

Finally, after capitalism, the future: In a genuinely communist society, the nature of art, like all other social phenomena, would change radically. (Clearly, I am not speaking of any of the present or former "socialist" countries; even in their own terms, these are/were at best transitional.) In such a society, the antagonistic and oppressive division of labor would be abolished; the workers would collectively own and democratically control the means of production; there would no longer be an owning class and a working class or an elite of mental workers set over manual workers. So too, art would no longer be professionalized. It would be practiced by all. And "the laws of beauty" mentioned by Marx could at last form the guiding principles of literature, permeating the work of a broadly creative populace, unaffected by economic exploitation, class antagonism, and ideological distortion.

# II

---

# Modern and
# Contemporary Theories

# Philosophy of Mind and Experience
## Phenomenology, Existentialism,
## Hermeneutics, Pragmatism

The most obvious and direct inheritors of the Romantic philosophical tradition are phenomenology and its offspring. The opening section treats the fundamental principles of phenomenology, as set out by Edmund Husserl, turning then to the most elaborate literary development of these ideas, that of Roman Ingarden.

There were two particularly important developments out of phenomenology, both associated with Martin Heidegger: existentialism and hermeneutics. The second section takes up existentialism, focusing on Heidegger and Sartre, with some attention to de Beauvoir. The third section begins with Heidegger's hermeneutics, continuing on to Gadamer and Habermas.

The fourth section takes up a range of literary theories—reception aesthetics (Jauss, Iser), reader response theory (Fish), intentionalism and related approaches (Hirsch, Ong, Knapp and Michaels)—that draw on one or more of the philosophical movements just discussed.

Though historically distinct from the other theories considered in this chapter, Pragmatism shows some striking similarities to the concerns of existentialism. In any case, it is clearly another philosophy of experience that has entered significantly into literary theory. The final section takes up Pragmatism, beginning with William James, but concentrating on Dewey.

## Phenomenology: Husserl and Ingarden

The phenomenological movement was a philosophical school that dominated continental philosophical thought in the first half of this century. Begun and developed by Edmund Husserl, it was further extended by such thinkers as Martin Heidegger, Maurice Merleau-Ponty, Jean-Paul Sartre, and others. Husserl conceived of phenomenology as a way of providing an absolutely certain grounding for the sciences. In this he no doubt failed. However, in pursuing his goal, Husserl examined the nature of the mind, of intersubjectivity, and of the relation of both to an objective world, and his views on these topics provided a starting point for much subsequent philosophy and literary theory. Indeed, the influence of Husserl's Phenomenological method was and is pervasive in continental literary thought. Husserl's work provides much of the ground against which both existentialism and deconstruction may be understood; it is a major source for modern hermeneutics; it constitutes a great deal of what is innovative in Lacanian psychoanalysis; it is at the very heart of German aesthetics of reception.

The first step in phenomenological method is "phenomenological reduction," the reduction of all experience to phenomena, to what is purely "given." This involves the "bracketing" of all issues relating to the real existence of the world; it involves an "epoché" or suspension of belief, in which we set aside all our presuppositions and consider only what is directly experienced. Take visual perception. I look before me and I see a lamp. That is the "natural attitude" or "naive" view, Husserl tells us. If I perform a phenomenological reduction, I must recognize that I experience only a certain shape, that presuppositions determine my inference that this shape is a lamp, a three-dimensional object with a range of properties, including another side that I do not now see. If I focus only on what is given in experience, I must recognize that no "lampness" is part of that experience. Indeed, this is clear if I merely "bracket" the existence of the lamp. For then I do not presuppose its existence *as* a lamp (or as anything else). If I bracket the existence of the lamp, I make no distinction between a real lamp, a hallucination, a dream, an optical illusion, and so on. Thus I may isolate precisely what it is I experience.

The crucial task of the phenomenologist is to describe how we come to know particulars. Husserl's motto was "To the things!" (quoted in Spiegelberg 109). And phenomenological method was intended to lead us back to the very basis of our experience of things. Let us return to the lamp before me. Setting aside presuppositions, as Husserl insists we can— bracketing the existence of the lamp—how do I come to know this lamp? First of all, I recognize that the lamp is not a series of discrete, unrelated perceptions. Rather, I understand it as a unity. Suppose I move around it, seeing it from different angles. I see the switch at the back, the cord with a two-pronged plug (one prong wider than the other), and so on. I see that the bottom of the base and the inner part of the shade are white, while the stem and switch are black; the base is hard and cool to the touch—and so on. I bring all of these different perceptions together into a coherent object that incorporates all these particular aspects. This process of synthesizing different aspects is called "constitution." In synthesizing these various aspects into a single object, I "constitute" that object.

Now, we may step back to a further level of abstraction, and observe not the lamp, but my constitution of the lamp. In doing this, we note that two elements are necessarily involved, an intending subject and an intentional object or constituted object: me and my (intentionally constituted) lamp. Note that I say "intending subject" here rather than "consciousness," and "intentional object" rather than "real object." As to the former, for Husserl, as for his teacher Franz Brentano, there is no such thing as simple or pure consciousness. Consciousness is always consciousness of something; it is always and necessarily directed toward an object. In other words, it is always "intentional." Put otherwise, it is always a process of "noesis" or thinking oriented toward a "noema" or object that is thought of. The noema is not the thing itself, as existing separately—that is precisely what is bracketed. Rather, the noema is the thing constituted in noesis, not the real object but the intentional object, not the object in the world but the object in the mind.

Husserl devoted considerable time to describing the operation of constitution—an enormously influential concept, as we shall see. First of all, he emphasized that constitution is a temporal process; it cannot be removed from time, which is its necessary medium. Specifically, intention always involves what Husserl calls both "protention" and "retention." "Retention" is what we hold in mind of what we have experienced. "Protention" is what we project with respect to what we are going to experience. Returning to the lamp, I see one aspect right now. But in constituting this object, I simultaneously hold in mind or retain the other aspects that I have seen previously. Moreover, as I move around the lamp, I expect to see certain things, and thus I protend (or project expectations) just as I retain. Put slightly differently, with the stress on the noema rather than the noesis, at each moment my perception involves what Husserl calls "horizons," the shading off of experienced aspects into other, unexperienced but suggested aspects, past and future (see, for example, *Ideas* 52)—the switch I saw a moment ago, but which is no longer visible, the plug that I expect to see when I pull up the cord.

But how do I come to see this as a lamp? How does it happen that, glancing at one aspect of the thing, I identify it as a lamp, expecting it to have a wide range of properties that I have not experienced? Initially, I do constitute a lamp through the process just described. Husserl refers to this initial constitution as a "primal instituting." I then, so to speak, retain this constituted object in memory until I encounter a similar object. The new experience evokes the prior constitution. This prior constitution, then, guides my current constitution, providing a wide range of expectations (or protentions), largely defining the horizons of this new noema, horizons that I may or may not choose to actualize by looking further at the lamp, walking around it, and so on. If I do choose to examine the new object, I will find that many of my expectations will be fulfilled. But some will be denied. Thus, I will constitute the new lamp in its specificity. But, at the same time, I will constitute a more general schema of a lamp, which is identical with neither the primal nor the present constitution.

For example, suppose that I have only seen table lamps with the switch on the stem beneath the bulb or on the base. I see a new lamp. This evokes my prior constitutions, giving rise to expectations as to the location of the switch. However, as I try to turn on the lamp, I do not find the switch in either place. Eventually, I discover the switch on the cord just below the base. Thus I constitute this particular lamp in this particular way—as having a switch high on the cord. But I also alter my more general or more abstract constitution of lamps, now allowing three possible locations for the switch rather than two.

Husserl saw this process (of constituting schemas) as part of the recognition of essences. Another aspect of phenomenology, and in certain works the most crucial aspect, is the systematic study of such essences. In order to isolate essences, Husserl maintained, one must further extend the phenomenological reduction until it is an "eidetic reduction," which is to say, a reduction to the essence of the thing. This is done through the free, imaginative variation of the intentional object in such a way as to isolate the limits of its identity as, for example, a lamp, a chair, a house. In other words, in free imaginative variation, we keep changing the lamp until it is no longer a lamp. And in doing so, we recognize what the essence of a lamp is.

A lamp is perhaps too complex to illustrate this point well. So let's take a cup. I look at the cup in front of me. It is beige, and cylindrical, and has a square handle; its height is slightly greater than its diameter, which is roughly two inches; it appears to be of some glazed ceramic material. I can imaginatively vary any of these aspects in order to judge the essence of cupness. For example, I may change the color or the shape of the handle or the height of the cup or the ratio between the diameter and the height.

Some of these, for example, the color, will not make a difference and are thus inessential. But others will make a difference. For example, as the ratio between diameter and height increases, the cup becomes a bowl; when the material is changed to marzipan, it becomes a dessert (in the shape of a cup), and so on. We continue this process of imaginative variation until we specify what cannot be changed if the (intentionally constituted) cup is to remain a cup. When we discover this, we have completed our eidetic reduction and defined the essence.

Up until now we have been speaking of the perception of physical objects. However, constitution—with its entire apparatus of retention and protention, horizons, primal institutings—applies to all experiences, including most importantly our experiences of ourselves and of others. The fact that we can withdraw from our act of noesis and observe it, indicates that we can and do constitute ourselves as noemata also. In other words, when I turn from observing the lamp to observing my observation of the lamp, I constitute myself as part of the noema, as one noematic object. I also constitute my act of constitution, for I synthesize my different acts of synthesis of the lamp, putting those acts together into a single activity. In all of this, I become an intentional object to myself. (In this, Husserl's indebtedness to German Idealism should be clear.)

Indeed, in saying this, I constitute myself at yet another level—the level of constituting my constitution of the lamp. This process can be repeated indefinitely—for I can constitute my constitution of my constitution of the lamp, and so on. Each such constitution has the next possible constitution as one horizon. It has this horizon, because each constitution has as its horizon the unconstituted subjectivity that performs the constitution. In other words, just as every noesis implies a noema, every noema implies a noesis. What is important here, however, is that this noesis *as such* is not an object to any subjectivity. Indeed, it "transcends" any possible experience, for it is by definition not what is experienced, but what experiences. At each level of constitution, it is not what is constituted, but what is constituting. This is what Husserl called the "transcendental ego" or "transcendental subjectivity," the ego or subjectivity that is doing the constituting when I constitute the lamp, or when I constitute my constitution of the lamp, or my constitution of the constitution of the lamp, and so on.

This constituting of myself as object, with its horizon of transcendental subjectivity, allows me to constitute Others as well, Husserl tells us. Specifically, I constitute myself as a corporeal object in relation to a physical world. Equally, I constitute the Other as a corporeal object. But the corporeality of that Other, Husserl says, "mirrors" my own corporeality, and thus evokes a common essential constitution, with common horizons (for example, I would have similar expectations of myself and of Others regarding behavior in certain situations—such as screaming or passing out upon suffering severe physical injury). But insofar as I (as noematic object) share the same horizons with Others (as noematic objects), they must share with me a horizon of transcendental subjectivity. Thus constituting myself and Others as objects—as bodies with particular properties, motions, and so forth—leads directly to constituting Others as transcendental egos, which is to say, unconstitutable subjectivities, who in turn constitute both themselves and me (as objects and as subjectivities). (Schelling presents a similar idea in a similar idiom when he speaks of the self "see[ing] itself reflected, catch[ing] sight of itself in the mirror [*Spiegel*] of another intelligence" [*System* 163].)

This process of the constitution of Others is not a matter of constituting a single individual. Rather it is a matter of constituting an entire community. Indeed, it is, at its most abstract level, the constitution of a community of what Husserl calls "transcendental intersubjectivity." Certainly, we constitute Others as individuals. But in doing so, we particularize them. We specify their traits, fill in and detail horizons of expectation. Thus we constitute Bill as having a specific, recognizable appearance; more importantly, we constitute him as having a certain history, certain character traits, and so on, and these lead us to have certain expectations (for example, that he will be on time or late for a meeting, that he will express certain opinions). This sort of constitution is tremendously important. However, it is preceded and allowed by a more general constitution: the constitution of transcendental subjectivity as such. More simply, we do not decide one by one that individuals have transcendental subjectivity, first noting this for Bill, then for Jane, then for Martha, and so on. Rather, we constitute the community of transcendental intersubjectivity and that is what permits our particularizing constitutions of Bill, Jane, and so on.

For Husserl, this constitution of transcendental intersubjectivity provides the necessary ground for the constitution of an objective world. While it may seem that we constitute others on the basis of an objective world, according to Husserl it is the intersubjective community that is the guarantor of objective reality. In constituting my experiential world, my immediate environment or "*Umwelt*" (the "world [*Welt*] around [*um*]" me), I constitute a complex of objects, the existence of which cannot be assumed outside of my constitution. If I imagine a world in which I am the only transcendental subject, Husserl insists, the world that I imagine may shrink to my constituted experience of that world. It is, in effect, indistinguishable from a dream. Though most obviously a version of Descartes' systematic doubt regarding the existence of an external world, this is also, in a sense, the problem of the Kantian noumenon, especially as developed by Fichte. If we take away the "form" of an object as provided by constitution, there seems to be nothing left but a mere manifold of sensation. How can this guarantee an objective world that will provide a philosophically secure ground for physical science? Again, one option is a Kantian principle of reason, an assertion that we have no choice but to assume the subjective purposiveness of nature. Husserl does not adopt the Kantian view, but rather sees the possibility of fixing transcendental objectivity (that is, the existence of an external world independent of our constitution) by reference to transcendental intersubjectivity.

Specifically, each of us constitutes an Umwelt or experiential world, but it is precisely the overlapping of these experiential worlds, the possibility of their coincidence, that defines for us an objective world. Thus, I see one aspect of the lamp while you see another. We both move around the lamp, constituting it as an intentional object—specifically, as a lamp of such-and-such properties (a red base, a red shade, a switch on the cord). For Husserl, it is crucial that our constitutions of an object coincide and that my experience of an object is never the only experience of it—at least potentially, innumerable noematic perspectives can be experienced simultaneously by different subjects. It is this that guarantees the objective existence of an object and, more broadly, the (transcendental) existence of an objective world.

As readers will immediately recognize from chapter 2, this is in part taken over from Schelling, who maintained that "The sole objectivity which the world can possess for the individual is the fact of its having been intuited by intelligences outside the self" (*System* 174). It remains as problematic in Husserl as it was in Schelling. Again, in order for this solution to work, we have to assume the noumenal existence of transcendental subjectivity. If we have reason to deny the noumenal existence of transcendental objectivity (objectivity per se, objectivity that transcends intention), then it would seem we have equal reason to deny the noumenal existence of transcendental intersubjectivity. Conversely, if we can assume the noumenal existence of transcendental intersubjectivity, there seems to be no good reason not to assume the noumenal existence of transcendental objectivity in the first place, in which case there is no problem.

A final point worth mentioning, before going on to discuss the literary use of Husserl, concerns the further articulation of Husserl's notion of community. Husserl allowed stages between the isolated transcendental ego and the absolute intersubjective community. Specifically, he allowed different levels of intersubjective community. The very highest level is that of the entire human community guaranteeing the objective world per se. But the most practically important is that of the narrower cultural community, or cultural communities. Thus, as Husserl puts it, "Objective Nature" is defined by "thereness-for-everyone." However, in some cases especially in the case of cultural objects ("books, tools, works of any kind, and so forth"), the guaranteeing community narrows; for example, it may be "the European or perhaps, more narrowly, the French cultural community, and so forth" (*Cartesian* 92), presumably down through various practical trades, philosophical schools, and so on. This range of communities and corresponding range of (communally shared) experiential worlds allows the introduction of historical and cultural study into phenomenology, a particularly important point for subsequent literary developments.

As already mentioned, Husserl's influence on literary theory is massive, though frequently unacknowledged by literary critics. Constitution has proven a particularly fruitful notion in the study of literature, especially after the work of Roman Ingarden. Ingarden was a Polish philosopher who developed a Husserlian literary theory in two important and influential volumes: *The Literary Work of Art* and *The Cognition of the Literary Work of Art.* Ingarden in effect introduced phenomenology into literary study and thereby largely determined the subsequent development of specifically literary phenomenology. Ingarden's work is not only valuable in itself; it provides a crucial background for a range of critics from René Wellek and Austin Warren in the United States to Georges Poulet in Switzerland to Wolfgang Iser and Hans Robert Jauss in Germany.

The phenomenological nature of Ingarden's project is clear even in the titles of his works. In *The Literary Work of Art,* he focuses on the noema; in *The Cognition of the Literary Work of Art,* he focuses on noesis. Specifically, in *The Literary Work of Art,* Ingarden sets out to determine the nature of a literary work through isolating its essential structure. He engages in a careful phenomenological description not of one literary work, but of any literary work—of what all literary works have in common. Specifically, he distinguishes four "strata" of this particular sort of cultural object: the phonic, the semantic, the objectal, and the schematized/aspectual. Anticipating more recent trends, he stresses the polyphonic nature of the literary work of art, its "multivoicedness" as we might say today, its plurality.

The phonic stratum is relatively straightforward. It is the stratum of sounds and sound patterns. Patterns of sound take on importance in literary art that, most often, they lack elsewhere. In constituting a literary work of art, then, we constitute or synthesize its sound patterns—from meter and rhyme to more subtle patternings.

The semantic stratum is highly complex, for it involves constitution at several levels. First of all, it involves the synthesis of nouns, verbs, and so forth, into sentences. This itself is a complex process, for each word involves a range of semantic elements; for example, nouns involve reference ("the chair" refers to a particular chair as defined in the larger context), concept (our idea of a chair involves properties of shape and function), category type (a chair is a type of furniture), and so on. Moreover, in a manner reminiscent of Abhinavagupta, Ingarden emphasizes that each word brings with it a range of relevant associations that may be activated by the use of the word in context, and thus contribute importantly to our experience of the work. Having constituted a semantic stratum at the level of the sentence, we must then synthesize sentences into larger units. In each case, Ingarden writes, we are constituting "intentional correlates" of the sentences or sentence complexes. In other words, we are constituting coherent meanings in increasingly large, coherent units.

This brings us to the object stratum. In constituting intentional correlates at the semantic level, we are inevitably led to constitute intentional objects. When we read the sentence "They arrested him late one night" (from the beginning of Alex La Guma's *In the Fog of the Seasons' End*), we first of all constitute an intentional correlate of the sentence. We understand that "arrested" means "took into custody" (not "halted," as in "that arrested his development"); we tacitly assume that "late" means "long into the night" (not "after they were supposed to"); we understand that several people arrested one person at a certain time (not that one person arrested several), and so on. All of this understanding is what is given in our intentional correlate. But we go further than the intentional correlate and begin to constitute an intentional world of intentional objects. Even in this sentence, we isolate the "they" as the basis for the subsequent constitution of two or more subjectivities, and the "him" as the basis for another subjectivity. The word "arrested" evokes our "eidetic" constitution of police, and we further constitute the "they" in accordance with this prior constitution.

Ingarden emphasizes in particular our constitution of time and space. Also in reading this sentence, we begin to constitute a sort of map, locating the place of the arrest and, as we read, the jail. We also constitute a series of temporal relations, defining what preceded what. In this novel, the opening sentence refers to events that are subsequent to the main action of the novel, and thus we must constitute this temporality as distinct from the temporality of our own reading experience (that is, we do not constitute the sequence of events as parallel to our experience of reading about those events, for the events occur in a different order from our reading).

More importantly, Ingarden stresses that the objects and situations we constitute are always partially indeterminate within the text itself. From the very beginning, we are filling in a wide range of properties and relations that are not explicitly stated in the work. Ingarden refers to this as "concretization." Our concretizations may be confirmed subsequently, or falsified, or neither. For example, knowing beforehand that *In the Fog of the Seasons' End* takes place in South Africa, and that it was written by a nonwhite political activist, we may begin tentatively to constitute the "him" as a political activist, probably nonwhite. As we read further, we find out that the "him" is indeed a nonwhite political prisoner. In this case, our concretization is confirmed by the text. However, much of our concretization falls outside of what is straightforwardly or definitively determined by the text. Consider the more complex case of Othello's motivation. One reader slowly, over the course of the play, constitutes Othello as a misogynist, his actions motivated by a deep hatred of women; another constitutes him as excessively passionate and prone to jealousy; another concretizes him as a man shattered by the racism of the world around him, and so on. None of these concretizations is simply verified or straightforwardly falsified by the text. That is because each of these readings relies not only on the text, but on various prior constitutings as well—constitutings of men (for instance, in relation to misogyny), constitutings of blacks (in relation to social racism), and so on.

On the other hand, this is not to say that one concretization is as good as another. For Ingarden, some concretizations are more adequate than others, for they take account of a greater part of the text. Indeed this is how we argue about concretizations. For example, I would argue that Othello is not excessively passionate, and that there are plenty of scenes in which he is calm even when others are violent (for example, the second scene, when Iago tries to anger him by reporting slander and when Brabantio physically attacks and vilifies him); thus a concretization of Othello as overly passionate does not really fit a large part of the play.

Ingarden also stresses that concretizations change historically. What we call the "life of the work" is its series of concretizations, changing with time and circumstance. These changes may be improvements—involving the development of more encompassing concretizations—but they need not be. This historicity of the work is of particular importance for subsequent German literary theory.

Finally, we have the stratum of schematized aspects. These are the elements that give an almost experiential particularity to the work, and thus play a crucial role in its aesthetic function, according to Ingarden. These are perhaps best understood as the sensible elements of our experience of the "quasi-reality" (277) of the object stratum. When we actually perceive an object, we see one aspect and we see this aspect in its particularity. But at the same time we link it with a schema. For example, we see an irregular red and black shape *and* we connect this shape with the schema of a lamp. So what we see is, in effect, a (concretized) aspect of a (schematic) lamp. Ingarden's point is that, in reading about a lamp, we do the same thing in reverse. We start out with the larger category or schema, then implicitly specify the particular, ending up with a schema concretized from a particular point of view in a perceptual quasi-reality.

Consider again La Guma's novel. In reading the first sentence, I automatically bring to bear certain visual and aural images on the scene. I not only concretize conceptually, but see and hear the scene—though in a way indirectly and indistinctly, as if through peripheral vision or in a partially remembered dream. This quasi-perception involves a series of "concretized aspects" (for instance, I see a black man, well built, in a bluish shirt, open, and a white undershirt, his hands behind his back, presumably cuffed). However, I have concretized these aspects from the schemas defined by the work itself. In mentioning "him," the novel defines a man, as I understand in my intentional correlate. I concretize that correlate both conceptually and perceptually. In other words, "man" evokes a schema or essence or prior eidetic constitution. This involves certain abstract properties (such as transcendental subjectivity) and certain physical properties. Moreover, this schematic "man" is, in turn, part of a larger complex, involving schemas not only for "arrest" and "night," but for "man arrested in apartheid South Africa." Indeed, it is the schema for this particular type of man that I concretize perceptually/aspectually in reading the novel.

In *The Cognition of the Literary Work of Art*, Ingarden analyzes the process of constitution of the literary work. This process necessarily follows the structure of the work itself (as noema) and thus there is considerable overlap between the two books. However, there are a few points worth mentioning in the latter work. First of all, Ingarden discusses the temporality of the reading experience, stressing the operation of retention and protention. Moreover, he emphasizes that retention and protention are in part determinative of present constitution as well; in other words, how we constitute a currently intended sentence correlate is in part determined by the sentence correlates we have already constituted and the sentence correlates we projected in the past and the sentence correlates we are now projecting for the future. My constitution of the meaning correlates, intentional objects, and so on, of the first sentence of La Guma's novel is clearly shaped by my prior constitutions regarding the novel and the expectations, or protentions, to which these have given rise. I would have understood the same sentence differently in the context of different retentions and protentions—for example, if it had been the first sentence of a newly discovered Arthur Conan Doyle mystery entitled *Sherlock Holmes Framed for Murder*. In keeping with all of this, Ingarden emphasizes that in reading literature the reader is "active" and "cocreative" (40).

### Existentialism: Heidegger and Sartre

Other than Husserl, the most important continental philosopher of the twentieth century is probably Martin Heidegger, and the single most important philosophical work is almost certainly Heidegger's 1927 *Being and Time*. It is difficult to overestimate the influence of this work on later humanistic and social thought. It changed the course of phenomenology, leading to such figures as Maurice Merleau-Ponty; it served as one of the founding texts in existentialism, exerting a major influence on such writers as Jean-Paul Sartre; it in effect gave rise to the hermeneutics of Hans-Georg Gadamer, Paul Ricoeur, and others; it deeply influenced Lacan, and largely formed Jacques Derrida's understanding of the philosophical tradition against which he was reacting; even such writers as Michel Foucault, Max Horkheimer, and Theodor Adorno developed some of their most significant ideas out of *Being and Time*; indeed, it is my view that *Being and Time* is one major, unacknowledged source of analytic philosophy after positivism (the views of John Austin, Gilbert Ryle, and Ludwig Wittgenstein have direct parallels in Heidegger's much earlier book) and of John Dewey's Pragmatic approach to art.

It is important to discuss the major ideas of *Being and Time* before going on to Heidegger's views on literature, and to the ideas of later thinkers. Within *Being and Time*, I shall begin with the objects or themes of Heidegger's study, turning to Heidegger's methodology in the following section.

*Being and Time* is, first of all, a study of Being—what it means to be, as such; not what it means to be this or that thing (say, a tree), but what it means that something is (full stop). This immediately faces Heidegger with a problem—how can we even begin to think about this question, much less answer it? First of all, we must turn to a more particular, more thinkable, kind of being—specifically, the sort of being we are, human being, or more exactly, the sort of being for which being is itself an issue (see *Being* 32). The being of a particular rock or tree cannot be an issue to that rock or tree. However, being can be an issue to me, to you, or to any other person—indeed, it is necessarily an issue, even if we forget it or deny it, for in our case it is identical with the issue of death. In other words, not to be is, for us, to be dead. Thus being and not being are issues for us, deeply important, fundamental issues. Following one standard usage in German, Heidegger refers to this being—that is, human being, being for which being is an issue—as "Dasein," literally "being there" (or "to be there"). I will follow the practice of Heidegger's translators in using the German term.

What, then, is the first thing to say about Dasein, the being for which being is itself an issue? The first thing to say is that the being of Dasein is always *Being-in-the-world*. This is absolutely crucial; it is perhaps the central insight of Heidegger's entire philosophy. Dasein (human being) is not isolated, walled off from other people and from things. Neither is it abstracted into a realm of pure thought. Dasein is always located in a world—always "thrown" into a world, Heidegger says, always "in the midst" of happenings and of doings. For Heidegger, this Being-in-the-world is the primary, the fundamental and definitive, mode of Dasein; all other ways of understanding Dasein must be referred back to this.

What is this Being-in-the-world? It is, in effect, our entire continuing experiencing and acting in relation to what we are not. It is our walking toward a certain place, to meet a certain person, to discuss certain matters; it is our dressing in a certain way, turning here rather than there, and so on. It is life—my life or your life—in its concrete richness and variety. As Heidegger emphasizes, it is, first of all, the "whole of this structure" (65). Our Being-in-the-world is always oriented toward and involved with the whole. Though local and specific at any given moment, it cannot be reduced to momentary impressions or isolated actions. It is, Heidegger says, a sort of "dwelling" (80). Our Being-in-the-world is like our living in a home, marked by the same thickness of feeling, expectation (for instance, expectation as to what items of furniture will be where, so that we sit down without any self-conscious thought about it), and so on.

On the other hand, Being-in-the-world is not in any way a passive inactivity, as the notion of dwelling might seem to imply. We are always engaged in "dealings" with the world; we are always "going about" the world (90). And we are going about the world because our relation to the world is a relation of *care* (84). We care about events, people, ourselves, objects. And we go about the world in this manner of care. (Heidegger emphasizes that our Being-in-the-world is also a Being-with Others; our relation to Others Heidegger sees as a particular form of care, "solicitude.")

All of this may seem to be either hopelessly vague or merely platitudinous. But the primacy of Being-in-the-world, thus understood, has highly significant consequences for a variety of philosophical (and thus literary) problems. Most importantly, we typically seek to understand a wide range of phenomena—from space and time, to language, to art—in isolation from our Being-in-the-world. We understand them in a derivative or secondary mode of being. Consider ordinary physical things. In philosophical reflection, we think of them as objects of contemplation or self-conscious and self-reflective study. For example, we may inspect them visually (as when we discuss constitution) or we might try to isolate their abstract essences (through imaginative variation or other means). In short, we focus on things as *present at hand*.

But in our dealings with the world, our relation to things is not, first of all, a relation to things present at hand; it is, rather, a relation to *equipment* that is *ready to hand*. We do not scrutinize the spoon, the hammer, the car. We eat with the spoon, strike with the hammer, drive the car. *This* is primary. We come to scrutinize these objects when they become "conspicuous"—which is to say, when we cannot use them, when they are broken or inaccessible. In short, our typical, philosophical way of conceiving of things is misguided. Philosophers try to understand things in their conspicuousness—as if they were *broken*, Heidegger says—when their primary being is in their inconspicuous readiness to hand. Think of our relation to a hammer when we are nailing something, then the change in that relation when the hammer breaks. Clearly, philosophical reflection is much more akin to the latter attitude than to the former—but the former is clearly primary.

This same sort of analysis can be applied to a wide range of concerns beyond hammers. For example, in a Heideggerian view, space is not primarily a Cartesian grid, latitude and longitude, a specific location on a map. Rather, space is primarily our Being-in-the-world ordered by our bodily sense of left and right, ahead and behind, by a sense of distance measured in such terms as "an hour's walk" or "a two-hour drive." Time too is primarily the time of Being-in-the-world, a time of expectation, waiting, arrival, culmination, and only derivatively the chronological time measured out by clocks.

Perhaps most importantly for our purposes, language is open to the same analysis. Signs are not disembodied and autonomous indicators of meaning or reference. They are not sounds, ideas, and objects (for example, the sound "cat," the idea of a cat, and a particular cat) tacitly conceived of as all present at hand—the usual way in which signs are understood, or misunderstood. Rather they are parts of our going about in the world. Specifically, a "sign is not a Thing which stands to another Thing in the relationship of indicating" (110); rather, signs are "items of equipment whose specific character as equipment consists in *showing* or *indicating*" (108). To understand signs—or to understand language—we must think of signs as part of our Being-in-the-world. "Cat" is not an isolated signifier that we scrutinize for reference; nor is it part of a system of objective linguistic relations that we scan for meaning. It is, rather, part of a warning ("Watch out for the cat's tail!" shouted out to the fellow on the rocking chair), a request ("Could you take care of our cat while we're away?"), or other dealings with people in the world. "Signs always indicate primarily 'wherein' one lives, where one's concern dwells, what sort of involvement there is with something" (111).

As we shall see, this is an insight that was developed at length by later analytic philosophers, without acknowledgement of Heidegger's work. In any event, it is a conception of language that indicates that many current debates about meaning may be ill-founded. Whether or not one fully accepts Heidegger's views on Being-in-the-world, it seems clear that he has indeed isolated a problem with dominant modes of discussing language, and much else. Language does indeed operate in and through our dealings with the world. To consider language as a system of signs existing in a Platonic realm is to remove it from its mode of operation and to give it the quality of being present at hand—to hypostatize or reify it, Marxists would say, to remove it from human, social life and transform it in one's mind to a static thing.

Heidegger's view of art is part of this same program of reorienting philosophical discussions toward the primacy of Being-in-the-world. The work of art too must not be conceived of as a thing, present at hand. But neither is it to be understood as equipment, ready to hand for use, and unnoticed precisely because it is ready to hand. In literary and aesthetic essays, such as "The Origin of the Work of Art," Heidegger maintains that art has a function closely related to that of Heidegger's own philosophical writings. (Unsurprisingly, philosophers often rediscover their own philosophical project in art.) Specifically, according to Heidegger, art discloses Being-in-the-world; it gives us access to the existential truth of Dasein, that is, the true Being of Dasein in its Being-in-the-world. It does this, not by *telling* us about that Being-in-the-World, but by allowing that Being to "emerge" into "unconcealedness" ("Origin" 36). For *"Beauty is one way in which truth occurs as unconcealedness"* (56). (In granting art the philosophical function of "disclosure," Heidegger's continuity with German Idealism is clear [cf. 79 on Hegel]. In keeping with standard Romantic bipolarism, Heidegger contrasts art with "the technical-scientific objectivation of nature" [47].)

Heidegger gives the example of Van Gogh's painting of a peasant's shoes: "from the dark opening of the worn insides of the shoes the toilsome tread of the worker stares forth. In the stiffly rugged heaviness of the shoes there is the accumulated tenacity of her slow trudge through the far-spreading and ever-uniform furrows of the field swept by a raw wind. On the leather lie the dampness and richness of the soil. Under the soles slides the loneliness of the field-path as evening falls" (34). The painting does not tell us any of this. But it allows us to see it. Put differently, "the work opens up a *world*" (44). It reveals to us the peasant woman's Being-in-the-world, not merely telling us about it, but engaging us with it.

One wonders about the degree to which any interpretation of this sort (for example, Heidegger's interpretation of Van Gogh) is truly and specifically a function of that work. In reading Heidegger, it is hard not to feel that a great deal of what Heidegger finds is, in fact, more in Heidegger than in the painting. Moreover, it seems that even what is in the painting could be more readily "disclosed" in a meditation on a pair of real shoes—or, better still, in work with peasant farmers. On the other hand, perhaps there is a way in which a work of art can "bring out" a world that, in its everyday reality, involves too many random elements to be truly revealing. *Othello* may be said to disclose the world in which racism eats away at the human soul, destroys human relationships. And it can disclose this world, because that is not a merely imaginary world; it is, rather, the world in which we have our Being. Yet, if we turn to "reality," we find that actual cases do not disclose the world in this way, because too much else enters; the world remains obscured. A superficially similar case, such as that of O. J. Simpson, is a complex of acts and objects merely present at hand, a cacophony of particulars and categories (sex, race, economic class, media exploitation, and so on) that does not reveal more than its own particularity—along with a handful of commonplace generalities (that some police are racist, that some men brutally beat their wives, that the American legal system favors the wealthy).

In addition to Being-in-the-world, there are a few other concepts that have had an impact in literary study and are important to mention, specifically those that cluster around the notion of "authenticity." Heidegger stresses the agency of Dasein, the freedom of Dasein in its "circum-spective" care. This emphasis on freedom became central to existentialist writers such as Sartre. Within Heidegger's own work, its greatest impor-tance is probably in relation to Dasein's "being itself," or more properly Dasein's choosing that possibility of being itself. "Dasein always under-stands itself in terms of its existence—in terms of a possibility of itself," specifically "to be itself or not itself" (*Being* 33). Thus we may be *authentic*, thinking and acting on our own free agency of care-full Being-in-the-world, or inauthentic, allowing our thought and action to be determined by something other than our own free agency.

Heidegger notes that we are not and cannot always be authentic. We often think or act in a standardized way, merely doing what "one" does: "We take pleasure and enjoy ourselves as *one* takes pleasure; we read, see, and judge about literature and art as *one* sees and judges" (164, modified). Indeed, in a discussion that may have influenced Bakhtin, Heidegger notes that Dasein may speak as "one" speaks; Dasein's speech may be "idle talk," a repetition of received opinion that "takes on an authoritative character" simply because it is so widely repeated. (A situation that is not uncommon in literary theory.) In all these cases, Dasein is dominated by the "one." In its most extreme form, such domination results in "the 'lev-eling down' of all possibilities of Being" for Dasein (165), their reduction to an "average everydayness" and a "publicness" in which Dasein loses its self-understanding in terms of its possibilities. In this condition, Dasein's "way of Being is that of inauthenticity" (166).

In the mode of inauthenticity, Dasein "forgets" its Being; Dasein loses its distinctive mode of being, for when Dasein is inauthentic, its being is not and cannot be an issue for it. (In other words, Dasein becomes mechani-cal—here we see a second instance of Heidegger's variation on the Ro-mantic theme of humanity versus mechanism.) Indeed, this is the function of the "one" (or the "they," as it is sometimes translated). Dasein's Being-in-the-world is necessarily a Being-towards-death, for (again) Dasein is precisely that mode of Being for which its Being is an issue. But our thrownness in the world and our Being-towards-death leave us invariably in a condition of *Angst*—a broad anxiety, not a fear of a specific event or entity. Inauthenticity is a *"fleeing in the face of death"*: "the 'one' [or the 'they'] provides a *constant tranquilization about death*" (298, modified) and thus a release from Angst. To say what "one" says, do what "one" does, think what "one" thinks, is to avoid thoughtful engagement with one's own care-full Being-in-the-world, and thus with death, which is always looming at the far horizon of that Being-in-the-world as its inevitable end.

If I consider my existential specificity, deciding what I think and what I want, considering my own care and my own world, then the image of the final end cannot be blocked out. I can forget death only when I think the current fashion (theoretical, religious, or whatever), mouth its platitudes, buy the house and car my colleagues buy, acquire the same sort of spouse, and so on. Authenticity for Dasein is, first and foremost, authentic Being-towards-death with all its *Angst* (310). When it achieves authenticity, Dasein finds its way out of *"lostness in the they-self* [or self defined by the 'one']" and is brought *"face to face with the possibility of being itself,"* but it does so only in **"freedom towards death**—*a freedom which has been released from the Illusions of the 'they'* [or the 'one']" (311), the freedom of one's own care-full Being-in-the-world, which reaches out to death at its farthest point.

As a number of readers have noted, Heidegger's discussion of authenticity and the "one," while not entirely novel, is nonetheless illuminating. But the link with death seems curious. It is not at all obvious how choosing to be oneself brings one face to face with mortality. Nor is it at all obvious how conformism involves a tranquilization about death. It does seem that choosing one's self may trigger broad anxiety and conformism may be motivated by a desire to evade anxiety. But it seems unlikely that the anxiety in question concerns death. It would seem, rather, to concern our need to feel that we are part of a community. It is particularly odd that Heidegger did not discuss authenticity in these terms as he treated this need for community at length in other contexts.

Indeed, this last point can come out particularly strongly when we consider a relevant literary work. We have already noted that *Othello* may be thought of as a work that discloses Othello's Being-in-the-world as, so to speak, Being-in-a-racist-world. Unlike some superficially similar historical or contemporary example, it discloses for us Dasein's existence in a world where the distinctive being of Dasein can be denied; it manifests or reveals to us the Being of a particular being whose distinctive character as Dasein is unacknowledged. Othello is *at best* equipment ready to hand. For most of Venice, Othello is a thing, "conspicuous," obtrusive in his blackness, an object merely present at hand. Only the Duke and Desdemona consistently conceive of him differently. And for the Duke, he is clearly an instrument; when Brabantio calls upon the Duke to contemplate Othello as a thing, the Duke responds by sending him to war, using him as equipment ready to hand. When Othello says that he has "done the state some service" (5.2.335), he indicates precisely that he has been its tool.

Except with Desdemona—and perhaps not even there—Othello has his Being in a world from which Being-with is absent. As Heidegger explains, "By 'Others' we do not mean everyone else but me—those over against whom the 'I' stands out. They are rather those from whom, for the most part, one does *not* distinguish oneself—those among whom one is too" (154). It is due to this likeness of Dasein with one another that "Being-in is *Being-with* Others" (155). But, at the end of the play, with Desdemona dead, Othello finds himself faced with an absolute absence of Being-with. In consequence, he succumbs fully to the mode of "fallenness" or inauthenticity. His suicide is not some free Being-towards-death. It is a complete submersion in the "one." It is a fleeing in the face of his own Dasein, even while embracing death, for he describes his suicide as the murder of a "Turk," the final stabbing as stabbing "him" (5.2.352), as if the body into which he plunges the dagger were someone else.

Then, in a final gesture, pathetic and yet indicative of a lingering sense of self, Othello seeks again the Being-with that he had lost forever in killing Desdemona, the Being-with that would allow him authentic Being-in-the-world, because it would allow him to be "among Others": "I kiss'd thee ere I kill'd thee. No way but this, / Killing myself, to die upon a kiss" (5.2.354–55). But, of course, this is a false hope of Being-with, known to be false. For, in killing her and in killing himself, Othello has become a mere thing, present at hand, and his Being-with Desdemona has been reduced to the mere contiguity in space of two broken objects. It is the complete triumph of Venetian society over the world of Othello, a world opened up for us through the play, and now closed again as Othello becomes the conspicuous, obtrusive thing that Venetian society had always made of him.

Given the way in which Heidegger's views illuminate the horrors of racism, one wonders how he could have become involved with German Nazism. Some critics have tried to see a link between Heidegger's philosophy and his political affiliations in the 1930s. Admittedly, there are writings (such as "The Origin of the Work of Art") in which some of Heidegger's ideas seem at least to parallel the nationalist mysticism and paranoia of fascism. (In a sense, Nazism was an extremely pathological form of Romantic nationalism; one can see suggestions of both in some of Heidegger's works.) But *Being and Time* reads like a thoroughgoing analysis and denunciation of Nazism.

Probably the most important development of Heidegger's emphasis on Being-in-the-world is to be found in the existential phenomenology of

Jean-Paul Sartre. Sartre takes up Heidegger's views almost point for point, revising them by focusing his attention more fully on consciousness and self-consciousness in the classic phenomenological sense. One could think of Sartre as taking Heideggerian "experientialism" and integrating it more thoroughly with Husserlian cognitivism. Or, to put it in less elevated terms, one could think of Heidegger's notion of Being-in-the-world as founded on experiences of hiking through the woods, while Sartre's notion of Being-in-the-world is founded on experiences of sitting in a café.

Sartre's fundamental ontological division is that between being-in-itself and being-for-itself. This parallels Heidegger's distinction between the thing that is present-at-hand and Dasein. However, the focus here is fully on consciousness, and thus it is closer to various distinctions drawn by German Idealists (see, for example, Fichte 17). The for-itself is conscious and self-conscious; the in-itself is, so to speak, mere being, without any self-consciousness. This division has several important consequences. First of all, the in-itself is necessarily a plenitude; it is what it is, without any lack or incompleteness. The for-itself, in contrast, is always lacking; it always carries *nothingness* with it in the form of what it expects or wants but cannot find. Sartre gives a simple example (40–42): I go to the café, hoping to see Pierre. But Pierre is not at the café. I see his absence; I see the nothing where Pierre should be. This is not a condition of the café. In itself, the café is, again, a plenitude. It is what it is. But for me, it is marked by lack. In this and similar cases, "Man is the being through whom nothingness comes to the world" (59).

Sartre develops a wide range of consequences from this distinction. Two are particularly important. The first concerns freedom. While the in-itself is (again) just what it is, the for-itself is always acting to fill a lack. In this action, the for-itself is completely free in the sense that it is not determined by the plenitude of its being. Unlike the in-itself, the for-itself cannot merely be carried along by the fullness of its being. It must choose; it must act. In "secret[ing] a nothingness," the for-itself achieves *"freedom"* (60). Or, rather, the for-itself is "condemned to be free" (186), for nothing about the for-itself fully determines its future, allows it to settle into a fullness of being without lack: "I choose myself perpetually and can never be merely by virtue of having-been-chosen; otherwise I should fall into the pure and simple existence of the in-itself" (617). This chair has no freedom. It cannot choose. And it cannot choose because it does not lack, being merely what it is *in itself.* But I, like every for-itself, do lack. And because I lack, I not only can, but *must* choose. My nothingness necessitates this freedom. (This idea also has its roots in Kant and the German Idealists, especially Fichte; cf.

Fichte's insistence that "the essence of transcendental idealism in general ... consists in the fact that the concept of existence is by no means regarded as a *primary* and *original* concept.... To the idealist, the only positive thing is freedom; existence, for him, is a mere negation of the latter" [69].)

Of course, this freedom does not occur in a void. It is always a freedom in a particular situation. The for-itself is always *situated*. And it is situated in circumstances that it cannot choose. For the for-itself "freedom is a *choice* of its being but not the *foundation* of its being" (616). As Heidegger said, we are "thrown" into the world. For Sartre, this thrownness places our freedom in "universal contingency" (616). I stake my existence on a choice, on a free act, doing this rather than that. But this choice occurs in a context that has no necessity, a context that could just as well have been something else. My most important, most definitive decisions, my fullest expressions of my freedom, are the result of accidents. (Think of marriage—what a matter of chance that I should have met this person at a certain time and a certain place, and thus have come to make this decision.) This absolute freedom in absolute contingency, "we may call absurdity" (616).

Sartre's views on freedom and absurdity have been extremely influential, not only in philosophy—where they formed some of the basic principles of existentialism—but in literature as well. Indeed, the absurdity of freedom within contingency, the absurdity resulting from the most meaningful decision founding itself necessarily upon the most meaningless conjunction of circumstances, is an important and widespread literary motif. One could productively consider Hamlet's much-discussed hesitancy about killing Claudius as a case in which the absoluteness of the decision becomes mired in meaningless contingency. This meaninglessness is brought home with particular force when Hamlet accidentally murders Polonius: Finally, Hamlet chooses and acts, but the sheer randomness of circumstance results in the pointless, indeed ludicrous death of Polonius.

The second development I should like to consider in Sartre is that of the Ego and the Other. Sartre's analysis of this relation has been extremely influential, and has been more or less taken up in its entirety by thinkers ranging from Jacques Lacan to Frantz Fanon. Specifically, for Sartre, the Ego is a "hypostasiz[ation] ... of the for-itself which is reflected-on" and made into "an in-itself" (156). In other words, it is the human self made into a static thing—for instance, a list of dispositions and character traits ("irritable," "gregarious," "sharp-tongued," or, for that matter, "good" or "evil") attached to the person like visible properties attached to a physical object. This Ego is formed, first of all, in relation to the Other. For the Other, looking at me, can make me into an object, can see me as an in-itself—as a body, as a list of character traits. For myself, in my worldly self-experience, I am not tall or short, friendly or unfriendly, good or bad. I am not a thing, but a continual acting, choosing, experiencing—in short, a continual be-ing-in-the-world: "To apprehend myself as *evil*, for example, could not be to refer myself to what I am for myself. . . . The qualification 'evil' . . . characterizes me as an *in-itself*" (365). But for the Other, I become these things: "Thus for me the Other is first the being for whom I am an object; that is, the being *through whom* I gain my objectness" (361).

This objectness has a wide range of consequences. Consider, for example, race. I do not directly experience myself racially. Race is a property of me as an in-itself, an Ego defined by the Other: "here I am—Jew or Aryan, handsome or ugly, one-armed, *etc*. All this I am *for the Other*" (671). As a result of this, "I encounter . . . a thousand prohibitions and a thousand resistances which I bump up against at each instant. . . . Because *I am a Jew* I shall be deprived—in certain societies—of certain possibilities" (671). Consider, again, Othello. At the end of the play, when he repeatedly refers to himself as "one," then kills himself as "a malignant and a turbaned Turk" (5.2.349), he has (in Sartrean terms) lost his character as being-for-itself. Entirely in keeping with Sartre's views, he has been hypostatized by the Other, by the gaze and by the words of Venetian society, reduced to a mere in-itself, a Moor, a Turk. The self-murder only makes this hyposta-tization real, fulfills it, transforming the experiential body of Othello (for himself) into the simple thing of a corpse (in itself). Our feeling of tragedy at the end of the play is Sartrean too, for, in murdering himself, and in murdering Desdemona, Othello has created a lack, formed for us a noth-ingness of the sort that cannot be filled with being, a nothingness that is at the center of all tragedy. This nothingness is all the more affecting because, however much Othello himself might be made of aery nothing, his tragic negation by the racist Other is all too real, all too common, in the actual, material world in which we live.

Before going on, it is worth noting a development of Sartrean thought that is arguably even more important than its original. Simone de Beau-voir drew on Sartre's distinction between the in-itself and the for-itself in order to formulate the pathbreaking feminist theories of *The Second Sex*. One of the central contentions of this wide-ranging treatise on biological, philosophical, literary, and other manifestations of sexism, is that women in patriarchal society are continually degraded to the condition of the in-itself. They are not viewed as having needs and freedoms themselves, but as fulfilling the needs and allowing the freedoms of men. This leads de Beauvoir to a particular view of the goals most appropriate for women's struggle. She does not set up economic parity or political enfranchisement or reproductive choice as a decisive aim. She, of course, advocates these. But she does so as part of a larger vision—the establishment of a society in which women are able to assume fully the status of for-itself—a society in which men do not prevent this; a society in which economic and political, educational and religious, social and familial structures do not impede this; finally, a society in which women themselves do not accept the status of the in-itself, for fear of the dangerous freedom entailed by the status of for-itself.

## Hermeneutics: Heidegger, Gadamer, Habermas

Beyond the thematics of Being-in-the-world, Heidegger's methodological principles have also been influential, giving rise to a wide range of "hermeneutic" theories. Probably the most fundamental principle of hermeneutic method is that all interpretation proceeds in a circle, the "hermeneutic circle." It necessarily begins with a "foreknowing" or "pre-understanding," a preliminary comprehension that guides our procedures. "Whenever something is interpreted as something," Heidegger tells us, "the interpretation will be founded essentially upon fore-having, fore-sight, and fore-conception" (191). But this foreknowing is not determinative. Indeed, it should always operate to direct our attention to the things themselves. A genuine hermeneutician will always attend closely to the object, never resting satisfied with foreknowing. Thus Heidegger contrasts hermeneutic attention with the inauthentic acceptance of authoritative discourse: "our first, last, and constant task is never to allow our fore-having, fore-sight, and fore-conception to be presented to us by fancies and popular conceptions," but must involve "working out these fore-structures in terms of the things themselves" (195).

Like most other interpretive methods, Heidegger's hermeneutics aims at truth. However, truth, for Heidegger, is not to be understood as the correspondence between an idea and a fact. This view of truth is secondary, derivative. It treats truth as a (present at hand) relation between two entities that are present at hand (see, for example, "Origin" 52). Rather, truth is an uncovering or disclosure, a bringing into unconcealedness—a quality to be found in art and philosophy more fundamentally than in science. Truth in this sense requires disclosure because, once experienced, it is invariably forgotten, covered over by (inauthentic) idle talk, standard opinions accepted by Dasein without any concern for the things themselves. This forgetting, this "falling" from an original authentic experience of truth into the "one," develops over the course of history—"a long tradition that has forgotten the unfamiliar source" ("Origin" 24)—and over the course of the individual's life. Someone has a certain experience, "discovers" something, then communicates this discovery to someone else—in, for example, a poem or a philosophical treatise. The discovery—or, rather, the statement of the discovery (that is, the poem, the treatise)—is passed on from person to person, assuming perhaps the status of authoritative discourse. Its experiential source is slowly obscured. On the other hand, this process of occlusion is never complete. In our foreknowing, we retain a sense of the unconcealedness of being, a hint of that most fundamental, but no-longer-familiar source.

Indeed, this hint of originary unconcealedness is what keeps the hermeneutic circle from being a vicious circle. There is, so to speak, an uncontaminated origin that we retain, if in concealment. Speaking of his own work in ontology, Heidegger writes, "Inquiry, as a kind of seeking, must be guided beforehand by what is sought. So the meaning of Being must already be available to us in some way" (*Being* 25). Later, he puts the point more generally, "Any interpretation which is to contribute understanding, must already have understood what is to be interpreted" (194).

This is not to say that hermeneutics is merely a matter of remembering what one already knows individually. First of all, it is, in part, a matter of turning to the things themselves by turning away from inauthentic tradition (what "one" thinks, does, and so forth), in the manner in which Husserlian phenomenology is a matter of turning to the things themselves by repudiating the "natural attitude." Perhaps even more importantly, it is also a matter of turning to the "concealed source" at the origin of human thought. For Heidegger, this origin is to be found in the earliest Greek metaphysics and in the earliest forms of words. He explains that "the ultimate business of philosophy is to preserve the *force of the most elemental words* in which Dasein expresses itself, and to keep the common understanding from leveling them off to that unintelligibility which functions in turn as a source of pseudo-problems" (262). For this reason, Heidegger frequently focuses his attention on etymologies of key philosophical terms or on the histories of key philosophical concepts. Whether looking at the development of a word or at the series of translations that shaped a philosophical concept, Heidegger notes a fairly consistent pattern—an originary unconcealedness is gradually transformed into an inauthentic and authoritative concept; an idea grounded in Being-in-the-world is altered into a concept of the merely present at hand.

Heidegger's view of truth as unconcealedness seems either implausible or trivial. If Heidegger merely means that our understanding of what is true is based on experience at some remove, then the claim is trivial. If, however, he means that (our understanding of) truth is a matter of a pure, direct experience of things themselves, then his view seems highly implausible—because our experience of things is always mediated and organized by cognitive structures; because most of what we know or wish to know (for example, any regularities of nature) is not even open to direct experience, and so on. On the other hand, Heidegger is no doubt correct to see interpretation as a (partially) circular process. We begin to interpret a text (or event or person) on the basis of presuppositions, developing and altering these as we read the text initially, modifying them further on subsequent rereadings, and so on. Hirsch argues, correctly I think, that this is not strictly circular, in that the foreknowing may be modified in the course of the interpretation (see, for example, his discussions of Heidegger and interpretive cognition at 3–6 and 31–35). Of course, hermeneuticians such as Gadamer would not disagree. Gadamer sees "prejudice," in the sense of foreknowing, as a significant and very valuable part of the hermeneutic circle; however, he explicitly denies that this disallows novelty or change that goes beyond recollection (see "Universality" 9). In any event, interpretation is, in broad terms, a process of the sort Heidegger describes.

On the other hand, Hirsch's comment tacitly points up the implausible "originalism" of Heidegger's hermeneutic circle. The idea that an originary experience has been lost does not seem to make much sense outside the context of biblical literalism. No doubt there is much truth that has been forgotten, in our individual and collective histories. But it seems likely that new truths have been replacing the old truths, that old falsities and inauthenticities have been forgotten with old truths, and so on. In consequence, we can hardly expect the history of a word or of a concept to lead us to a pure source and unconcealed truth. And yet, one cannot deny that the sort of conceptual and lexical histories that Heidegger undertakes are often very illuminating. An entire history of thought about a concept can be re-understood by looking at the way the concept has been translated, by tracing the subtle (and not so subtle) differences between, say, a Greek term and its Latin "equivalent"; some fine shades of meaning, some revealing social or psychological implications can be uncovered by tracing an etymology. Our discussion of *pity* and *fear* in Plato, Aristotle, the Arabic theorists, and later writers, provides a partial example of this sort of linguistic/conceptual history.

A number of thinkers have developed Heidegger's hermeneutics, often combining Heidegger's views with those of Husserl, as well as other phenomenologists. For example, Paul Ricoeur has developed hermeneutics in relation to a range of topics in spirituality, literature, psychoanalysis, and other areas. His early work, *The Symbolism of Evil*, has clear relevance to literary study, as does his very important phenomenological/hermeneutic study of Freud, and his more straightforwardly literary work on metaphor. At a more general level, Ricoeur has usefully distinguished between hermeneutics that set out to dispel illusion and hermeneutics that set out to reveal a hidden truth (see chapter 2 of *Freud*). The former, he terms "the hermeneutics of suspicion." This critical hermeneutics is practiced by Heidegger when he sets out to "destroy" the metaphysical tradition (which conceals the originary unconcealedness of Being), by Derrida when he "deconstructs" the metaphysical tradition including Heidegger's notion of an originary unconcealedness, by Marxists when they engage in ideological critique, and so on. Beyond the hermeneutics of suspicion, Ricoeur posits the "hermeneutics of recollection of meaning," what might more briefly be called the "hermeneutics of revelation." This almost celebratory hermeneutics is practiced by Heidegger when he sets out to disclose Being in its origins, by scriptural hermeneuticians when they set out to reveal the meaning of "God's word," and so on.

Perhaps the most influential theorist to have developed hermeneutics after Heidegger is Hans-Georg Gadamer. Gadamer derives from Heidegger a concern for returning our attention to experiential Being-in-the-world, a focus on art as revelatory of truth, and so on. However, his central focus is on developing our understanding of hermeneutics as a process of understanding "distant" texts, primarily texts from other periods within our own culture. Gadamer's central point in this regard is that hermeneutic reflection is not merely a matter of eliminating errors; it is not merely a matter of isolating and correcting distortions, correcting tradition by reference to the things themselves or an originary disclosure. Rather, it is always and necessarily a matter of integrating the past text into our own current concerns in the context of our being toward the future, which is to say, in the context of our projects. Interpretation, according to Gadamer, must involve "the transformation of something alien and dead into total contemporaneity and familiarity"; it "consists not in the restoration of the past but in *thoughtful mediation with contemporary life*" (*Truth* 163, 168–69).

More exactly, all interpretation is a matter of putting questions to texts. While the text may be the same text for different questioners, the questions—and thus the answers, the interpretation—will change, because "the particular research questions . . . that we are interested in pursuing are motivated in a special way by the present and its interests" (284). In this way, all interpretation is a matter of "prejudice"—not in the sense of "irrational bias," but in the sense of foreknowledge, expectation, prior belief. Gadamer is adamant that prejudice, in this nonjudgmental sense, is crucial to understanding—it is what allows us to ask questions in the first place. Thus, far from ridding ourselves of prejudice, we need to recognize the importance of prejudice. Indeed, Gadamer goes so far as to say that *"the prejudices of the individual . . . constitute the historical reality of his being"* (276–77).

In connection with this, Gadamer takes up the traditional hermeneutic distinction between *understanding, interpretation,* and *application.* Understanding is our direct grasp of the meaning of a text; interpretation is our self-conscious investigation and articulation of that meaning; and application is our linking of that meaning to our current situation. Consider a parable in the Bible. We understand the literal meaning of the prodigal son story. In a first interpretation, Jesus himself articulates its spiritual point, altering our understanding. We in turn interpret it further, drawing out its implications. Then we try to apply it to our lives. We try to decide whether it applies to a particular dilemma in our life; if so, we ask ourselves what action it counsels us to take, and so on. In undertaking this application, our understanding and interpretation of the parable are further developed and altered by reference to the case at hand. The situation is the same in law. In legal hermeneutics, we understand the literal meaning of a statute, interpret its implications, and seek to apply it to new cases. Here too understanding leads to but is at the same time altered by interpretation, and interpretation leads to but is at the same time altered by application. Moreover, note that application is absolutely crucial in both cases. No biblical or legal interpretation is of any value unless it leads to application, unless we can connect it with the case at hand. Note also that this application is not arbitrary or fanciful, but neither is it a mere restatement of the original text. It is, or should be, both accurate to the original and adapted to the current situation. Gadamer's argument is that all interpretation, including literary interpretation, is the same. Application to present circumstances is crucial, and that application affects our interpretation and understanding, just as it is affected by them.

More exactly, according to Gadamer, we approach any distant text with our own horizons determined by our own "historically effected consciousness" ("the consciousness effected in the course of history and determined by history, and the very consciousness of being thus effected and determined" [xxxiv]). We do not seek to suppress our horizons and substitute those of the work, escaping from history. Rather, we seek a "fusion of horizons." But how does the historically effected consciousness achieve this fusion of horizons? It does so by relying on its "prejudices," specifically on that set of "prejudices" that go to constitute the living tradition that it shares with the historically distant text—the prejudices they hold in common. In other words, we interpret a distant text, we fuse horizons with it, on the basis of the continuing life of tradition (304).

As this indicates, Gadamer does not view tradition skeptically, as does Heidegger. Quite the contrary, in fact. For Gadamer, tradition necessarily has a sort of presumptive authority. Though parts of tradition are always subject to invalidation, it is simply impossible to validate or invalidate all of tradition—for we must presuppose it at every moment: "That which has been sanctioned by tradition and custom has an authority that is nameless, and our finite historical being is marked by the fact that the authority of what has been handed down to us—and not just what is clearly grounded [roughly, not just what is philosophically or scientifically established]—always has power over our attitudes and behavior" (280).

It is not clear that tradition is as encompassing and as continuous as Gadamer maintains. For example, it is not clear that contemporary Americans share a tradition with Euripides or even Chaucer in any significant degree. Indeed, it is difficult to understand what sharing a tradition might mean concretely. Moreover, in this context, Gadamer's notion of a fusion of horizons is obscure. If we understand a distant work by reference to a shared tradition, it would seem that we understand only that part of the work that is maintained by the tradition, that part that is common to both sets of horizons. In this case, it would seem, we do not fuse different horizons, augmenting our horizons with those of the text, rather we reduce both sets of horizons to the few horizons they hold in common. Conversely, if we are to augment our horizons with the different horizons of the text, it is not clear how this can be done from the basis of a common tradition. Relying on continuous tradition seems, by definition, to exclude such augmentation, because it necessarily excludes difference of horizons (difference of horizons being precisely what is not carried down by tradition).

On the other hand, Gadamer is right that we cannot question everything about tradition, that we have to rely on some traditional ideas. More importantly, his emphasis on application (in the hermeneutic triad of understanding, interpretation, and application) seems a salutary corrective to the emphasis of many writers on original authorial or historical meaning. Even when we are seeking original authorial or historical meaning, we seek it from our own perspective, guided by our own interests, from the position of our historically effected consciousness. We always and necessarily interpret distant works in the context of the horizons provided by our own tradition—and, in this sense, we do "fuse horizons." For example, even when we interpret for the original social meaning of *Othello*, we do so by way of the horizons of contemporary Shakespeare and Renaissance studies, the current moment of a continuing interpretive tradition, as well as social, political, and other horizons. Indeed, it is crucial to recognize this, if we are to make any sense out of our interpretive, evaluative, or other practices.

A simple illustration of Gadamer's general point may be found in the interpretation of *Othello* presented above. Racism is a pressing issue in the United States today. In asking the text questions about racism, I am bringing it into the present, making it part of our current horizon. But this does not mean that the answers are arbitrary, that I can give my questions any answer whatsoever. I ask the question, "What is the text's representation of race?" In answering the general question, I turn necessarily to a part of the text—the murder of Desdemona, perhaps. I then return to my question and refine it: "Does the text represent Othello stereotypically as an excessively passionate Moor?" I then return to the text, continuing in the hermeneutic circle, examining parts of the text relative to this more specific question, and so on. In doing this, I should ultimately achieve a sort of fusion of horizons—my horizons maintained by the questions, the horizons of the text maintained in the details that respond to those questions. The interpretation incorporates both those questions and those details and thus fuses the horizons. Indeed, we may even see in this a relation to tradition, for both contemporary racism and antiracism are part of living traditions that extend back, through many changes, to Elizabethan England, to the earliest European contacts with and stereotypes about Africans—though, again, it is not clear that this tradition is as consistent, or as necessary, as Gadamer supposes. (Indeed, in emphasizing shared tradition, Gadamer in some ways does his theory a disservice. The same principles apply to "cross-traditional" interpretation, as may be seen clearly in the case of the Arabic Aristotelians.)

Another important thinker who has been strongly influenced by Heidegger and hermeneutics is Jürgen Habermas. The range and complexity of Habermas's ideas, and their orientation toward social science rather than literature, prevent anything like a general explication of his work. However, it is worth mentioning some of the basic principles of his thought insofar as they derive from the theories we have been considering. In his important early text, *On the Logic of the Social Sciences*, Habermas follows the influential hermeneutician, Wilhelm Dilthey, in sharply distinguishing the methodology of the social sciences from that of the physical sciences, or, as Habermas calls them, the "nomological sciences." Habermas's primary contention in this regard is that the social sciences must deal with Being-in-the-world while the nomological sciences deal with things present at hand in the world, though he does not put it in precisely these Heideggerian terms.

More exactly, Habermas sees social science as focusing on value-oriented human action in the context of a social value system. In keeping with Gadamer and others, Habermas insists that "historical reflection" concerns "the subjectively intended meanings" of human action (including speech and other human "communicative action") and the "traditional significations" linked to these actions (32); it avoids technical-scientific objectification and the reduction of meaningful human intentional action to mechanical causality. Indeed, historical understanding is not an analysis of causes, but the telling of a story (33), a story in which the past event is, as Gadamer says, continually reunderstood in the context of a tradition and in relation to current concerns.

According to Habermas, each human act is animated by an individual *Sinn* or "sense" and that Sinn is itself the manifestation of a social *Bedeutung* or "meaning." The Sinn of a given action is, for Habermas, necessarily situation specific (43). The Bedeutung is necessarily broader, covering a wide range of specific situations, though it is also historically variable, changing from period to period. To take a very simple case, the Sinn of the word "big" changes from situation to situation, from communicative act to communicative act (contrast "big baby," "big debt," "big man on campus"). The Bedeutung, however, is roughly constant (for any given historical period; it does change historically). Bedeutung involves a range of generalities from "grammatical rules" to "social roles" (76; recall that all human actions have Sinn and Bedeutung, not just the utterance of words and phrases). It is important to note that these rules and roles are a function of intersubjective expectation, not of law-like behavior (65). Our use of "big" is not a matter of some natural law that absolutely determines our behavior. It is, rather, a matter of knowing how people expect us to use "big," what they will understand by it.

To take a slightly less straightforward example, suppose we want to understand why someone has dressed in a certain way. We might imitate the physical sciences and try to define some law that is universally applicable and that will determine that someone will dress in a certain way under certain circumstances, much as an object will fall to the ground with a certain acceleration. This would follow the nomological model. In contrast, we might try to figure out the individual Sinn and collective Bedeutung of the clothing. Thus we may note that the Bedeutung of a black suit is "in mourning," with the Sinn in this particular case being "my uncle has died." Or the Bedeutung of the piece of clothing may be "semiformal, sexually alluring," with the Sinn being something along the lines of "wants to be attractive to Smith."

In sum, to understand a social event is to engage in a "step-by-step explication of contexts of meaning," not "the explanation of individual events through their subsumption under laws" (36). (In fact, in formulating things this way, Habermas shows that, like most post-Romantic humanists, he does not really understand the notion of law in the natural sciences. Laws are merely the strictest known formulations of regularities, and they may apply in all cases or only in a certain percentage of cases.)

According to Habermas, the contexts of meaning through which we understand a social event are always linguistically organized. Human action, for Habermas, is, again, intentional action with Sinn. And intentional action with Sinn is linguistically formulated action. If I go to the grocery store, that action has Sinn, a personal intention that I formulate, in part, as "going to the grocery store." Moreover, the social Bedeutung of this act is a function of its linguistic description. In other words, it is not my physical actions that have Sinn or Bedeutung. Rather, the act has the Bedeutung, "going to the grocery store," precisely and only insofar as it is formulated as "going to the grocery store." (Though Sinn and Bedeutung are different, they are clearly related and to a great extent overlap. Here, it is only the sameness, the overlap, that is relevant.) Note that the very same observable behavior, the very same motions of my body—getting in the car, driving along a certain route—could equally result if I set out to stalk my neighbor (who happens to be going to the grocery store). To understand my action in each case is to understand its contexts of meaning, its Sinn and Bedeutung. And, clearly, these are different for "going to the grocery store" and for "stalking my neighbor"—even though the physical action in the two cases is identical. In consequence, these contexts of meaning are specifically linguistic. As Habermas puts it, "the boundaries of action are drawn by the boundaries of language" (72).

The determinative position of language in human action makes communication or "communicative action" central to any social scientific analysis: "We grasp the structure of individual lifeworlds only through communication experienced in a social context" (113). Much of Habermas's later work focuses on the theory of communicative action. Habermas is particularly concerned with the ways in which communicative action is constrained in societies structured by economic class hierarchy. In relation to this, he seeks to determine the social conditions that would have to obtain in order to foster truly free communicative action and, correlatively, the ways in which critical reflection might loosen communicative constraints even within contemporary society and thereby foster the development of liberatory social conditions. As this indicates, Habermas is not only a hermeneutician, but, to some extent, a Marxist. In keeping with this, he diverges from Gadamer on the issue of tradition. As we have seen, while Gadamer hardly advocates the unquestioning acceptance of tradition, he does grant to tradition a prima facie authority. In Ricoeur's terms, Gadamer's attitude toward tradition is primarily revelatory. Habermas, in contrast, adopts a predominantly suspicious attitude toward tradition in class society (see 169).

Yet, it is unclear how exactly this suspicion can operate to critique tradition, given Habermas's view of language as defining the limits of action and specifying a worldview. (Presumably, the latter is what Habermas intends by his references to "the linguistic worldview" [173]). Specifically, Habermas insists that, through "the power of reflection," we can "reject the claim of traditions" (170). In other words, through hermeneutic reflection, we can free ourselves from constraints on communicative action, constraints tied to the class structure of society. It is easy to see how this could be true "locally," so to speak. In other words, it is easy to see how, by Habermas's principles, reflection could reject one or another traditional alternative *within a broader linguistic worldview*, how one could choose this or that option within, say, capitalist or patriarchal ideology. But, it is hard to see how reflection could go further (for example, how it could lead to a broad rejection of capitalist or patriarchal ideology)—and this is what Habermas seems to have in mind. For example, Habermas writes that "Hermeneutics comes up against the limits of the context of tradition from the inside. Once these limits have been experienced and recognized, it can no longer consider cultural traditions absolute" (172).

The problem here is twofold. First of all, Habermas, following in the tradition of German Idealism, seems to overestimate the cognitive power of reflection. In fact, the human ability to take a sort of mental step back from its own thought and scrutinize its prejudices seems minimal. Even our most basic introspections concerning habits or feelings are highly fallible, as Nisbett and Ross have shown at length. In short, we have little reason to believe that "Controlled distancing (*Verfremdung*) can raise understanding from a prescientific practice to the status of a reflective process" (166). This does not mean that prejudices are absolute. It means that they can be disputed only by systematic empirical investigation, ideological analysis, and so forth—unless, of course, these too are constrained by a "linguistic worldview," unless their boundaries too are drawn by the boundaries of language.

Which leads us to the second problem with Habermas's claims here—his overestimation of the degree to which language can define thought. Habermas does acknowledge that language is not rigidly determinate itself. For example, he writes that "language spheres are not monadically sealed but porous, in relation both to what is outside and to what is inside" (149). He even goes so far as to say that a language "can in principle incorporate everything that is linguistically foreign and at first unintelligible" (151). The problem is that, given what Habermas says elsewhere, it is not at all clear how one can start out with the initial unintelligibility of, for example, some foreign idea or practice, and move from there to the incorporation of that idea or practice into one's own language. Habermas indicates that we do this through translation (see 147–48). But if our language defines for us a worldview, limiting our action (including our communicative action), it is difficult to see how we could translate at all or even study other traditions per se. It would seem that we would always be, in effect, studying or translating our own worldview, never that of the other language.

Conversely, if language is indeterminate enough to allow the incorporation of any foreign element (and, with perhaps some slight qualifications, I agree with Habermas that it is), then language is also indeterminate enough to allow the definition of any worldview. And that means that language itself cannot possibly impose one particular worldview over another. Of course, we do assimilate ideologies in part through language. But that does not mean that those ideologies are defined by language— after all, we critique the ideologies in the very same language. Moreover, it seems highly unlikely that, even in practice, any language community or even any individual person is confined to one worldview. In other words, the idea of a worldview itself seems problematic. Even in ordinary daily activities, there is a wide range of social practices and ideologies, in the classic Marxist sense, that define the partial, and contradictory, ways in which we conceive of and act in the world.

On the other hand, given this conception of language as *non*determinative—basically, a consistent working out of Habermas's view of language as "porous"—some of Habermas's practical conclusions become more plausible. It is, in fact, possible to translate other languages more or less adequately and to experience other traditions, and in this context to question some of our prejudgments and reject some of our prejudices (see 147–48, 166). Though the possibilities for this "comparative culture" approach to overcoming prejudice remain very limited, they are probably not insignificant. Moreover, Habermas's focus on communicative action, on the ways communication is undermined by systematic distortion in class society, and so on, usefully draw our attention to aspects of political relations that we might otherwise ignore.

Finally, these considerations are far from irrelevant to the study of literature. Consider, for example, the ways in which unequal social relations of race and sex systematically limit and pervert the communication between Othello and Desdemona—permitting her to derogate his color without understanding his reaction (and without him articulating a reaction) and permitting him to silence her claims of fidelity. *Othello* could be seen as a tragedy of communicative action. Had there been no stifling hierarchy of race and sex, the communicative understanding between Othello and Desdemona would not have been so thoroughly shattered. Indeed, it would be an interesting exercise to go through the play, examining the ways in which the tragedy results from the many small but systematic distortions of communication from dialogue to dialogue and noting the degree to which these distortions result from patriarchal and racist social structures and practices.

### Reception Aesthetics, Reader Response, and Intentionalism

In discussing Roman Ingarden, we noted his stress on the reader's creative function and on historical changes in concretization. Despite this stress, Ingarden tends to be more concerned with what is determinate in a literary work than with what is indeterminate, just as Husserl tends to be more concerned with the absolute, transcendental, and objective, than with the various contingencies of the Umwelt explored by Heidegger. The theorists of the "Konstanz School" of "reception aesthetics" have further developed the ideas of Husserl and Ingarden. However, in doing so, reception aestheticians have focused on the variables and variations in the reading, interpretation, and evaluation—that is, "reception"—of literary works, often drawing extensively on Gadamerian hermeneutics. The major figures in this school are Wolfgang Iser and Hans Robert Jauss.

Iser is explicitly phenomenological in his approach and acknowledges his great debt to Ingarden. Having reiterated Ingarden's claims about the creative aspect of reading, he goes on to explain that the pleasure of the reader is to a great extent a function of that creativity. But creativity, he tells us, is pleasurable only to the degree that it is creativity within a constitutable (thus comprehensible) context. As Iser puts it, "In this process of creativity, the text may either not go far enough, or may go too far, so we may say that boredom and overstrain form the boundaries beyond which the reader will leave the field of play" (275). In the first case (boredom), the text is predictable. In the second (overstrain), it is incomprehensible.

In this context, Iser discusses the importance of "gaps" in a text. Not mere vagueness requiring concretization, gaps involve a particular "frustration of [protentive] expectations" which "blocks the flow of sentences" so that "we are led off in unexpected directions" where we must "bring into play our own faculty for establishing connections—for filling in the gaps" (279–80). One of Iser's examples is drawn from Henry Fielding's *Joseph Andrews*. Lady Booby is trying to seduce her footman, Joseph. But, Iser explains, Joseph "recoils, calling loudly upon his virtue" (37). Fielding then goes on at some length explaining that there is no way the reader could "receive such an idea of surprise as would have entered [his/her] eyes had they beheld Lady Booby when those last words issued out from the lips of Joseph" (quoted in Iser 37). As Iser explains, "The non-description of Lady Booby's surprise, and the insistence on its inconceivability, create a gap in the text," a gap that must be filled by "the reader's imagination" (38).

In connection with this, Iser makes a number of ancillary points. For example, in reading we continually seek unity and thus are forced to alter our reading when we encounter gaps; he argues that in general the more we are forced to change our reading, the greater our sense of the reality of the story. He also maintains that in forming (provisional) unities, we are guided by "two main structural components within the text": (1) "a repertoire of familiar literary patterns and recurrent literary themes" and (2) "techniques or strategies used to set the familiar against the unfamiliar" (288). This is another way of saying that the literary work draws on our expectations (as represented in schemas, eidetic constitutions, and so forth) and at the same time undermines those expectations or the tentative conclusions we had based on those expectations. These expectations and conclusions may be undermined simply by not being fulfilled; by being implied, then contradicted; by being ironized, and so on. Consider the last possibility, irony. Iser uses a scene from Joyce's *Ulysses* as an example. Leopold Bloom is engaged in an argument. Joyce structures the scene in such a way as to link Bloom's cigar with a fiery weapon used by Odysseus when he defeated the Cyclops. This "heroic weapon" is one element of our literary "repertoire." However, the scene evokes this element only to ironize it (in one interpretation anyway). Iser goes on to identify this undermining of standardized expectations (in its various forms) with "defamiliarization" (288—again, the standard romantic motif).

Hans Robert Jauss draws on a wider range of theoretical resources, and in fact gives relatively little attention to phenomenology. However, his major theoretical work may be seen as a radically historicist development of phenomenological principles, primarily by way of Gadamerian hermeneutics. In his seminal essay, "Literary History as a Challenge to Literary Theory," Jauss sets himself the task of defining a genuine literary history— not an economic or political or other history that makes reference to art, and not a mere chronology of literary works, but an historical account of literature as such. A genuine history of this sort, Jauss argues, must focus on "the experience of the literary work by its readers" (20; compare Gadamer's claim that "the work of art is one with the history of its effects" [*Truth* 477]). The reception of works, changing across cultures and across times—across Husserlian communities and experiential environments— is what ultimately determines not only the survival of past literature, but the development of new literature as well.

But how is this reception to be understood? Jauss explicitly rejects psychological analysis and opts instead for a description of the work "within the objectifiable system of expectations that arises for each work in the historical moment of its appearance" (22), most particularly what Iser refers to as the "repertoire of familiar literary patterns and recurrent literary themes" (288)—in other words, the "preunderstanding" of the work through various eidetic constitutions of genre, character, and so on.

In connection with this, Jauss defines the concept of "aesthetic distance" as "the disparity between the given horizon of expectations and the appearance of a new work" (25). Much like Iser, Jauss is concerned with the degree to which a new work fails to fit our protentions, frustrates our expectations, alters our horizons—somewhat like the lamp with a switch on the cord rather than the stem or the base, in our earlier example. The more we are required to alter our horizons in reading a given work, the greater our aesthetic distance from that work. Our response to a given work is, then, in part a product of our aesthetic distance; we may find the work either inaccessible or predictable, as Iser noted—too distant or not distant enough. More importantly, the reception of a work in a given period or country is bound up with this distance, which varies historically and culturally, not just individually.

For Jauss, then, true literary history is the history of aesthetic reception, involving an analysis of horizons of expectation, aesthetic distance, and so on, across particular societies and periods. But this history cannot focus on a single literary work in isolation. Rather, it must locate that work in the context of the reception of a wider range of literary works. Horizons of expectation do not change for one work alone. Rather, they change for literature as a whole, or for a given genre, and so on. Thus, if we are to study the different responses to, say, Shakespeare's sonnets over the past four centuries, we must look not only at the responses to the sonnets per se, but to the more general expectations concerning lyric poetry, or literature in general. For example, many of Shakespeare's sonnets shamelessly mix metaphors or embed quite different metaphors in one another. In a period when the horizons of expectation involve consistent and uninterrupted development of single metaphors, the aesthetic distance from Shakespeare's sonnets is likely to be considerable. In periods when the disruption of any continuous conceptual development has entered our horizons of expectation as a possibility, our aesthetic distance from Shakespeare's sonnets is likely to be diminished.

Finally, Jauss argues that we must ultimately situate this literary history in a broader social and political history. For our horizons of expectation in literature are not unrelated to "the horizon of expectations of [our] lived praxis," our daily life, our understanding of and relation to the larger world. Returning once again to Shakespeare's sonnets, we may contrast the moral horizon of expectations that, for example, distanced many Victorian readers from the homoerotic motifs of the sonnets, and the very different moral horizon of expectations that defines many contemporary academic readings.

Though Jauss and Iser are the major contemporary theorists to have developed explicitly phenomenological ideas, a range of other writers have practiced literary criticism and written literary theory under the banner of phenomenology. For example, Georges Poulet has taken up the phenomenological notion of the mirroring and "identificatory" constitution of the Other. He has argued that the task of the critic is to enter the author's subjectivity, to relive the author's noesis in creating the literary work. In keeping with phenomenological motifs, Poulet addressed his most important book of criticism to the subject of human time, which he sought to describe phenomenologically in its noetic detail for a number of different writers.

Among American critics focusing on reception or response, the work of Stanley Fish is probably the most influential, and perhaps the closest to phenomenology and reception aesthetics. In fact, Fish's work shows striking parallels to phenomenology at various points, though it is difficult to say whether phenomenology was a significant influence on Fish. It is standard to divide Fish's career into an early and a late period. In the early period, Fish's most influential theoretical work was on the temporality of the reading experience. Specifically, he examined the reading practices of his students, discovering that the actual process by which students understand literature does not conform to Wimsatt and Beardsley's view that the responsive experiences of the reader are irrelevant to the meaning and value of a literary work. In short, he found that the "affective fallacy" (as Wimsatt and Beardsley termed it) is ubiquitous in literary experience and understanding. Fish concluded that it is not the students, but Wimsatt and Beardsley, who are wrong. Specifically, one's temporal expectations are part of the work, he insisted, and the disruption of expectations is central not only to our experience of the work, but to the very meaning of the work. This disruption might occur through plot or sentence structure or the division of poetic lines—as in J. P. Clark Bekederemo's lines on Death "Claiming a lady nobody knew / Attracted him."

Fish's conclusion that temporal expectations are themselves part of the meaning of a work seems to be a non sequitur. However, the examination of temporal expectations is by no means necessarily irrelevant to our understanding of the meaning of a work. Indeed, close attention to the temporality of reading, as examined by Fish, can make us more sensitive to the precise development and details of a work's meaning. For instance, in the lines by Clark Bekederemo, the initial misunderstanding—that "nobody knew" the lady—does not entail that nobody knew the lady. In fact, the poem makes it clear that a larger community did know her, and attended to her illness. However, this misunderstanding helps to draw our attention to that community—its misunderstanding of her condition, its sense of loss and fear at her death—making us aware of the community in a way that we would have been otherwise. It helps to make the community enter the poem as a thematic focus.

This early work of Fish is closely related to phenomenological studies in the temporal constitution of the literary work, the disruption of horizons of expectation, and so on. Later Fish shifted his attention from the individual reader to the "interpretive community." By "interpretive community," Fish refers to a group of readers who share certain approaches to and views about literary works. For Fish, there is no question of these readers being right or wrong, because there is no fact about literary works independent of interpretive communities. In Husserlian terms, the existence and nature of particular cultural objects (in this case, literary texts) are constituted by this intersubjective community. For example, Freudian critics share a wide range of presuppositions about the nature of literature and literary study. Through these shared presuppositions, they constitute an intersubjectively shared world. As Fish puts it (evidently drawing on phenomenological vocabulary), "the fact of agreement, rather than being a proof of the stability of objects, is a testimony to the power of an interpretive community to constitute the objects upon which its members (also and simultaneously constituted) can then agree" (338).

For example, in Fish's view, there is no fact as to whether Desdemona is or is not a scapegoat figure, as in Frye's theory, or a "mother imago," to take a psychoanalytic concept. She is a scapegoat figure or a mother imago if an interpretive community constitutes her as such. Thus she may be a scapegoat for a Fryean interpretive community and a mother imago for a psychoanalytic interpretive community, but neither for an interpretive community of cognitive scientists or deconstructionists or Marxists.

Fish's idea of interpretive communities has obvious parallels in Husserl's notion of the constitution of cultural objects in communities. However, it does not have Husserl's notion of a final grounding of such communities in the encompassing human community and Husserl's resultant objectivism. Fish's theory also has links with earlier Romantic and Idealist theories, such as that of Schelling, though it does not have Schelling's idea of a "preestablished harmony" of intelligences (Schelling, *System* 164). This leaves Fish in an apparently contradictory relativism, according to which interpretive communalism is true for a Fishean community, but false for all other communities. Indeed, the very meaning of the theory changes across communities and thus need not even entail that meaning is a function of interpretive community. If there is an interpretive community that says Fish is an intentionalist, then he is an intentionalist. Indeed, if there is a community that says Fish is Northrop Frye, then he is Northrop Frye.

Moreover, it is difficult to say precisely what constitutes an interpretive community, how one enters such a community, how subgroups or individuals can be said to share meanings, truths, and so forth, within such a community. After all, if Fisheans and Freudians define different communities with different objects and different truths, the same should be true for different types of Freudian, for different subtypes of these types, and ultimately for different individuals, everyone forming his/her own interpretive community of one. (For a cogent criticism of Fish's theory, see Scholes.)

On the other hand, Fish is right to emphasize the degree to which the criteria for determining and evaluating interpretations vary considerably across communities. Indeed, what seems obvious to members of one community may seem entirely implausible to members of a second community and downright incomprehensible to members of a third community. We do not all come to literary texts with the same presuppositions, concepts, aims, or attitudes. Indeed, the differences appear at times so great as to be irreconcilable. Thus it is important, both theoretically and practically, to recognize the function of communities in determining what is and what is not accepted, what is and is not considered acceptable, as an interpretation. Despite what we might like to think, the evaluation of theories and interpretations is not simply, and perhaps not even primarily, a matter of reason and textual evidence. In practice, literary interpretation—and academic evaluation in general—may be very close to what Fish has described. (We will return to this idea in connection with both Marxism and the philosophy of science.)

The approach most obviously opposed to response theory is intentionalism. Intentionalism is the doctrine that the meaning of a text, and thus the proper object for interpretation, is the intention of the author. Like American response theories, intentionalism begins with a repudiation of New Critical doctrines. However, these two reactions to New Criticism move in antithetical directions. Given this "similarity in difference," it is worth saying a few things about intentionalism in this context, especially as some intentionalists have been strongly influenced by phenomenology. Indeed, we have already noted an instance of intentionalism—a very extreme instance—in Poulet's (phenomenological) view that the critic should seek to make his/her noesis coincide with that of the author. Not all forms of intentionalism are this severe.

Probably the most famous advocate of intentionalism is E. D. Hirsch. Though not a phenomenologist, Hirsch has drawn significantly upon phenomenological ideas. His theory of interpretation rests on a distinction between "meaning" and "significance." Meaning, for Hirsch, is definite and invariable. The meaning of any text is fixed at the moment of its utterance, and it is defined by the intention of the author. Directly contrary to Wimsatt and Beardsley's doctrine that the author's intention is irrelevant to the interpretation of a literary work, Hirsch's theory insists that the author's intention is the only possible object of such interpretation. Of course, for Hirsch the best evidence regarding authorial intent is to be found in the literary text, along with the historical circumstances of its production. Nonetheless, meaning cannot reside in the text itself or in those historical circumstances. In isolation from a speaker, any given text is devoid of meaning; it is merely a sound or mark. Indeed, it is only the speaker that ties an utterance to a particular language or to a particular historical period. Consider the word "napkin." We might say that its meaning is a matter of whether it is American English or British English or Scots English, seventeenth century or twentieth century, and so on. But a specific use is located as, say, twentieth-century American English only because a speaker used it in the twentieth century as American English, that is, used it with a particular intention. Correlatively, we interpret Shakespeare's words as having a particular meaning precisely because we have tied them to Shakespeare. *Othello* is not somehow intrinsically fixed in a certain period or a certain country. It is located in England in the early 1600s precisely and only because it is linked to Shakespeare. Moreover, it is not linked to some physical action of Shakespeare's—for example, his writing out the words, which could be the work of a copyist. Rather, it is linked to his intent in uttering those words.

On the other hand, Hirsch recognizes that the reader brings a great deal to his/her experience of a literary text—associations, evaluations, and so on. The reader's experience of literature is not merely reconstructive. And this is important. But for Hirsch it is not part of the meaning of a text. Rather, this is what Hirsch calls the "significance" of the text, its relevance or importance for a particular reader or group of readers.

There is a wide range of non-Hirschean approaches to intentionalism (for instance, that of speech-act theorists, such as Mary Louise Pratt). Two critics particularly worthy of mention are Steven Knapp and Walter Benn Michaels, primarily because their view of intentionalism is very unusual and has been highly controversial. In a widely read article titled "Against Theory," Knapp and Michaels have argued that intentionalism should be understood not as a normative theory, but as a mere description. According to Knapp and Michaels, we are all intentionalists, whatever we might think. When we interpret any text, we necessarily posit an authorial intention that conforms to our interpretation, whatever theory we may be invoking around that interpretation (in other words, independent of whether the theory we are invoking is or is not intentionalist). Thus there is no point in having a theory of interpretation at all (hence the title, "Against Theory"). Whatever theory we put forth, we still end up being intentionalists in practice. (This focus on our actual practices, and what does or does not make a difference to those practices, links Knapp and Michaels with Pragmatism, to which we turn in the next section.)

This is not an entirely invalid point. For example, on the first day of one recent graduate course in literary theory, I began by asking students to discuss what sorts of things they find important to an interpretation, what criteria they would invoke in judging the validity of an interpretation, and so on. Some talked about textual evidence, some were concerned with history, a number talked about the importance of individual response; in short, the class included advocates of all the major interpretive theories— except intentionalism, which no one at all advocated. I then handed out the text of a song by Tori Amos and asked the students to interpret the poem. I did not do this with an ulterior motive, as I did not know what would happen. Though I strongly suspected that there would be a difference between the theories the students advocated abstractly and the principles they followed in actual interpretation, I had no idea as to what that difference would be. To my surprise, virtually everyone set out to interpret the poem in intentionalist terms—they kept referring to what Amos "had in mind," what her "typical concerns" are (as expressed in other songs); they referred to interviews and biographical material (sometimes in the form of quandaries only—"It would be interesting to find out if Amos ever . . ." or "Did she do any interviews on . . . ?").

Walter Ong's much earlier, and now classic essay, "The Jinnee in the Well Wrought Urn," is relevant here, and is interesting in both its similarities to and differences from Knapp and Michaels. In this essay, a response to New Criticism, Ong argues that, however much we try to make the poem into a "pure" artistic artifact, we will fail, for the author will inevitably intrude on our concerns. However, this is not because our interpretations are necessarily, pragmatically intentionalist. Rather, it is because our human feeling for the work always draws us back to the human being who was the originator of that work.

In any case, Knapp and Michaels are no doubt right to emphasize our un-self-reflective tendency to interpret intentionally, whatever our self-conscious theoretical stance. However, we have little reason to accept their global assertions that we never interpret counterintentionally and that theory cannot affect interpretive practice. First of all, there are many cases of nonintentional interpretation in, for example, law, cases where a particular statute simply has to be interpreted inconsistently with authorial intent. Think of a law that refers to "free persons of this state." If it was written in a slave state prior to emancipation, the author would have intended it to refer only to whites. However, it must now be interpreted to refer to all people of the state, independent of race. Secondly, even intentionalist interpretation may be guided by theories. For example, one theory may limit intention to consciousness, while another may seek unconscious intent; one may remain at a commonsense level, while another might employ the technical principles of speech-act theory.

But, again, their emphasis on the discrepancy between our interpretive theories and our interpretive practices—and the tilting of these practices toward intention—is important. Indeed, it is *theoretically* important, though they may not be pleased with that idea.

### Pragmatism: James and Dewey

Pragmatism is a movement in American philosophy that, in certain forms, has many significant parallels with existential phenomenology, despite some obvious differences in origin and style. The major early exponents of Pragmatism were Charles Sanders Peirce, John Dewey, and William James. One of the primary tasks of early Pragmatist writers was to turn philosophers away from philosophical speculation and Idealism, and to distinguish genuine and resolvable philosophical issues from pointless philosophical banter and obscurantism (see, for example, James 49–50). In recent years, some of its central principles have been reiterated and redeveloped by Richard Rorty and others. We will turn in a moment to the major Pragmatist work that bears directly on literary theory—John Dewey's *Art as Experience*. However, it is worth considering briefly some of the major tenets of Pragmatism more generally.

In late 1906 and early 1907, William James delivered a series of lectures that set out to define and explain Pragmatism. These lectures, published under the title *Pragmatism: A New Name for Some Old Ways of Thinking*, remain an excellent introduction to the topic. As James explains, Pragmatism is first of all a philosophical method that turns our attention to the broad practical consequences of any doctrine or theory or idea. When faced with any dispute over words or concepts or claims or hypotheses, a Pragmatist asks first of all: What difference does it make to our lives? Note that this question encompasses the question of what difference the dispute could make to our observations of the world—in, for example, experiments (see, for example, 49). But it is not confined to this. For, James emphasizes, our lives are much broader than experimental observation. A doctrine that makes no observational difference may make a huge difference to our attitudes and feelings. As James puts it, "The pragmatic method . . . is to try to interpret each notion by tracing its respective practical consequences. . . . If no practical difference whatever can be traced, then . . . all dispute is idle" (45). These different practical consequences are of two sorts, "sensations" and "reactions" (47)—the passive or objective and active or subjective aspects of our experience.

This view has some consequences that are worth noting. First of all, it leads to a conception of truth that has little to do with a correspondence between claims and facts. The Pragmatist conception of truth is homier. In effect, if it works, it's true. This is called an "instrumental" conception of truth. As James puts it: "any idea that will carry us prosperously from any one part of our experience to any other part, linking things satisfactorily, working securely, simplifying, saving labor, is true just so much . . . true *instrumentally*" (58). Indeed, this view leads logically to the view that blatant illusion can be truth. It has, however unintentionally, a sort of Orwellian aspect. Ultimately, for an idea to "work," it must benefit us in our experience. Thus if an illusion is "enabling" for our practices, it is true, by the Pragmatist account. Putting the theory in the worst light possible, we could say that if soldiers fight better when they believe their Fatherland is the ideal state, then it is true that their Fatherland is the ideal state. As James puts it later, "an idea is 'true' so long as to believe it is profitable to our lives" (75). In short, we should believe in any idea that it would be *"better for us* to believe in" (76). For example, since we feel better about the future when we believe in God, then we should believe in God (and, by implication, our belief is, thereby, true—which is to say, "true instrumentally").

It is easy to see what a writer such as Marx would have said about this theory—that it is in effect a justification of dominant ideology, ideology that operates to keep oppressed people satisfied and cooperative. It is interesting, in this context, that James's own rhetoric is thick with capitalist imagery. It is, I think, no accident that his view of truth is, in effect, the view of truth in a factory: Truth is whatever increases the efficiency of production and distribution. If an innovation makes manufacture swifter or increases monetary gain, then the principles on which it relies are "true," for they are true in the marketplace, and there is no higher court of appeal. It is no accident that James emphasizes "linking things" (as in an assembly line), "working," "saving labor," instrumentality; that he stresses how all this must proceed "prosperously" (58); that, in his view, truth is anything "profitable" (75), and so on. (In fairness, however, I should note that James was at times highly critical of the actual effects of capitalist practices; for a more politically sympathetic interpretation of James, see chapter 2 of Lentricchia.)

It is also worth remarking that there is a certain incoherence in James's position, and it is not unrelated to his capitalist model. Specifically, James could be saying that the Pragmatist notion of truth is (only) *instrumentally* true, or that it is "really" true. In other words, he could be claiming that it is in our best interest—it is most "profitable" for us to believe the Pragmatist notion—or he could be claiming that the Pragmatist notion of truth is just the way things genuinely are. Presumably, however, he isn't claiming the second, because for him the only notion of truth is the first. Thus he must be claiming that we must believe the Pragmatist notion of truth because it is the most profitable. This is circular, of course, but that is not a problem—all notions of truth are circular. There are, however, subsequent problems.

First of all, it does not seem that he could actually claim this. After all, he claims that we should believe in God because it improves our outlook on life. But, suppose we adopt the Pragmatist view of truth and believe that "God exists" means only that believing in God improves our outlook on life. In this case, we would not actually believe that an omnipotent and benevolent deity exists in any objective sense; the Pragmatist conception of truth eliminates this as a possibility. But it would seem that believing in God will have the desired beneficial effect only if we believe that an omnipotent and benevolent deity exists objectively. Thus it would seem that, to live profitably, we must ultimately reject the Pragmatist notion of truth, that is, we must conclude that it is untrue. Perhaps even more importantly, all judgments about what is better for us must themselves be judgments about facts. But the theory does not allow this. Thus, James says that people will live better if they believe in God. Clearly, he means that this is a fact about the world. But, according to his theory, he can only mean that he himself lives more profitably if he believes that people will live better if they believe in God (cynically—he will give more lectures, publish more books, and so forth).

There is a great deal of value in the Pragmatist insistence that we should always relate our theoretical debates to the human world, that ideas should not and indeed cannot be mere bodiless abstractions, but must always be a part of our practical/sensory life; to treat ideas as free of gross matter and untied to action is to distort those ideas, to suppress the context in which they arise and have meaning. But full-fledged Pragmatism, at least as developed by James, appears to be theoretically self-contradictory and to have questionable ideological consequences.

Interestingly, few of these problems seem to arise for Dewey's work on the theory of art and literature. While *Art as Experience* maintains the Pragmatist focus on "practical, human-sensuous activity" (to borrow Marx's phrase from the fifth "Thesis on Feuerbach"), it has little connection with many of the major Pragmatist themes. Indeed, in this work, Dewey seems as close or closer to Heidegger than to James. And this is no coincidence. In the early 1930s, when Dewey was revising *Art as Experience,* he expressed "considerable interest in Heidegger" to Sidney Hook (as recounted in Spiegelberg 336–37)—one of many instances of Heidegger's unremembered influence. Dewey's entire approach is reminiscent of Heidegger's project of reorienting philosophy toward the study of Dasein's Being-in-the-world. Moreover, there are passages in Dewey that seem to echo Heidegger's analyses quite narrowly—for example, his treatment of space as "a comprehensive . . . scene within which are ordered the multiplicity of doings and undergoings in which man engages" and time, not as a "succession of instantaneous points," but as "the rhythmic ebb and flow of expectant impulse, forward and retracted movement," and so on (23). (On the other hand, there are elements in Heidegger's work that are reminiscent of James's ideas as well.)

In any case, whatever its Heideggerian connections, Dewey's theory of art is explicitly founded on the Pragmatist view that art is not separate from life. First of all, this means that the pleasures of art are no different from the sorts of pleasures we experience in everyday life. Aesthetic experience is not some rarefied and isolated phenomenon, but an "intensified" form of everyday experience (3). "[T]he work of art," Dewey tells us, "develops and accentuates what is characteristically valuable in things of everyday enjoyment" (11). (In a similar way, in "Texts and Lumps," Richard Rorty argues that our understanding of literary texts is of exactly the same sort as our understanding of anything else in human life, including our understanding of objects in physical science.) Indeed, originally, art was obviously, fully, and directly integrated into human life. The statue was part of a temple and involved in ceremony; the poem was recited at a festival. It is only with the rise of capitalism that art has become "museumized," separated off from practical life, alien, elite, untouchable. In connection with this emphasis on the experiential quality of art, Dewey anticipates reader response criticism, insisting that when we experience a work of art, we actualize it in our different individual ways by integrating it into our own world: "A new poem is created by every one who reads poetically" because "every individual brings with him, when he exercises his individuality, a way of seeing and feeling that in its interaction with old material creates something new" (108).

Art, then, is part of experience, and is itself, therefore, experience—experience that is unusually developed and intensified, but not fundamentally different from our ordinary experiences of life. More exactly, all experience is a matter of our simultaneously active and passive relation to the environment—human practical-sensuous activity, "doings and undergoings," Dewey puts it (103). In what we call "an experience," these doings and undergoings are structured into a process of desire, tension (due to the resistance put up by the world), and growth as a result of working through one's desire in interaction with the world. A simple example would be eating. I begin with hunger, a desire for food. The world does not automatically offer me food. So, in order to satisfy my desire for food, I engage in practical-sensuous activity, doing and undergoing—I cook. This is active, in the sense that I chop, stir, saute, bake, but passive in that I am constrained by what foods are available, how long they take to cook, and so on. Thus I work through a particular sort of active/passive engagement with the environment in order to produce food, which I then eat (itself an active/passive engagement as well).

This example of cooking is, in fact, more germane to Dewey's theory than is initially evident. Most importantly, the whole development of my experience here may serve as a sort of paradigm of the aesthetic experience and its relation to everyday life, for "the esthetic . . . is the clarified and intensified development of traits that belong to every *normally complete* experience" (46, emphasis added). Specifically, hunger/cooking/eating is a process of tension, progress, and resolution, which, Dewey tells us, provides us with a type of *aesthetic* pleasure. Aesthetic pleasure in art and literature, aesthetic pleasure per se is, ultimately, nothing other than an intensified version of our ordinary feeling of resolution after desire, tension, and working through. Whenever I set out to do something, work on it, and bring it to a conclusion, the sense of wholeness or completion that I feel is, according to Dewey, essentially the same in kind with the feeling I have on seeing a play or reading a novel (see, for example, 14–15).

Too often, however, everyday experience does not resolve; it is "inchoate" (35), disrupted and disorganized, a jumble of ideas, feelings, and desires never followed through. At other times, it is arrested, a mere repetition of conventions that involve no desire, no tension, but mere routine. These tendencies of life, Dewey tells us, are the source of the two greatest dangers in art: incoherence and cliché (40). Art fails precisely when it fails to make an experience. And it fails to make an experience in precisely the way life fails to make an experience—through random dispersion or mechanical repetition. (With respect to the latter, Dewey's view is clearly a revision of Romantic antimechanical dehabituation. As Dewey puts it, "Art throws off the covers that hide the expressiveness of experienced things" and "quickens us from the slackness of routine" [104]. We shall return to this point below. Dewey is unusual, though not unique, among Anglo-American philosophers in the degree to which his work is—like the work of continental theorists—continuous with Romanticism.)

Indeed, these flaws are not only to be found in the work itself. They may also vitiate our experience of a work, for this experience must itself be a fully worked through doing and undergoing. The reader of a literary work, or at least a particular reading of a work, may be faulted in just the same way as the work itself may be faulted. Thus Dewey writes that "That which distinguishes an experience as esthetic is conversion of resistance and tensions, of excitations that in themselves are temptations to diversion, into a movement toward an inclusive and fulfilling close" (56). In connection with this, Dewey distinguishes between perception and recognition. Recognition is the mere identification of an object, usually toward some practical end, as when we recognize a door, then use it to enter a building. Perception, in contrast, is a working through of what one senses, an engagement with the tension between object and expectation. For example, if I genuinely perceive the door and do not merely recognize it, I note the details of its shape, color, design, condition, the way it sounds when opened, how it shuts, and so on. The same distinction applies, more significantly, to art. Just as life may be inchoate or routine, and just as a literary work may be incoherent or clichéd, our approach or response to a literary work may be irresolute (we may be distracted, not pay attention) or merely recognitional. The most obvious literary examples of the latter come from evaluation based on fashion or common opinion. For instance, someone might admire a critical analysis because its terminology allows him/her to recognize that it is poststructural (and thus "sophisticated") without genuinely perceiving the analysis, working through its argument, and so on. Or one might deplore a work because its structure allows one to recognize that it is postmodern, without attending to the specific properties and structures of that work.

Unsurprisingly, the same types of problems affect artistic creation as affect aesthetic response, the structure of the work, and life more generally.

Specifically, Dewey takes up the Romantic view that literature crucially involves the expression of emotion. On the other hand, he insists that no literary work can be a mere pouring out of chaotic feelings (nor can it be the mechanical representation of unfelt feeling, which is not art, but artifice [63]). The "welling up" of emotion "must be clarified and ordered." And this can be done only "through objects of the environment that offer resistance to the direct discharge of emotion and impulse" (61). Here Dewey distinguishes between discharge and expression: "To discharge is to get rid of, to dismiss; to express is to stay by, to carry forward in development, to work out to completion" (62). Clearly, only the latter allows the development of art. And it does so, because it alone defines a complete experience comprising impulse, tension, working through, and resolution.

Finally, the same broad pattern of active/passive desire and interactive working through is to be found in criticism—criticism, in this context, being merely a more formal, more fully articulated, more social, and more socially regulated version of interpretive perception. Specifically, criticism must involve absorption in the work. "But absorption in a work of art so complete as to exclude analysis cannot be long sustained," he insists; there must be "a rhythm of surrender and reflection" (144). Thus criticism too is an active/passive engagement involving a working through. For example, various published interpretations of *Othello* serve as prelude to my absorbed rereading of the play, which itself results in the production of my own critical reflections, which I must work through with the text, in alternating reflection and absorption, until my analysis resolves itself in a manner that gives me (and, perhaps, some others) a sense of a complete or satisfying experience.

Significantly, this circuit is not only drawn from everyday life, but feeds back into everyday life, making worldly experience less clichéd and less chaotic, less a matter of mere recognition and more a matter of perception, even making life more of a whole experience. Here Dewey's Pragmatist (and Heideggerian) approach leads back to Schillerian Romanticism, for the function of criticism and of art becomes the training of sensibility, aesthetic education: "The function of criticism is the reeducation of perception of works of art; it is an auxiliary in the process, a difficult process, of learning to see and hear" (324). And, "The moral function of art itself is to remove prejudice, do away with the scales that keep the eye from seeing, tear away the veils due to wont and custom, perfect the power to perceive" (325). He even goes so far as to see art as "the incomparable organ of instruction" (347), centrally involving imagination, for "the ideal factors in every moral outlook and human loyalty are imaginative" (348).

These links with Romanticism are developed further when Dewey returns to the isolation of art from practical life, the "museumization" he set out to debunk. In explaining this museumization, he takes up the standard Romantic opposition between art and science, with its secondary opposition between art and business. The "isolation of art that now exists," he explains as the result of "two forces . . . natural science and its application in industry and commerce" (337). This leads him to social conclusions that are close not only to Schiller, but to Marx. Specifically, he insists that art can only be reincorporated into life through "a radical social alteration, which affects the degree and kind of participation the worker has in the production and social disposition of the wares he produces," for this alone "will seriously modify the content of experience into which creation of objects made for use enters" (343). Indeed, he goes on to argue that art will not be "secure" until "the mass of men and women who do the useful work of the world have the opportunity to be free in conducting the processes of production and are richly endowed in capacity for enjoying the fruits of collective work." It is these social and economic conditions that are crucial. Not only for political, but for aesthetic reasons, "the material for art should be drawn from all sources whatever and . . . the products of art should be accessible to all." Beside this, he concludes, "the personal political intent of the artist is insignificant" (344).

Perhaps the most surprising aspect of Dewey's theory, however, is not its connection with Schiller (whom he discusses little) and with Marx (whom he does not discuss at all), but with Abhinavagupta (to whom he never refers). Dewey elaborates a theory of aesthetic emotion that is, in effect, a version of Abhinavagupta's account of rasadhvani. He explains that "when excitement about subject matter goes deep, it stirs up a store of attitudes and meanings derived from prior experience." These "elements that issue from prior experience . . . proceed from the subconscious" (65). Moreover, these memories are "not necessarily conscious but retentions that have been organically incorporated in the very structure of the self" (89). Indeed, there are even terminological parallels. Dewey explains that in "esthetic experience . . . the material of the past" does not fill one's attention, as in recollection. Rather, "elements coming from past experiences . . . are organically absorbed into the perception had here and now" such that they give the work "its *suggestiveness*" (122–23, emphasis added). (By the 1930s, there were many sources from which Dewey could have picked up the principles of rasadhvani theory. Dewey was reading some Indic materials while writing *Art as Experience*, as indicated by the fact that he wrote a brief introduction to Jagadish Chatterji's book on the Vedas [see Dewey "Introduction"]. Though it is possible that he formulated these ideas entirely independently, it seems that he came upon them somewhere—even if only when reading an overview of Indian art, the introduction to an Indian play, the production notes for an Indian dance performance, or whatever.)

One final point from Dewey is worth mentioning in connection with the study of literary theory. One purpose of the present volume is to expose readers to the remarkable breadth of literary theory. Too often, courses in literary theory seem to be confined to a few recent and fashionable figures. The problems with this approach are clearly indicated by Dewey. (Though Dewey is speaking of art, not theory, the point still holds.) Dewey notes that it is important to familiarize oneself with as many schools and as many traditions as possible. If we are familiar with only one tradition or with only a few schools, we run two risks. First of all, we are likely to underestimate the value of works from other traditions or schools. Secondly, we are likely to overestimate the value of works from the tradition or schools with which we are familiar. As Dewey puts it, "Knowledge of a wide range of traditions is a condition of exact and severe discrimination" (312). Thus, "Through knowledge of a variety of conditions, the critic . . . is saved from the snap judgment that this or that work is . . . wrong because it has matter to which he is not accustomed, and when he comes across a work whose matter has no discoverable precedent he will be wary of uttering an offhand condemnation" (311).

It is important to stress this point, and to stress (in Pragmatist fashion) that it has practical consequences. Consider, for example, a tenure committee that criticizes a candidate's work on Abhinavagupta and the Rama legends, despite the fact that no one on the committee has any idea who Abhinavagupta might be or what the Rama legends were about (not to mention how they developed, were varied, and so forth). Despite a total lack of competence, we often feel fully confident that our judgment represents "high academic standards" rather than ignorance, narrow-mindedness, and bias. Though one must admit that multicultural education is often badly done, this is this sort of problem that such education is aimed at alleviating.

# 4

---

# Social and Political Philosophy

Ideological Critique, Feminism, Theories
of Culture and Power, Postmodernism

While phenomenology is the obvious inheritor of Kant and German Idealism, prominent social and political approaches to literary theory are the
obvious inheritors of Marx and, in some cases, Nietzsche. The first section
takes up an element of Marxist thought developed extensively in the modern period and with particular relevance to literary study: the critique of
ideology.

Perhaps the most influential aspect of ideological critique in literary
study, however, has not been that associated with Marxist class analysis,
but that which derives from feminism. Though relatively little feminist
literary theory falls into the category of technical philosophy, it is certainly
the most significant and influential form of social and political analysis
practiced by literary critics today. The second section presents a sort of
anatomy of feminism and of its relation to literary study.

After Marx, Foucault is the single social philosopher whose work has
had the greatest impact in recent literary theory. The third section begins
with a treatment of Foucault, then turns to a movement largely inspired
by Foucault's work—New Historicism, as developed by Greenblatt, Montrose, and others. This section ends with Bourdieu, whose work has both
significant affinities with and differences from that of Foucault.

The final section turns to a controversial and slightly more recent development in social and political philosophy and literature, postmodernism,
considering work by Baudrillard, Lyotard, Haraway, and Jameson.

## Ideology and the Critique of Ideology

In part due to the influence of Marx, the forms of social and political philosophy that have been most influential in literary study tend to focus
on the ways in which social organization systematically privileges some

groups at the expense of others. One aspect of this study is materialist, the analysis of the nature and history of class relations—and, by extension, relations between the sexes, relations between different racial or ethnic groups, and so on. Such an analysis necessarily leads to an examination not only of domination itself, but of the means by which domination is maintained. In consequence, it is in part an analysis of *repression*, the use of physical force or threat to maintain or extend domination—the suppression of workers' movements, the patriarchal stifling of women through physical brutality, the European military conquest of Africa, and so on. But there is another aspect to this sort of study that has perhaps been even more central to the study of literature—the analysis of "internal coercion," the analysis of ideas that operate to preserve and extend social hierarchization outside of repression. These ideas are referred to as "ideology." (Actually, "ideology" is used in a wide range of senses. For overviews, see Geuss, Parekh, or Boudon. Here and below, for the sake of clarity, I shall confine my use to the more restricted sense.) Insofar as they operate to further capitalist domination, they are termed "capitalist ideology"; insofar as they operate to further patriarchy, they are termed "patriarchal ideology," and so on.

More exactly, I follow Raymond Geuss in distinguishing epistemic, functional, and genetic senses of "ideology." Or, rather, I see ideology as having an epistemic component, a telic component (not explicitly distinguished by Geuss), and a functional component. Unlike most authors, I do not view the genetic component as important; indeed, I believe that an emphasis on genesis is more often than not misleading. (We shall return to this below.) Within this scheme, then, ideology may be understood, roughly, as a set of false ideas (epistemic) and/or aspirations (telic) that function to preserve social hierarchies of class, sex, race, and so forth (functional).

It is worth considering this definition in more detail. Beginning with the epistemic component, let us consider the simplest case—straightforwardly false ideas. Perhaps the bulk of any ideology is made up of erroneous beliefs. For example, patriarchal ideology involves such false ideas as *women cannot do math, women cannot do logic, women cannot do science, women are not aggressive enough to succeed at business,* and so on. Note that these are not ideological simply because they are false. James Joyce evidently believed that women do not like soup (see Ellmann 463). As there is no evidence that women like soup less than men, this is a false statement about women. But it is not ideological as it has no consequences for social hierarchies. In contrast, beliefs about women's abilities in math, science, and business operate to discourage women from entering the most high-paying and most powerful professions in capitalist society, to discourage parents from aiming their female children toward these professions, and so on. In other words, they have a *function* in sustaining oppressive hierarchies. Other straightforward examples could be taken from U.S. foreign policy (for instance, the popular belief, held by a wide range of ordinary people during the Gulf War, that Kuwait was a democracy, a false belief that clearly served to increase support for the war [see Jhally, Lewis, and Morgan 51]).

There are many other ways in which ideologies may be epistemically faulty as well. For example, we have a range of tacit and "operational" beliefs, beliefs that guide our action, but that we would not explicitly affirm. For example, many white Americans no doubt tacitly believe that black men are dangerous. If asked, they would deny believing this. But their behavior is clearly based on such a tacit belief. For example, they might consistently avoid being alone with a black man, even one they already know, while they would have no such qualms about being alone with a white man or anyone else; they might avoid walking down a street where they see a black man, and so forth. Similarly, one might have a tacit belief that women are intellectually flimsy. While asserting that one believes men and women are intellectually equal, one might repeatedly pass over women's comments in meetings, ignore women's suggestions and arguments, and so on. In both cases, it is fairly clear that the tacit belief functions to maintain social hierarchies.

One particularly important form of epistemic error is to be found in the excessive limitation of alternatives—what is called the establishment of a "problematic." A problematic is not a single belief, but the range of beliefs that are "in the field," the range of possibilities open to debate. Often, the problem with an ideology is not so much that everyone holds one particular (false) belief as that the entire debate is constrained in such a way as to exclude plausible options from consideration. Sometimes a problematic is explicitly formulated via governmental statements and media analyses. For example, at one point during the Gulf War, the State Department issued a statement that it would either begin a ground offensive right away or continue intensive aerial bombardment for another week before beginning a ground offensive. The major news media then went out and polled people, asking, "Should we begin a ground offensive right away or should be continue bombing for another week before undertaking the offensive?" Experts discussed the options on television and radio, and so on. One result was that the American people strongly supported continued aerial bombardment. But, as those of us involved in antiwar actions continually stressed, this way of phrasing the issue simply left our position out of the debate. Replacing bombardment with an embargo, and scrapping the whole idea of a ground offensive, was simply not an option.

Indeed, this case illustrates the issue of the problematic in another, more subtle way as well. As those of us in the peace movement were well aware, even this focus on Iraq involved a skewing of debate on U.S. foreign policy. However bad the Iraqi invasion of Kuwait, it was insignificant in comparison with, say, the U.S.-supported destruction of East Timor by Indonesia, or any number of other U.S.-armed atrocities going on in the rest of the world. Even our proposal of an embargo (rather than the mass murder of Iraqi civilians) focused attention on Iraq as if it were the most important topic of concern in world politics, as if the invasion of Kuwait were the gravest crime against humanity committed in the world at that time. In this sense, though we managed to escape from the narrow problematic of "bombardment versus ground offensive," we found it almost impossible to escape from the more encompassing problematic defined by the focus on Iraq.

Telic considerations are closely related to the delimitation of problematics. Specifically, ideologies involve not only beliefs, tacit beliefs, and problematics, but ranges of desire, interest, aspiration. These aspirations, emotions, and interests typically involve false beliefs and thus could in principle be considered under that category, but they are worth considering separately. Specifically, a social hierarchy allows one certain possibilities for betterment, but disallows others. Ideology operates to channel one's aspirations into the narrow range defined by social hierarchies and to discourage aspirations outside of that system. Consider, for example, the early South African gold mining system, presented, for example, in Peter Abrahams' novel, *Mine Boy*. Black miners could not take skilled (and thus higher-paid) mining positions. These were reserved for white miners. They could, however, aspire to various positions in the hierarchy of black miners—for example, they could become mine police, or "boss boys" in charge of groups of black miners, or compound guards. In this way, they could aspire to advancement within the system, and this served to some extent to channel their aspirations away from rebellion against the system and toward success within the system. Thus, in Abrahams' novel, during a strike of black miners, it is precisely the privileged compound guards who refuse to join the other blacks, but remain loyal to the white owners and managers.

Perhaps a more obvious example is that of women. Through the repeated presentation of women in limited roles on TV and in movies, through stereotyped children's stories and games, girls come to have a limited set of career options defined for them—a sort of implicit problematic of aspirations. At least until fairly recently, these would include secretaries, but not business executives, nurses, but not doctors, and so on. It still includes poets, but not physicists. Note that this need not involve any explicit belief to the effect that women can be nurses, but not doctors. It more importantly involves the formation of ideals, the imagination of possibilities, that are severely limited. In the operation of a "problematic of aspirations," it may simply not occur to a young woman that she might become a physicist, rather than a poet (or a doctor, rather than a nurse). Here, too, it is clear that these limitations are functional, for in these cases, women's aspirations are limited to the lower-paying and less powerful positions in medicine, business, and so on.

While the functional component is perhaps clearer than the epistemic and telic components, there are still some complications worth spelling out. The first concerns a common misunderstanding. Ideology does not function to celebrate the dominant class. Rather, it functions to preserve the system of relations of domination. In other words, it is not necessarily, and not typically, a self-aggrandizement of the dominant class. Indeed, it may even involve the aggrandizement of the dominated group, as in the version of patriarchal ideology that places women "on a pedestal." Thus, the ideological function of a belief or aspiration cannot in any way be judged by the attitude it expresses toward dominant and subordinated groups. It can only be judged by an examination of its actual operational effects in social structure.

The second point about functional analysis concerns its specifically Marxist form. By the tenets of historical materialism, a functional analysis is not necessarily complete when it has isolated a hierarchical relation served by the beliefs or aspirations in question. It must further explain this hierarchical relation in economic terms. Thus, for example, it is not enough to note that various ideological beliefs in South Africa preserve the domination of whites over blacks. One must further relate that domination to economic conditions. Consider, again, racist ideology in the South African gold mines. The division between white and black workers, as well as the "micro-hierarchization" of black workers (into boss boys, camp police, and so forth), had the function of fragmenting the working class, preventing coordinated action, and making it highly unlikely that any group could strike successfully—as indicated at the end of Abrahams' novel, when the black workers strike, but without the cooperation of the black guards and the white workers. In short, the delimitation of "system internal" aspirations (e.g., to be a boss boy, rather than to change the system; or, for a white person, to be a skilled miner, rather than to change the system) functioned as part of the system of racial hierarchization, certainly. But that system itself functioned to preserve the encompassing system of capitalist exploitation, and we do not fully understand the racial hierarchization unless we extend our analysis to this economic conclusion.

Ideological critique is, as one might expect, the systematic analysis of these epistemic, telic, and functional components. In its most general form, it begins with epistemic or telic evaluation: the isolation of false beliefs—both explicit and tacit—and the demonstration of their falsity, the delimitation of problematics and articulation of plausible alternatives, the recognition and expansion of excessively limited aspirations, and so on. Following evaluation, it proceeds to functional analysis, first determining the exact relation between the ideas in question and one or another social hierarchy, then (at least in Marxist ideological critique) further analyzing that social hierarchy in relation to economic conditions.

On the other hand, this general statement may make it appear that ideological critique is largely an academic exercise. It is not. The entire point of engaging in ideological critique is to produce political effects. Thus it is not merely a matter of engaging in an isolated analysis; it is a matter of gearing an analysis to an audience in such a way as to foster a broader understanding, critical of capitalism and its attendant hierarchies (for example, racial stratifications), to encourage a broader range of aspiration, including aspirations to transform the social structure itself, and so on. For example, the response to racism in 1940s South African gold mines would not be an abstract argument that blacks and whites are equally human or a critical analysis of racist pseudoscience. Of course, it could involve this sort of approach for a very small segment of the population—perhaps some well-educated, petit bourgeois educators who have no direct economic interest in black hyper-exploitation and who might be persuaded to let these academic considerations influence their vote in elections. For the vast majority of people, however, such an argument would be effectively irrelevant, inconsequential in practical terms. With black miners, for example, it would be most important to stress the necessity of improving the common lot of the miners, or at least of the black miners—to clarify how accepting the fragmentation into boss boys, mine police, and so forth, weakens them as a group and thus harms them all as individuals, for it prevents them advancing their overwhelmingly more important common interests. With black domestic workers, it would involve discussing how their own wages are tied directly to those of the mine workers, and thus how their own well-being is bound up with that of the miners. With white workers, it would involve stressing that their higher wages in no way compensate for the devastation to health caused by work in the mines, that they could never hope to strike successfully for improved conditions as long as they refuse to join in solidarity with the black workers, and so on.

Each case here is a matter of analyzing validity and aspiration in relation to function in preserving a hierarchy. But, it is also a direct response to that function. In short, one is not doing ideological critique if one does not aim to undermine the social hierarchies isolated in the functional analysis. As a result, the articulation of ideological critique is almost necessarily tailored to particular situations, groups, and so on. This is not to say that it is duplicitous. Of course, it may be, but then it is more properly referred to as "propaganda," not "ideological critique." Rather, this is merely a matter of focusing on what parts of a (valid) analysis are relevant in particular social and historical conditions. The same point clearly applies to literature. Ideological critique is likely to involve one sort of response in a composition class, another in a graduate seminar, another in an essay for a popular outlet, another for a Marxist academic journal, and so on.

There are two obvious ways of engaging in ideological critique in literature. The first is to analyze ideological beliefs and aspirations as developed (ideologically) in the work. The other is to consider how the work might bring up such beliefs and aspirations only to critique them itself. To advert to Ricoeur's distinction, the former might be thought of as the "suspicious" form of ideological critique; the latter might be thought of as the "revelatory" form. Our discussion of *Othello* as an antiracist play is in effect a version of the latter approach. For an example of the former approach—which is arguably the more important of the two—we may consider Alan Paton's *Cry, the Beloved Country,* a particularly good example, because its partially racist ideology is largely implicit, and at odds with the self-consciously antiracist aims of the book.

Paton's novel has been a favorite of liberal media and instructors since its publication in 1948. The *New Republic* and the *New York Times* both published highly laudatory reviews, and the book is (or was until recently) required reading in some high schools. Paton has not only been celebrated by liberals in this country. He himself has been active in liberal politics in South Africa. He has opposed the brutal exploitation of blacks in South Africa, and his novel is in large part a liberal critique of that treatment.

However, it is at the same time a paternalistic critique. Specifically, Paton develops the entire novel around a tacit belief about the relation between whites and blacks, white culture and black culture, a sort of homology by which blacks are to whites as children are to adults. Frequently, the whites are vicious and perverse adults, and sometimes the blacks are innocent, even holy children; but they are adults and children nonetheless. Added to this, he repeatedly assimilates African culture to blindness and Christian European culture to sight—another ideologically functional idea.

The novel concerns a black priest, Kumalo, a simple, childlike man who goes to the big city in order to find his lost son and sister. His sister, it turns out, is a prostitute, and his son has murdered a white liberal—Jarvis, the absent hero of the book. Kumalo also meets his brother, who is a corrupt politician. The novel paints the following picture of South Africa: Many, perhaps most, blacks are degenerate. The young men are thugs and murderers, or alcoholics, or both. The young women are prostitutes. As Jarvis puts it, "Our natives today produce criminals and prostitutes and drunkards" (146). The older men are corrupt and treacherous—except those who are priests. This is not too great a departure from earlier African culture, which was filled with "violence and savagery . . . superstition and witchcraft" (146). In contrast, whites are of two sorts: those neglectful of black problems, and those (liberals and paternalists) who help blacks.

The first point to make about this portrait is that it is grossly inaccurate. In fact, the vast majority of violence and crime perpetrated in South Africa has been by whites against blacks. Of course, blacks may have been more responsible for small-scale street crime, as is typical of disenfranchised groups. Part of the problematic of the novel—and of South African society at the time and of U.S. society—involves the tacit redefinition of "crime" so that it refers primarily to small-scale street crime, with the large-scale, systematic criminality of the state or the dominant classes effectively excluded from consideration. Secondly, the implication of this portrait is that black culture is barbaric and white culture civilized. Finally, the novel implicitly poses the question: What is wrong with blacks? In this respect, it begins to establish a problematic in which the poles of debate are marked by the (right-wing) view that blacks are inferior racially and the (paternalistic liberal) view that they are only inadequately educated and acculturated. Ultimately, this problematic is rendered explicit, and Paton opts for the paternalistic liberal view. But what is in some ways most important is not which position Paton takes; rather, it is this fallacious problematic itself. If there is an issue, it should be: what is wrong with whites? After all, they are the ones who have dispossessed and brutalized blacks, not vice versa. Paton's liberal problematic constrains debate to entirely implausible, but obviously ideologically functional, positions.

Ideological critique is in some ways very simple. It may appear to lack subtlety and sophistication when compared to some more recent, more opaque modes of social analysis, currently in favor in academic circles. Literary critics like to focus on barely perceptible subtleties of language, nuances of tone. Ideological critique focuses on blunter matters. But, for the most part, oppression is not a matter of barely perceptible subtleties of language, and nuances of tone. Overwhelmingly, what is of deepest concern to the vast majority of the world's population concerns the validity of large, humanly consequential beliefs and aspirations, the broad social function of those beliefs and aspirations, and, most importantly, the material conditions that underlie all this—material conditions of almost continual suffering for most people in the world today. While there is clearly value in going on to analyze other aspects of culture and social hierarchy, it seems to me that anyone genuinely committed to real social amelioration for ordinary people must recognize Marxist ideological critique as the primary tool of cultural analysis. That it has largely fallen into desuetude in literary criticism indicates something approaching a dereliction of our duties as both literary critics and social beings.

Before going on to some more recent developments in political and social philosophy and literature, however, it is worth returning briefly to the "genetic" component of ideology, which we mentioned at the outset, but then left aside. Typically, ideological ideas/aspirations are understood to have arisen within the dominant class (this being the "genetic" component) and to have been imposed on the dominated class by the broad cultural hegemony of the dominant class. Though intuitively plausible, this is in fact a highly doubtful assumption. As Jon Elster points out, the ideologies that are most effective in stifling subaltern rebellion are often endogenous to the subaltern group. In other words, both the oppressor and the oppressed generate false beliefs and aspirations that serve the status quo. The oppressor does so to justify his/her oppression of others. The oppressed do so in order to make sense of their oppression by others, and to do so in such a way as to make their condition bearable. Thus, colonized Irish, Indians, and Africans generated their own ideologies concerning their relation to the English—viewing themselves as more sensitive, emotional, spiritual, poetic, or whatever. And these ideologies often operated to support the political and economic hierarchies then in place.

Of course, the ideologies of the oppressed are not wholly endogenous. They are at least in part influenced by ideologies of the dominant group. The point is that they are not wholly exogenous either—and, more importantly, their functional character is in no way contingent on exogenesis. In other words, ideologically functional beliefs and aspirations need not arise in the dominant group. They may arise among the dominated themselves. In consequence, identifying the origin of a belief or aspiration is insufficient grounds for identifying that idea as ideological or counterideological. There is a tendency among literary critics to adopt a facile geneticism, identifying "male" ideas (ideas that, evidently, originated with men) as patriarchal and "female" ideas (ideas that, evidently, originated with women) as revolutionary. One obvious problem with this view of things is that women have been contributing to "male" ideas from the outset and that women have been equally influenced by men, so that identifying ideas as male or female seems entirely senseless. But more importantly, this form of genetic claim is implausible in any case. It cannot legitimately be considered a form of ideological critique. Indeed, it is far more likely to reinforce ideologically functional beliefs and aspirations than to combat them.

### Varieties of Feminism

As already noted, most feminist theory would not fall into the category of what one usually refers to as "philosophical literary theory." This is primarily because few varieties of feminism derive from movements one would normally include in the discipline of Philosophy. There are, of course, individual exceptions—such as Simone de Beauvoir and Luce Irigaray. But even these cases are complex. For example, one might reasonably argue that Irigaray's most influential work is more appropriately categorized with psychoanalysis.

On the other hand, feminism is probably the most important influence on social and political literary study in the last half century. Feminist political activism, feminist literature, feminist theories and analyses, have radically altered the way in which many of us think about society and about literature. Due to feminist work, the questions we ask about literature, the literary works we read, the constitution of our faculties and student bodies are very different today from what they were fifty years ago. In short, feminist work has made it much harder for literary critics to leave half the population out of consideration, in theory and in practice.

Thus it seems crucial to include feminism in a chapter on social and political philosophy. However, our representation of feminism would be very skewed if we were to focus this section on those few feminists who are closely associated with technical philosophy. Therefore, in this section, I have sought to present an analytic of feminism today, or, to advert to a concept we will examine in the following section, a sort of Bourdieuian mapping of positions in this social and intellectual field. For perhaps the first thing to say about feminism is that it is not monolithic. The term "feminism" covers a range of "feminisms." Feminism is, in effect, many different things—some of them mutually exclusive. This is, of course, not a criticism of feminism. It merely means that feminism is a large, developing field of social and intellectual endeavor. Thus, like most other intellectual fields, it cannot be encompassed by a single dogma (a point made by a number of feminist writers, such as Sheila Rowbotham [45], Deborah Cameron [4], and others).

There is a problem, however, when people do not recognize that feminism is many different things, as most feminist theorists acknowledge. Specifically, the evaluation of various theories can become a matter of supporting or opposing a particular label. Those who, for whatever reason, dislike the word "feminism" will tend to oppose what is labeled "feminist," whatever its content, while those who like the term will have the opposite response. Thus, I frequently find undergraduate women students who would never refer to themselves as "feminist," not necessarily because of political disagreement, but rather because, for them, the word "feminist" calls up images of compulsiveness, dogmatism, mean-spiritedness, or various sorts of personal preference that they do not share. They often identify it with the hatred of men, Stalinistic political correctness, and ugly pants.

A couple of years ago, for example, I had two undergraduate women students planning on pursuing doctorates and careers of teaching and research in the social sciences; they absolutely refused to view themselves as feminist. At the same time, I had a student who argued adamantly that women with children should stay home, because, she insisted, a woman's place is with her child; this student was equally adamant in insisting that she herself is a feminist. No doubt, I could have found converse examples as well—probably in the same class. Indeed, I have known graduate students and university faculty members who have been simultaneously enthusiastic about Luce Irigaray, Deborah Cameron, Elaine Showalter, Julia Kristeva, and Anne Fausto-Sterling, despite the fact that there is little these authors have in common other than the name "feminist." Correlatively, I have no doubt that there are students and professors who are indiscriminately disdainful of all these thinkers. In both cases it would seem to be the identification of the writers as "feminist" that is most important—and not the specific arguments, programs, and so on, that they present.

Perhaps the most intellectually and practically valuable response to this problem is to detail the conceptual varieties of feminism, clarifying and organizing our diverse understandings of feminism. In this section, then, I would like to specify what I see as the most important of these varieties and the relations between them. Hopefully these specifications will leave the resultant terms—"standard feminism," "feminism of gender difference," and so on—more open to clear, precise conceptual and referential use, and less open to emotive and associative reduction. Moreover, the same conceptual distinctions apply, with slight changes, to the political and intellectual work of minority, gay, lesbian, anticolonial, and other subaltern activists, though theoretical work in these fields—especially literary theoretical work—is more recent and less developed. Thus, a parallel structure of conceptual alternatives—including, for example, "standard antiracism," "anticolonialism of difference," and so forth—should help us to understand these fields as well.

Across a broad range of writers, activists, and ordinary people, the term "feminist" appears to be used most consistently with respect to a particular set of political aims. While it is probably impossible to plot out a minimal program shared by all people who call themselves "feminist," there is a cluster of goals most of which would be shared by most people who think of themselves as feminist. Thus virtually every feminist advocates actions to reduce or, ideally, eliminate rape, wife abuse, the sexual molestation of young girls, female infanticide, underfeeding of girls, restrictions on reproductive freedom, and so on. There are, of course, differences here—for example, in the case of abortion, where there is an entire organization of women who refer to themselves as pro-life feminists, though others would take a pro-choice outlook to be a sine qua non of feminism. Despite such differences, women's basic physical rights to health, nutrition, and so on, as well as their right to exercise control over their own sexual and reproductive lives, seem to be almost universally affirmed by feminists. Moreover, feminists in general share the (certainly correct) belief that women have been deprived of these rights in a manner and degree to which men have not. Only the most narrow-visioned feminists fail to recognize that in the course of human history most men have been deprived of such rights as well—often due to race and class (the most frequently cited factors), but also to age, nationality, sexual preference, intellectual capacities, physical disabilities, or less systematic factors, such as personality or appearance. This, however, does not change the fact that women *as women* have been systematically deprived, while men *as men* have not—and some conception of this seems crucial to feminism of all sorts as well. Beyond physical concerns, feminists also share economic, social, and intellectual concerns. Virtually all feminists agree that women should not be underpaid relative to men, and thus they support equal pay for equal work. Most feminists would in addition support comparable pay for comparable work, though this is more controversial if only because comparable work can be difficult to define. Similarly, feminists universally or nearly universally oppose preferential hiring or promotion for men based on sex. They also oppose the unequal division of housework between men and women, at least when the spouses work the same amount of time outside of the home. In addition, virtually all feminists believe (correctly) that there are in fact pay discrepancies between men and women, that men are commonly hired or promoted unfairly, and that housework is not equally divided between working spouses. More generally, while not all feminists support the idea that it is important for women to work outside of the home, all do appear to hold that there should not be inequalities (either at home or at work) for those that do. Let us use the term *basic feminism* to refer to these social and economic aims, combined with the physical concerns discussed above, and the relevant beliefs in both cases. (The parallels for "basic antiracism," "basic anticolonialism," and so forth, should be fairly clear.)

Despite specific aims common to basic feminism, there is at least some disagreement about both the means by which these aims may be achieved and about the larger social transformations to which these might contribute. Thus most feminists support affirmative action programs. But not all feminists who support equality in hiring believe that this is best achieved by such programs. Moreover, in many cases, empirical issues arise that are not uncontroversial. The relation of affirmative action to the eventual elimination of hiring discrimination against women (or minorities) is a case in point. Another case is that of the relation between sexual violence and pornography. Those who believe that pornography of certain sorts encourages violence against women—for example, rape—will consider the elimination of pornography to be one means of fighting such violence. Those who do not share this analysis of pornography will not see its elimination as contributory to ending the sexual abuse of women. Moreover, there are some feminists who believe that pornography does contribute to violence, but who still oppose its suppression, primarily on civil libertarian grounds.

However, this is not to say that there are not dominant views on at least certain issues. There are. For example, the majority of feminists do indeed seem to support affirmative action and oppose at least certain sorts of pornography—though the majority of feminists may not support the legal suppression of pornography (I just don't know). We might use the term *standard feminism* to refer to basic feminism supplemented by majoritarian views on the means directly relevant to the achievement of the goals of basic feminism. (As these majoritarian views are likely to vary across groups, one might wish to qualify this term, for example, in national terms—standard feminism in the United States, standard feminism in India, and so forth.)

Those who accept basic feminism and even standard feminism often diverge on the question of broader social transformations. Some feminists advocate the large-scale structural transformation of society, frequently in a socialist, perhaps even anarchist direction. Other feminists advocate little or no program of change beyond that of basic feminism, perhaps along with some comparable concerns for other oppressed groups (for example, basic antiracism). These are frequently referred to as the revolutionary and reformist or radical and liberal versions of feminism. But, in fact, those advocating structural change are not necessarily more revolutionary or radical on central issues. Moreover, it seems odd to term common aims "liberal" or "reformist," and oppose these to a social vision that does not repudiate but incorporates and expands them. Thus I shall instead refer to these alternatives as *minimal feminism*, which is to say, feminism that does not advocate larger social transformation beyond the implementation of basic feminism, and *utopian feminism*, feminism that does advocate such transformation, whether communist, anarchist, religious, or whatever. Again, there are direct parallels in minimal and utopian antiracism, antihomophobia, and so on.

As the preceding list indicates, there are various sorts of utopian feminist. For the most part, the distinctions between these varieties are irrelevant to our present anatomy for they involve categories that apply indifferently to feminists and nonfeminists alike. However, there are two broad evaluative distinctions that are important for our analysis and that greatly affect utopian feminism. Some feminists believe that men and women cannot live together because any group of men will necessarily dominate or seek to dominate the women with whom they are associated. Whether this male will to power is conceived of as socially or biologically determined, it is seen as overwhelming. The conclusion of such feminists is that only through separation from men can women lead genuinely happy, fulfilling lives. Other feminists do not agree. Members of the latter group feel that, while some men are no doubt incorrigible, others can be made self-conscious about their sexism, and some are already in effect feminist. Indeed, certain feminists of this sort would claim that much the same can be said about women—that some women are incorrigibly attached to patriarchal ideology, that others can be made self-conscious about their sexism, and that some are feminist. Thus there is no reason to advocate the separation of the sexes and to deny men (and women) the physical, emotional, and intellectual pleasures of interaction with the other sex.

The first position, I will refer to as *feminist separatism;* the second as *feminist integrationism.* Advocates of the first seek a purely female society in which the present partial isolation of men and women is absolutized. Advocates of the second seek a fully integrated society in which the present partial isolation of men and women is reduced to a minimum, a society in which something like Aristotelian friendship is extended across sexes. Of course, here, as elsewhere, there are intermediate cases. For example, some feminists are separatist for one generation only; they believe that men raised in sexist society are incorrigible, but that male children raised from birth in a female society would be free from patriarchal distortion and could, therefore, fully participate in an ideal polis. Other less extreme views might involve the advocacy of all-women's businesses or societies or institutions within a generally integrated society. These various positions characterize important tendencies among other subaltern activists as well. For example, there is a directly parallel development in the division between black separatists, black integrationists, and those in between who advocate black business, black cooperatives, and other black enterprises.

Before discussing the underlying principles that guide the formation of particular feminist (and other subaltern) goals, it is important to make one further evaluative distinction, closely related to, but not identical with, that between separatism and integrationism. Some feminists believe that the world would be better off if it were ruled by women. Other feminists find this view shocking—not because they see less good in women than in men (they do not), but rather because they fail to see less evil in women than in men. The former believe that it is men who cause war and oppression and that women not only do not, but, if in power, would not; the latter believe that women have not caused very much war and oppression only because they have not had very much opportunity to do so. The first group I will call *female supremacists;* the second, *feminist egalitarians.*

Supremacism is most often utopian in orientation and may be separatist, but need not be (as the idea of women governing the world—not merely women's communities—indicates). As described above, integrationism was implicitly egalitarian; it may also be supremacist, though clearly any form of supremacism (male or female) puts limits on the possible extent of integration, as is clear from our own society. Unsurprisingly, then, female supremacism, as well as black and other subaltern supremacisms, include the same variety of aims and attitudes as the dominant supremacisms (male, white, and so forth); these range from benign paternalism (maternalism?) to the violence of groups that advocate, in bell hooks's words, the "extermination of all men" (33)—for example, SCUM, the Society for Cutting Up Men, an American group (cited by de Beauvoir, "From an Interview" 144).

Having said this, it is important to emphasize that, despite the existence of such groups, women are *overwhelmingly* more likely to be victims of cross-sex violence than perpetrators.

Turning to the principles of decision underlying much feminist thought about goals, the basic and extremely important distinction in this area is that between those who base their decisions primarily upon considerations of *solidarity* and those who base their decisions primarily upon considerations of *justice.* The distinction I have in mind here was most famously debated, outside of feminism, by Michel Foucault and Noam Chomsky, and has been taken up by a range of other theorists (for instance, Frederic Jameson who, in *The Political Unconscious,* maintains the solidarity position [see, for example, 290]). This is fundamentally a distinction between criteria of decision that are applied universally and criteria that vary depending upon the sex (race, sexual preference, and so forth) of those involved; put differently, it is a matter of whether our decisions are determined by universal ethical principle or by a generalized support for the members of one group. Of course, there are many situations in which questions of ethical principle simply do not arise. In these cases, there is no possibility of choosing one criterion over the other. Moreover, when we are concerned with oppressed groups, even in those cases in which questions of principle do arise, criteria of justice and criteria of solidarity will often lead to the same conclusions. Indeed they will almost always lead to the same conclusions in the issues of most importance to basic feminism, basic antiracism, and so on. However, they will frequently lead to different decisions about means even in these cases *and* they will frequently lead to different decisions about goals falling outside of basic feminism, and so on.

A good example of this difference may be found in the reactions of ordinary feminist women to the case of the Central Park jogger (who was raped and beaten with particular brutality). As, for example, Joan Didion has argued, a number of feminists saw the case primarily as a battle between women and a patriarchal judicial system; in this context, they "took the side" of the woman by calling for conviction and severe punishment of the defendants. Other feminists certainly agreed that the judicial system is patriarchal and that rape is undoubtedly a heinous crime that should be severely punished. But they were disturbed by what they saw as injustice done to the defendants (misuse of evidence, dubious police methods, and so forth). Thus they could not necessarily support conviction. (For discussion of this case in relation to feminism, see also J. James.) I will refer to these alternatives as *feminism of solidarity* and *feminism of justice.*

We come, finally, to empirical beliefs. For the most part, empirical beliefs relevant to feminism concern the nature of sex and gender (those relevant to antiracism and anticolonialism concern race and ethnicity, and so on). However, some feminists do hold that beliefs relating to a broad range of other topics are or may be feminist or nonfeminist. Thus, for example, Anne Fausto-Sterling maintains that holistic science is feminist (208–13); Luce Irigaray maintains that a physics of solids is patriarchal (see 106–18); I have heard some feminists claim (in oral debate, if not in writing) that the study of mother/daughter relations in literature is feminist, while the study of father/daughter relations is nonfeminist, perhaps even antifeminist. There appears to be so much diversity in this area that I see no useful and unifying way of categorizing it. Indeed, it is often difficult to see precisely what claims are being made. Thus, while I certainly favor holistic science, I do not see how a claim about the putative feminism of holistic science could be true or false. It appears to be something more like a declaration that one approach to scientific inquiry is politically correct—or, in the other cases, that one object of inquiry in physics or literary criticism is politically correct. In this sense, such declarations are more like normative principles than like empirical claims—though it is unclear what the force of these normative principles might be, or what they may be based upon. In any case, it is important to be aware that there are feminists who extend feminist claims to a range of empirical disciplines in ways that do not in any obvious sense touch upon gender issues. (This seems less true in other areas of subaltern theory, though it is not unheard of.)

For the most part, however, feminist concern about empirical matters focuses upon issues of cognitive, affective, moral, and other similarities and/or differences between men and women. The first distinction I should like to make is that between feminists whose approach to these matters is oriented toward research, and feminists whose approach is oriented toward theoretical or personal reflection. Thus there are feminists who base their claims about gender upon their own intuition, usually supplemented by appeals to common experience, or to principles of speculative philosophies, such as deconstruction. They often distrust systematic empirical inquiry as inadequately theorized. Writers such as Hélène Cixous, Luce Irigaray, Gayatri Spivak—and many others—fall into this category. However, there are also feminists who seek to base their generalizations upon archival, historical, statistical, experimental, or other studies. Writers such as Mary Hiatt, Anne Fausto-Sterling, Cynthia Fuchs Epstein, and Deborah Cameron—along with many others—fall into this category. They distrust intuition, frequently viewing it as nothing more than the expression of sexist ideology, the substitution of stereotypes for facts; moreover, they are often suspicious of what goes by the name of "theory," finding it to be little more than unsupported speculation. I shall refer to the former group as advocates of *reflective feminism* and the latter group as advocates of *empirical feminism*.

Within each group, there are further significant divisions. Thus reflective feminists may be *intuitionist* or *speculative,* hence narrowly personal/experiential or aimed toward larger philosophical conjecture. Similarly, empirical feminists may be *historicist* or *statistical/experimental* in orientation, depending upon whether they focus on historical narratives or on various experimental, statistical, and other studies. Of course, these distinctions need not be absolute. For example, it is not uncommon to find feminists combining philosophical speculation with historical research. However, these are distinct tendencies, and in many specific cases they are indeed mutually exclusive.

Clearly, feminists not only have different methods of determining the validity or invalidity of beliefs concerning sex and gender, they have different beliefs that they take to be valid or invalid. The most obvious division here is between feminists who maintain that there is a broad range of significant cognitive, affective, moral, or other differences between men and women, and feminists who maintain that there are very few such differences and that these are overwhelmed by the similarities between the sexes. Thus some feminists claim that women are irrational and humanistic, men rational and impersonal; others disagree. Some feminists claim that women are more emotionally bonded; others claim that any apparent difference in emotional bonding is simply a function of immediate social and economic circumstances. Some feminists claim that women's morals are interactive and personal, whereas men's are abstract and absolute; others claim that this division has no basis in fact and is simply the by-product of biased research methods. I shall refer to the former group as *feminists of gender difference* and the latter as *feminists of human diversity,* for such writers tend equally to emphasize individual difference and human similarity.

Feminists of gender difference often assimilate the opposition between male and female—in intellect, emotion, morality, and so forth—to the great Romantic opposition between order, reason, mechanism, on one hand, and revolutionary disruption, feeling, organicism, on the other. A good example of this is Hélène Cixous. Her idea of *écriture féminine* represents feminine expression as decentering male order, overturning male hierarchy, and so on. "I-woman am going to blow up the Law," she insists ("Laugh" 257). The law is oppressive in a way directly related to masculinity, for the male body "gravitates around the penis" and, in consequence, male anatomy "engender[s] that centralized body (in political anatomy) under the dictatorship of its parts" ("Laugh" 259). Moreover, since "Woman," Cixous insists, "is body more than man is" ("Sorties" 95), this writing is linked with organicism as well.

Of course, Cixous is not at all alone in this. There is a similar, if more constrained, Romantic pattern in Carol Gilligan's distinction between the putatively male ethics of rights—"formal and abstract," based on "rules" and "separation"—and the putatively female ethics of care, which are "contextual and narrative," based on "relationships" and "connection" (19). Gilligan's opposition emphasizes the analytic/synthetic, form/sense (in Schiller's terms), and human/mechanical contrasts, but not the hierarchizing/disrupting contrast, which is so important to Cixous.

Among feminists of gender difference, it is important to distinguish those who believe such differences to be *biological,* and those who believe them to be *social.* In addition, it is important to note that advocates of socially determined gender difference most often allow for significant differences within genders according to broad categories such as race, class, and sexual orientation. Indeed, it is valuable to go beyond such categories to questions of degree and type of social determination. A social difference between men and women may be deeply ingrained due to processes of socialization or due to psychoanalytic factors, such as the castration complex. On the other hand, a social difference may be superficial and have to do more with immediate and changeable economic and social circumstances than with psychological structures. A subaltern may not speak aggressively because he/she has been socialized to be timid, or he/she may simply fear reprisal, given current power relations. Related to this, it is important to distinguish between differences of principle and differences in output. Two people following the same principles, but placed in different circumstances, will behave differently. In other words, the outputs of the principles will differ, despite the fact that the principles are the same. A simple example would be the following: Suppose, as seems likely, that people identify with literary characters who have experiences similar to their own. Given that men and women have some different types of experience in our society, it follows that in certain cases they will identify with different literary characters. Thus men and women will be following the same principle, but the principle will lead to different outputs in the two cases.

Many feminists, and many other subaltern theorists, focus on these differences in output and the circumstances that generate them. In other words, they focus not on deep and abiding differences of principle between men and women, nor on the absence of such differences. Rather, they concern themselves with such things as women's experience and women's culture. I will call these thinkers and activists *feminists of cultural identity*. Feminists concerned with cultural identity may ultimately believe that differences of circumstance and output are the result of differences of principle, or they may view these differences in circumstance and output as the result of sameness of principle as worked out in an oppressive society. In other words, they may be difference feminists or diversity feminists. However, their focus is not on difference, in this sense, or diversity, but rather on experience and culture (or cultures, usually distinguished by race, class, and sexual preference). Indeed, difference and diversity are less important categories for other subaltern thinkers (for example, African-American theorists), while cultural identity is enormously important for them. This is presumably because such groups are more fully isolated, and thus have a more clearly distinct cultural identity (for example, in the United States, blacks and whites live in relatively separated communities; this is clearly not the case for most men and women).

Historically, most subaltern attention to identity has fallen under the category of "affirmation of cultural identity." For example, a wide range of feminists of this sort have been concerned to record and valorize unique aspects of women's life and work. More recently, however, some theorists have drawn on deconstruction, Lacanian psychoanalysis, Foucaultian historiography, as well as Marxist and related theories, to examine the complex ways in which identities are imposed on us, rather than discovered and affirmed by us. This view—which might be termed cultural constitution or construction of identity—remains close to some concerns of previous theorists regarding identity, but approaches identity by way of ideological critique, in effect combining the two tendencies.

Feminist literary practices are too multiple and diverse to catalog or exemplify here, especially as they do not easily fit into the main topic of the book—*philosophical* literary theory. It is worth noting, however, that a number of the preceding divisions have direct parallels in literary study. Basic feminism, with its concern for fair and equal treatment of women and men, corresponds most obviously to the work of feminists to have more women hired, tenured, and promoted in a range of educational institutions, to have them achieve equity in pay, and so on. But basic feminism also leads directly to feminist concerns with canon revision—the fair and equitable treatment of female authors. In a sense, canon revision is basic literary feminism. (Once again, there are parallel practices for African American, postcolonial, gay/lesbian, and other subaltern politics.)

A moderate form of feminist separatism has its most obvious counterpart in the development of women's studies programs. However, the intellectual principles that underlie and give academic force to the study of women's literature as such are at least parallel to a very moderate separatism. Consider, for example, the important study of literary relations among women writers, their implicit formation of a women's tradition partially distinct from the "mainstream" tradition of predominantly male authors. This study involves a qualified—and temporary—segregation of women authors in order to examine their various connections, influences, and so forth, and to compensate for prior critical biases and misrepresentations.

As we noted in the preceding section, feminist concerns often figure prominently in ideological critique. Such "feminist critique," as Elaine Showalter calls it, may focus on various aspects of a literary work or a body of literary works—the stereotypical denigration of women, the confinement of women to a narrow range of professional possibilities, the simple underrepresentation of women, and so on. This sort of critique arises most obviously out of the feminism of justice or the feminism of solidarity. In connection with this, we should also note that the various utopian feminisms parallel the many combinations of feminist criticism with other socially oriented theories, as in Marxist-feminist criticism, ecofeminist criticism, and so on.

Statistical/experimental feminism is not only parallel to some forms of literary study, it leads directly to such work as Mary Hiatt's stylistic studies of male and female writers. The same may be said of historicist feminism, in that literature is one primary area for the study of women's history, the development of an historically based understanding of gender, and so on. Both intuitionist and speculative feminisms bear importantly on literary study as well. The former is perhaps of more significance for pedagogy than for scholarship, as it tends to focus on the relation of literary works to the experiences of individual women readers. The speculative approach, in contrast, tends to be highly theoretical, as is clear in some of the more narrowly philosophical feminist critics, such as de Beauvoir and Irigaray, as well as those who make extensive use of philosophy, such as Gayatri Spivak and Judith Butler.

Feminism of difference too plays a prominent role in literary study, manifesting itself in many studies of putative differences between the styles or narratives of female and male authors, the responses of male and female readers, and so on. The feminism of human diversity, in contrast, has led most obviously to ideological critique—including critique of feminists of difference (see, for example, Susan Faludi's outstanding *Backlash*). Finally, feminists of cultural identity have been particularly important in literary study in recent years. One strain of this may be found in the work of Elaine Showalter and others investigating women's culturally distinct practices, experiences, professions, communities, and so on. This strain is typically integrated with historical feminism. Another strain, often more speculative in orientation, concerns the "construction of gender," the ways in which society—its discourses, institutions, sciences, arts—shapes and orients the categories through which we think and enact, or "perform," femininity and masculinity. Prominent theorists of this sort would include Judith Butler and Teresa de Lauretis.

As the last comments suggest, these literary approaches may be and are combined in a variety of ways. Once again, feminism is a broad, multifarious, and changing field of study. Indeed, this breadth and dynamism are part of the reason it is, perhaps, the most influential field of literary theory as well.

## Power, Science, Culture: Foucault, New Historicism, Bourdieu

Michel Foucault was a French social historian and philosopher of history loosely associated with both structuralism and poststructuralism. He is perhaps best known for his highly influential analyses of power. Part of the importance of Foucault's work in this area is that he did not limit his study to state power, or even focus in particular on state power. Rather, he addressed a wide range of power relations in a wide range of social structures. Moreover, he linked power to what he called "knowledge"—not "justified true belief" per se, but, roughly, systems of research, analysis, theorization, and so forth, claimed to yield or approximate such justified true belief; Foucault's concept of "knowledge" is, in this way, closer to "science" than to "justified true belief." In any case, for Foucault, power is not merely the strength of the state, and it is not merely brute force; it is a relation existing in all social structures and it is bound up with thought, study, systematic theorization. Conversely, "knowledge" (or science) for Foucault is not pure understanding; it is implicated in the power relations of social structures.

More exactly, from his earliest works on the insane asylum and the medical clinic, he was concerned with institutional structure, the way institutions arose and developed, how they changed, how they were associated with "knowledges" or sciences, how they currently operate, and so on. During the 1960s, the heyday of structuralism, his work moved more and more in a structuralist direction. He became concerned more narrowly with the structures of discourse in intellectual disciplines—including disciplines that did not have any obvious basis in institutions such as the clinic or the asylum. During this period, he sought to analyze the intellectual conditions that permitted and structured the development of fields of knowledge or sciences, ranging from economics to biology to linguistics. In doing so, he considered how these fields were defined, how they established authority, how methods of inquiry and theorization were developed, and so on. After 1970—in part as a slightly delayed response to the popular uprisings of the late 1960s—Foucault returned to institutions, and now focused more intensely on power.

All three "periods" of Foucault's work share certain characteristics. Primarily, they all involve the division of European history into periods and the isolation of a set of rules that putatively govern the knowledges/sciences dominant in each period—or, rather, each "episteme," which is to say, each historical period in which systematic theorization is defined by such a set of rules. (To say that the Renaissance episteme differs from that of the Classical episteme is to say that the set of rules governing the "production of knowledge" or articulation of theories in the Renaissance is relatively consistent and is different from the rules governing such production or articulation in the Classical period.) Moreover, all periods of Foucault's work involve a critique of standard views about scientific development. For Foucault, the changes in the ways theories are developed cannot plausibly be viewed as a matter of intellectual progress. In the structuralist period, Foucault does not focus on the reasons for these changes, but in his work on institutions, he argues that the changes are primarily a matter of institutional power (much as Marxists might argue that they are a matter of economic relations). It is also worth noting that in the structuralist period he emphasizes the differences between periods, indicating that they are marked by virtually unbridgeable ruptures. In other works, particularly those of his last period, he recognizes a greater degree of continuity between periods, tracing, for example, important views of the modern period back to Classical and Renaissance precursors, an intellectual continuity usually sustained by some sort of institutional continuity.

More exactly, in most of his works, Foucault develops a tripartite periodization of European history since the Middle Ages: the Renaissance, the Classical Age (roughly 1660–1800), the Modern period. This periodization governs both the structure of theories and the structure of institutional power. In the Renaissance, Foucault argues, knowledge was based upon "resemblance" and "interpretation." Objects and events were related by similarities that had a significance requiring interpretation. Thus human reason may be understood by its similarity to divine wisdom as a reflection of God in the human soul (*Order* 19); the walnut may be used to treat injuries of the head because its shape is so similar to that of the human brain (27); the length of the line on one's palm resembles the length of one's life and thus may be used to predict one's longevity (28), and so on. Viewed from the Modern episteme, Renaissance beliefs appear incoherent, a bizarre combination of theology, medicine, and superstition. But they fit together perfectly well in an episteme based on resemblance and interpretation—all structured and guided by divinity.

In keeping with this intellectual structure, relations of power in the Renaissance were focused on the power of the sovereign and on the "spectacle" of his/her power. In the Renaissance, punishment was a great staging of the power of the king or queen; the absolute power of the executioner over the condemned man resembled the absolute power of the monarch over all his/her subjects and was an interpretable symbol of that power. The expulsion of madmen from the cities, their confinement in ships or in the city gates, were interpretable symbols also, based on resemblance (the gate of the city resembling the liminal state of the insane), and so on.

In the Classical period, the episteme shifted away from resemblance understood through interpretation and became a matter of strict categorization based on analysis into components. This episteme defined knowledge as the exhaustive systematization of elements (such as the parts of a plant in botany), often graphically represented in tables. Foucault refers to this as "representation" in that it replaces a set of natural, interpretable resemblances between objects with a system of "signs" that functions to define and systematize such objects.

Power in the classical period is not a matter of symbolic expulsion or the staging of sovereignty, but rather of (systematic) confinement, on the one hand, and the manipulation of "representation," on the other. Specifically, it was during the Classical period that madpersons and criminals came to be confined in large numbers—in a sense, analyzed out of society at large, organized into prisons (as knowledge is organized into tables), rather than offered up for interpretation. In keeping with the general structure of the episteme, criminal law was gradually "rationalized" in the course of the Classical period—turned into a system of grading or tabulating offenses and punishments—and this was done in order to deter criminality by associating in people's minds the representation of crime with the representation of punishment, the fear incited by the latter serving to block action based on the desirability of the former (for example, the fear of prison serving to deter people from stealing something they desire but cannot buy, the representation of prison being associated with the representation of stealing in their minds).

In the Modern period, knowledge shifted to what is "outside" of representation, what provides its conditions, its invisible, underlying causes. Two such conditions came to have particular significance: language and the human subject or "man." The nineteenth- and twentieth-century sciences are deeply concerned with the status of language and of the human subject. Both are understood as highly internally structured and as providing the pattern of all knowledge, experience, and action.

In keeping with this focus on the internally rule-governed subject, power in the modern period has turned toward what Foucault terms "discipline." Discipline is the intensive focus on the training of subjects to think and behave in a strictly defined manner. Institutions in the Modern period are increasingly organized to foster such an intensive focus on individual subjects. In prisons, in mental asylums, in clinics—indeed, in schools and factories—power comes to be manifest in a sort of intensifying micromanagement of the actions and thoughts of the inmates (prisoners, madpersons, patients, students, workers).

Thus, prisoners and the insane are no longer hidden from view, analyzed out of the society, organized into cubicles. Rather, they are placed under continual, centralized observation (graphically represented in Jeremy Bentham's "Panopticon," a circular structure in which all the inmates are visible from a central point occupied by some institutional authority, some representative of institutional power). Moreover, in conjunction with such continual observation, inmates are subjected to the authority of criminal psychologists, psychiatrists, and others, who prescribe strict regimens to guide and restructure thought and action. First of all, these authorities define norms against which all subjects are measured. Then, insofar as someone deviates from the norms, his/her individual subjectivity is investigated in an effort to uncover the hidden cause of deviancy—in the unconscious ("He steals because he suffers from a compulsive disorder"), in social conditions ("She cannot do her schoolwork because she comes from a deprived background"), and so on.

It is important to stress that, in Foucault's view, this sort of investigation is not undertaken in order to "correct" deviancy. Rather, it is done to extend power. And the extension of power often involves sustaining and even furthering deviancy within an institutional structure. For example, Foucault points out that the prison system has never actually functioned to rehabilitate criminals. It has functioned, rather, to create a system of "delinquency" or habitual criminality which is in effect incorporated into the "carceral" system of power—the judiciary, the police, the penal institutions, and so on. This system of delinquency serves a number of functions. For example, by establishing contacts between the police and criminals, it helps to systematize police corruption (in, for example, complicity with drug trafficking or prostitution) and at the same time extend police surveillance (by establishing a system of informants made up of released convicts). Moreover, by way of police corruption, surveillance, and so forth, this system of delinquency helps to undermine revolutionary criminality, diverting the energies of the poor away from criminality aimed at class and property relations and toward nonpolitical criminality. This is not peculiar to the carceral system and criminology. All the "human sciences" and their related institutions operate similarly—not to rectify deviancy, but to maintain and extend relations of institutional power.

In keeping with this, Foucault argues that the authority of psychiatry, criminology, and so forth, is not the authority of truth, but rather that of power. That power, Foucault maintains, is becoming increasingly ubiquitous in modern society. Supported by the human sciences, society is becoming increasingly "disciplinary," increasingly organized by a structure of authority, norms, observation, the training of thought and behavior. (We shall return to this topic below.)

Needless to say, none of this is uncontroversial. As Foucault is often misunderstood as a sort of Idealist, it is worth noting that he does acknowledge that there is something distinct from discourse, and that it may be possible "to uncover and free . . . 'prediscursive' experiences [such as madness] from the tyranny of the text" [*Archaeology* 47]. His hesitancy on this matter is not, I take it, a matter of idealism or thoroughgoing relativism; it is not a matter of rejecting the very idea of "the Real," of saying that all ideas are equally valid/invalid, and so on. Rather, it results from his recognition of the ubiquity of power and the thorough interweaving of power and knowledge or theorization, an interweaving that makes such an "uncovering" overwhelmingly difficult. His concerns on this score are well founded, as much research has indicated (see my "Teaching and Research" and citations for some relevant studies), though he does at times seem to overstate the case and thus to risk undermining the truth-claims of his own theory.

The plausibility of his historical analysis is more questionable. Even when Foucault acknowledges continuities across periods, it is not at all clear that the periods he isolates maintain the internal coherence he assumes. There are two problems here. First of all, Foucault's major categories are so vague that it seems almost anything can be made to fit under them. "Resemblance" and "interpretation" are broad and somewhat amorphous concepts; so are "order" and "analysis." It would seem that the confinement of madpersons in the Classical age could easily be seen as a matter of resemblance open to interpretation—they are physically removed from the light of the sun and from the vision of society just as they are psychologically removed from the light of reason and from the community of reasonable people. Similarly, the internment of the insane in the city gates may be seen as a matter of ordering and categorization, a physical placement at a point in the city directly comparable to a representational placement in a table. Secondly, insofar as the categories are well enough defined actually to differentiate attitudes, thought patterns, and so forth, they do not apply so univocally to one period only. There seem to be so many exceptions to Foucault's divisions—even in Foucault's own account—that one is justified in wondering whether any general way of thinking is, in fact, more characteristic of one period than of another. For example, one wonders if it is really true that early schooling today is more "disciplinary" than that of the Renaissance or the eighteenth century. Perhaps it is, but Foucault doesn't really present us with evidence of this— most often, he presents us with examples or illustrations that clarify his point, but do not really support it. After all, it would be very easy to come up with examples from the twentieth-century schoolroom that make it seem lax and anarchistic, and much less disciplinary than the Renaissance schoolroom.

But, again, Foucault's broad analysis of the general relations between power and knowledge, as well as his concept of discipline and related ideas, are highly plausible and illuminating. Indeed, Foucault not only presents concrete historical analyses, he formulates a broad theory of "knowledge production," which is relatively independent of those analyses and which is perhaps of greater importance to literary theory. During the structuralist period, the central concept of this theory is that of the "episteme," which we introduced informally above. In *The Archaeology of Knowledge* (a transitional work between structuralism and the later institutional studies), Foucault provides us with a technical definition of "episteme" as "the total set of relations that unite, at a given period, the discursive practices that give rise to epistemological figures, sciences, and possibly formalized systems; the way in which, in each of these discursive formations, the transitions to epistemologization, scientificity, and formalization are situated and operate; the distribution of these thresholds, which may coincide, be subordinated to one another, or be separated by shifts in time; the lateral relations that may exist between epistemological figures or sciences in so far as they belong to neighboring, but distinct, discursive practices" (191).

For Foucault, a science such as linguistics or psychiatry is defined in part by a certain discourse and in part by institutional relations. A discourse includes several components: A set of ideas—for example, the idea that schizophrenia has a neurophysiological component, the idea that schizophrenia is a particular mental illness, even the idea that illness is an appropriate model for various mental phenomena; a vocabulary—for example, in modern psychiatry "schizophrenia" is a legitimate category, and is therefore part of the vocabulary, but "demonic possession" is not; rules of authority, or criteria determining who can speak authoritatively—for example, in psychiatry, authorities do not include priests, but do include psychiatrists; and so on. Each separate discipline constitutes a "discursive formation" along these lines. Simply put, the episteme is what all discursive formations have in common during any given period (such as a basis in resemblance and interpretation during the Renaissance).

Rules of authority provide a clear juncture between what might seem purely verbal or discursive, on one hand, and what is practical, concrete, institutional, on the other, for it is institutions that define authority in Foucault's sense. For example, it is medical schools and hospitals that define and sustain medical authority. In connection with this, one may distinguish authoritative discourses, such as medicine, from nonauthoritative discourses. As Foucault notes, in the cases he most often addresses, "none may enter into discourse on a specific subject unless he has satisfied certain conditions or if he is not, from the outset, qualified to do so." However, there is more variation across discourses than this implies. Specifically, "not all areas of discourse are equally open and penetrable; some are forbidden territory (differentiated and differentiating) while others are virtually open to the winds and stand, without any prior restrictions, open to all" (224–25). Unsurprisingly, this is not a constant situation. What counts as authoritative varies from period to period. Meteorology may provide a good example of a discourse that has only recently achieved the status of authoritative discourse. In Foucault's view, the scope of authoritative discourse is continually expanding (compare Dreyfus and Rabinow 48). More fields of study are coming under the control of authoritative "knowledge," and thus more ordinary relations are being subjected to institutionally structured relations of power. Given the nature of the discourses and institutions in question, this in turn makes society increasingly disciplinary; put differently, discipline (in Foucault's technical sense) spreads across greater and greater areas of social life. Psychiatry, once confined to severe dysfunction, now covers daily moods and motivations; certified authorities in nutrition and marriage appear where there were none before, then expand their treatments beyond illness and dysfunction to ordinary routines.

Another important concept articulated by Foucault in connection with his analysis of authority is the *énoncé*, or statement. The statement, in Foucault's use, is an utterance made by an authority in an authoritative discourse and understood in relation to the system that defines and authorizes that discourse. An example may be found in a psychiatrist's pronouncement that a given individual is criminally insane. This pronouncement is a statement by an individual who has a position of institutional and professional authority and through this authority is part of a system of power relations that may lead to incarceration for the individual in question.

Archaeological literary criticism, based on such works as *The Archaeology of Knowledge* or the more narrowly conceptual/structuralist *The Order of Things: An Archaeology of the Human Sciences*, may undertake a number of tasks. Most obviously, it may seek to locate a literary work within the episteme of its time, investigating, say, the various discourses in that work. For example, it might be of interest to examine Iago's "prosecution" of Desdemona in light of the English Renaissance discursive formation of jurisprudence, including contemporary notions of evidence and weight of testimony, rules as to who could testify, and so on. The lack of authority granted to Desdemona's words might be related productively to women's lack of a legal right to testify in court (see Maclean 77), to the development of "feminist" jurisprudence in the sixteenth century (see Maclean 79–81), or to other practices surrounding the testimony of defendants. This examination could be connected further with the marriage of Othello and Desdemona and with the "hearing" before the duke where both Othello, the alien defendant, and Desdemona, a woman, are allowed to testify in response to Brabantio's accusations.

Returning to Foucault's theory, the internal difficulty with Foucault's archaeological work is that it continually points toward a study of power as crucial to understanding epistemic structures, but it does not lead to or even clarify the nature of such a study. After *The Archaeology of Knowledge,* Foucault tries to compensate for this imbalance, focusing more on power as the central component of authoritative discourse (that is, of "knowledge" or science). As he put it in *Discipline and Punish,* "power and knowledge directly imply one another . . . there is no power relation without the correlative constitution of a field of knowledge, nor any knowledge that does not presuppose and constitute at the same time power relations" (27). He does not discard his earlier concerns with discourse, but he more strongly emphasizes the location of discursive formations in relations of power: "the subject who knows, the objects to be known and the modalities of knowledge must be regarded as so many effects of these fundamental implications of power-knowledge and their historical transformations" (27–28).

In this later work—usually termed "genealogy," in opposition to the preceding "archaeology"—Foucault introduces a number of new technical terms, such as "apparatus" (see "Confession"; see also Dreyfus and Rabinow 120–22). The apparatus is a complex of mutually supporting power-knowledge relations linking intellectual disciplines with institutional and related force. In terms of archaeological theory, the apparatus is the intersection of a discursive formation, such as psychiatry, and a set of relations of power, such as those that define an asylum. (Foucault adds that the apparatus arises historically from a particular, strategic goal, such as the treatment of indigents in the case of the asylum [195].) The apparatus is an important notion because, again, for Foucault power and knowledge are inseparable. A central part of the genealogist's task is necessarily "deciphering" the apparatus, analyzing the relations that define this complex of power-knowledge.

Of course, the most important concept of Foucault's last period is that of power itself. As Foucault continually emphasized, power in this context is not a solely negative concept. Power does not merely forbid, it also positively constitutes actions. As Foucault put it in an interview in 1977, "What makes power hold good, what makes it accepted, is simply the fact that it doesn't only weigh on us as a force that says no, but that it traverses and produces things, it induces pleasure, forms knowledge, produces discourse" (*Power/Knowledge* 119). The power relations of the asylum do not merely operate to limit the action of certain mental patients. They equally produce theories, courses of education and certification, systems of observation and interpretation, a range of pains and pleasures for the patients, and so on.

In his late essay "The Subject and Power," Foucault wrote that the analysis of power relations has five components (223). The first is determining "the system of differentiations," which is to say the criteria that distinguish groups so that one group may "act upon the actions" or control the behaviors of members of other groups. This system would include all gradations within an institution—even such minor hierarchical distinctions as "Administrative Assistant," "Secretary," and "Temporary Support Staff"—as well as larger divisions within society as a whole. The second component of such analysis is the determination of the objectives of the authorities "who act upon the actions of others"—for example, "the maintenance of privileges, the accumulation of profits," and so on. The third component involves attention to the "means of bringing power relations into being," "according to whether power is exercised by the threat of arms, by the effects of the word," and so on.

The fourth component of the analysis of power is the delimitation of the "[f]orms of institutionalization." This includes the variety of institutions, whether, for example, asylums are distinct from hospitals and prisons, whether there are different institutions for the "criminally insane" as opposed to the insane who are not criminal (or for the criminally insane vs. criminals who are sane), whether there are different institutions for those whose illness is judged organic versus those who are thought to suffer from a primarily nonorganic mental disorder, and so on. It also includes different types of institutional structure—for example, residential versus nonresidential, voluntary versus forced, and so on. The final component is the determination of the "degrees of rationalization," which is to say, the degrees to which the relations of power have been organized into systems of explicit, regulated, standardized procedures. Systems of this sort would include, for example, those governing admission to or release from a mental hospital, the routinization of daily life in the hospital, the limitation and regularization of patients' relations with the outside world, the structuring of administering medication, and so on.

Foucault's theorization of power and its five components may be applied to fictional apparatuses (say, fictional asylums) just as readily as it may be applied to real apparatuses. It may also be applied to looser social structures. For instance, the military structure of *Othello*'s Venice could be analyzed valuably in these terms. The system of differences, for example, is crucial, defining the initial conflict between Iago and Cassio. Moreover, this itself is in part a result of the fact that rationalization of military procedures reaches a sort of limit in the discretionary powers of the general (Othello). Indeed, one could argue that one problem in the play is that consideration of evidence is blocked repeatedly by the discretionary power given to institutional authority. For example, had the duke pursued Brabantio's case further, rather than closing it through his discretionary authority, perhaps Iago's plot could have been revealed earlier. Othello's decision about Desdemona's infidelity is a more obvious case. Indeed, the family or household (the relations between husband, wife, attendants, and so on) could be reunderstood in this theoretical context—then further related to such discursive formations as that of law, as noted above. This would, of course, involve not only textual analysis, but extensive work in social history as well.

Moreover, Foucault's ideas here may be applied not only to literature, but to the apparatuses of literary study. It is in some ways even more revealing to consider Shakespeare studies, or *Othello* criticism, as a locus of power-knowledge, than to consider *Othello*'s Venice in these terms. The systems of education, hiring, promotion, publication, and so forth—in short, the entire structure of the profession—is a clear case of a system of power-knowledge. It involves hierarchical distinctions at each level, with those higher in the hierarchy—dissertation directors, hiring committees, tenure committees, editorial boards, readers for presses—able to act upon the actions of others in the sense of deciding whether those actions have resulted in an acceptable dissertation, publishable article, teaching quality adequate for tenure, and so on. The examination of objectives would raise the issue of the degree to which this hierarchy does or does not serve to advance disinterested intellectual inquiry, as widely claimed, and the degree to which it too operates to "maintain privilege, accumulate profits," and so on. The examination of forms of institutionalization would draw our attention to the operation of power in the systems of state and private education, in the distinctions between university, college, and community college. A focus on rationalization leads us to consider the codified rules governing academic evaluation in tenure, promotion, hiring, the awarding of degrees, as part of a system of institutional authorization, and so on, as well as the points at which these rules are limited by the discretionary powers of institutional authorities.

If there is anything that Foucault teaches us, it is that we can hardly understand a system of "knowledge" without understanding the relations of power that traverse it. And this does not apply merely to psychiatry or criminology, to disciplines we are not in and people we do not know. It applies with all its critical force to us as well and to the discipline of literary study.

The literary movement most closely associated with the thought of Foucault is New Historicism or Cultural Poetics. In its broadest sense, New Historicism encompasses all historically oriented literary criticism that is simultaneously influenced by contemporary literary theory (such as Foucault and Derrida). More narrowly, it refers to a group of writers, including Stephen Greenblatt, Louis Montrose, and others, who combine elements of Marxism (the notion of historical determination), deconstruction (the idea that meaning is a function of differance), Foucault (the view that discourse and power are inseparable), as well as various feminist and other subaltern concerns. (Whether these theories are mutually consistent is not clear.)

The basic tenets of New Historicism would include the following (for a fuller discussion, see Veeser): First of all, every work of literature is firmly bound to its history and culture. Indeed, it is a part of that history. Thus history cannot be considered a mere background to a literary work, any more than the literary work can be considered background to political, legal, or other history. Indeed, all this political, legal, and other history is textual, or textually constituted (at least now). There is and can be no question of reliving the past. There can only be a reading of texts that define that past for us (in many ways, a Gadamerian point). New Historicism is, in part, a reading of political, legal, literary, and other historical texts through one another, as part of one history, or as part of culture (hence the name Cultural Poetics). As Louis Montrose puts it, critics need to stress both *"the historicity of texts,"* namely, "the cultural specificity, the social embedment, of all modes of writing," and *"the textuality of history."* In using the latter phrase, Montrose explains, he has in mind two things. First, "that we can have no access to a full and authentic past, a lived material existence, unmediated by the surviving textual traces of the society in question." Second, "that those textual traces are themselves subject to subsequent textual mediations when they are construed as the 'documents' upon which historians ground their own texts, called 'histories'" (20).

As this quote hints, despite their focus on the mutual relations among texts or histories, New Historicists stress the incoherencies within and across these texts and histories, their discontinuities. Montrose puts the point deconstructively, asserting that "the meaning of a text cannot be stabilized" (23). More broadly, there is no overarching organic unity to any given text and there is no standard worldview (or related unifying principle) for any given historical period. All historical periods and all texts are always already internally disrupted, internally disunified, and contradictory. This is in part due to (Marxist/feminist) conflicts of sex, race, and class, conflicts that may be repressed in a given text, but not eliminated, as well as other (Foucaultian) conflicts of institutional or disciplinary power; it is also due in part to the (Derridaean) disseminative, hierarchy-disrupting nature of language, or representation more generally (which we will discuss in the next chapter).

In keeping with these ideas, Greenblatt, the most influential of the New Historicists, follows Foucault (and Pierre Bourdieu) in situating literary texts within a field of power relations and in maintaining that these power relations are not merely negative—they serve "as the enabling condition of representation itself" (*Shakespearean* 2). Yet, he insists, these power relations are not simple; it is crucial that we "resist the integration of all images and expressions into a single master discourse" (2–3). (This may seem to be an anti-Foucaultian point. However, the target of such assertions is not Foucault's concept of the episteme, but the traditional notion of the worldview. Greenblatt's point is that we should not assume everyone or almost everyone in the Renaissance believed the same things about the monarch, the nature of society, religion, and so on. He does not appear to be addressing the Foucaultian notion that different discursive formations share abstract structural principles, such as a focus on resemblance and interpretation.)

More exactly, as to the relation between literature and history, Greenblatt notes that "Inquiries into the relation between Renaissance theater and society have been situated most often at the level of reflection: Images of the monarchy, the lower classes," and so on (11). In other words, the relation of a Shakespeare play to contemporary English culture has been conceived of narrowly in terms of how a given person or group or institution is represented in that play and how that representation relates to the real conditions of that person, group, or institution (for example, how Catholics are represented and how that representation relates to the actual condition of Catholics at the time). Greenblatt argues that the relations between literary text and history should be understood more broadly.

This seems a perfectly reasonable idea, though it is difficult to make much sense of the list of relations Greenblatt goes on to present. The first is "appropriation," the taking of things in the public domain, the "prime example" of which is "ordinary language," as in "Lear's anguished 'Never, never, never, never, never'" (*Shakespearean* 9). The second is "purchase"; here Greenblatt includes stage props and costumes (9). The third is "symbolic acquisition," either through "simulation" (an imitation of some historical/cultural act, such as a royal pardon), metaphor (for example, the substitution of pagan marriage for Christian marriage), or metonymy/ synecdoche ("performing one part or attribute of a practice" [11]). To my mind, this is a pretty incoherent typology of relations between text and history. It is neither consistent across types nor complete within a type. The complex, historical and cultural resonances of a work—its ideological presuppositions, its political implications, its tacit manifestations of cultural relations and traditions, its dhvani, its takhyīl—seem here reduced to a bizarre mixture of the notion that playwrights use language, that actors use props, and that scenes in plays imitate some cultural events, directly or indirectly, in whole or in part. In some ways, Greenblatt seems to have defined historical relations in such a way as to make them even more narrow, and even more crudely mimetic, than the traditional views he criticizes.

On the other hand, Greenblatt's purpose in drawing up this schema is to turn our attention to particular aspects of historical relations that he has found useful to examine in interpreting Shakespeare. The schema makes more sense if it is understood not as systematic theory, but as practical advice ("I've found that one can make surprising discoveries by looking at how and where a company got its costumes—from impoverished nobles, from defunct monasteries, etc."). Moreover, understood in this way, it is easier to see how such a schema can contribute to the striking and unexpected insights that one often discovers in New Historicist writing.

In terms of literary practice, New Historicists such as Greenblatt have taken up Foucault's practice of beginning their work with an "exemplary" anecdote that putatively characterizes the period in question—say, Elizabethan England—forcing us to see it as outside the limits of our own way of thinking. Foucault interprets various historical and literary cases as exemplars, teasing out cultural/historical implications through what is finally a sort of symbolic interpretation, though Foucault would no doubt reject this characterization. For example, Foucault begins *Madness and Civilization* with an analysis of the symbolism of the "Ship of Fools" in the Renaissance; *The Order of Things* starts out with a detailed interpretation of a Velasquez painting; *Discipline and Punish* begins with an exemplary execution.

As New Historicists have recognized, this practice is similar to what the American anthropologist Clifford Geertz calls "thick description"—the description of a social act that places it within a "hierarchy of meaningful structures" (Geertz 7) that give the act significance within a particular society. On the other hand, the parallel is not exact. Geertz's theory—or, rather, concept—is somewhat vaguely formulated and is ultimately a rehearsal of the hermeneutic valorization of interpretation over empirical investigation (itself a version of the Romantic dichotomizing of art and science). It is not clear that opposing interpretation and empirical study in this way makes much sense, and thus it is not clear that such an opposition really tells us anything about interpreting social phenomena, or anything else. In contrast, Foucault's analyses preserve some of the structuralist precision of *The Archaeology of Knowledge* in their integration of exemplar interpretation into a larger, theoretically well articulated system of discourse and power; moreover, again in keeping with his (limited) structuralist affiliations, Foucault does not stress the pseudo-opposition between empirical study and interpretation.

In any event, the attempt to read large social patterns out of a single case or a handful of single cases is highly dubious, for we have no reason to believe that the properties of any given event can be generalized. On the other hand, this sort of careful attention to a single exemplar can lead an interpreter to notice details that would go unnoticed if he/she were looking at a larger body of cases (from which broad patterns could be more validly inferred). And, again, it is the discovery and elaboration of just these unnoticed details that makes New Historicist writing valuable.

After recounting an anecdote along the lines of Foucault, New Historicists typically go on to consider a literary work in relation to that anecdote and, as Foucault might say, the discursive formation that surrounds it. For example, in a famous essay, Greenblatt takes up English Renaissance views of exorcism. He then considers, in relation to this, Edgar's pretense of being possessed—Shakespeare's "symbolic acquisition" of possession and exorcism in *King Lear*. He discusses not only how Shakespeare is drawing on the tradition of possession and exorcism literature, but how he simultaneously undermines the tradition, how this relates to the reception of Shakespeare by various audiences, and so on.

Specifically, Greenblatt notes that Shakespeare drew in particular on an anti-Catholic treatise by Samuel Harsnett in portraying putative demonic possession as a sort of theatrical fakery. Indeed, "*King Lear*'s relation to Harsnett's book is one of reiteration" (*Shakespearean* 120) in having Edgar falsely and theatrically mimic demonic possession. And yet this is an uncertain, self-undermining reiteration. It is not, like Harsnett's treatise, anti-Catholic propaganda. Quite the contrary. For example, considering the play as part of history, rather than as something merely to be placed against history as background, Greenblatt discusses the degree to which Catholics in England evidenced an interest in the play. And, looking to the narrative development of this faked possession, we find that Catholic engagement with the play is not surprising. After all, Edgar is not condemned in the play for his pretense of possession. Indeed, he is elevated, especially in contrast with characters such as Edmund, whose fakery is political and personal rather than religious. More exactly, Edgar's false possession is fully in keeping with what Harsnett says about Popish fakery, but Edgar has all our sympathy in this. In consequence, Greenblatt notes, the play involves—among much else—a "current of sympathy" for Catholics, which "is enough to undermine the intended effect of Harsnett's" treatise (*Shakespearean* 122).

Going further, Greenblatt argues that, while "Edgar's possession is a theatrical performance exactly in Harsnett's terms," Shakespeare's presentation differs from Harsnett's more broadly in offering "no saving institution." It cannot offer such an institution because, for Shakespeare, "the force of evil" cannot be confined to and identified with specific individuals or institutions. Thus everything becomes uncertain, questionable. As Greenblatt puts it, "In Shakespeare, the realization that demonic possession is a theatrical imposture leads not to a clarification—the clear-eyed satisfaction of the man who refuses to be gulled—but to a deeper uncertainty, a loss of moorings, in the face of evil" (127). By this analysis, then, Shakespeare is simultaneously asserting and subverting dominant views—manifesting the internal disruption and contradiction that has marked his and every historical period. Greenblatt goes on to note that this scene continues to speak to us today because we, in our own contradictory condition, feel the need for ritual and for the clear delimitation and expulsion of evil, but cannot believe in any such ritual, delimitation, or expulsion (128).

It is not at all clear that any of these conclusions is warranted. As to the "current of sympathy" with Catholics, the play does present fake possession as unobjectionable for an individual in extreme circumstances. But that hardly means that it in any sense justifies or defends what is reputed to be a systematic and exploitative use of fake possession by an institution. (By Greenblatt's reasoning, a story about a starving person who steals bread could be seen as involving a current of sympathy for the mafia.) On the other hand, this cuts both ways. In representing a single case of fake possession, the play can hardly be said to assert that possession is always or generally a theatrical pretense. In other words, it does not seem to take any stance on Catholicism and possession. (By Greenblatt's reasoning here, we could conclude that, for Shakespeare, being male is theatrical fakery, that everyone is really a woman—after all, some female characters fake being men, just as Edgar fakes being possessed.) Finally, as to identifying evil with specific individuals, the play seems to come pretty close in the cases of Goneril, Regan, Cornwall, and Edmund. But these are perhaps more objections to a specific reading than to New Historicist theory in general.

Regarding the literary works we have been considering, the "trial" scene of *Othello* (1.3) seems particularly appropriate for New Historicist analysis. As Maclean indicates, the laws and practices concerning trial procedures were not entirely consistent at the time the play was written and performed—an idea perfectly in keeping with New Historicist presuppositions. Nonetheless, there were laws and there were dominant theories underwriting those laws—theories that posited some sort of female inadequacy or inferiority, even when put forth in defense of women. For example, some aspects of law concerning women were justified by the view that women "act often against their own best interest because of weakheadedness" (Maclean 79).

The trial in the first act of *Othello*, it can be argued, finds its place in the very center of Renaissance jurisprudence, and at the very point of its contradictions. Brabantio accuses Othello of bewitching his daughter, convincing her to act against her own best interest. In doing this, he is implicitly claiming the authority of a guardian to decide what is best for a woman who is unable to decide for herself (presumably due to feminine weakheadedness). However, the status of guardianship was highly contested at the time (see Wiesner 4). More importantly, Desdemona herself enters as a witness on behalf of Othello and her testimony is taken as definitive. Indeed, she and Othello are the rational and truthful participants in the trial—a representation patently at odds with the paternalistic elements of contemporary jurisprudence.

The trial scene, then, may be understood as operating to challenge and disrupt the patriarchal theories on which much contemporary jurisprudence rested—though it did so on the basis of what were no doubt already a wide range of incoherencies in legal principles and practices. Moreover, it is not only located passively in an historical context. It is part of the discursive history in which the speech of women and the status of that speech is contested. The play in effect takes a position in the debate by reversing the standard patriarchal hierarchy of marriage law, vesting legal authority in the rational testimony of a woman and not in the hysterical accusations of a male guardian. (A genuine New Historicist reading would involve considerable elaboration of historical details—for example, in relation to specific laws or legal practices concerning elopement, abduction, etc.—and perhaps reference to relevant aspects of seventeenth-century responses to the play.)

Needless to say, a large number of theorists beyond Greenblatt, Montrose, and others have come in recent years to write on culture, expanding their discussions of literary texts beyond "high art" and the elevated history of monarchs, to include a far wider range of social phenomena and to consider literature as one such social/cultural phenomenon. One particularly influential writer who has sought to theorize the relations between various "levels" of culture—to understand their genesis and function—is Pierre Bourdieu. Given his recent importance among literary critics (including New Historicists), it is worth briefly considering some of the basic principles of his work, in part for their intrinsic value, and in part to give an example of another sort of work in philosophical culture study, beyond that of New Historicism or cultural poetics.

Perhaps the two most fundamental concepts in Bourdieu's theory of cultural production are the "field" and the "habitus." The field is the set of social restrictions, possibilities, roles, and rules that define any given area of culture. One could think of this in relation to, for example, basketball. The field would be the rules of the game, including the definition of five positions, each with a particular (relative) location and a particular function. Bourdieu argues that any given field is "independent of . . . politics and the economy," though it can be more or less "autonomous" (*Field* 162, 163; citations of Bourdieu refer to this work unless otherwise noted). Basketball, or rather professional basketball, is clearly embedded in the encompassing economic field. This does not affect the definition of the field itself (for example, the number of positions does not vary depending upon economic conditions). However, the operation of the sport—who plays for what team in what game, how many games are played, what the conditions of play might be—may be more or less governed by internal concerns or political/economic concerns, thus making the field more "autonomous" or more "heteronomous." For example, the structure of the season might be determined by what is most likely to identify the team that is best at playing basketball, or it might be determined by what will yield the highest profits in terms of ticket sales, commercial endorsements, and so on. In the former case, the field would be operating autonomously; in the latter case, it would be operating heteronomously.

Note that the very same principles apply to, say, literature as a field, if somewhat more loosely and implicitly. Literary works are organized into particular genres and subgenres, with distinct conventions, evaluative criteria, and so on. More significantly, people active in the field are organized into authors, editors, reviewers, publishers, each having specifiable roles and functions. Moreover, literature too may be more or less autonomous, more or less guided by literary concerns or economic imperatives.

The habitus is the set of individual behavioral dispositions, cognitive and perceptual schemas, and so forth, that guide individual action within a field. It would involve, for example, the rules and plays internalized by a particular basketball player. In literature, it would include what one is sensitive to or takes note of in reading a literary work (aspects of action or romance, aspects of characterization, aspects of dialogue, aspects of style or narrative structure, moral implications or themes, and so on) and, related to this, how one judges a literary work (for example, if one evaluates it in terms of excitement, or ethics, or stylistic complexity). Note that this is not merely a matter of one's profession. It extends to the various fields in which one lives one's life more generally and includes such matters as how one spends or saves money, what sort of house, furniture, car, clothes one buys, what sort of games one plays—not only what one can afford, but what one notices about a house, furniture, or whatever, how one evaluates these things, how one plays a particular game, and so on.

These dispositions are not necessarily open to introspection or choice. In some ways, they are similar to the internalized rules of a grammar (a connection made by Bourdieu, as Randal Johnson notes [5]). We are guided by the rules governing pluralization, but we cannot really introspectively determine these rules (most people, when asked, say that plurals in English are formed by adding "s," which is true only for words ending in unvoiced nonsibilants). Moreover, like grammar in Chomsky's theory, these dispositions are individual.

On the other hand, what is perhaps most interpretively important about the habitus is that it falls into clear patterns according to social category. Thus members of one economic class will share certain dispositions not shared by members of other classes; people living in the countryside will share certain dispositions not shared by people living in the city, and so on. For example, people in one social class will be more inclined to notice action and romance in a movie, and judge the movie in relation to these, while people in another social class will tend to notice and evaluate montage, and people in a third social class will look to moral themes; people in one social class will prefer one sort of furniture, and so on; people in one social class will focus on perfecting minute details in their work, play, while others will have broader or different concerns (see *Distinction* 173–74).

Bourdieu's first point of importance to literary study is that, in examining an author's development, we should turn first to the literary field in which the author was working. In other words, we should not begin with individual biography, noting the idiosyncratic details of the author's private life, but with an understanding of the social possibilities in which the author's life took place. Moreover, if we turn to biography, our focus should be on the habitus of the author, usually by reference to the various groups of which he/she was a member—his/her economic class origin, and so on.

Consider Shakespeare. I have been arguing that there is a sort of tacit antiracism in *Othello*. In a Bourdieuean analysis, I might go on to examine the range of positions available on race. (This may not strictly be a Bourdieuean analysis as attitudes on race probably would not constitute a field in the strict sense; however, the spirit of the investigation would be the same.) For example, I might determine that there are four or five different positions white writers standardly adopted on race: (1) an "animalist" position in which blacks are seen as lacking a human soul, (2) a sort of "chosen race" position in which blacks are viewed as having a soul, but as having been rejected by God, (3) a Christian universalist position in which blacks are judged to have immortal souls which should be saved by conversion to Christianity, and so on. I would seek to isolate these positions by examining a very broad range of writings—literary and nonliterary—dealing with race. From here, I might wish to go on to examine what led Shakespeare to the Christian universalist position. Our lack of knowledge about Shakespeare's life would not be too inhibiting from this point of view as we could look at characteristics of the various groups to which he belonged (economic class, place of birth, occupation), seeking relevant, and explicable, patterns. Was one view more likely to be held in towns (as opposed to cities or rural areas), by the petit bourgeoisie, and so on? Moreover, I might extend this to characters. Iago certainly invokes the animalist position when informing Brabantio about Desdemona's marriage. Does this fit his class origin? And what of Brabantio, who seems to accept this position easily?

In addition to this general theory of field and habitus, Bourdieu has set forth a specific theory of the way in which "the field of cultural production" (including the field of literary production) works. In at least some of his writings, this more specific theory is, I believe, marred by Bourdieu's somewhat inconsistently maintained assumption that hierarchy in the autonomous part of the cultural field "reverses" the "economic world" of ordinary commodities and thus of popular literature (see 29; see also *Rules* 81, 83). In this view, a work is, roughly, judged valuable in the cultural field insofar as it is not valued in the larger economic field, or at least does not make immediate appeal to a mass audience. There is certainly an element of this in much elite evaluation. Indeed, if elite evaluation merged too systematically with popular response, it would lose its distinguishing characteristic and thus would no longer mark an elite. However, the situation seems more complex. Specifically, one might argue against Bourdieu that elite cultural evaluation is bound up with economy and thus with audience in a way that does not differ essentially from popular cultural evaluation. There is, of course, some difference between the evaluation of elite and popular works. However, this is not, it would seem, a matter of one set of cultural works (the popular) appealing to consumers and another set of cultural works (the elite) not doing so. Rather, it is a matter of one appealing to one audience, while the other appeals to a different audience. Issues of prestige can certainly go along with this—as they do with foods, such as cream cheese and caviar. But cream cheese and caviar remain commodities that operate economically in much the same way.

Bourdieu addresses the issue of different audiences—or markets—in terms of "restricted" and "large-scale" production. Elite cultural works are generated by restricted production for a limited audience. Popular works are generated by large-scale production for a general audience. Bourdieu sometimes identifies the limited audience of elite works as "producers of cultural goods" (115)—artists, writers, critics, and so on. There are certainly cases where this is true—for example, when works of elite literature find their primary market in the university. Indeed, it may even be true in general that "producers of cultural goods" form the primary market for elite literature. However, first of all, this does not support the

view that elite literature does not participate in the same economic relations as popular literature. Everything here is economic in the usual sense.
Teachers are purchasing a product, and they choose that product based on
a number of factors—what will draw students, what will be suitable for
filling class time, what is most amenable to the generation of publishable
articles, and so on. Moreover, as Bourdieu notes elsewhere, there are not
simply two types of literature and audience. Rather, there are different
levels of "avant-garde" art, "works of bourgeois art aimed at the nonintel-
lectual fractions of the dominant class," "works of middle-brow art aimed
at various target publics" and "crowned by the big literary prizes," and so
on (127). In this way, even the broad distinction between elite and popular,
between restricted and large-scale production, appears overly simple.

On the other hand, even if the division between elite and popular, restricted and general, must be understood as a distinction of degree, not of
kind, it is clear that there are tendencies in cultural production of just the
sort described by Bourdieu, and that they are very important for our understanding of literature, art, and so on. Moreover, the elitist function of
the various gradings of art—their function in allowing some people the
status of a cultural elite—is clear and consequential as well, as Bourdieu
has discussed at length in *Distinction.*

In any case, Bourdieu's theory is not confined to this broad contention
about the relation between elite and popular culture. As part of this theory,
he develops several valuable and influential concepts, prominently including consecration, symbolic capital, legitimation principles, and cultural capital.

Consecration is the simplest to define. It is merely the establishment of a
work or individual or group as authoritative within a field. It is roughly
equivalent to the colloquial "canonization," but one can reserve the latter
term for the academic variety of consecration, which most often develops
quite slowly. As Bourdieu points out, there is typically a significant "time
lag between cultural production and scholastic consecration." The distinction is valuable as schools are among the "institutions of cultural conser-
vation" (124). One could think of canonized works as both consecrated
and conserved.

Symbolic capital is the status or prestige of the consecrated objects or
persons in a field relative to one another or relative to objects or persons
excluded from consecration. For example, consecrated authors such as
Toni Morrison have more symbolic capital than unconsecrated authors
such as Sidney Sheldon; or, to take an example from the academic field, a
Harvard professor has more symbolic capital than a professor at a state

university, who, in turn, has more symbolic capital than a professor at a community college. Bourdieu specifies his general contention about mass and elite culture in relation to symbolic capital, maintaining that there is a "negative relation . . . between symbolic profit and economic profit, whereby *discredit* increases as the audience grows" (48); "the artist cannot triumph on the symbolic terrain except by losing on the economic terrain . . . and vice versa" (*Rules* 83).

Again, this seems to be an oversimplification. Indeed, Bourdieu acknowledges that symbolic capital has economic and political elements that are simply denied in "bad faith" (a concept we will discuss in a moment): "'Symbolic capital' is to be understood as economic or political capital that is disavowed, misrecognized . . . a 'credit' which, under certain conditions, and always in the long run, guarantees 'economic' profits" (75). In connection with this, he stresses that the economic cycle for elite works is long rather than short (that is, an elite work may sell well in the long run, but not in the short run [see 97–101]). Once again, however, this economic situation is best accounted for by seeing elite cultures as defined by different markets from popular cultures, rather than seeing them as defined simply against popular market success.

Legitimation principles are the principles by which consecration is guided. According to Bourdieu, authority in the cultural field is defined by a broad legitimation principle according to which new consecration is bestowed by already consecrated authorities in the field (that is, previously consecrated authors, critics, and so on), or, more exactly, previously consecrated persons with a high degree of symbolic capital. Thus, well-established, long-consecrated authors and critics praise a new author—especially perhaps one who has not achieved popular market success or, more properly, one whose works are addressed to the appropriate (restricted) audience. This new author then comes to be "consecrated" him/herself—winning prizes, giving prestigious lectures, entering course syllabi, achieving scholastic consecration or canonization, and judging still newer authors him/herself.

Within the cultural field, the establishment of consecrated authorities necessarily implies that these authorities have authority due to some sort of expertise. Their judgment must somehow be distinguishable from that of ordinary folk. In part, this is a matter of symbolic capital—which is, of course, entirely circular (they have authority because they are consecrated because they have prestige, and so on). In part, however, it is a matter of a type of competence, which is manifest in one's writing, conversation, and so on. In the case of literature, this might involve a certain sort of familiarity with literary history, movements, schools, and so on, an understanding of the usual rankings of various works (that is, a knowledge of which writers and what works have been consecrated), a fluency in the idioms of literary discussion, and so on. Note that this is not only, or even most importantly, a matter of serious disciplinary knowledge. It is, rather, largely a matter of fluency in conventions that are in many ways similar to etiquette. For example, this sort of competence in literary study would involve knowing that currently one is expected to deplore New Criticism and celebrate historicism, to speak of "texts," not "books," to discuss "construction," rather than "inference," and so on. This competence, acquired especially in family upbringing and in formal education, Bourdieu calls "cultural capital." (It is worth noting that Bourdieu's concepts may be applied outside the cultural elite. In some groups, competence respecting football would count as cultural capital; competence respecting ballet would not.)

Bourdieu emphasizes that the consecrated elite in the cultural field see themselves as underprivileged relative to those unconsecrated writers and artists who have achieved material success, usually through acceptance by the bourgeoisie and petit bourgeoisie. Put simply, cultural and symbolic capital just do not grant the same social power as economic capital. In connection with this, Bourdieu introduces the notion of "homology." He argues that the elite fraction of the class of "cultural producers" (writers, artists, and so on) sees its position as parallel to that of economically dominated classes because its economic position within the field of cultural production is homologous to the position of the working classes within society as a whole. Simplifying somewhat, we could represent the idea in the following manner: bourgeois (heteronomous) writers/elite (autonomous) writers//bourgeoisie as a whole/proletariat as a whole. As a result of this homology, the cultural elite often expresses solidarity with the economically oppressed, at times even going so far as to view its own artistic endeavors as "revolutionary" in exactly the same sense that worker agitation is revolutionary. The cultural elite, in short, often comes to see itself as the cultural wing of a broad revolutionary movement; indeed, it often comes to see itself as the most truly revolutionary part of that movement.

Anyone who has read any literary theory will immediately recognize the truth of Bourdieu's claim here, at least with respect to certain groups in certain periods. It is not clear that revolutionary claims are quite as widespread as Bourdieu seems to imply. For example, as Bourdieu stresses, elite culture is simultaneously opposed to bourgeois and to popular culture. The resentment of the cultural elite is, in consequence, as likely to express itself in antipathy toward the economic masses as antipathy toward the economic elite. Moreover, it is not clear that revolutionary claims, when they do occur, are principally the result of homology. They might with equal or greater reason be said to result from market concerns about producing new and innovative works (in other words, claims about a revolutionary approach to the novel or to literary interpretation have much the same function as advertisements that boast "a revolutionary new concept in hair styling"), combined with resentment against a common enemy (the bourgeoisie, or more generally anyone with money), and related factors. Nonetheless, claims of this sort do occur with surprising frequency. For example, in recent years, cultural elites in the universities have regularly insisted that the newest, hyper-elite literary theory is truly revolutionary, the genuine vanguard of the liberation of the oppressed. Even more importantly, anyone with any critical sensitivity will equally recognize the truth of Bourdieu's analysis of this revolutionary zeal as a matter of bad faith.

"Bad faith" is a concept that Bourdieu draws from Sartre. Sartre distinguishes bad faith from both sincerity and simple deceit. Bad faith is, in effect, deceit of others that is equally self-deceit—not repression in the psychoanalytic sense, but a refusal to admit to oneself what one fully recognizes. Consider a tenure committee looking at the cases of two candidates, a standard case of legitimation. One of the candidates is personally well liked by the committee; the other is not. The committee lavishly praises the first candidate, with little attention to his record. However, they begin to scrutinize the record of the second candidate, questioning everything she has done. First, they ask if the book manuscript was actually done by the candidate—maybe her husband worked on it. When it turns out that she did the work herself, they then wonder if the manuscript was really refereed by the press that is publishing it, even though it is an academic press. When it turns out that the manuscript was refereed, they begin to look for problems in the candidate's teaching—maybe her evaluations are misleadingly high, and we can prove this with an unannounced classroom visitation, and so on. The members of the committee are clearly setting out to harm the second candidate. However, in most cases, they will say that they are "upholding academic standards" (or even "upholding academic standards against affirmative action," if the candidate happens to be nonwhite). Clearly, this is not a sincere statement. If they were "upholding academic standards," in however misguided a fashion, they would raise the same questions about other candidates. Indeed, this sort of super-critical scrutiny often occurs when a candidate has less symbolic capital than competitors—when the candidate is nonwhite, is a woman, has graduated from a state school rather than an Ivy League school, and so on. On the other hand, it seems unlikely that this is a simple case of deceit in which the tenure committee members fully recognize what they are doing and just lie about it. It seems most likely to be bad faith. They are lying to others and to themselves. (For Bourdieu's views on bad faith in education, which fit quite well with the preceding example, see Jenkins 158–60 and citations.)

### Postmodernism

"Postmodernism" is a term used to refer to a range of practices, conditions, and theories putatively distinctive of the current time. The term "postmodernism" derives, first of all, from the name of one tendency in literature and art after World War II. This tendency is generally understood as a revolt against certain aspects of "high Modernism," including various formal and aesthetic features (such as its seriousness), but primarily its elevation of art as a way of piecing together a fragmented world, a way of understanding, structuring, making sense of life. It is not that postmodern writers question the possibility of *art* accomplishing this goal. Rather, they question, or even deny, the possibility of anything accomplishing that sort of encompassing synthesis or meaningful unification of life.

Contemporary theorists of postmodernity draw on this literary meaning of the term, but qualify and reorient it in various ways, which it is important to keep in mind. Specifically, "postmodern culture" is the culture that gives rise to the "postmodern condition" of fragmentation, meaninglessness, and so forth—though fragmentation and meaninglessness of which we are in effect unaware, as there is and can be no state of unity, meaningfulness, and so forth, with which this could be contrasted. "Postmodern literature and art" and "postmodern theory," in contrast, are works that represent and reflect upon postmodern culture and the postmodern condition—sometimes to celebrate, sometimes to criticize, sometimes to understand without any overt evaluation. Thus "postmodernism" refers to a sense or experience of human life ("postmodern condition"), a set of cultural phenomena that give rise to that sense or experience ("postmodern culture"), a set of artistic representations of that postmodern condition and/or culture ("postmodern literature and art"), and a discursive analysis of all this ("postmodern theory").

This division into condition, culture, literature, and theory marks a conceptual distinction, but it should not necessarily be taken to constitute a sharp division in reality. Specifically, one tenet of much postmodern theory is that, in postmodern society, all discourse, indeed all thought and action, are encompassed by postmodern culture and are part of the postmodern condition. In other words, literature, art, and theory do not and cannot stand above culture, in a position from which they can analyze and critique it without being caught up in it. Literature, art, and theory are all part of the same incoherence and meaninglessness.

Of course, there are ambiguities. For example, many writers, contrary to their theoretical claims, tacitly privilege literary art as allowing us some special insight into culture, as implicitly comprehending that culture rather than merely expressing or reproducing it. Moreover, in practice, even the most radical postmodern theorists necessarily assume that their own theories somehow escape "co-optation" by postmodern culture, that their own writings do at some level make sense of postmodern life—otherwise there would be no point in putting forth such theories. Clearly the ideas summarized in this section are attempts at analyzing postmodern culture, efforts at understanding and even ameliorating the postmodern condition (though without necessarily trying to give "meaning" to postmodern life), efforts at adopting a theoretical stance that is, in some sense and in some degree, removed from the postmodern chaos.

More exactly, postmodern theorists see the postmodern condition as one of meaningless incoherence in which everything becomes "free-floating, ecstatic and haphazard," as Jean Baudrillard put it (*Transparency* 10). There is nothing that links our diverse momentary experiences, nothing that synthesizes the "manifold of experience." There is only "a profusion of images *in which there is nothing to see.* . . . They leave no trace, cast no shadow, and have no consequences" (17). The phrase underscored by Baudrillard, "in which there is nothing to see," is the crucial one. It is not merely that there is fragmentation—of experience, of thought, of society. More importantly, in this view, there is nothing beyond this fragmentation, nothing that the fragments are or were part of. (We will return to this point below.)

For some postmodern theorists, such as Baudrillard, the postmodern condition radically alters the structure and function of the human mind. According to Marx, the industrial revolution gave rise to a new sort of alienation, to fetishism of commodities—the reduction of relations between persons to relations between commodities; it effectively made the human being into an extension of the machine. Subsequently, the industrialization of culture—the transformation of music, narrative, visual art, and all other aspects of human cultural life into mass-produced commodities—gave rise to a "one-dimensional man," in Marcuse's phrase. A one-dimensional person is so thoroughly alienated that he/she is not aware of any dissatisfaction with the current order; the structure of things as they are so entirely usurps his/her understanding, and destroys reflection, that it produces "a false consciousness which is immune against its falsehood" (Marcuse 12), immune to what is called "consciousness raising." (Consciousness raising here is a—in my view, highly problematic—form of ideological critique that relies on an appeal to an oppressed person's experience of oppression, as when a worker comes to an awareness of the exploitative relations between workers and capitalists by recognizing and articulating his/her own experience of exploitation in a factory.) In a similar way, in Baudrillard's analysis, the postmodern condition produces a human being who is, one might say, a mere extension of the media around him/her, a sort of computer terminal. As Baudrillard puts it, "The cybernetic evolution, in view of the equivalence of brain and computer, places humanity before the crucial question 'Am I a man or a machine?'"

This is, obviously, a romantic dilemma, opposing humanity to mechanism. Postmodern thought in this way is an extension of Romanticism (with the significant difference that the "cyberneticization" of humanity is as likely to be welcomed as regretted by postmodern theorists). Part of the reason for this continuity is that both postmodern theorists and Romantics are deeply Kantian. For example, Baudrillard's idea of a "free-floating" and "haphazard" postmodern experience—a conception of the present that he shares with many contemporary thinkers—is a sort of technological version of Kant's "manifold of experience," the fragmentary whirl of unsynthesized sensations. Indeed, postmodern theory is in many ways an extended meditation on the very problems addressed by Kant—the possibility of a synthesis of a manifold of experience, the existence of a transcendental object or reality independent of this synthesis, the possibility of a teleology of nature, and so on. However, postmodern theorists conceive of these as problems of the particular historical moment of the postmodern, the result of specific technological and related developments, not as general epistemological dilemmas.

More exactly, we may organize the claims of postmodern theorists into four broad categories. The first concerns our experiential environment, the Umwelt of Husserlian phenomenology, what we directly synthesize (or fail to synthesize) in experience. The second concerns the objective reality corresponding to that experience. The third category focuses on the subject's sense of personal identity and purpose; like the first category, it concerns synthesis, but synthesis of one's own subjectivity, rather than synthesis of the objects of experience. The final category concerns the broader principles that structure life and underlie personal identity and purpose. These categories are, again, roughly Kantian. Thus, we could say that the first category concerns the manifold of experience and the synthetic activity of the understanding. The second category concerns the noumenon. The third category concerns the transcendental subject. And the final category takes up purposiveness, both the subjective purposiveness of nature (or the objectal world) and the ethical purposiveness of the transcendental subject (a crucial part of Kant's system, examined in his second critique, *The Critique of Practical Reason*). On the other hand, the claims made by postmodern theorists are more Hegelian than Kantian. First of all, they concern a problem that is historical rather than universal and social rather than individual. Secondly, they tend to deny or at least ignore the noumenon.

The most fundamental assertion of postmodern theorists is that, as Jameson puts it (drawing on Husserlian terminology), "the subject has lost its capacity actively to extend its pro-tensions and re-tensions across the temporal manifold and to organize its past and future into coherent experience" (*Postmodernism* 25; unless otherwise noted, subsequent citations of Jameson refer to this text). Specifically, in the postmodern period, we are all subjected to a vertiginous flux of unsynthesized and unsynthesizable experiences, crashing in upon us from everywhere. These experiences are not direct, of course, but mediated by television, cinema, video, audio recording, computer. We look at the television and see something happening right now in Bosnia, something that happened yesterday in Somalia, something that happened fifty years ago in Italy; driving in the car, we hear reports on or recordings of a similar range of events, while passing huge billboards with faces of people from somewhere else at some other time. There is no way we can make sense of all these phenomena, put them together. They won't fit; too many pieces are missing. They lack even the most basic coherence in space and time, the fundamental organization given by the Kantian forms of sensible intuition. In this way, these experiences all seem, to a degree, unreal. Indeed, they are mixed up or intertwined with more straightforward or conventional unrealities. We see a news report on Washington only a few minutes before the beginning of a situation comedy taking place in Washington. Worse still, the situation comedy is more developed, more coherent. Fictional, shallow, and implausible as it may be, the situation comedy appears to us more real than the news bulletin, a bulletin that is itself all staging, a scripted show, created for effect and for sales—just like a sitcom.

Thus reality begins to fade. We know that some experiences purport to be real and others purport to be fictional, but they are no longer strongly marked, clearly distinguishable. There are no longer any clear cases. Our whole life comes to be pervaded by a sense of irreality. Fabricated, broadcast, digitalized, cabled, computer-mediated sensations and words usurp any more direct experience. We drive to work listening to the radio, interact all day by telephone or video console, return home and watch television all evening, then sleep. Everything comes to have the same tone—uncertain, undifferentiated, a twilight world between waking and sleeping. Jameson refers to this as "the *derealization* of the whole surrounding world of everyday reality" (34). Contrast another sort of experience: You walk to work, interact face-to-face all day, go to the park or the pub, perhaps go to a puppet show (a fiction unmistakably marked off from reality) or some other popular, live entertainment. (Of course, most of us do have face-to-face interactions, and manage to synthesize billboards. Moreover, one might legitimately ask if an evening of reading is not as unreal as an evening of TV. The contrast may be much less than it seems.)

As I mentioned a moment ago, postmodern theorists tend to deny or to ignore the noumenon, or at least they are widely interpreted in this way. Indeed, the basic premises of postmodern theory indicate that reality is, in effect, a nonissue. For the whole point is that the vast encompassing media society operates to seal us in a sort of prison of images. On the other hand, as critics such as Christopher Norris have pointed out, this does not prevent reality from proceeding without us—along pretty horrific lines. Even if it is true that "we" Americans and Europeans, or "we" Americans and Europeans of a certain class, can no longer synthesize the manifold of experiences foisted upon us by the media, and even if we no longer have any clear sense of reality distinct from the hyperreality of mass media and cyberneticization, there are still things going on in Bosnia, Somalia, and Washington. After the Gulf War, Baudrillard wrote that the war never took place (*La guerre*). Christopher Norris takes this claim to mean just what it says, that the war did not take place, or that its taking place or not taking place is irrelevant because the media-constructed appearance, the "simulacrum" (as Baudrillard says), replaced the reality (see Norris). In consequence, he criticizes Baudrillard's claim harshly for its intellectual incoherence and moral irresponsibility.

On the other hand, perhaps Baudrillard meant merely that the Euro-American perception of the war did not "take place" in the sense that it did not operate in a real location, a *place* and physical reality, that it was, rather, entirely fabricated, a simulacrum. And perhaps this is the way in which we should interpret his claims more generally. Under this interpretation, Baudrillard was, to a great extent, correct: most Europeans and Americans experienced the war as moments of video games flashed on screens between Pepsi commercials in a senseless and unsynthesizable array. Indeed, those who conducted the war also conducted their campaign primarily within the imaginary space of virtual reality. This may well be what Baudrillard had in mind, for he acknowledges the real horrors of the war—the deaths, the human suffering. Insofar as Baudrillard had this in mind, Norris's objection does not hold. Baudrillard's evident denial of reality is not a denial of its existence or of its importance, but of its broad accessibility, and thus its function in general human life.

Of course, even under this interpretation, he still overstates the point. The falsity and ideological function of government propaganda about the war were discoverable with a little research; the facts about the war were available to anyone who sought them (and Baudrillard, to his credit, sought them). Moreover, Baudrillard has a highly objectionable tendency to forget that not everyone in the world lives in hyperspace—consider, for example, the hundreds of thousands of dead and wounded Iraqis, or, for that matter, the American veterans suffering from the "Gulf War Syndrome."

Still, there may be a certain point to Baudrillard's claim—the near ubiquity of the simulacrum may produce a phenomenon akin to that of Marcuse's one dimensionality. It so thoroughly isolates many of us from any nonideological experience, and so saturates us with dominant ideology, that it can render "consciousness raising" almost impossible, at least in certain areas.

Again, postmodern theorists not only insist that we are unable to synthesize the Umwelt of experience or to gain any sense of a reality underlying that experience, they also stress that we are no longer able to achieve a sense of continuous personal identity, defined by goals or even desires. Baudrillard insists that we no longer have anything to pursue because of "the very availability" of what "we had been pursuing" (*Transparency* 4). At one level, this is a wild exaggeration—and a cruel one, in a world where tens of thousands starve to death every day (according to Oxfam America, 40,000 children alone die every day of hunger). But for the middle classes in bourgeois democracies, it is not an unreasonable claim. We have what we need. Our lives cannot be organized by a struggle to survive, or even by a struggle for comfort. Our sense of self is not, often, a function of achieving some long-term plan, unless that plan is "Get lots of stuff!" We seem to consume for the sake of consuming. Or, rather, we consume things that are there to be consumed because they are presented to us for consumption, and because we believe that other people are likely to consume them (because they believe we are likely to consume them, and so on). To paraphrase Jameson, we might say that we retrospectively think that we have needed or wanted something because we are given a name for that thing that other people seem to be using to refer to something they retrospectively needed (see Jameson xiii)—"Wow, PEPSI, just what I wanted!" With each new name, our desire and our sense of self, shift again ("Wow, high resolution TV, just what I wanted!").

In connection with this, Baudrillard has distinguished three stages of value: "a natural stage (use-value), a commodity stage (exchange-value) and a structural stage (sign-value)" (*Transparency* 5; see *L'Échange* 17–19). In the first stage, we simply use objects; for example, we eat the food we grow, live in the dwelling we build, and so on. In Marxist terms, this is the first ("primitive communist") stage of social organization, prior to accumulation, private ownership, and so on. In the second stage, we accumulate commodities and exchange them for other commodities, either directly or through the use of money. However, this accumulation and exchange always leads to use; we accumulate and exchange in order to acquire something else that we will, in fact, use. In the third stage, we exchange purely in order to exchange. In the first and second stages, exchange-value is ultimately parasitic upon use-value in that all exchange must lead to some use. In the third stage, however, the use of commodities is, precisely and solely, for exchange. There is no use distinct from exchange, merely a continual circuit of exchange within a system that defines relative exchange-value. This is the "structural" stage of "sign" value in that it is akin to a pure system of signification removed from any relation of reference whatsoever. Indeed, in this stage, all forms of circulation (economic, linguistic, and so forth) no longer operate primarily at the level of representation, making reference to some distinct reality (a use-value for a commodity, a literal referent for a linguistic sign); rather, they operate at the level of "simulation," a sort of massive and encompassing pseudo-reality. We purchase commodities (from vegetable dicers to exercise machines) which we do not use, but which we have seen actors and actresses pretend to use on television—a simulation of use value. The language of news, sitcoms, docudramas, advertisements, all makes a show of reference. But it never does, ultimately, refer. It is a cacophonous or melodious sequence of jingles and sound bites which repeat words that are supposed to be repeated, but which connect to nothing except other words: "revolutionary new product," "fiscal responsibility," "high academic standards." (Subsequently, Baudrillard adds a fourth, "fractal," stage [see *Transparency* 5], in which there is a complete loss of value; even the equivalence relations of exchange-value are replaced by "pure contiguity" [5]. However, it is not clear that this is substantially different from the structural stage as explained in *L'Échange*. For example, he explains both in terms of simulation and lack of reference [see *L'Échange* 18 and *Transparency* 5–6].)

There are a number of problems with this view of things. First of all, most of us do in fact use the vast majority of what we buy. We eat the food we buy, drive the car we buy, sleep in the bed we buy. Moreover, it is not clear to me that words are used far less referentially today than before— after all, the vacuous use of words has always been one symptom of sophistry. On the other hand, it seems that Baudrillard and other postmodern theorists have isolated some significant issues here, especially with respect to commodities. Upper-middle-class people, especially those of Europe, North America, and Japan, but also those from other parts of the world, are in what is probably an historically unique situation. Their immediate needs and wants are easily satisfied, leaving them with disposable income and a baffling array of consumable items. Indeed, even many of those people who cannot be sure of satisfying their needs and wants— and it is very important to remember that such people constitute the vast majority of the world's population—are still caught up in this system of consumerism. For example, in Delhi, I have seen televisions operating in hovels made of rags by the side of the road. This pathetic development does not show that the people living in these hovels were economically irresponsible. Rather, it shows that they could never hope to save enough money for a decent place to live, and thus decided to spend what little they had accumulated on an old television, and that even in India the society is structured by a mass proliferation of consumer goods that go beyond need or natural desire. Moreover, in many cases (though, again, far fewer than Baudrillard indicates), people do purchase these commodities and never use them, or use them once, then pack them into a closet or basement.

Postmodern theorists emphasize that this rampant consumerism is linked to the total loss of larger structures, "fundamental rules," "criteria of judgement," and so on (Baudrillard, *Transparency* 14). It is part of the disintegration of purposiveness (to come, at last, to our final Kantian category). It is part of the loss of what Jean-François Lyotard calls "master narratives." It is, in effect, the substitution of consumption for more encompassing, vital, human goals and life structures that are now lost.

Specifically, Lyotard argues that there are two ways of knowing: narrative and scientific. (Again, the Romantic opposition of art and science.) Narrative knowledge is practical, communal, traditional, contextual. Manifested in proverbs, tales, and so on, it guides members of a community in speaking, hearing, and acting (21). Scientific knowledge, in contrast, is abstract, antitraditional, and so on. In earlier periods, narrative knowledge was dominant. People were able to structure their lives—understanding themselves and the world around them—by reference to overarching stories. These stories made sense out of life, gave it coherence, goals, meaning. In short, these were stories people could use to guide and evaluate their lives. The most obvious plots of this sort (though not mentioned by Lyotard) are religious. The Christian story of faith, suffering, salvation, and eternal bliss, when truly believed, gave meaning and purpose even to the most banal acts of everyday life. Great revolutionary ideologies served the same purpose. And, less grandly, so did such tales as "The American Dream," a story of hard work or a good marriage leading to financial security and years of joy in the bosom of a happy family.

While these narratives are clearly important in all sorts of ways, Lyotard is concerned more narrowly with narratives that have operated to legitimate scientific knowledge. According to Lyotard, these narratives are of two sorts: (1) those claiming that science leads to truth, and (2) those claiming that science leads to human betterment. The point can be generalized, for these are the primary justifications of religious and social movements as well.

In any event, Lyotard tells us, no justifying or "master" narrative is available any longer. "Modernism" involves an attempt to maintain such master narratives; "I define *postmodern* as incredulity toward metanarratives" (xxiv). Lyotard here seems to indicate that, now, God is dead—and so are the divine narratives of truth. The revolutionary ideal of practical emancipation was killed in the Gulag. The bourgeois dream of "success," endless human betterment through higher paychecks and a family that bowls together, ended in divorce, the loneliness of retirement centers—and pointless consumerism. The postmodern condition is, then, once more, a condition of "haphazard" experience, random desire (or pseudo-desire), fragments, unsynthesizable due to the absence of any larger structure (any master narrative) into which they might be integrated.

In addition, according to Lyotard, in "the postmodern world," "Most people have lost the nostalgia for the lost narrative" (41), which can be a bad thing or a good thing. One result of the loss of master narratives, according to Lyotard, is that "performativity" becomes the only criterion for evaluating knowledge. Knowledge is no longer a matter of either absolute truth or liberation, but of simple productivity; it is reducible to monetary profits and losses. In the university, for example, knowledge is not a matter of articulating a correct theory; nor a matter of educating students so that they can be free. Rather, it is a matter of producing the ideas and the people needed for capitalist production (specifically, for information production, as postmodern capitalism is more a matter of information than of industry [see 48]).

On the other hand, the loss of master narratives, if accompanied by a loss of nostalgia, can lead equally to a more positive result, the acceptance of diversity: "Postmodern knowledge is not simply a tool of the authorities; it refines our sensitivity to differences and reinforces our ability to tolerate the incommensurable" (xxv; again, a Romantic idea—it enhances negative capability). In other words, master narratives give "meaning" to our lives in part by devaluing all alternatives (racial, cultural, sexual); the loss of such narratives—and the loss of desire for such narratives—means the loss of "meaning," but also, perhaps, the loss of ethnocentrism, heterosexism, and so on.

I for one am not at all sure that Lyotard is right on either count. It is unclear that society today is any more performative than it ever was, for knowledge was always bound up with class interests; and it is not at all evident that there is a greater acceptance of difference today than formerly, for tolerance seems to have varied a great deal historically. Nonetheless, there are a number of writers who share Lyotard's views on the problems and possibilities of postmodernity.

One similar perspective is developed by Donna Haraway in her influential essay "A Cyborg Manifesto: Science, Technology, and Socialist-Feminism in the Late Twentieth Century." Here, Haraway takes up the common postmodernist metaphor of the human who is half machine; however, unlike some other writers, she uses it as a positive image for overcoming the oppressive "politics of identity" which base political action on group identity (identity as a man or woman, as white or black, and so on). In Haraway's view, "we are all . . . hybrids of machine and organism" (150). While this condition could be repressive, it might also be a valuable "confusion of boundaries" which could contribute to a "postmodernist . . . world without gender" (150). By undermining rigid distinctions, such a "cyborg" (non)identity might allow us to eschew all oppressive identities (those of race, class, sexual preference, and so forth). However, such undermining of identities need not reduce us to uncoordinated and fragmented individuals unable to work in political solidarity, for, as cyborgs, we are all part of an "integrated circuit" (149); we are all linked in a network that operates to undermine individualist boundaries. In Haraway's view, then, the postmodern condition allows new possibilities for overcoming domination, both through the concrete circumstances in which it places us (the integrated circuit of communications technology) and through the "Cyborg imagery" which this makes available to inspire the deconstruction of identity politics and the establishment of "a powerful infidel heteroglossia" (181), a heterodox multiplicity of voices.

The connections between literature and postmodern social theory are clear in general terms. However, a number of writers have analyzed literary postmodernism directly and extensively. For example, having treated postmodernism and knowledge in "The Postmodern Condition," Lyotard considers the function of postmodern literature in "What is Postmodernism?" Postmodern literature retains the general characteristics of postmodernism, specifically its lack of unifying master narratives. However, according to Lyotard, it does not have the dual character of postmodern culture in general. Rather, postmodern (or avant-garde or experimental) literature is linked with the tolerant strain of postmodern culture, which values difference. In addition, it is opposed to literary realism, which, in Lyotard's view, is linked with performativity and uniformity.

Specifically, Lyotard sees realism as a nostalgic and, crucially, consumerist substitute for the master narratives, an item made salable by its stabilizing representations of identity and of reality, representations that operate to make life appear unified, simple, communicable (see 74, 75). Think, for example, of situation comedies about devoted friends and loving families who live well-structured, stable lives, and who go through minor crises that are easily and warmly overcome within thirty minutes; or consider the way television melodramas structure terrible suffering and personal crisis into well-packaged stories about "the healing care of loved ones" or "the struggle for hope" or "using one's own suffering to do good for others."

Indeed, using these last three examples—which I jotted down at random—we could extend Lyotard, noting that each such effort at stabilization could be seen as a sort of "performatively" simplified version of a prior narrative or sub-narrative, which has now lost its function. Each is, in a sense, the fragment of a master narrative, now retold not for its truth (which almost no one honestly affirms) and not for its edifying effects (which almost no one honestly considers), but merely for its sales. Thus "the healing care of loved ones" may be understood as deriving from the bourgeois narrative of marriage and family, with changes to accommodate, and mitigate, their palpable disintegration; "the struggle for hope" is, in effect, a mundane version of the Christian combat against despair, the soul-destroying sin of Judas; and "using one's own suffering to do good for others" is a kind of commercial revision of the story of Jesus.

In any event, in contrast with all this, Lyotard tells us, avant-garde experimentalism disrupts our sense of identity and of reality, bringing us face-to-face with the disunified, complex, and incommunicable.

Clearly, what Lyotard is claiming here has much in common with the theories of the Romantics. His conception of "performativity" is similar to, for example, Schiller's notion of the modern mechanization of sense. And his idea of the function of avant-garde experimentalism is close to Schiller's notion of aesthetic education. It is no surprise, then, that Lyotard invokes Kant's seminal idea of the sublime in order to explain the function of avant-garde experimentalism. This experimentalism operates to undermine unity, simplicity, and so forth, precisely because it is not beautiful, but, in being sublime, evokes what is beyond conception—thus certainly what is beyond performativity.

Of course, not all postmodern theorists agree with Lyotard here. Indeed, according to some theorists, postmodern culture is so pervasive that it virtually co-opts everything. In other words, it is so all-encompassing that it can take any "oppositional" idea or action and immediately use it toward its own ends, for its own self-perpetuation. In this view, then, there can be no truly oppositional avant-garde in Lyotard's sense. Experimental techniques from literature, cinema, art, and music are immediately incorporated into commercials selling cars or perfume, without causing the slightest disruption to the system.

This co-optation is in part a function of the pervasive irony, or even self-parody, of postmodern culture. Advertisements involve self-mocking exaggerations. Celebrities and politicians play roles that teeter on the edge of being parodies of those roles (as when Rush Limbaugh appears on *Late Night with David Letterman* in an obviously fake commercial for a fictional pork product; he holds a meat tin aloft, smiles, and announces: "Big Ass Ham"). Almost nothing is quite straight. Almost everywhere, there is an edge of irony (except in the banalized master narratives of melodrama, and perhaps even there). In a culture of pervasive irony, what solemn belief or practice could avant-garde art take as an object of attack?

In this view, challenging postmodern culture through experimental art is like fighting shadows or the air. There is no hard surface there to resist the blows, and thus to be overcome. This argument seems to have a good deal of truth in it. (For an insightful discussion of co-optation, see Graff.) However, it finally shows, not the impossibility of challenging contemporary social structures, but the vapidity of claims that this challenge is most effectively undertaken by experimental art involving radical formal innovation. In my view, it points back to the necessity for ideological critique.

Lyotard's concern with performativity, like the concern of other postmodern theorists with consumerism, serves to link postmodernism closely with capitalism. At several points, Lyotard draws attention to this connection and stresses its importance. Frederic Jameson takes up this theoretical link and develops it influentially in his award-winning volume, *Postmodernism, or the Cultural Logic of Late Capitalism*. Specifically, Jameson believes that there is coherence underlying the discontinuous flux of postmodernism: "I want to suggest that our faulty representations of some immense communicational and computer network are themselves but a distorted figuration of something even deeper, namely, the whole world system of a present-day multinational capitalism" (37). Our bewilderment in the vortex of postmodern society is a "symbol and analogon of that even sharper dilemma which is the incapacity of our minds, at least at present, to map the great global multinational and decentered communicational network in which we find ourselves caught as individual subjects" (44; Jameson uses the phrase "cognitive mapping" to refer to the structural understanding of complex phenomena—an understanding we have not been able to achieve in postmodern society/multinational capitalism).

Multinational or "late" capitalism is, for Jameson (following Mandel), the full development of capitalism, its conquest of all areas of life, the reduction of all value to exchange-value. As Jameson explains, "This purer capitalism of our own time thus eliminates the enclaves of precapitalist organization it had hitherto tolerated" (36). It invades all areas of culture, in effect totalizing the culture industry as discussed by Horkheimer and Adorno, so that there are no longer any cultural "footholds for critical effectivity." Now, "not only punctual and local countercultural forms of cultural resistance and guerrilla warfare but also even overtly political interventions like those of *The Clash* are all somehow secretly disarmed and reabsorbed by a system of which they themselves might well be considered a part" (49). Again, every form of resistance is immediately co-opted. Jameson, however, does not see the situation as hopeless. Rather, he calls for a "new political art" which will achieve "a breakthrough to some as yet unimaginable new mode of representing" the "world space of multinational capital"; thereby allowing us to "regain a capacity to act and struggle which is at present neutralized by our spatial as well as our social confusion" (54).

There are many questions that one might raise about this analysis. Even leaving aside the issue of whether we are really living in the postmodern condition as characterized by Jameson, Baudrillard, Lyotard, and others, one might take exception to Jameson's leap from analogy to causal connection. After all, the fact that we are unable to synthesize the vast network of multinational capitalism and the fact that we are unable to synthesize the manifold of daily experience does not, in and of itself, indicate that the latter is a result or instance or dialectical development of the former. Indeed, one might reasonably ask if either form of disorientation is unique to the postmodern condition. Did medieval peasant farmers synthesize their daily experiences, or the larger economy? Can we even say that Scholastic philosophers did? Similarly, one might question Jameson's broad assertions about cultural co-optation, as well as his specific example (a rock band)—might not various organized social movements (from the women's movement to the peace movement), even individual marches or actions, even individual people involved in those movements (such as Noam Chomsky), have been more appropriate cases for consideration? One might also wonder whether "we" really do lack "the capacity to act and struggle" at present, especially as some people at least seem to be acting and struggling. On the other hand, Jameson is certainly correct that the consumer economy of today is at least in certain respects quite different from the capitalist economy of, say, the nineteenth century. And, insofar as we do live in a postmodern condition, this economic change is clearly relevant.

In applying postmodern theory to a literary work, we may consider the work to *express* the postmodern condition, to be caught up in that condition and defined by it, or we may consider the work to *represent* the postmodern condition, in other words, to approach it critically, with the aim of understanding it. If we are considering a work as an expression of postmodernity, then we are likely to examine it for characteristic signs of the postmodern condition—meaningless fragmentation, and so on. If, however, we consider a work as a representation of postmodernity, we will look for an understanding of the phenomenon more along the lines of a theory of postmodernism.

For example, we might consider the events recounted in Ali's "I Dream It Is Afternoon When I Return to Delhi" (see appendix) as an instance of a postmodern inability to act in a world where there is no clear distinction between illusion and reality, dream life and waking life, the images produced by postmodern culture (cinema, journalism) and the direct but incomprehensible images of real social life. All experiences are fragmentary. In the culture industry, he sees the ending of the film without the beginning, reads headlines isolated from their stories at the *Times of India*. In social "reality," he hears a disembodied voice, sees disembodied hands and handcuffs. There is nothing to hold all this together, to give it coherence and meaning. The only form of coherence is mere repetition, circularity—or, rather, a repetition of social practices deprived of function, a recurrent waiting for a bus that never comes, or comes but never reaches a destination. What the speaker is continually offered instead of social and personal coherence or meaning is money, or the threat of punishment for nonpayment. All things, all experience and expectation, all constraint (silver handcuffs) and reward (silver rupees), are thus reduced to exchange-value, to economy, though an economy that (in keeping with Jameson's views) is itself entirely fluid, unreal, uncertain, mysterious, unmappable.

# 5

# Philosophy of Language and Linguistic Autonomism

## Formalism, Bakhtinian Dialogism, Structuralism, Deconstruction

The mainstream of philosophical literary theory in recent years has been based in various forms of continental philosophy of language and linguistics. The first section addresses two relatively early instances of this: Russian formalism, especially the work of Jakobson, and Bakhtinian dialogism. The next section turns to one of the most important interdisciplinary movements of the modern period: structuralism. The section begins with the linguistic principles of de Saussure, which remain pervasive in literary theory. It then turns to one exemplary instance of a formal semantic approach to literary study, that of Greimas. The section concludes by considering some elements of Chomskyan linguistics and the related interpretive theories and practices of Claude Lévi-Strauss. The final section takes up the work of Jacques Derrida. Deconstruction, which develops directly out of structuralism, has had virtually unparalleled influence in literary theory over the past twenty-five years.

### Russian Formalism and Bakhtin

Russian formalism developed in the early years of the twentieth century. Suppressed by the Soviet government, it virtually disappeared in the USSR. However, it exerted considerable influence in Europe, both indirectly (through its influence on structuralism) and directly (through translations and applications). Though not, strictly speaking, based on philosophy of language, formalism centrally involved linguistic theory and was highly influential on more narrowly philosophical theories, for which it provides necessary background. Formalism was the first widely influential scientific approach to literature. Like all other literary movements, it includes a diversity of views and approaches within its ranks; but all formalists shared a concern to isolate and systematize the definitive features of literature. For this reason, formalism tends to be a theory of literature rather than a theory of interpretation, though it does involve interpretive elements.

Formalists were first of all concerned with understanding the unique or distinctive characteristics of poetic language, what set poetic language apart from ordinary speech. For the most part, the formalists took up the Romantic view that literature makes things strange, allows us to see what had become ordinary and thus invisible. It "defamiliarizes." Thus Victor Shklovsky focused on the "habitualization" that characterizes our ordinary relation to the world, and that desensitizes us to events, objects, people. Art operates to make this world "unfamiliar"; "art exists that one may recover the sensation of life" (741). This is, clearly, a variation on a common theme extending back to Schiller and others.

Roman Jakobson, a major figure in both formalism and structuralism, and a member of the Prague School of linguistics (which was, in effect, intermediate between Russian formalism and French structuralism), emphasized a different aspect of making strange. In developing a "science of literariness" (that is, a science of the uniquely literary qualities of literature), Jakobson stressed the internal structure of the literary work rather than its relation to human experience. Jakobson distinguished six elements of any communicative situation: (1) the sender (or speaker), (2) the receiver (or hearer), (3) the message, (4) the code in which the message is sent (that is, the language), (5) the context or referent of the communicative act, and (6) "a physical channel and psychological connection" between the sender and the receiver (66). According to Jakobson, different types of language use emphasize different communicative elements. For example, ordinary communication places emphasis on the verbal and nonverbal context. Poetic language, in contrast, emphasizes or "foregrounds" the message itself, the verbal particularity of the communicative act at all levels of complexity—phonological, morphological, and so on.

In connection with this, Jakobson set out to examine in detail the linguistic devices employed in poetic language. Interpretively, he sought to understand the significance of syntactic, morphological, and other narrowly linguistic patterns in particular works. In ordinary speech, a pattern in the use of, say, present participles, plural sentence subjects, or subordinate clauses has no importance beyond its functional relation to contextual matters, such as responding to a question or directing someone's attention. In the present paragraph, for example, I have thus far begun three of the four sentences with a prepositional phrase. And two of these four sentences have singular pronouns for syntactic subject. However, this is all purely incidental to my "referential" aim. In other words, in writing this paragraph, I set out to express my ideas about a certain object or topic clearly. I then choose words, phrases, and so on, that I believe will achieve this task. I do not pay any particular or separate attention to the form the words take as I write. (For Jakobson, there is, in ordinary communication, some concern with the message per se, but it is not primary, as in poetry.)

In poetry, however, this is not the case. If I were writing poetry, I would be very concerned with the form of my expression, not merely in the sense of looking at meter, but in the broader sense of attending to formal properties of words, phrases, and so forth, in themselves and in relation to one another. Moreover, according to Jakobson, the resulting linguistic patterns are not only important in themselves, they are relevant to an interpretive understanding of the poem.

Due to its linguistic focus, Jakobsonian analysis of these foregrounded patterns could easily fall under structuralism. Indeed, Jakobson's most famous analysis of this sort is contained in his article on Baudelaire's "Les Chats" (chapter 11 of Jakobson), co-authored with Claude Lévi-Strauss and considered a paradigm case of structuralism. However, due to its emphasis on the formal properties of poetic language, this approach fits equally well under formalism. I should like to illustrate it by discussing Agha Shahid Ali's poem (see appendix). This is clearly a poem about loss, the emigrant's loss of his/her native country and culture; more broadly, the loss of one's past. Semantically, the poem develops this theme by establishing a situation in which the speaker desires a return to his past or, equivalently, desires a cycle of time in which the past does not disappear. But he continually finds his desire frustrated. Though it is not immediately obvious, the formal devices of the poem contribute directly to the development of this theme.

Consider, for example, the use of verbs. The overwhelming majority of the verbs in the poem are continuous present; in thirty-nine lines, Ali uses over a dozen continuous present tense verbs or present participles (in effect, an adjectival form of the continuous present-tense verb). Though each of these is justified "locally" by the referential context, this accumulation, this pattern also functions separately. The continuous present in English conveys process and continuity, but a sort of narrow continuity, the continuity of a current action that necessarily does not extend far back into the past. Moreover, it indicates a lack of completion. We use the continuous present when we are engaged in an act that is not finished. The sense of incompletion fits perfectly with the speaker's sense of loss—or, rather, his sense that he cannot return in a fulfilling or resolving way, that the future excludes any possibility for completing his incomplete past in his native country.

Almost all the other verbs are present tense as well, reinforcing the focus on the narrow, futureless current moment. The past tense is used only four times: "I've saved this change for you," "you haven't changed," "it was your voice," and "I've bought an extra ticket." The first, second, and fourth are present perfect. They concern an act in the past (as indicated in the past-tense inflection of the main verb), but the act leads to a current state or condition (as indicated in the present tense of the auxiliary verb). This is precisely the state of irresolution that is treated referentially: he is given money and a ticket, but cannot use them; he has not changed, but all of India has changed.

Perhaps the most revealing use of tense in the poem is that of the future. Though "The film is about to begin" has a sense of futurity, it is actually present tense and refers to a present state. Thus the only true future tense verb in the poem is contained in the line "Any moment she'll be buried alive." It is important that both these sentences refer to a very immediate future. The poem contains no vision of a distant future, of any longer term. Moreover, the only genuine future tense is also in passive voice: she will be buried. The future is not an action, but an imposed condition to be suffered. Finally, if we take account of the referential context here, we see that the future is specifically loss—not real death, but living death. Anarkali was being led away from the man she loved and who loved her, separated from him against her will and against his. The future envisioned in this poem, the future of the exiled speaker, is a future of separation and confinement.

Clearly, none of this is absent from the referential communication of the poem. But the linguistic devices of the poem—here, the uses of tense—while coherent with that reference, do not seem to be a mere by-product. They are patterned in such a way as to have independent significance.

Other members of the Prague School similarly focused on formal linguistic features and on the differences between the use of language in poetry and in ordinary speech. For a theorist such as Jan Mukarovsky, poetic language is defined by its violation of the norms of ordinary language. As he put it in "Standard Language and Poetic Language," "the standard language is the background against which is reflected the esthetically intentional distortion of the linguistic components of the work" (861). For Mukarovsky, ordinary language is "automatized," much as ordinary life is "habitualized" for Shklovsky. (In the development from Shklovsky to Mukarovsky, we witness another instance of the increasing emphasis on textualism, the movement from a focus on subjectivity to a focus on language, which has marked much literary theorization over the last century.) The foregrounding of poetic language, then, functions to make us aware of language; it operates to make language strange, to defamiliarize it. Thus it is crucial for Mukarovsky that poetry violate the norms of ordinary speech. On the other hand, poetry itself can become automatized—poetic innovations become conventions; what was once innovative becomes banal, the object of widespread imitation. Thus the norms of poetic language too must be violated.

Mikhail Bakhtin is almost the precise antithesis of formalists and Prague theorists such as Mukarovsky. Where the formalists studied the ways in which literary language was different from ordinary language, Bakhtin was concerned with, and valued, those literary works that encompass what he saw as the diversity and vitality of ordinary language. Where the formalists saw the literary work as an isolated verbal object, Bakhtin valued literature precisely insofar as it incorporated and was incorporated into dialogue. Where the formalists focused their attentions on poetry, Bakhtin devoted himself to the novel. Writing at about the same time as the Formalists, Bakhtin—some of whose work was also suppressed by Soviet authorities—in some ways came much closer to deconstruction and New Criticism, though in other ways his work is very different from these as well.

More exactly, in the standard post-Romantic fashion, Bakhtin draws a broad distinction between two types of discourse. The first sort, the "discourse of authority," is the unquestionable discourse of dominant people and dominant ideas (religious, moral, political, scientific, and so on). According to Bakhtin, this is linked with "epic" works of literature. "Epic," in Bakhtin's sense, may include works that are not long poetic narratives. Epic is more importantly defined by a series of other properties. Thus epics, for Bakhtin, present themselves as having a definite, fixed meaning that is completely determinate. They concern events that take place in a distant inaccessible past, a past that is historically unrelated to the present and that is entirely unfamiliar or strange to contemporary readers, but that is presented as unquestionably superior. These works most often rely on a sacred and putatively infallible tradition for subjects and themes, and present the official view of the ruling elite. Finally, they have a solemn tone and employ a stylized language. One might think here of Milton's *Paradise Lost*. It concerns a distant and ideal past, removed from historical time. It addresses a traditional and sacred topic with a solemn tone and elevated diction. Its message is presumed to be clear, determinate, and complete—to "justify the ways of God to men" (1.26).

The second sort of discourse isolated by Bakhtin is "internally persuasive discourse." This is a discourse that convinces us, a discourse that we are inclined to accept as a basis for thought and action—not because of some supposedly authoritative origin (the State Department, the pope), but because of what it says. Related to this, internally persuasive discourse is a discourse with which we interact, not one imposed on us from above. It is open, antidogmatic, and contemporary or at least linked with our current situation and experience (that is, it is "relevant," as we might say). On the other hand, we do not simply accept an internally persuasive discourse once and for all—that would turn it into a dogma, an authoritative discourse. Rather, we continually bring it into *"struggle* with other internally persuasive discourses" (346). In the process, the internally persuasive discourse is "questioned . . . put in a new situation in order to expose its weak sides, to get a feel for its boundaries, to experience it physically as an object" (348). We do this in order to define our "own discourse" and our "own voice" and not merely to accept an "alien discourse," even one that is internally persuasive (348). This is necessary, Bakhtin maintains, for, "An independent, responsible and active discourse is the fundamental indicator of an ethical, legal and political human being" (350).

Consider, for example, literary theory. The dominant theory at any given time, or the dominant premises shared by a range of theories, are very likely to be maintained and repeated in a discourse of authority. Today, particular presuppositions about the nature of language—for example, the presupposition that it is structured by difference in a roughly Saussurean/Derridean manner—are likely to be presented as unquestionable truth. This authoritative discourse is perhaps most visible in the use of certain phrases, for example, "As Derrida has taught us," "As we now know," and so on. Note that the authoritative presentation of a given theory does not in any way imply that the theory in question is intrinsically authoritarian—Bakhtinian zealots may well say "As Bakhtin has taught us," but this hardly means that Bakhtinian theory is itself necessarily or inherently an authoritative discourse. Note also that a theory may be repudiated in an authoritative discourse. When New Criticism is dismissed as "naive" or as "reactionary," as is standard today, it is unquestionably and absolutely devalued through an authoritative discourse.

In contrast, a theory may be presented in such a way as to encourage readers to explore its insights and its problems, to examine its arguments, to study its possibilities for application. A theory may be presented in such a way as to encourage readers to think about the claims and implications of the theory, to work through them. It may be presented in such a way as to allow readers to consider whether or not it is internally persuasive, or how it should be revised. In other words, it may be presented in such a way as to foster in each reader a concern with defining his/her own voice.

The struggle of different discourses is associated by Bakhtin with the novel and, by extension, with all works of literature that share the novel's definitive characteristics (that is, all works that have been "novelized," as he puts it). The novel is, according to Bakhtin, an endlessly changing genre, always open, flexible. Its meaning is always rent by uncertainty, indeterminacy, difference, or heterogeneity. In contrast with the epic, the novel does not address a distant and inaccessible past, but a living present or a historically related past; there is always a "zone of contact" between us and the events of the novel, a zone that is crucially "familiar" to us. Perhaps the most crucial property of the novel is linguistic. Unlike the rarefied language of epic literature, the language of the novel and of novelized literature is not removed from daily interaction. Indeed, it is entirely submerged in such interaction.

Everyday speech is always embedded in dialogue, both "externally" and "internally." Externally, it is always a response to earlier speech, and it leads to later speech. John says something in response to Jane, who in turn replies, and so on. Internally, everyday speech incorporates the ideas, discourses, "voices" of many others in a tense interrelation. As Bakhtin puts it, "any concrete discourse . . . is entangled, shot through with shared thoughts, points of view, alien value judgments and accents" (276). For example, when I say something about Bakhtin, my speech incorporates the voice of Bakhtin with many other voices from my past—for example, deconstruction, to which I compared Bakhtin earlier, but also contemporary linguistics, cognitive science, and other voices that have gone to form my own voice (now speaking about Bakhtin in a particular way, with particular purposes, and so forth). Thus, I necessarily speak in such a way that Bakhtin is partially altered, partially challenged, partially supported. I engage in *"dialogic interaction"* with Bakhtin's voice. Moreover, I may consciously undertake to further this interaction—as, for example, when I set out to apply Bakhtin to Shakespeare. In this case, I "take [Bakhtin's discourse] into new contexts, attach it to new material, put it in a new situation in order to wrest new answers from it, new insights into its meaning" (346), or so I hope.

Speech, then, is naturally *dialogic,* and its natural dialogism can be extended and intensified in this way. Only the discourse of authority can stifle this dialogue, making speech *monologic,* the assertion of an incontrovertible doctrine. The novel and all novelized literature are, according to Bakhtin, dialogic. Conversely, epic literature is monological. Bakhtin writes that "Within the arena of almost every utterance an intense interaction and struggle between one's own and another's word is being waged, a process in which they oppose or dialogically interanimate each other. The utterance so conceived is a considerably more complex and dynamic organism than it appears when construed simply as a thing that articulates the intention of the person uttering it, which is to see the utterance as a direct, single-voiced vehicle for expression" (354–55). The discourse of authority and "authoritarian" (287) epic literature seek to reduce the utterance to "direct, single-voiced . . . expression." The epic poet seeks to make language "an obedient organ, fully adequate to the author's intention" (286), "unitary and singular" (287). The epic poet "strips the word of others' intentions" (297), in effect de-dialogizing language. In novelistic genres, in contrast, the author sets out to multiply and intensify the diversity of voices, the variety of discourses. Unlike the epic writer, "a prose writer can distance himself from the language of his own work . . . can make use of language without wholly giving himself up to it" (324). The novelist can "express authorial intentions . . . in a refracted [rather than direct] way" and thus can use *"another's speech in another's language,"* creating a discourse that is "double-voiced" and "dialogized" (324).

Related to dialogism is Bakhtin's notion of heteroglossia. While dialogism is a function of any (unstifled) speech within a given community, heteroglossia is more specifically a dialogic incorporation of that which is linguistically and culturally different or outside. (Actually, heteroglossia may be nondialogic as well—if the different languages and cultures are merely catalogued or otherwise gathered into a static structure that does not involve mutual interaction [see, for example, 287–88 and 295–96]. However, as this is not the typical case, at least not in the novel, Bakhtin at times ignores this difference and treats heteroglossia as necessarily dialogic.) Heteroglossia arises when "The period of national languages, coexisting but closed and deaf to each other, comes to an end" (12), when, in other words, dialogism is no longer confined to single speech communities, but operates across such communities. For Bakhtin, the novel exhibits a "multi-languaged consciousness" and came to prominence during the period when Europe emerged "from a socially isolated and culturally deaf semipatriarchal society" and entered "into international and interlingual contacts and relationships." At this point, a "multitude of different languages, cultures and times became available" (11). Moreover, this hetero-glossia operates not only inter-linguistically, but across different communities intra-linguistically, across different "languages" within a national language, by incorporating and dialogizing regional "languages" (or dialects), "languages" of different social classes, of different trades and occupations, of different generations, and so forth (see 291). In keeping with this, Bakhtin notes that the conception of language relevant to hetero-glossia is necessarily much broader than that implied in the phrase "national language." As Bakhtin explains, "We are taking language not as a system of abstract grammatical categories, but rather language conceived as ideologically saturated, language as a world view" (271). For Bakhtin, this heteroglossia of ideologically saturated languages, of worldviews, is also definitive of novelized literature.

According to Bakhtin, in order for the novel to arise as a dialogic and heteroglot genre, the monologic and monoglot epic and all that which is fixed, sacred, authoritative must be in some way be undermined: "the flowering of the novel is always connected with a disintegration of stable verbal-ideological systems and with an intensification and intentionalization of speech diversity that are counterpoised to previously reigning stable systems" (370–71). For Bakhtin, the undermining of monological systems occurs initially and most significantly through the various modes of laughter, including such literary modes as satire and parody, which deflate the pretensions of official discourse. As Bakhtin puts it: "It is precisely laughter that destroys the epic, and in general destroys any hierarchical (distancing and valorized) distance," because "Laughter demolishes fear and piety before an object" (23). But heteroglossia is not based simply on derisive glee. It derives also from "the eternally living element of unofficial language and unofficial thought (holiday forms, familiar speech, profanation)" (20). In other words, the novel is closely linked with popular practices and celebrations that operate to overturn standards and rules, break rigid social strictures, open spaces for unofficial voices and views, even if only very briefly. It is linked with such practices as the carnival, which is, for Bakhtin, the paradigm case of a heteroglossic disruption of authoritative discourse.

In recent years, Bakhtin's views have been very influential, though not uncontroversial. His notion that literature dealing with the mythical past is closed, hierarchical, and so forth, seems at the very least overgeneralized, as does his rather blunt valorization of the novel and denigration of the epic. (Bakhtin does qualify this division by allowing for different types of novel and for the novelization of other genres—including narrative verse—but this seems to weaken his claim almost to triviality. Sure, novels are heteroglot if we have decided to use "novel" simply to mean "heteroglot work," even when the "novel" in question is long narrative poem in twelve books.) Moreover, insofar as he is correct in his claims about the novel and the epic in the narrow senses of these terms, he seems to repeat the standard Marxist division between feudal and bourgeois art without the explanatory clarity of the Marxist view (which takes economic context into account beyond discourse context). Finally, his widely cited ideas about the carnival and laughter seem implausible. For example, his theory seems to commit him to the view that racist cartoons of Africans are dialogical, destroy hierarchies, and are a good thing, while African celebrations of indigenous myth and religion in epic are monological, hierarchic, and a bad thing.

Nonetheless, his stress on the dialogic nature of all speech, and the heteroglot nature of modern literature, is suggestive and useful, as is his distinction between the discourse of authority and internally persuasive discourse.

Shakespeare provides an excellent example of the sort of literature Bakhtin referred to as novelized. Shakespeare repeatedly presented a broad range of class and regional dialects in his plays, and a correspondingly broad range of characters. He mixed tragedy with wit and laughter—even with the sort of bawdiness closely associated with carnival. He frequently dealt with current problems (as in, for example, *Othello*) and repeatedly brought historical events into the "contact zone" of his contemporaries by explicitly or implicitly relating these events to current concerns (compare Queen Elizabeth's statement concerning Shakespeare's *Richard II*: "I am Richard II. Know ye not that?" [quoted in Greenblatt, "Introduction" 1057]). Moreover, his plays are notoriously ambiguous and ambivalent, even contradictory, impossible to fully "close" or determine. Indeed, they are so thoroughly dialogized that some have been read by both Protestants and Catholics, loyalists and rebels, misogynists and feminists, as advocating their particular views.

In a Bakhtinian reading of *Othello*, one might argue that the tragedy of the play ultimately results not from Iago's deceptive actions, but more importantly from the failure of Othello to fully dialogize his discourse about and with Desdemona, and from Desdemona's prior inability to engage the heteroglossia implied by Othello's very presence in Venice. Specifically, by calling him "the Moor," Desdemona implicitly relegates Othello entirely to another culture, outside the discursive context in which her own speech takes place; in this way, her discourse fails to manifest the heteroglossia that would dialogize the relation between those cultures. In consequence, she does not engage in dialogue with Othello, but closes him off, fixes his identity in an epic tale of heroic deeds. Correlatively, Othello does not dialogize Desdemona's speech, especially that protesting her innocence. He does not consider it, incorporate it, apply it. Rather, he merely seeks to stifle it, to subsume it under his own monologue, his own (epical) discourse of authority. Suffocating her with a pillow is particularly revealing in this regard, for it is precisely the breath of her speech that he has denied. In this reading, Othello's final appeal takes on added poignancy. He pleads with writers of his story, implicitly including Shakespeare: "Speak of me as I am. Nothing extenuate, / Nor set down aught in malice" (5.2.348–49). He has learned the dangers of the epic mode. It is the mode in which Desdemona, and all of Venice, conceived of him. And it is the mode in which he conceived of himself at the moment when he murdered Desdemona. At least in death, he hopes, he can be treated otherwise.

Indeed, this sort of reading is doubly Bakhtinian, for it not only focuses on dialogism and heteroglossia within the (novelized) drama, it simultaneously brings the drama into our contact zone. It tacitly dialogizes the play itself by "re-accentuating" it in relation to contemporary concerns about race. This dialogization in critical analysis is, for Bakhtin, as crucial as the internal dialogization that defines novelized genres themselves. As Bakhtin argues, in a passage that anticipates the views of such writers as Gadamer and Jauss, "The historical life of classic works is in fact the uninterrupted process of their social and ideological re-accentuation . . . against ever new dialogizing backgrounds," such that "each new era" uncovers "ever newer aspects of meaning" and the "semantic content" of the works "literally continues to grow" (421).

## Structuralism

Structuralism was an interdisciplinary movement that developed in the 1950s and 1960s, primarily in France. It encompassed work by anthropologists, such as Claude Lévi-Strauss, sociologists such as Lucien Goldman, psychoanalysts such as Jacques Lacan, developmental psychologists such as Jean Piaget, and writers in a range of other fields—including, of course, philosophy. Though not formally affiliated, all these thinkers shared an interest in rethinking and re-theorizing the human sciences on the model of linguistics, specifically the linguistics of Ferdinand de Saussure.

Though his theories are generally considered outmoded by contemporary linguists, understanding Saussure's ideas is crucial to understanding structuralism.

Saussure did contribute enormously to the development of modern linguistics. Specifically, Saussure introduced a number of important distinctions into linguistic theory. These distinctions allowed him to reorient linguistics away from the philological study of narrowly focused linguistic history (for example, etymology) and toward the study of language as a system in which all the parts are related. (At one level, Saussure was taking up Romantic organicism with respect to language.) Perhaps Saussure's most important contribution to linguistic study, and his most significant legacy in literary structuralism, was this. Prior to Saussure, European linguists tended to focus on localized aspects of language, such as the history of particular words. Saussure insisted that we could come to no real understanding of any localized elements considered in separation from the entire structure of which they are a part. Structuralist followers of Saussure, if they share nothing else, share at least this conception of language—and the view that language, thus understood, is the most appropriate model for studying all aspects of human mental and social life.

The first of Saussure's influential distinctions is that between synchronic linguistics and diachronic linguistics. Simply put, diachronic linguistics studies language history, while synchronic linguistics studies a cross-section of that history, the state of a language at any given time. However, the terms imply more than this. And to understand these further implications, we have to understand another fundamental distinction, that between language (*langue*) and speech (*parole*). Speech is anything anyone says or writes. For example, everything in this book is speech. Language is, in contrast, the system that allows for speech. Language determines vocabulary, syntax, phonology, and so on. It is what allows words and sentences to have meaning and to communicate ideas. Considered in and of itself, language is in effect an atemporal structure (within a given historical period). Speech, in contrast, is always necessarily temporal. The rule governing plural formation in English is, in effect, atemporal (in, say, the modern period). In contrast, my use of any given plural (for example, "structures") necessarily unfolds in time—the time of my utterance, the time of an auditor's or reader's reception. It is the interaction between speech and language that makes language historical, that makes language change. But language changes only systemically; it shifts as a structure. Synchronic linguistics is, then, the study of any atemporal system. Diachronic linguistics is the study of the structural shifts of such systems.

Take, for example, the difference between aspirated and unaspirated *t*—the former is pronounced with a little puff of air, the latter without. (Put your hand in front of your mouth and say "top," then say "stop"; you should feel a little puff of air accompanying the *t* in "top," but not that in "stop.") In many languages, aspiration is a "phonemic" property; it can be used to distinguish between two different words. In modern English, aspiration is not a phonemic property, but voicing—the use of one's vocal chords—is. For example, the only difference between *t* and *d* is that in pronouncing *d* we use our vocal chords, whereas in pronouncing *t* we do not. Because this difference is phonemic, "dip" and "tip" can be different words in English. However, "stop" and "st$^h$op" (t$^h$ = aspirated t) are not and cannot be different words in English—though they would be different in a language in which aspiration is phonemic. Aspiration is, in fact, phonemic in many Indian languages. Given this, it is easy to imagine Indian speakers of English implicitly distinguishing between aspiration and non-aspiration in their speech. For example, they might come to use "t$^h$op" for a spinning toy and "top" for an upper surface. Through immigration, the expansion of English usage in South Asia, and other factors, this could ultimately lead to a major shift in the language such that aspiration becomes phonemic in English wherever it appears. In this case, the phonological structure of the language would have changed. Synchronic linguistics studies this structure (langue) at either point—when aspiration is not phonemic or when it is. Diachronic linguistics studies the relation between these two (synchronically understood) structures (or langues) and the transition from one to the other by way of parole (here, initially, the various paroles of Indian speakers of English).

Saussure further explains the nature of the linguistic system by isolating the sign as the central unit of language, and then analyzing the sign into two components: the signifier and the signified. Signs are words or meaningful parts of words, what contemporary linguists refer to as "morphemes." Sometimes the use of the word "sign" is extended to larger units, such as idioms. Thus the simple word "pave" is a sign (in English); the prefix "re-" is also a sign; the composite word "repave" is a sign. In addition, we might consider the phrase "pave over" to be a sign, the idiom "pave the way (for)," and perhaps even the commonplace "The road to hell is paved with good intentions." The signifier is the sensible aspect of the sign—the sound pattern, the pattern of marks in writing. The signified is the concept to which the signifier is linked. Thus the sound [kat] is a signifier linked with the concept of a cat (a small, furry animal) as its signified. Or to take a perhaps clearer, because unfamiliar example, the sound [treš] is a signifier in Kashmiri, but not English. It is not a signifier in English because it lacks a signified. In Kashmiri, however, it is linked to the concept of thirst. Thus the signifier [treš] and the signified idea of thirst together form a sign in Kashmiri.

For Saussure, all linguistic elements are defined by two sorts of relations. On one hand, an element is defined by its relations with all similar and dissimilar elements within the system of language. On the other hand, it is defined by its place in a temporal sequence of speech. Thus the word "pave" is in part defined by its relation to such words as "blacktop," "surface," and so on. But it is also in part defined by its place in such speech sequences as "We have to repave the road" or "I don't want to just pave over our disagreements." These two relations may be represented graphically as two axes, such as those in the Cartesian coordinate system. The vertical axis represents the relations in language and is called "paradigmatic" or sometimes "substitutive." The horizontal axis represents the relations in speech and is called "syntagmatic," or sometimes "combinative." (See below.)

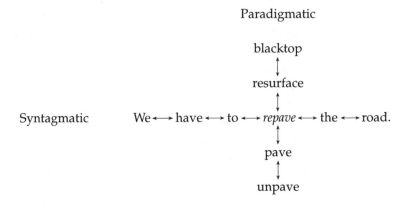

Figure 1.

These notions are in fact somewhat more complicated than is usually granted in literary theory. It is probably best to consider them in relation to several different aspects of language. This will involve some technical linguistics. But the concepts are derived from technical linguistics and one cannot fully understand them if they are not related to that context.

Since a good deal of structural linguistics focused on phonology—the study of language sounds—it is perhaps best to begin with this. We have already noted that the sounds [t] and [tʰ] are not phonemic in English. However, they are distinguished in English. Specifically, they count as alternative versions of a single phoneme—"allophones" of that phoneme—used in different phonetic contexts. More exactly, [tʰ] is the pronunciation we use at the beginning of syllables, while [t] is the pronunciation we use elsewhere. In terms of the two axes, [t] and [tʰ] are *paradigmatic alternatives* for a single speech sound. At the beginning of syllables, [tʰ] is inserted in the sequence of sounds along the combinative axis; elsewhere, [t] is inserted. One could think of it in the following terms: I proceed along the combinative axis saying, "I had to stop the spinning top." I come to the "t" in "stop" and am faced with the paradigmatic alternatives [t] and [tʰ]. Because the *t* is not at the beginning of a syllable, I choose [t], not [tʰ]. In contrast, when I come to "top," I find the *t* at the beginning of a syllable, thus I choose [tʰ]. (Obviously, this is not a matter of reflective choice; I put it this way to illustrate the relation between the paradigmatic alternatives and the combinative sequence.)

But how is it that [t] and [tʰ] count as one phoneme, whereas [t] and [d] count as two? What determines phonological identity? Here structural linguistics gives an answer that has had far-reaching consequences in literary theory: Phonemic identity, and indeed all forms of linguistic identity, are determined by a structure of differences. In other words, [t] and [tʰ] count as one phoneme simply because the system does not count aspiration as a phonemically differentiating factor. [t] and [d] count as different phonemes simply because the system does count voicing as a phonemically differentiating factor. [t] and [tʰ] are no more intrinsically identifiable than [t] and [d]—as can be seen from the fact that aspiration is phonemic in some languages (for example, Hindi) while voicing is not phonemic in some languages (for example, Hawaiian). Moreover, even these sounds are not simple positive identities. For example, the sound [t] includes a wide range of pronunciations. In pronouncing [t], one's tongue may be placed at various points on the alveolar ridge (just behind the upper teeth)—some more forward, some more back, some off-center, and so on. All of these pronunciations count as [t], simply because they are not defined by the system as differentiating phonemes or allophones. In this way, identity is merely the residue of a system of differences.

Moreover, in structuralist linguistics, this system of differences has a specific form. It is composed of bipolar oppositions. In other words, each difference is defined by the presence or absence of a certain feature. A sound is either voiced or unvoiced, for example. Thus, a system defines voicing as a differentiating feature and then defines each speech sound as falling on one side of the polarity: + voicing/-voicing. Thus language structure is in large part a matter of polar oppositions, with one category defined by the presence of a differentiating feature and the other category defined by its absence. This too has been an enormously influential principle in later literary theory.

Because of their great influence, it is worth saying a couple of things about these ideas before continuing. First of all, most phonological features are in fact not bipolar (except trivially). For example, consonants are defined by three features. One is voicing. Another is place of articulation. The third is manner of articulation. As to place of articulation, consonants may be alveolar, palatal, bilabial, labiodental, interdental, velar, or glottal. And as to manner, they may be stops, fricatives, affricates, nasals, lateral liquids, retroflex liquids, or glides. Any English consonant has one and only one place of articulation, and one and only one manner of articulation. Thus each consonant is defined by one feature that is part of a dual opposition (voicing) and two features, each of which is part of a seven-way opposition (place and manner of articulation). Bipolar opposition is a significant part of language structure, but it by no means pervasively defines that structure.

More importantly, the phonology of a given language is not a system of pure differences lacking positive features, as is sometimes asserted (most famously by Saussure [120]). Rather, the phonology of a given language is a system of real, positive features that are given a function in the system by being defined as differences of specific sorts. The system of language does not create voicing, for example. There is a real, worldly difference between vibrating and nonvibrating vocal chords. Similarly, there is a real, worldly difference between producing a puff of air (aspirating) and not producing a puff of air. There are also real, worldly similarities between a [tʰ] and a [t] or between a [d] and a [t], and, of course, between the various ways we pronounce [t]. None of this is created by a system of language. Rather, a system of language counts certain of these features as phonemic, others as allophonic, still others as neither. All this is a matter of selection and emphasis, not creation. In other words, the voicing of [d] is not created by the system of language; the voicing of [d] is a real feature of its pronunciation—the use of vocal chords. However, the voicing of [d] is selected and rendered phonemic by the system of language.

Finally, these phonological analyses (and related morphological analyses) have been widely used to draw conclusions about meaning. Unfortunately, we have little reason to believe that linguistic meaning is in any way directly analogous to linguistic sound. For example, even if phonology were a system of pure, bipolar differences, this would have no clear consequences for semantics. In other words, it would not follow that meaning is a system of pure bipolar differences.

On the other hand, this does not mean that a semantic theory is valueless simply because it is based on a structural linguistic model of phonology. Indeed, the assimilation of semantics to phonology has been central to the development of structuralist literary theory, and it has often operated in illuminating, if problematic, ways. In general terms, Saussure and subsequent theorists in the structuralist tradition have tended to see the meaning of a given term as a function of both a system of paradigmatic differences and a syntagmatic context. We will discuss what is currently the most influential case of this—deconstruction—in the following section. But writers such as Claude Lévi-Strauss and A. J. Greimas have developed theories along these lines as well. Greimas in particular has developed an entire theory of structural semantics, both linguistic and literary, on this foundation.

Specifically, for Greimas, the signified (or meaning) of a sign is constituted by a series of "semes" or semantic units. These are "constituents" of meaning, analogous to the phonological features that define speech sounds (for instance, the feature "+ voiced"). These semes are always part of binary oppositions, and are not analyzable (that is, they are "basic" and thus do not consist of further, "smaller" semantic units). Greimas's semantic theory has two components: a series of elements (the semes) and a series of rules governing the relations between elements. The semes for "man," for example, would be "+ male" and "+ human." "Male" is part of a bipolar opposition with "female," and so on.

According to Greimas, semes fall into two categories. There is, first of all, a "semic nucleus" (sometimes called a "semantic core") of central, definitional semes—for instance, "male" and "human" for "man." There are, in addition, various clusters of "contextual semes." These are possible meanings for a given term, and are picked out by context. In other words, contextual semes form a paradigm set (also structured by bipolar oppositions) from which one element is chosen in the (syntagmatic) course of an actual utterance. Greimas uses examples such as "head." According to Greimas, the semic nucleus of "head" consists in the semes "extremity" (being at one end) and "superativity" (being on top or at the front; see 51). In any particular context, however, "head" will be further specified as the context will select items from polar oppositions that define possible contextual semes. Thus in the phrase, "John's head," the "human" alternative will be selected from the alternatives "human versus nonhuman." In "the head of the hammer," in contrast, "nonhuman" will be signaled, then, from the nonhuman sub-opposition "animate versus inanimate," "inanimate" will be signaled as well.

Extending Greimas somewhat, we might find a perhaps more interesting example in "man." "Man" might include contextual semes ranging from "strong" and "brave" to "domineering" and "sexist." In the following sentence, "strong" and "brave" might be triggered: "When the bear attacked his family, Karl showed that he was a man." Clearly, this sentence does not merely mean that Karl demonstrated he was both + male and + human. Similarly, "domineering" and "sexist" might be triggered by the following sentence: "When he voted against instituting a women's studies program, Karl showed that he was a man."

Greimas argues that particular semes are repeated in a range of terms within a text and that this repetition defines a level of coherence in the text. Indeed, that level of coherence is precisely what picks out the appropriate semantic elements to begin with (as in the cases we just considered). For example, a feminist text dealing with a patriarchal institution is likely to include a range of terms that contain such semes as "domination" and "sexism" (or, rather, the clusters of semes that define these terms; "domination" and "sexism" are presumably not unanalyzable semantic elements). These semes do not form a level of semantic coherence (or "isotopy," as Greimas calls it) on their own, however. Rather, they are necessarily linked with their polar opposites. It is these sets of oppositions, most often formed into homologies ("A is to B as C is to D"), that form the levels of semantic coherence in the text. (These oppositions themselves may subsume "sub-oppositions," as when "nonhuman" is opposed to "human," but is itself analyzable into "animate versus inanimate.")

For example, suppose we take the polar opposite of sexism to be feminism, and the polar opposite of domination to be equality. These polar oppositions will help define one level of coherence in the text. Specifically, the text will be stressing sexism, domination, the relation between the two, and the way that both are opposed to feminism and equality. In other words, we establish a parallel between the two oppositions such that domination/equality = sexism/feminism ("Domination is to equality as sexism is to feminism"). Following this homology through the course of the work—in connection with imagery, character, and so forth—allows us to isolate one level of semantic coherence.

As an example of this sort of analysis, we might look at Othello's thoughts before the murder of Desdemona (5.2.1–15):

It is the cause, it is the cause, my soul.
Let me not name it to you, you chaste stars.
It is the cause. Yet I'll not shed her blood,
Nor scar that whiter skin of hers than snow,
And smooth as monumental alabaster.
Yet she must die, else she'll betray more men.
Put out the light, and then put out the light.
If I quench thee, thou flaming minister,
I can again thy former light restore,
Should I repent me; but once put out thy light,
Thou cunning'st pattern of excelling nature,
I know not where is that Promethean heat
That can thy light relume. When I have plucked the rose,
I cannot give it vital growth again;
It needs must wither. I'll smell thee on the tree.

This speech includes a number of polar oppositions that form a level of semantic coherence. Most obviously, there is the opposition death/life. This is linked with darkness/light. However, the relation between the two oppositions is not a simple one. For the purpose of the comparison is to show not only how darkness and death are similar, but how they are different: the candle can be relit, while life, once gone, cannot be restored. Thus darkness/light//death/life is itself mapped onto another opposition, reversible/irreversible (that is, darkness/light is mapped onto reversible, death/life onto irreversible), yielding something like "darkness/light is to reversibility as death/life is to irreversibility."

Cold/hot is another standard comparison that Shakespeare uses, but skews through the manipulation of homologies and bipolar oppositions. Heat is linked with life, but Desdemona is connected with snow, and thus cold, while still alive. This is at least in part the result of there being two sorts of life and death at issue—one physical, the other spiritual. Desdemona is linked not only with physical life, but with spiritual death, thus with (physical) heat and (spiritual) cold. More technically, we could take "spirit versus flesh" as the opposition most properly definitive of the isotopy on which we wish to focus. Each of these terms subsumes the subopposition of "life versus death," and in each case the context "heat" selects "life" and "cold" selects "death." Graphically:

## Desdemona

*Spirit vs. Flesh*

life vs. death  life vs. death

heat vs. cold  heat vs. cold

There is a sort of reconciliation of these various homologies, which indicates the pivotal importance of the spiritual/physical opposition, when Othello, in his semi-delusional state, imagines his murder as a sacrifice that will prevent Desdemona from sinning in the future and that will thus save her soul (see 5.2.6, 26–32, 65). In this way, the murder is (for Othello) based upon a homology of death/life, not with darkness/light, but with light/darkness; in the context of sin, physical life is parallel to spiritual death (thus darkness and cold), while in the context of deathbed remorse and confession (see 5.2.53), physical death is parallel to spiritual life (thus light and heat). Graphically:

## Desdemona

*Flesh vs. Spirit*

life vs. death  death vs. life

heat vs. cold  cold vs. heat

light vs. darkness  darkness vs. light

Or, equivalently, (physical life and heat and light)/(spiritual death and cold and darkness)//(physical death and cold and darkness)/(spiritual life and heat and light). ("Physical life and heat and light are to spiritual death and cold and darkness as physical death and cold and darkness are to spiritual life and heat and light.") Moreover, the opposition between reversibility and irreversibility enters here as well. For, despite Othello's explicit statement, his example of the flame may indicate that physical states of any sort are reversible, or at least limited. But spiritual states are not reversible. They are an eternal, infinite death, cold, and darkness—or an eternal, infinite life, warmth, and light. Hence Othello's insistence that he will kill her body, but "I would not kill thy soul" (5.2.32).

This complex homology functions not only in speech, but in action. When Othello smothers Desdemona, he treats her as if she were a flame— thus physical light and heat—for one puts out a flame by smothering it. Moreover, Desdemona revives briefly, only to die immediately. This is a seemingly implausible sequence of events, from a realistic point of view. But it serves to emphasize that, unlike a flame, she cannot physically live a second time. Yet, at the same time, her physical death is limited, temporary—like her physical existence, but unlike her spiritual existence. Put differently, the flame of her physical life flickers once more, briefly, showing that it cannot continue. But this is not a permanent expiration. It leads instead to unending spiritual life: "the more angel she," as Emilia puts it (5.2.129). The ending, of course, continues the structure—but reverses it. For, in killing himself, Othello—by the Christian doctrine attached contextually to his act of suicide—kills also his immortal soul, thereby inverting the homology with Desdemona and realigning physical and spiritual demise.

In a Greimasian reading, then, we see a passage as forming a semantically complex, and highly internally tense structure of oppositions, homologies, and even oppositions between homologies, in a level of semantic coherence. In much of his work, Claude Lévi-Strauss engaged in this sort of analysis as well. Indeed, Lévi-Strauss's work is one of the prime sources of Greimas's theories. However, Lévi-Strauss also developed a broader, more flexible approach to the study of structure, in some ways more closely related to the linguistic theories of Noam Chomsky than to those of Saussure. In the four volumes of *Introduction to the Science of Mythology*, Lévi-Strauss developed a method of analysis that, while ultimately organized in terms of bipolar oppositions, allowed the interpretation of more diversely structured sequences. Specifically, for Lévi-Strauss a body of myth will contain a range of complex narrative structures that are superficially dissimilar but fall into clear patterns when their relations are understood. These relations involve particular sorts of "transformation" triggered by context.

In linguistics, a transformation derives the specific sound, word, or sentence we utter from an abstract "underlying" form. The transformation produces what we actually say. Take, for example, the sounds [t] and [tʰ]. According to Chomsky, these are different surface realizations of a single underlying phoneme. The underlying phoneme has no sound of its own. It is purely abstract. It is transformed into an actual sound—either [t] or [tʰ]—by a transformation rule, something like: "At the beginning of syllables [tʰ]; elsewhere [t]." Or consider the plural morpheme, a case from morphology rather than phonology. We tend to think of the plural morpheme as simply s. In fact, English has three plural morphemes, or rather three surface realizations of the plural morpheme: [s] for words such as "cap," [z] for words such as "cab," and [əz] for words such as "lash." Here the transformation rule would be something like: "After sibilants (s, z, š, ž, č, ǰ) add [əz], after unvoiced nonsibilants add [s], elsewhere add [z]."

In Lévi-Strauss's theory, the notion of a transformation is somewhat looser, and the contextual features are less strict, less formalizable. However, the idea is much the same. Just as [s], [z], and [əz] are different surface manifestations of the same morpheme, several stories or myths or parts of stories or myths may be different surface manifestations of the same underlying meaning. To illustrate (somewhat oversimply), a tale about a herd of buffalo that lives at the bottom of a lake may be a different surface manifestation of the same meaning manifest in a story about a school of fish that lives on the plains. The transformation rule might make reference to the cultures in which the stories are told, as when one is a fishing culture and one is a herding culture; or it might simply make reference to different story contexts within a single culture. In other words, the underlying structure would be something along the lines of "finding a food source in an impossible environment" (perhaps as part of a myth concerning a utopian world of plenty). In the context of fishing, this would become "finding fish living on the plains"; in the context of herding, this would become "finding buffalo living at the bottom of a lake."

Or, to take a real example (in slightly simplified form), we may consider Lévi-Strauss's treatment of three myths about the origin of mortality. Lévi-Strauss shows that these myths have a common structure, but in one this is related to sound (occurs in the context of sound), in another to smell, in the third to taste. The underlying or abstract element in each case is the experience of decay seen as the source of mortality. The transformations match the decaying objects with a sense organ—hearing, taste, or smell—determining them by reference to (or in the context of) a way of entering the human body. In other words, the underlying meaning is the abstract notion of decay, unspecified in terms of physical manifestation; it is transformed to one surface structure or physical manifestation in the context of entering the body through hearing, another in the context of entering the body through smell, a third in the context of entering the body through taste. In the first case, then, the surface manifestation is noise; in the second, it is stench; in the third, it is (the taste of) opossum flesh, which is associated with feces (presumably, a substitution along these lines was necessary because, while people hear noise and smell stench, they do not literally eat feces and thus some close approximation was required).

Lévi-Strauss ultimately aims to establish "transformation sets," sets of tales, myths, or whatever, which can be understood as transformations of identical underlying patterns. Note that this leads Lévi-Strauss to a project that is neither a typology (as we find, for example, in Northrop Frye) nor a listing of constant surface elements (as in, say, Vladimir Propp). Lévi-

Strauss is instead seeking basic underlying structures and rules relating those underlying structures to surface structures. Thus the surface elements themselves become relatively insignificant. A morphologist does not group all [s]'s together—linking the nonmorphemic s in "spot" with the third person singular morpheme in "jumps" and the plural morpheme in "caps." This would be bad morphology indeed. Instead, the morphologist groups all instances of the plural morpheme together, however different their surface manifestations. Likewise, Lévi-Strauss will not group together all instances of, say, water imagery or parent/child conflict. For two water images or two instances of parent/child conflict may be as different as the s in "spot" and that in "caps."

A Lévi-Straussian analysis of this sort might be applied to a large body of work, or to a single work with complex internal structures. For example, the corpus of Shakespeare's plays could be profitably considered in these terms. For a brief illustration, however, a single work, such as Ali's poem, is obviously more appropriate. This short poem contains four distinct and parallel surface sequences of events. These sequences form a transformation set. As Lévi-Strauss points out, each plot sequence in a transformation set is likely to be incomplete and thus opaque. By mapping the sets onto one another and understanding their transformational relations, we should be able to understand their underlying significance more fully. Using the same letter for the parallel elements, we may summarize the four sequences in the following manner:

a. speaker is waiting alone for a bus
b. bus comes (presumably it is crowded) and stops
c. speaker's hands are empty/he has no money
d. unrecognized voice shouts for speaker to board bus
e. hand offers silver money
f. policeman has silver handcuffs
g. policeman asks for ticket
h. speaker leaves the bus

a'. speaker runs alone to cinema
b'. speaker stops outside cinema
(c', having no ticket, is implied)
d'. Sunil is there and does not say anything, but speaker now recognizes
his voice on the bus
e'. Sunil gives speaker a ticket to the cinema

g'. the usher says that the ticket is invalid
(h', speaker leaves cinema, is implied)

e". movie heroine leaves earrings (implicitly, with husband)
h". she is led away (implicitly, by armed men)
i". she is buried alive

a'''. speaker is waiting alone for a bus
c'''. his hands are empty
b'''. many busses come, now empty and not stopping
d'''. unknown beggar women and children appear
e'''. they offer the speaker money
j'''. they weep for him

   Clearly, this categorization is in part a reflection of interpretation; it does not rely solely on surface similarity. While it is relatively clear from surface considerations that a, a''', and even a' are parallel, it is far from clear that what I have called j''' is in fact a final element, subsequent to i", itself an unparalleled element, and so on. This sort of interpretive categorization is a necessary part of structural analysis; it is a necessary part of grouping sequences by inferred underlying structures. In short, Lévi-Straussian structural analysis does provide well-defined methodological principles, but is not by any means a mechanical procedure.
   Turning to the interpretation, we find that the initial elements of these sequences involve the speaker, alone, seeking entrance to some public sphere where he becomes part of a group. This is clearly related to the frame of the poem: the speaker dreams of returning to Delhi (that is, he is alone, dreaming, but imagines entering into a community). In the first and second cases, a temporary union is achieved: he enters the bus, and the cinema. Moreover, in the third sequence, the scene occurs in a movie following a marriage. Specifically, the lovers had been separated, but were allowed to marry. Thus, in the movie also, we find isolation leading initially to a form of community, in this instance through the marriage ceremony.
   In each case, however, this union is temporary. The frame is illusory because it is merely a dream. The three plot sequences are more detailed. Specifically, in the first and second sequences, the speaker receives a gift from Sunil—silver rupees and a cinema ticket, respectively. This gift is what allows the speaker to enter the community. But in each case there is

something wrong with the gift and the speaker is forced, by an official representative of social authority, to leave the communal space. In the third sequence, most of this is implicit and must be brought in from a knowledge of the movie. But it is much the same. Anarkali is married to the prince. She can be married only because she is given the proper jewelry; she herself is too poor to own appropriate finery. However, just after the marriage, as the husband sleeps, the wife is taken away (by the king's guards). Before leaving, the wife removes her jewelry, leaving it behind with the husband. In short, she is forced by social authority to leave the marriage, in order to be buried alive, the image implying not only eventual death, but a complete isolation from human community prior to death.

The first three sections, then, manifest the speaker's sense of unbridgeable isolation from his home, his inability to return to India and be reintegrated into that community. This is particularized by reference to the singularly important loss of his friend Sunil. Moreover, both the general and the particular separation derive from some intervention by social authority. More exactly, in the first and second sequences, the speaker escapes authority. The third—Anarkali—sequence (embedded into the second sequence) results in irreversible isolation. The final sequence in effect accepts this. In this sequence, there is no possibility for entering into a communal space (the busses are empty and do not stop). The speaker is offered money, but not by Sunil, and not as a way of entering society. Rather, he is offered money by women who have no money and who, as beggars, are themselves excluded from society. Moreover, these women weep for him, almost as if he were dead, or buried alive, like Anarkali, or separated from a beloved who is dead or buried alive—for he is sleeping, just as Anarkali's husband sleeps in the film. In keeping with this connection, the generosity of the beggar women is, it seems, a grim parody of the Indian practice of showering money on newlyweds.

Put differently, underlying these four structures is a series of homologous bipolar oppositions that define the concerns of the poem: home/exile; love/law; social union/social isolation. The speaker desires what is represented by the first term in each opposition. But these oppositions are all, in turn, mapped onto other oppositions: past/present, temporary/permanent, and, ultimately, dream/reality. These final oppositions define the speaker's desire as unfulfillable, reducing home, love, and union to aery nothing, an insubstantial, irrecuperable memory, congealing exile, law, and isolation into inexorable facts.

## Deconstruction

Deconstruction is, first of all, a philosophical movement founded on the writings of Jacques Derrida, in large part as a development and criticism of structuralism and phenomenology (including Heidegger's phenomenological hermeneutics). In general terms, one might say that deconstruction examines the implications of a given theory, drawing them out until they undermine or contradict that theory itself. In the case of structuralism, Derrida sets out to demonstrate the "instability" of a system of binary oppositions. In other words, he argues that the structure posited by structuralism—which he takes to be the structure of language itself—cannot fix meaning, cannot itself be fixed. Thus the structuralist project of unearthing structures, whether in myths or kinship systems or psychoneuroses (in the case of Lacan), is doomed to failure. As to phenomenology, Derrida argues that the very processes of perceptual and conceptual constitution undermine the possibility of the presuppositionless insight into essences—the ultimate goal of Husserl's phenomenology. Husserl set out to establish "a *universe of absolute freedom from prejudice*" (*Cartesian* 35; compare Heidegger's statement that "Everything that might interpose itself between the thing and us in apprehending and talking about it must first be set aside," "Origin" 25). The phenomenological method was to create such a universe and to allow the phenomenologist to experience "truth" with absolute certainty as "perfect clarity" (*Ideas* 181). But, according to Derrida, phenomenological method itself disallows this.

More exactly, Derrida takes up the structuralist conception of meaning as defined by system and sequence. In Derrida's phrasing, system defines meaning by "difference" and sequence modifies that meaning by deferral. Take a simple phrase: "the cat on the mat." The word "cat" derives its systemic or language meaning by its difference from other terms in the system—"dog," "tiger," "feline," "kitten," and so on. At the same time, it is part of an ongoing sequential or utterance meaning. (I avoid the word "speech" for reasons that will become clear.) This utterance meaning is in the process of being constructed at each moment of the utterance of the sentence. Thus the meaning of cat, in the utterance, is not complete with the articulation of the word "cat." Rather, it is deferred. We do not know which cat, or what about the cat. We wait, continuing to synthesize the meaning, until the next word: "on." But the meaning is still incomplete; it is still deferred, now to "the," then to "mat," then beyond the phrase, even beyond the sentence. Thus, meaning is always the product of a system of differences and a process of deferral. Combining the two terms ("difference" and "deferral"), Derrida coined the word "differance" (pronounced: "differance with an 'a'"). Meaning is, then, differance.

A crucial aspect of Derrida's argument is that neither the difference nor the deferral can be limited. There are always further differences and there is always some possible future utterance to which meaning is deferred. For this reason, meaning is never fully fixed; it is always to a degree indeterminate. And because of this, meaning is never fully *present*—not to the receiver of the message, not even to the sender of the message. Meaning is always partially elusive.

More exactly, the system of difference is infinite. "Cat" is different from everything—"tiger," "pet," "meat," and so forth, not merely "dog." Moreover, even if it were different only from "dog," this would not fully determine the meaning of "cat," for the meaning of "dog" itself is a function of difference—difference from "cat," and so on. Thus, there is no way of ultimately pinning down an absolute and definitive meaning, which exists positively, on its own. This sort of meaning, which would exist apart from the system and which would serve to define any given element in the system, is what Derrida calls a "transcendental signified." There is, he argues, no signified (that is, no meaning) that transcends the system of differences. Thus there is nothing to render the elements of that system fully definite and present.

As to deferral, the same point holds. The chain of speech is unending. At each moment, a new utterance is modifying, recontextualizing all the speech that preceded. Here too there is no transcendental signified in the sense of a final stopping place for speech; there is no period or full stop that would put an end to all possible modification in the future. It should be clear that this is connected with phenomenology. Our understanding of the meaning of an utterance is a process of constitution. Reading a sentence, we retain the past, intend the present, protend the future. But that constitution is never closed. Despite Husserl's insistence on the possibility of experiencing perfect clarity, and thus perfect truth, constitution is always a temporal activity, endlessly open to modification, and never at any point fully fixed. (In fact, Husserl and Sartre came close to this view; see, for example, Sartre 176.)

Derrida makes a similar point about perception. According to Derrida, perception too is defined by differance. (Derrida says that he does not believe in perception, which comes to the same thing.) Specifically, my experience of any physical object is the product of my isolation of the object as different from other objects and my temporal synthesis of its temporally experienced aspects. Take, for example, the leg of a chair. In order to experience this as an object, I must distinguish it from the floor, from the surrounding atmosphere, from the seat of the chair, and so on. Moreover, in doing this I am locating the leg of the chair in a system of differences—indeed, I am locating it in the system of linguistic differences, insofar as it is this linguistic system that distinguishes chair legs from chair seats, and so on. I then look at different aspects of the leg in sequence, synthesizing them. The system of differences—perceptual and semantic—is, again, endless. The sequence of constitution is, again, endless. No perception, however clear, involves direct and immediate contact with a transcendental object, a Kantian thing-in-itself fully experienced, fully present. Perception, like conception, involves only difference and deferral.

According to Derrida, the entire history of Western metaphysics stands in opposition to this view of meaning and perception as functions of differance. Here, Derrida employs the standard Romantic emplotment of history in which his own work constitutes a radical and revolutionary break with everything that went before—even as he insists that any such radical break is in a sense caught up in the metaphysical presupposition it overturns. Specifically, the history of Western metaphysics is the history of a "metaphysics of presence," a conception of meaning and perception according to which meaning and being are fixed in a transcendental signified, a transcendental signified that may be made fully present to an observer. All doctrines of such metaphysics are, as deconstructionists frequently put it, self-deconstructing in that they inevitably and necessarily posit a transcendence and a presence that their own principles cannot determine or even, ultimately, allow.

Husserlian phenomenology is a prime example. According to Husserl, as we have noted, objects are defined by essences. These essences function therefore as a transcendental signified, fixing the meaning of relevant terms (thus the essence of cups fixes the meaning of "cup"). Finally, essences can be made fully present to any observer who adopts the phenomenological method. However, eidetic reduction is necessarily an endlessly differantial activity. Eidetic reduction always necessarily involves determining an entity's difference from other entities, an essence's difference from other essences, but that in turn relies on a prior definition of the contrasting essences. (To limit the essence of a cup through imaginative variation, I contrast it with a bowl. But to do this, I need to have determined the essence of the bowl. But to do that . . . .) Moreover, any eidetic reduction necessarily involves the deferral of an entity's final constitution in the temporal synthesis carried out through free imaginative variation. Thus, in both ways, eidetic reduction itself necessarily undermines the possibility of any full, definitive presence.

In a sense, then, the primary project of deconstruction is the undermining of the metaphysics of presence in its various manifestations, or rather the demonstration that the metaphysics of presence is "always already" undermined by differance. It is important to recognize that Derrida's project here is closely related to Heidegger's hermeneutic of suspicion, which Heidegger himself referred to as a "destruction" of Western metaphysics (see, for example, *Being* 44; for a discussion of Heidegger's use of this notion and of its relation to "deconstruction," see Rapaport 3–9). However, Derrida's deconstruction seeks to undermine not only the metaphysical tradition, but the pure presence that Heidegger seeks at the origin of that tradition. Indeed, that is the point of Derrida's insistence that presence is "always already" undermined: there was never a point when there was a pure presence available to unimpeded phenomenological observation; there was never a time when, in Heidegger's phrase, "*truth occur[red] as unconcealedness*" ("Origin" 56).

Derrida develops this critique further in a structuralist direction primarily by interpreting the philosophical tradition (of the metaphysics of presence) in terms of bipolar oppositions. For Derrida, these are invariably hierarchized, but, at the same time, they are self-undermining in that hierarchization. Specifically, in a bipolar hierarchized opposition, one term, the "secondary" term, is defined by its relation to the other, "primary" term. However, the secondary term can derive its meaning from the primary term only if that primary term is independently fixed, only if it has meaning outside of the system of differences, only if it is linked to a transcendental signified. Thus "dog" cannot be fully defined by its difference from "cat" unless "cat" has meaning that is not a function of the system of differences of English. For, if "cat" is defined by the system of differences of English, then the meaning of "cat" is as much a function of its difference from "dog" as the meaning of "dog" is a function of its difference from "cat." But, in Derrida's view, there is no transcendental signified. Thus, no bipolar hierarchized opposition can ultimately have structural or semantic validity, for no term can have a fixed meaning, no term can be primary. Whether a bipolar opposition is understood as structuring society or as structuring a poem, it is necessarily unstable.

More exactly, metaphysicians of presence really have only one way of maintaining their view of presence. In order to hold that relations of meaning are stable, they must hold that the differences that structure language are not perfectly reciprocal. In other words, they must hold that bipolar oppositions are, indeed, hierarchized, that some terms are primary and others secondary, that primary terms have meaning in and of themselves, while secondary terms derive their meaning through their difference from the primary terms. Thus the metaphysics of presence establishes the linguistic system as a structure of hierarchized oppositions. Literary authors, like philosophers and other metaphysicians of presence, regularly seek to establish this stability in their writings. One main task of deconstructive literary criticism is to expose and investigate the ways in which that effort, like all efforts of the metaphysics of presence, is self-deconstructive, the ways in which the putatively stable and stabilizing hierarchies are disrupted by differance, despite the author's intent.

Derrida identifies three main forms of the metaphysics of presence, and each is associated with a particular dual hierarchized opposition. The first, and most general, is logocentrism. Logocentrism is the conceptual/perceptual version of the metaphysics of presence that we have been discussing. It is the view that meaning is fixed by a transcendental signified, that such a signified is or can be fully present, that the perceptual world has intrinsically defined noumenal existence, and that this noumenal existence can be present to us as such, unmediated by system or sequence. Both sorts of presence are experienced as absolute clarity and give rise to absolute certainty—as exemplified by Husserl.

Again, each centrism has a definitive hierarchy. With each such hierarchy, Derrida sets out to demonstrate its invalidity. This involves a series of steps. First of all, Derrida seeks to revalue the "disparaged" or secondary term by establishing it as the defining or primary term. This "deconstructive reversal" in turn leads to an undermining of the hierarchy itself, a demonstration that no such hierarchization is viable. In the case of logocentrism, this hierarchical opposition is that between identity and difference or identity and differance, with identity established as the definitive, positive, or transcendental term. (It should be clear that this opposition and, more generally, that between deconstruction and the metaphysics of presence, are variants of the great Romantic opposition between formal stability and disruptive force, limitation and infinitude.) Derrida seeks to reverse this standard metaphysical view and establish difference or differance as the definitive term, with identity merely derivative, merely that which is not difference and is produced by difference (for instance, the identity of "dog" is not positive, but a result of its being different from "cat"). But this reversal must lead to the complete disruption of the hierarchy, just as the notion of differance must lead to an endless, if partial, semantic indeterminacy—even with respect to the term "differance"—for the notion of differance itself undermines stability and hierarchy of any sort (even a hierarchy of differance over identity) by dispensing with the transcendental signified on which the hierarchies rest.

The second major centrism is phonocentrism. This is perhaps best understood as a specification of logocentrism. In the phonocentric view, presence is manifest most fully in oral speech, in the human voice. It is in oral communication that we come into direct contact with meaning and with one another. Oral speech or voice, then, is the definitive term in the fundamental bipolar opposition of phonocentrism. The other term is writing, the absence of voice, the loss of presence through the deferral of communication. Derrida argues that the metaphysics of presence results in a consistent valorization of oral speech and denigration of writing in philosophy, literature, anthropology, linguistics. This opposition is, furthermore, linked with a historical and cultural division between societies believed to be primarily oral, and "modern" societies submerged in writing. In this extension of phonocentrism, it is not merely oral speech or voice that allows presence and writing that denies it. Rather, true presence is to be found only in those "primitive" societies that are entirely oral, that have not been "corrupted" by writing. These societies live in unity with nature, in internal harmony, in a state of perfect presence. Thus phonocentrism is associated with a nostalgia for a lost past, and is a particularly prominent feature of Romanticism.

Derrida's argument here is much the same as it is with respect to logocentrism. Specifically, he argues that the very discourses that assert the full presence of oral speech are self-undermining, that speech is "always already" marked by the absence and deferral that characterize writing. Indeed, speech is, in effect, a form of writing (which thus becomes, briefly, the definitive term), for it always already exceeds one's intent or understanding, always already fails to produce presence, and so on, precisely because it is always partially indeterminate, always differantial, always a function of infinite difference and endless deferral. Moreover, there is and can be no perfect state of pristine unity with nature and with others, for the union with nature is always already rent by the differance of perception; the union with others is always already shattered by the differance of meaning.

The final sort of centrism is phallocentrism. This term has both a general and a specific use. In its general use, it may be identified with androcentrism. In this sense it is the establishment of a hierarchy in which "man" is the primary term and "woman" is defined by difference from "man." In its more specific use, it refers to the particular way in which androcentrism (putatively) manifests itself in psychoanalysis. In this sense, it defines a hierarchy in which the phallus alone has positive meaning, and the female reproductive organs are defined as a mere absence or lack of the phallus. Clearly, the two senses are related. Moreover, it should be clear how each of these polarities is homologous with the polarities of logocentrism and phonocentrism. In phallocentrism, the phallus and man are present and define identity, whereas the female genitalia and woman are defined by absence and difference. Moreover, according to Derrida, in this manifestation of the metaphysics of presence, man is identified with oral speech, and woman with writing. Because of these homologies, deconstructionists sometimes refer to the three collectively as "phonologophallocentrism." Unsurprisingly, the overturning of this hierarchy operates in the same manner as the other two.

Before going on to illustrate deconstructive literary criticism, we should consider a few theoretical difficulties. As we have already indicated, the structuralist theory of meaning is inadequate. First, a differential conception of meaning does not yield a disseminative or unstable meaning; it yields no meaning at all. To say that "groex" is the opposite of "gluaz" is to say nothing about any meaning for either. Clearly, meaning is not *only* a matter of difference and deferral. Nor is it *primarily* a matter of these. Knowing what "dog" means does not consist most importantly in placing "dog" in a series of oppositions. Rather, it involves being able to recognize paradigm and nonparadigm cases of dogs—from Great Danes to poodles. Indeed, when we use oppositions, it seems that we do so merely to signal specific positive meanings. Suppose you mention "foot" and I ask, "Do you mean 'foot' as opposed to 'hand' or 'foot' as opposed to 'stanza'?" The oppositions here do not differantially define meanings. Rather, they allow us to isolate one positive, nondifferantial meaning from a series of alternatives. Finally, as we shall discuss in the last chapter, most contemporary linguistic theorists follow Chomsky in repudiating the entire idea of an autonomous linguistic system such as that unquestioningly presupposed by Derrida. In sum, meaning is positive and human, not differantial and autonomous/systemic (or idealist); it is a part of our Being-in-the-world, as Heidegger would say, not an abstract play of signs. The meaning of "cat" is primarily a matter of what we do with cats; it has little if anything to do with polar oppositions in autonomous language.

Other problems arise in connection with the three centrisms. There is, first of all, the problem of all structuralism—the tendency to reduce complex sets of relations to a binary opposition. And, of course, the entire notion and critique of logocentrism rests on Derrida's differantial conception of meaning. As to phonocentrism, his ideas here are historically implausible as well. In fact, written languages have virtually always been privileged above purely spoken languages and literates have been privileged above illiterates; written speech defines prestige forms in a language, and purely oral forms are denigrated in comparison (see my *Politics* 77–78 and citations). Derrida is correct that speech is generally considered historically primary, but (1) in this case, that makes sense (that is, historically, oral speech developed first) and (2) that only goes to show that historical primacy and social domination cannot be automatically identified. Moreover, he is correct that speech has, periodically, been celebrated as superior to writing. But that merely indicates that celebration and actual social value are not identical—as should be clear from patriarchal celebrations of women, European celebrations of "primitives," and so on.

As to phallocentrism, while men have, indisputably, dominated women in social, political, and economic structure, it is not clear that the definitional relation of "man" and "woman" is central or even very relevant to this domination. A wide range of social institutions and a complex of ideological beliefs and practices seem far more important than the issue of whether we define the term "woman" by reference to the term "man." Nor do the complexities of patriarchy and sexism seem well explained by the idea that, in phallocentrism, man is seen as primary and definitive, while woman is viewed as secondary and derivative. After all, "woman" is seen as primary and definitive in housework, child-rearing, and other forms of uncompensated work. Indeed, it is even arguable that "woman" is primary and definitive more broadly, in being linked with nature and birth and life—none of which makes much of any difference to the real lives of women. Moreover, the assertion that meaning is differantial—and thus that linguistic hierarchies are unstable—does not seem a particularly cogent response to patriarchy and sexism as real systems of exploitation. Indeed, the linguistic point seems to have no consequences whatsoever. After all, by Derrida's system, there can be no (linguistic) hierarchy between "rapist" and "rape victim." This "binary" is endlessly self-deconstructing. Neither term has its meaning fixed by a transcendental signified. But this clearly should not have any consequences for our social and legal reaction to men who are rapists and women who are rape victims. Finally, it is clear that, historically, women have been linked with oral speech, not with writing and that their real oppression has been closely connected with illiteracy, exclusion from writing and publication, and so on. Like virtually all other oppressed people, their suffering has been exacerbated not by some putative philosophical valorization of speech over writing, but by the real, historical valorization of writing over oral speech.

But, once again, this does not prevent deconstructive ideas from proving fruitful in indicating some problematic areas or inadequacies in earlier theories or in analyzing literary works. Ali's poem provides a good illustration. It is, in many ways, a poem about presence and absence, identity and difference, loss and nostalgia. As we have already noted, it is organized around a series of oppositions: home/exile; love/law; social union/ social isolation; temporary/permanent; past/present; dream/reality. But the poem itself repeatedly undermines the possibility of this series establishing itself as a stable structure. The poem seems to equate home with love, union, and marriage, and to tie all to a lost past. But it is the past itself that defines exile, law, isolation, and death. Anarkali's execution was an historical incident. Indeed, it was ordered by the greatest of the Mughal emperors during what is often seen as an historical golden age. Thus the primary metaphor for separation suffered in the present—the speaker's separation from his home and his friend—characterizes the past precisely in terms of exile, law, isolation, and death, indicating that home, love, and union are always already lost, always already absent.

This reversal operates elsewhere in the poem as well. The line "PRISONERS BLINDED IN A BIHAR JAIL" recapitulates the opposition of love and law, and the link between law and isolation (through both imprisonment and blinding). But it associates all of this with India (through the synecdoche of Bihar, a state in India), thus with home, so that home itself defines isolation and a sort of internal exile. This reversal is repeated in the other headline: the untouchable villagers have been driven from their homes by landlords; their home in the larger homeplace of India is no longer and thus never truly was their home. In India, the speaker's lost home, unity and identity were always already rent by caste opposition, by difference.

The poem also plays with the identification of voice and presence. In the first stanza, the speaker hears a voice; it calls to him, opening the possibility of presence; it repeats its invitation: "The voice doesn't stop." But there is only absence: "There's no one I know." Later, in the cinema, the speaker turns to Sunil, only to find him absent. All that remains is a ticket, a trace of the past, with a bit of writing, an inscription, a date showing absence, difference: "my ticket is ten years old." What should have been voice and presence is merely a fragment of writing, a token of absence, a mark not of identity, but of difference—even differance, for it equally involves an endless temporal deferral of home, of union, of love, of all the plenitude of being and meaning which is not only absent now, but which is and was always already lost.

# 6

---

# Philosophy of Language and Cognition

## Analytic Philosophy, Chomskyan Linguistics, Cognitive Science, Empirical Poetics

The Anglo-American philosophical tradition is as rich and complex as that of the Continent, though it has not had the same degree of influence in literary study. One important basis for Anglo-American philosophy is logical formalism. In order to understand writing in this tradition, one has to be familiar with some basic principles of this formalism, which I introduce in the first section. The section continues by addressing a selection of prominent, formally oriented philosophers, from logical positivists such as Ayer, to Russell, Quine, Davidson, and the possible worlds theorists. Another strain of Anglo-American philosophy has focused not on logic, but on ordinary language. The second section takes up this approach, treating Wittgenstein, Anscombe, Grice, Austin, and Searle.

In the late 1950s, Noam Chomsky revolutionized linguistic theory. In work over the next four decades, he developed his linguistic theories in ways that have caused profound changes in disciplines ranging from neurophysiology to musicology. The next section takes up Chomskyan linguistics and the related philosophy of language and their significant implications for literary study. The fourth section then turns to cognitive science, an interdisciplinary field, based in part on Chomskyan principles. In the last three decades, cognitive science has developed into one of the most important and influential areas of research in the academy. It has recently begun to have very considerable impact in literary study. However, cognitive science cannot be wholly speculative or interpretive. For cognitive science to develop in any field, theorists must have recourse to empirical research. The final section considers the empirical study of literature, as it is now, and as it might develop in the future.

## Anglo-American Philosophy of Language (I): Formalism

Though most often ignored by literary theorists, Anglo-American philosophy has developed a rich tradition of linguistic study of direct relevance to literary theory. Indeed, language has been the major focus of Anglo-American philosophy in the last century. The Anglo-American or "analytic" tradition has two major strains. One group, including Bertrand Russell, the logical positivists (such as Rudolph Carnap and A. J. Ayer), Willard Quine, Donald Davidson, and the possible worlds theorists (prominently Saul Kripke), sought the model for linguistic study in mathematics and formal logic. The other group, including Ludwig Wittgenstein (in his later work), Elizabeth Anscombe, the ordinary-language philosophers and philosophers of "communication-intention" (such as Peter Strawson and Paul Grice), and the speech-act theorists (prominently John Austin and John Searle), turned away from mathematics and logic to a careful study of practical speech activity. In the present section, we will consider the ideas of the former group, turning to the communication theorists in the following section.

Mathematics and formal logic advanced strikingly in the early part of this century. A particular milestone was Russell and Whitehead's *Principia Mathematica*, which demonstrated that mathematics could be reduced to formal logic plus some set theory. While humanists tend to use the word "reduce" pejoratively, this is not the case in science. Indeed, a reduction is valuable in science, for to reduce one field to another is to improve our theories. Reduction in this sense is (roughly) a matter of taking two sets of data ("a" and "b"), and two associated theories ("A" and "B"), and showing that both sets of data can be accounted for by one theory alone (for instance, that a and b can be accounted for by A alone, without reference to B). The advances of Russell, built on the earlier advances in logical formalism by George Boole, Gottlob Frege, and others, created an atmosphere in which it seemed that almost anything was possible for formal logic, that formal logical analysis would allow the solution of a wide range of problems—especially when combined with the physical sciences, which were advancing at an equally impressive pace. This focus on formal logic may be of little direct relevance to literary analysis. However, it is enormously valuable for promoting clarity of thought and rigor of argument. And that should be as important to literary theorists as it is to writers in the sciences.

Before beginning to discuss any of the specific doctrines of these thinkers, however, it is important to define some terms that are common in their writings, terms that are drawn primarily from logic and mathematics. The very first term to define is "logic." Logic is narrowly and specifically defined as a set of rules determining possible relations of truth and falsity among propositions. Put differently, it is a set of rules determining what propositions can be true simultaneously and what propositions cannot be true simultaneously. That is all logic is. It is not a way of looking at the world, or of conducting one's life; it is not an attitude of objectivity, or lack of emotion; it is not a belief in current theories of physics. Most of what Mr. Spock claims to be logical or not to be logical really has nothing to do with logic in this technical sense.

Suppose a student—Biff—says, "I may get a lower grade if I skip school today, but I'll do it anyway." Biff may be being imprudent, but he/she is not being illogical. However, suppose Biff says, "Everyone who skips school, without exception, receives a lower grade. I will skip school. I won't receive a lower grade." In this case, he/she is being illogical. This is because there is a logical rule such that, if all As are also Bs, and Q is an A, then Q is a B. In this case, if all people who skip school (A = people who skip school) are also people who get a poorer grade (B = people who get a poorer grade), and Biff (Q = Biff) is a person who skips school (Q is an A), then he is also a person who gets a poorer grade (Q is a B). Logical principles show us that Biff's statements cannot all be true. At least one of his sentences is false. Either (1) some people who skip school do not receive lower grades or (2) Biff will not skip school or (3) Biff will receive a lower grade.

This example brings us to several other terms of crucial importance in logic and analytic philosophy. The first of these is "implication" or, equivalently, "entailment." At its simplest, an implication is a relation between two propositions, p and q, such that if p is true, q must also be true. In this, technical sense of the term, most of what we ordinarily call "implication" is not implication. For example, "Biff is a citizen of the United States" does not imply "Biff lives in the United States," because it is possible for "Biff is a citizen of the United States" to be true while "Biff lives in the United States" is false; more simply, Biff can be a nonresident citizen. However, take the following sentences. The first two sentences conjunctively imply the third sentence:

If (1) Biff is a citizen of the United States.
And (2) All citizens of the United States live in the United States.
Then (3) Biff lives in the United States.

This is a genuine or true implication because the conclusion cannot be false if the premises are true. Note that it does not matter that the premises are in fact false. Logic is not concerned with actual truth or falsity, but with relations of possible truth or falsity among propositions.

A notion related to that of implication is "bi-implication." A bi-implication is a relation between two propositions such that if one is true, the other is true, and if one is false, the other is false. Note that the preceding example is not a bi-implication; it is perfectly possible for Biff to live in the United States while not a citizen or while some citizens are nonresidents (that is, #3 can be true while #1 and #2 are false). In contrast, "Biff is of average height or short" and "Biff is not tall" imply one another (that is, form a bi-implication). If "Biff is of average height or short" is true, then "Biff is not tall" is true; if "Biff is of average height or short" is false, then "Biff is not tall" is false. A bi-implication is most often marked by the phrase "if and only if," thereby contrasting it with a simple implication, marked by "if" alone or "if . . . then." Thus we might say, "Biff is of average height or short if and only if Biff is not tall." And we might say, "If Biff lives in Minnesota, then he lives in the United States." But it would be wrong to say, "Biff lives in the United States if and only if he lives in Minnesota."

Another way of thinking about the difference between implications and bi-implications is in terms of necessary and sufficient conditions. An implication gives necessary or sufficient conditions, but not both; a bi-implication gives both. Since humanists are frequently unfamiliar with these terms, it is worth discussing them briefly. K is a sufficient condition for L if the occurrence or existence of K in and of itself leads to or involves L. K is a necessary condition for L if L cannot occur or exist without K. Thus we would say that decapitation is a sufficient condition for death; in other words, if Biff is decapitated, he dies. However, decapitation is not a necessary condition for death, because there are many other ways of dying. We cannot conclude that Biff was decapitated from the fact that he died. Being alive, in contrast, is a necessary but insufficient condition for dying. If something dies, it must have been alive; but being alive does not, in and of itself, make people die. Note that in both cases the relation is represented by an implication. In contrast, living in one of the fifty states or the District of Columbia is both a necessary and sufficient condition for living in the United States. Moreover, the relation between these two sentences is one of bi-implication. Someone lives in the United States if and only if he/she lives in one of the fifty states or the District of Columbia. Another way of putting this is to say that living in one of the fifty states or the District of Columbia "exhausts the logical possibilities" of living in the United States.

Above, we used the word "conjunction." Like "implication" and "bi-implication," this names a "logical connective," which is to say, a logical relation between propositions. A conjunction is a combination of two or more propositions (p *and* q, or p *and* q *and* r). It is true if and only if all the propositions in the conjunction are true. A disjunction (p *or* q, p *or* q *or* r) also is a combination of two or more propositions. However, it is true if at least one of the propositions is true. Thus "Biff is a citizen and Biff is a resident" is true if and only if Biff is both a citizen and a resident. "Biff is a citizen or Biff is a resident" is true if Biff is a citizen or if Biff is a resident or if Biff is both. Note that this is slightly different from our ordinary language use of "or." In common usage, "Biff is a citizen or Biff is a resident" is true if Biff is a citizen or if Biff is a resident, but *not* if Biff is both a citizen and a resident. In logical parlance, the latter, ordinary language relation is referred to as an "exclusive disjunction," because the truth of one proposition is taken to exclude the truth of the others.

In defining various logical connectives ("or," "and," "if . . . then," and "if and only if") we have used letters in place of various particulars. For example, we have used "p" and "q" to stand for sentences, so that "p and q" means "the conjunction of two sentences." These letters are called "variables" because they may be replaced by a variety of sentences—"Biff is a citizen (p) and Biff is a resident (q)," "All dogs eat meat (p) and the president is from Arkansas (q)." These sentences are called the "values" of the variables. The use of such variables is called "formalism" because "p and q" gives only the *form* of the conjunction. (Note, therefore, that "formalism" in this sense is different from "formalism" in the sense of chapter 5.) The substitution of a particular set of values for the variables—"Biff is a citizen" for "p" and "Biff is a resident" for "q"—is called an "interpretation" of the formula or an "instance" of the formula (equivalently, it "instantiates" the formula).

Once interpreted, formulas of the sort we have been discussing acquire a "truth-value," which is to say, they are either true or false. A true sentence has a truth-value "T" ("true"); a false sentence has a truth-value "F" ("false"). The laws of logic define formulas that are necessary truths. No matter what sentences we substitute for the variables, these formulas will remain true. However, other formulas—such as "p and q"—are true only under certain interpretations. For example, "p and q" is true under the interpretation "Clinton was elected president and Clinton was elected governor of Arkansas," but not under the interpretation "Clinton was elected president and Clinton was elected governor of Nebraska." Here we say that the truth-value of the formula "p and q" is a "function" of the truth-values of p and q; in other words, the truth-value of "p and q" is determined not by purely formal properties, but rather by the values of the variables. In contrast, consider the law of noncontradiction. This states that no proposition is both true and not true in the same sense at the same time; more formally, "-(p and-p)." This entire formula is true by reason of its form alone. There is no interpretation of "p" that would make this formula false. For example, it is true for p = "Clinton was governor of Arkansas" and for p = "Clinton was governor of Nebraska."

Philosophers in general distinguish between *a priori* knowledge and *a posteriori* knowledge. A priori knowledge is knowledge for which we do not need any empirical evidence; it may be justified without research into actual conditions in the world (though the discovery and demonstration of a priori truths may involve extensive and highly complex inferential reasoning; to say that a truth is justified without empirical research is not to say that it is self-evident). Logical truths are all a priori. A posteriori knowledge is knowledge that can be justified only through such research. Empirical truths are all a posteriori. Note that, despite the phrasing here, this is not a matter of temporal priority. We do not learn a priori truths first, then learn a posteriori truths. To say that logical truths are a priori is to say only that they are truths by reason of their form alone. To say that empirical truths are a posteriori is to say only that their truth or falsity is contingent upon conditions in the world.

This division seems to imply that all a priori truths are purely formal, that all a priori truths are logical truths, that no interpretations of logical formulas are true a priori. But in fact there are certain instances of implication that seem to be true independent of any conditions in the world, even though the implication is not true by form alone (that is, there are instances of "if p then q" that seem to be true a priori even though the general form "if p then q" is not true a priori). Specifically, following Kant, a number of Anglo-American philosophers have maintained that there are not only logical and empirical truths, but also truths derived from the analysis of concepts, and these too are a priori. Thus "If L is a bachelor, then L is an unmarried man," is an "analytic" truth, true a priori by the meanings of the terms alone. In contrast, "If L is currently President of the United States, then L likes to eat at McDonald's," is an empirical truth (when uttered in 1999), contingent on historical circumstances.

Another way of looking at this issue of truth and meaning is by reference to mathematics. Again, mathematics is not reducible to logic alone, but to logic plus set theory. And set theory has some significant implications for our understanding of semantics. Specifically, the distinction from set theory that has proven most important for semantics is that between the set itself and the class concept. A set is any collection of individuals (or other sets). A class concept is a criterion for forming that set. We may apply these ideas directly to ordinary language. "Dog," for example, involves a class concept (our definition of what constitutes being a dog—"a barking quadruped, commonly domesticated") as well as a set (consisting of all individual dogs). Semantically, we refer to the class concept as the "sense" or "meaning" or "definition" of the word and the set as the "extension" of the word.

Note that one set may conform to different criteria at any given time, and that one criterion will almost certainly define different sets at different times. For example, at one time "Irish-speakers" and "Irish people" would have defined the same set, though they represent different class concepts. Today, they define very different sets. Even more obviously, "Irish people" defines a different set today than it did a century ago. Note also that a set may have only one member. For example, "The green book on my desk" and "Volume 2 of Anscombe's *Collected Philosophical Papers*" happen to define the same set, a set with one member—that particular book. Of course, if I remove Anscombe's book from my desk and replace it with Russell's *Logic and Knowledge*, then these descriptions define different sets. Specifically, "The green book on my desk" now defines Russell's book, not Anscombe's.

This brings us to another distinction directly parallel to that between sense and extension—the distinction between sense and referent or, more exactly, between a name or definite description, on one hand, and a referent on the other. (The distinction between sense and referent was most famously drawn by Gottlob Frege; the present discussion does not strictly follow Frege, but extends his ideas in ways that have become standard in Anglo-American philosophy.) A definite description is a description specifying a single item or a set with one element, for example, "The green book on my desk." A definite description specifies a single item by defining a series of sets that intersect for one item only. (The intersection of two or more sets is their overlap; it consists in the elements they all share.) Thus, "the green book on my desk" may be interpreted in set theoretic terms as something like "The intersection of the set of green things and the set of books and the set of things on my desk," such that these three sets share only one element. Similarly, a name ("Bertrand Russell" or "Gottlob Frege") refers to a single item, though not by way of defining sets. (Actually, names can be understood as tacit definite descriptions, roughly "the intersection of the set of people named . . . and the set of people relevant to the current discourse [for the present context, the set of logicians and related philosophers].") The *referent* of a definite description or a name is the object to which the description or name refers. It is directly parallel to the extension of a common noun.

As already mentioned, for the most part these distinctions will not bear directly on our analysis of literature. However, they provide us with tools for clarifying and critiquing literary arguments. Many people trained in analytic philosophy feel that arguments and analyses in literary theory are frequently hopelessly muddled. Such arguments often confuse necessary with sufficient conditions, sense with extension, mere consistency with logical implication, and so on. Thus such arguments end up with mistaken or even paradoxical conclusions. Consider the confusion of consistency with entailment. Literary critics often conclude, implicitly or explicitly, that a theory is valid because it "applies" to a number of literary works. But such applicability is a matter of consistency only, not a matter of entailment.

Beyond this clarification of thought and argument, the principles of formal logic provide us with background necessary for understanding influential developments in formal analytic philosophy—first of all, logical positivism. Since much current literary theory is based upon continental metaphysics, such as that of Derrida, logical positivism provides a sharp contrast with typical modes of thought in literary theory. Thus, it may be particularly useful in questioning these modes of thought—whatever one's final conclusions about either logical positivism or continental metaphysics. The first thing to mention here is that logical positivism has been more thoroughly travestied than any other movement discussed in this book. Indeed, virtually any objectionable or naive position may be referred to as "positivist." The most common accusations, however, are that positivism is naively foundationalist, absolutist, based upon a sense of complete intuitive certainty, and opposed to all forms of discourse that are not scientific. In fact, none of these statements is true. For example, A. J. Ayer insisted that only tautologies are known with certainty; at best, other propositions are mere probable hypotheses (38). And Ayer, Russell (not a logical positivist in the strict sense, but a closely related "logical atomist"), and others were quite clear that the sort of foundational project envisioned by Descartes and Husserl, and based upon intuitive clarity, is impossible (see, for example, Russell, *Human Knowledge* 156). As to nonscientific discourses, Ayer was careful to explain that nothing in the logical positivist theory implies that poetry is nonsense or lacks meaning (44–45).

Logical positivism was, rather, a movement that sought to extend the sorts of analysis we have been considering. Specifically, for logical positivists, there are only two kinds of truth: (1) tautologies and (2) empirical truths. Tautologies are of two sorts: (a) logical truths and (b) analytic truths. Thus there are three sorts of rational task: (1) the development of logic, (2) semantic analysis, and (3) empirical research. Any claims or theories that rest on something other than logic, semantic analysis, and empirical research, are not rational pursuits, and cannot be true. Specifically, metaphysics—for example, discussions of "Being" or "the Absolute"—is not a rational pursuit and cannot be true. The same holds for normative aesthetics or ethics. On the other hand, aesthetics or ethics understood as, say, historical or cognitive phenomena are perfectly reasonable objects of study for a logical positivist. Moreover, literary theory is a perfectly reasonable pursuit. However, it is a pursuit that must be based upon logic, analysis, and empirical research. It must eliminate vague and unsupported claims, follow rigorous modes of argument, and so on.

The logical positivists further developed these views in formulating their conception of meaning as verifiability. They have been widely criticized for holding to the apparently absurd idea that a sentence can have meaning only if it is definitively verifiable. (Indeed, Russell criticized the logical positivists for just this.) But in most formulations the claim was much weaker. For example, Ayer insists only that "some experiential propositions can be deduced" from a given empirical (thus neither logical nor analytic) proposition (39). By "experiential propositions," Ayer meant something very specific—"observation sentences," sentences that make reference to direct experience or "sense data." The idea that sense data are fully isolable, directly experienced phenomena has been rejected by most recent schools of analytic philosophy. On the other hand, the basic idea of a "verifiability" criterion is not absurd. The important principle here is that a sentence that does not concern meanings or logical relations should have some empirical consequences if it is to be open to rational consideration—not, I think, an indefensible view.

In recent years, Donald Davidson has taken up and developed what is perhaps the central insight in this theory. In a series of influential papers, he has argued that a theory of meaning is reducible to a theory of truth. According to Davidson, to know the meaning of a sentence is to know the "truth conditions" of the sentence. "Truth conditions" are the conditions under which a statement would be true. More technically, Davidson draws on Alfred Tarski's definition of truth: "p" is true if and only if p. For example, "Snow is white" is true if and only if snow is white. To understand the meaning of the sentence, "Snow is white" is simply to know the conditions under which it would be true that snow is white. While one might argue that Davidson overestimates the value of truth conditions in meaning and interpretation, it seems clear that the determination of truth conditions is an important aspect of understanding meaning—especially of understanding the meaning of theories, literary or otherwise. It also seems clear that this is an aspect of semantics almost entirely ignored by the continental theorists who dominate literary theory.

A more broadly influential principle of the logical positivists, and the related logical atomists such as Russell, was the notion of linguistic analysis as a crucial means of resolving metaphysical dilemmas. The elimination of metaphysics as a legitimate discipline left these philosophers with a difficulty: If metaphysics is nonsense, why do so many people find the problems of metaphysics so pressing? If debate over these issues is pointless, even meaningless, why are people so deeply concerned with these issues? The answer is that there may be real issues there, real problems, and thus legitimate concerns; however, they have arisen in a metaphysical, and thus unresolvable, form because they have not been correctly analyzed. In short, our grammar can mislead us. Perhaps the crucial terms are ambiguous or vague; perhaps certain idioms lead us to a false analogy; maybe the form of the words causes us to think of experiences or events as if they were material objects. As Russell puts it in *Principles of Mathematics*, statements about certain abstract entities are not necessarily false or nonsensical (his examples are mathematical—points and numbers—but such metaphysical concepts as "goodness," "beauty," or "being" would have done equally well). Rather, "they need interpretation which shows that their linguistic form is misleading, and that, when they are rightly analyzed, the pseudo-entities in question [for instance, ' Being'] are found to be not mentioned in them" (xi).

In my view, this sort of analysis is absolutely invaluable. I have tried to practice it throughout this book, insofar as that is consistent with explicating theories of other writers. For example, one could understand the preceding delimitation of varieties of feminism as an analysis of this general sort. On the other hand, I do not take this to be a matter of determining the contents of a preexisting, autonomous meaning. Indeed, I would argue that the logical positivists' idea of meaning is metaphysical in precisely the sense they deplore. It is an hypostatization based on a misleading linguistic form. Meaning, implicitly understood as a substantive, external thing, is a "pseudo-entity" in Russell's sense. More exactly, I have argued elsewhere that there is and can be no such thing as "the meaning" of a term, sentence, or whatever (see chapter 1 of *On Interpretation*). The gist of my argument is the following. Any given term may be explained by a meaning or by an extension. If I want to explain what a dog is, I may give a definition ("A furry, four-legged mammal that is often domesticated as a pet") or I may point to a number of dogs, thereby indicating (part of) the extension of the term. Now if we want to say that a particular definition is correct or incorrect, we can do so only relative to an extension. For example, we might object to the preceding definition of "dog" on the grounds that it excludes wiener dogs (which are not furry) and includes all cats (which are furry, four-legged, and domesticated). In other words, as a class concept, it picks out the wrong set. On the other hand, we can judge the truth or falsity of an extension only relative to a definition. For example, we determine whether a given animal is a dog or a kind of wolf by reference to the definitions of "dog" and "wolf." Since we can judge definitions only by reference to extensions and we can judge extensions only by reference to definitions, no definition and no extension can be judged true or false "absolutely." A definition is true or false only relative to an extension. An extension is true or false only relative to a definition. In consequence, one or the other must be fixed arbitrarily. One or the other must be *stipulated*, either explicitly (as is done with technical terminology) or implicitly (as in ordinary language).

Thus no definition of any term is right or wrong unless we choose to make it so. There is no such thing as what a term "really means." Consider, for example, the word "meaning." Theorists often debate whether meaning "really is" authorial intent or individual reader response or historical reception, or whatever. By the argument just presented, these debates are pointless. They are "metaphysical" in the logical positivists' sense. Meaning isn't "really" any of these things. We are free to stipulate any of these objects as the variety of meaning with which we are concerned in a given interpretation. Indeed, it is incumbent upon us to do so if we are to follow clear and rigorous procedures in our interpretations. Moreover, as prolegomena to stipulation and interpretation, we need to isolate the varieties of meaning that might be stipulated—for there are many varieties beyond those ordinarily set out in interpretive theories, and these different varieties lead to different interpretive concerns and practices. For example, even if we consider only those varieties of meaning defined by reference to the author alone, we may distinguish literally intended word and sentence meaning, intention regarding the meaning of metaphors or symbols, broad thematic aim or purpose, evaluative attitude toward characters or events, associated unconscious fantasy, and so on. Clearly, each of these varieties of meaning will involve different interpretive practices and lead to different interpretive conclusions—even though they are all varieties of authorial intention.

In this view of interpretation, then, the isolation (and systematization) of varieties of meaning (along with relevant methodological principles), is perhaps the central task of a theory of interpretation. Of course, this is not logical positivism. Nor is it analysis in the technical sense. However, it is clearly a view that has developed out of the analytic project of logical positivism.

Needless to say, formal analytic philosophy does not end with logical positivism and logical empiricism. The most important contemporary analytic formalist is no doubt Willard Quine. Quine has accepted some views of his analytic predecessors, but he has criticized more than he has accepted. Perhaps most importantly, Quine has argued, in extremely influential work, that there is no such thing as an analytic truth, because meaning is not strictly separable from empirical belief. As this idea may appear completely implausible, it is worth illustrating the general point before going on. It seems, intuitively, that "male" is analytic with respect to "father"—indeed, "Fathers are male" would seem to be a paradigm case of an analytic truth. However, sex change operations make it possible now to have a father who is a woman. In other words, it is now possible to say, truthfully, "Some fathers are women." Thus a medical development (sex change operations) has in effect demonstrated that something we all thought of as definitional or analytic was, in fact, an empirical belief.

Quine's argument, however, does not rest on such examples. Rather he draws his conclusion from a conception of the way theories work. According to Quine, theories operate as wholes. We do not believe individual propositions, but rather entire complexes of propositions, entire theories. This "holism" leads Quine to the view that no segment of a theory is completely isolable from the rest of the theory. Changes in one part of the theory will have ramifications throughout the theory. "Meanings" cannot be, so to speak, quarantined from such changes. More generally, meanings cannot be quarantined from experience. What we call "meaning" is merely that part of the theory which we are least willing to revise due to experience. It is not a part intrinsically immune to such revision.

Quine not only believes that there is no such thing as pure meaning. He also believes that there is no such thing as pure experience. There are no such things as pure sense data. All observation is, as he puts it, "theory laden." In other words, an observation is already located in a theory; it is already integrated into a "conceptual scheme." For example, to observe that something is red is to have divided up the world in a certain way. We happen to have isolated a certain range of experiences as "red," another as "orange," and so on. This division, however, was not preordained as absolutely necessary. It is not a product of direct experience, but rather the creation of our conceptual scheme. Invoking the concept "red" is invoking a conceptual scheme, a theory of the world. This conclusion too follows from Quine's holism. As Quine puts the more general point, "the contribution which linguistic meaning makes to knowledge and the contribution which sensory evidence makes to knowledge are too inextricably intertwined to admit of a sentence-by-sentence separation" (*Ways* 139).

As a development of his view that there is no completely isolable analytic meaning, Quine has put forth his widely discussed thesis of "the indeterminacy of translation." According to Quine, there can be no such thing as a completely correct translation, even for single words, whether across languages or within a language (in the latter case, we would be more likely to say "interpretation" than "translation," but the point is the same). The reason for this is simple. There is no such thing as meaning per se. There are only holistic conceptual schemes. Thus translation is not a matter of isolating and pairing specific meanings in one language with directly equivalent meanings in another. Rather, it is a process of mapping one conceptual scheme onto another. And this can be done in many different ways. There is no single correct way of mapping one conceptual scheme onto another.

Quine's example is the (fictional) word "gavagai." Suppose we are field linguists working on a previously unknown language (a language known by monoglot speakers only). Our informant points toward a rabbit and says, "Gavagai." We may translate "gavagai" as "rabbit" or as "undetached rabbit part" or as "moment of rabbit existence." Whichever alternative we choose will have consequences elsewhere. If we translate "gavagai" as "rabbit," this will require us to translate other terms in specific ways. If we translate it as "undetached rabbit part," we will have to translate those other terms in different specific ways.

According to Quine, then, nothing can be correct or incorrect except relative to a theoretical structure or conceptual scheme. "Gavagai" does not "really" mean "rabbit" or "undetached rabbit part" or anything else. Rather, it means "rabbit" in one scheme, and "undetached rabbit part" in another, and so on. Quine compares a conceptual scheme to a Cartesian coordinate system. Readers who have forgotten their geometry may prefer as an analogy the grid on a map. On one map, Baltimore may be in G4; in another, it may be in L16; in another, it may cover the entire area of S3,

S4, T3, and T4. There is no right answer as to where Baltimore is located, except relative to a grid. In the first grid, Baltimore is at G4; it would be wrong to say that it is at L16. But the reverse is true in the second grid.

Donald Davidson has taken up Quine's ideas and argued (convincingly, I think) that there is no such thing as a conceptual scheme. The "grid" (or, equivalently, the "frame of reference") is nothing other than language itself. In consequence, Quine's view that the truth of a proposition is relative to a conceptual scheme reduces to the commonplace that the truth of a proposition is relative to the language in which it is uttered. In other words, Quine's seemingly radical and relativistic view ultimately implies only the triviality that a sentence is true "relative" to what it means. Any meaningful assertion—for example, "My lamp is red"—is as nonrelativistically true or false as we could imagine. The only "relativism" here is that to be true or false, an utterance must first of all be a meaningful assertion. Consider again a map. Even though some people might refer to it as "G4" and others as "L16," the location of Baltimore is as factually determinate as one could possibly imagine. Put differently, there is no relativism of facts here or of which truth conditions obtain in the world. The only "relativism" is a matter of which utterances have what truth conditions.

Note that none of this entails that "G4" and "L16," or any two words, must have the same meaning, or even the same extension, nor that they must be fully definite. "G4" and "L16" might cover very different areas, though both include Baltimore. Moreover, they may be vaguely defined— think of maps that do not include visible grid lines. Clearly, the same holds, even more strongly, for words of natural language, which are even more various and vague. But none of this affects Davidson's point. For none of it affects Baltimore.

The same arguments apply equally well to other versions of Quine's view, including those that pay more attention to literature and art—for example, Goodman's theory of frames of reference and world versions. Beginning from the premise that no statement is true except relative to a "frame of reference" (2–3)—that is, relative to a conceptual scheme, in Quine's terms—Goodman concludes that there are many "world versions," each defining "a world of our own making" (10), with no "real" world that might be discovered beneath or beyond these world versions. In addition to the Davidsonian problems with this view, Goodman may be faulted on the ground that his notion of world versions is perniciously vague. World versions range from cultural formations to scientific theories to art. The Eskimo view of snow defines a world version (8–9), as do contemporary theories in physics and biology (4–5), as do the paintings of Constable or the novels of Joyce (5). It is difficult to see how these quite different "frames of reference" might be understood as part of the extension of a coherent class concept. Perhaps Goodman is simply referring to the ways they affect saliency, the ways they change what we notice or pay attention to, which would make some sense. It is indeed true that vocabulary (such as the number of words for snow), theories in natural science, paintings, and novels all affect what appears most salient to us. And that is a significant point. But this does not appear to have any of the relativist consequences claimed by Goodman.

But neither this reply to Goodman nor Davidson's rejection of conceptual schemes fully responds to Quine's argument that meaning itself is indeterminate, that "gavagai" could equally mean "rabbit," "rabbit stage," "undetached rabbit part," and so on. In connection with this, Davidson has set forth an intriguing theory of interpretation. Specifically, in interpreting (or translating), he argues, we seek to preserve maximum agreement. We seek to make others "right, as far as we can tell, as often as possible" (136). Of course, Quine could retort that mere habit is not an argument that an approach is correct. Yes, we interpret other languages in terms of our own; that does not make our interpretations correct. But Davidson's point is a Kantian one. This is not a matter of particular hermeneutic contingency. It is a matter of general epistemological necessity. As Davidson explains, "What justifies the procedure is the fact that disagreement and agreement alike are intelligible only against a background of massive agreement" (137). Indeed, "Given the underlying methodology of interpretation, we could not be in a position to judge that others had concepts or beliefs radically different from our own" (197).

Here Davidson is in part arguing against such conceptual relativists as Sapir and Whorf, who maintained that Hopi and other native Americans conceive of the world entirely differently from the way Europeans conceive of the world. Davidson's argument is that Sapir and Whorf—and the contemporary cultural theorists who hold similar relativistic views—are making a claim that makes no interpretive sense and that, unsurprisingly, is inconsistent with their own arguments. Specifically, Whorf argues that Hopi and English concepts are radically different and he does so by explaining Hopi concepts in English. Whorf lands himself in the contradiction for Davidsonian reasons. When Whorf tries to demonstrate a discrepancy between Hopi and English with respect to one particular concept or set of concepts, he has no choice but to assume broad similarities between

Hopi and English on other concepts. Without that presupposed "background of massive agreement," we could not discuss or even conceive of conceptual divergence.

My own view on the issue is broadly Kantian as well, and in a sense encompasses Davidson's view. Specifically, all theory construction, including all linguistic interpretation, is partially guided by simplicity considerations. Given a range of alternatives, we implicitly choose that hypothesis which appears to be the simplest—roughly, that hypothesis which appears to account for the greatest range of data with the fewest posits and principles. For example, in the absence of recalcitrant data, it is simplest to assume that all cultures use animal terms (such as "gavagai") to refer to whole animals (for example, whole rabbits), rather than assuming that some cultures use these terms to refer to undetached animal parts. Insofar as our judgments are guided by simplicity criteria, this is not because the simplest theory is most likely to be true. In fact, it is difficult to say what this would even mean, how probability could be calculated in this context, and so on. Rather, we follow simplicity criteria for the Kantian reason that we have no choice but to follow simplicity criteria, much as we have no choice but to follow certain basic logical principles—however badly we might do so, especially in complex cases. (Needless to say, we often err in simplicity evaluations, sometimes severely.) In other words, it is not that simplicity criteria are "true"—whatever that might mean. We just cannot undertake an analysis or argument without them. Lacking simplicity criteria, even the most ordinary interpretive or inferential acts would be baffled by an inadjudicable proliferation of alternative hypotheses, such as those noted by Quine—for the quandary about whole rabbit versus undetached rabbit part applies not only to "gavagai" but to "rabbit" itself. Simplicity criteria are, in that sense, akin to Kant's transcendental principles. (For a fuller discussion of this, see chapter 1 of *On Interpretation*.)

Note that, in many cases, simplicity criteria will lead to the same conclusions as Davidson's "assumption of maximal truth" criterion. In other words, it is often simplest to assume that a speaker's words are maximally truthful. However, there are cases where we do not follow Davidson's criterion. Sometimes we assume that speakers are wildly mistaken in their claims (as when an unmedicated schizophrenic patient, who has no connection with Iran, speaks of an Iranian government plot to murder him/her). In these cases, it is fairly clear that we are following simplicity criteria.

It is worth noting that Davidson has been one of the few formal analytic philosophers who has had any impact on literary theory. For example, Reed Way Dasenbrock has argued that Davidson's antirelativism provides a powerful response to such currently influential theories as that of Stanley Fish. And Paisley Livingston has drawn on other aspects of Davidson's work to reconsider aspects of intentionalist interpretation. (Davidson insists that "in the end the sole source of linguistic meaning is the intentional production of tokens of sentences" ["Locating" 298]; he further argues that intention is a complex phenomenon, involving several distinct components.)

However, the school of formal analytic philosophy that has been most influential in literary theory has no doubt been possible worlds theory. Possible worlds theory developed out of the formalization and interpretation of "modal" logic, as worked out by Rudolf Carnap, Ruth Marcus, Saul Kripke, and others. Modal logic is a branch of formal logic that concerns necessity and possibility as "modal operators," explicit indicators of the "mode"—possibility, necessity, impossibility, or nonnecessity—of a proposition. Basic formulas of modal logic would include, for example, "It is necessary that p if and only if it is not possible that not p" (for example, "It is necessary that Socrates is mortal if and only if it is not possible that Socrates is not mortal"). Interpretations of ordinary logical formulas refer to the actual world. But, in terms of its reference to the actual world, "It is necessary that Socrates is mortal" is apparently indistinguishable from "Socrates is mortal." Put differently, the truth conditions for "It is necessary that" are unclear. In order to define truth conditions for modal operators, a number of theorists have interpreted such operators in relation to "possible worlds." A state of affairs is necessary if it occurs in all possible worlds; it is possible if it occurs in at least one possible world.

But what are possible worlds? Possible worlds are simply possible states of affairs. Most often, possible worlds share a history with the actual world, diverging only after a certain point. For example, suppose I begin to talk about how my life would have developed had I remained a mathematics major. I am considering a "counterfactual" situation, and thereby creating a possible world. But this possible world—in which I take a b.s. in mathematics—is identical with the actual world up until the point at which I (in the real world) decided not to continue in mathematics. In the counterfactual/possible world and in the actual world, I am born on the same day, do everything exactly the same all through infancy, early childhood, and so forth, even up through the beginning of college. It is only after a certain point that the two "world lines" or sequences of events become distinct.

After the bifurcation of the world lines, there are two Patrick Hogans—and, indeed, two of everyone else: the actual person and the counterfactual/possible person. Thus I would have a "counterpart" in the possible world (Patrick Hogan, the mathematician), and other people would have counterparts also. Some people—actual or possible—may not have counterparts. For example, suppose that, as a mathematician, I had children. As I have no children now, these counterfactual children would not have actual counterparts.

Note that possible worlds are not complete in the way the actual world is complete. They have "gaps." In other words, there are aspects of possible worlds that are indeterminate. Possible worlds are usually conceived of as identical with the actual world except as indicated. However, this cannot cover all cases. Take the possible world in which I become a mathematician. All the composition courses that I taught as a graduate student in English would still have to be taught, but by someone else. The teacher of those courses—as well as everything that went on in the courses—is a gap in that possible world. Moreover, it is a gap that may be filled in a number of different ways, each of which would define a distinct possible world.

Note also that only in the rarest instances will a possible world not share a history with the actual world. Even if the possible world is focused entirely on people with no counterparts in the actual world, or on a place with no such counterparts—that is, even if the people and the place are purely fictional—it is still likely to share with the actual world a good deal of public history. Also, every possible world must share a certain number of principles with the actual world (for example, principles of physics and biology and psychology). To advert to Davidson's views on translation, a possible world can be understood only if it is similar to the real world in a wide variety of ways.

There are two basic sorts of relations between worlds: those defined by history and those defined by concept, those of temporal sequence and those of similarity. Possible worlds theorists refer to these relations as "accessibility" and "proximity." One possible world is accessible from the actual world at any point at which it could split off as a separate world line. Moreover, one possible world is accessible from another possible world in the same way. Thus my continuing to major in mathematics defined a possible world accessible from the point prior to my decision no longer to major in mathematics. My becoming a professional mathematician is not itself directly accessible from the actual world at any point. However, it is accessible from the possible world in which I continue to major in mathematics. Had I decided to do so, I *could have* continued to major in mathematics; and, had I continued to major in mathematics, I *could have* become a professional mathematician. In each sentence, the "could have" marks a point at which a possible world was accessible.

Proximity is merely a relation of similarity. Two worlds (both counterfactual or one actual and one counterfactual) are more proximate to the degree that they are more similar. At one end, proximity becomes so great that the worlds are indistinguishable, hence identical. At the other end, proximity becomes so slight that one world is no longer conceivable, and is thus not a possible world at all. For example, a counterfactual world in which I wore a different shirt this morning is highly proximate; a counterfactual world in which all sentient beings are liquid is not proximate at all.

A number of literary critics have made use of possible worlds theory, for example, Umberto Eco and Thomas Pavel. Perhaps the most obvious use of possible worlds theory for literary study is in the application of its vocabulary to various problems of the relations between literature and the world. For example, a literary work is not a creation out of nothing, with no connection whatsoever to the real world. On the other hand, to describe the work as "imitation" or "mimesis" seems to many people either vague or overly constricting. Perhaps it would be better to conceive of a literary work as defining a possible world. Having said this, we are free to determine the degree to which this possible world shares a world line with the actual world (for example, the degree to which it presupposes specific historical events). Moreover, we are free to examine the degree to which it is or is not proximate to the real world. Indeed, the notion of proximity, understood as a relation of degree, might profitably replace the notion of realism. Realism is too often understood as a simple property. Thus we say that a work is or is not realistic. But the options are clearly much more complex than this. A possible worlds conception of literary works leads us to a different, more refined, and more accurate, view: All literary worlds deviate from the actual world, but they do so in varying manners and degrees.

Consider, for example, the particular case of fictionalized history. Clearly, the nature of the genre is not well captured by saying that it is realistic or highly mimetic or the like. It is much more clearly definable using possible worlds terminology. Specifically, we begin with an account of the actual world that has gaps. Our written history is, in fact, a possible world that we assume to be identical with the actual world, except that actual history is complete, whereas written history, like all possible worlds, is incomplete. A fictionalized history, then, is a possible world that is one (possible, that is, accessible) specification of the (less fully definite) possible world of written history.

Another potential use of possible worlds theory would be for conceptualizing plot coherence or necessity. Aristotle argued that the events in a plot must form a probable or necessary sequence. However, many literary works involve events that are impossible in the actual world, and yet are perfectly plausible within the plots in which they occur. This may seem to pose a problem for Aristotle. However, we could rephrase Aristotle's criterion in terms of possible worlds: In a successful plot, each event must determine a possible world accessible from the possible world of the preceding event. This allows for a determination of possibility or necessity within possible worlds that is different from that of the actual world—and thus more obviously in keeping with our experience of necessity in literary works. For example, this allows magic to have causal efficacy in appropriate works. Note that this criterion (of accessibility of possible worlds within the sequence of events in the plot) is not constrained by any fixed degree of proximity between those possible worlds and the real world. The requisite degree of proximity is fixed in the work itself—more in fictionalized history, less in fantasy.

Having said all that, however, it is worth sounding a caution. Possible worlds are ontologically hazy, somewhat mystical entities. They seem to be a prime case of the sort of metaphysical excess decried by the logical positivists. Clearly, they do not exist, for if they did exist, they would be the actual world. But if they do not exist, how, precisely, do we explain anything by referring to them? They may provide us with a model for rethinking certain literary issues. And they may be very valuable in that capacity. But it seems doubtful (to say the least) that they can provide any sort of genuine explanation of literary phenomena. (Unless perhaps we adopt David Lewis's Twilight Zone–like view that reality is world-relative—for example, in the world where I am a mathematician, *that* world is real and this world, where I am a literary theorist, is merely possible. On the other hand, one suspects that this sort of theory might create more problems than it solves.)

## Anglo-American Philosophy of Language (II): Meaning in Use

As we have already indicated, there was a large group of analytic philosophers who argued that meaning is best understood not in terms of a mathematical formalism, but rather as a socially functional means of communication. The views of these writers are frequently summed up in the slogan "Meaning is use," that is, use in communication with others, use within society, use toward specific practical purposes. The division here is in some ways parallel to that between psychologists who do research in laboratories and psychologists whose research is focused on real situations in the real world. The advantage of the first approach is that it allows the researcher maximum control of variables, though in an artificial situation. The advantage of the second approach is that it allows us to consider real situations, though with many uncontrolled variables. A similar point could be made about theories based on formalism and theories based on use. Each is valuable, but partial.

Bertrand Russell was one of the first writers to emphasize the importance of use. In 1919, well before the development of ordinary-language philosophy or any other theory of communication-intention, he wrote that "A word has a meaning, more or less vague; but the meaning is only to be discovered by observing its use: the use comes first, and the meaning is distilled out of it" (300). In the 1940s, Ludwig Wittgenstein took up and developed this idea in his *Philosophical Investigations*, though he did so in a way far more reminiscent of Heidegger than of Russell. (Wittgenstein was familiar with Heidegger's work and saw its value, even in his earliest, most positivistic period [see Monk 282–83 and 310].)

Wittgenstein had begun his philosophical career as a sort of logical positivist, albeit a peculiarly mystical one. In the *Tractatus Logico-Philosophicus*, he set out to determine what could be discussed meaningfully and to indicate how that could be discussed precisely and lucidly. But, unlike other logical positivists, his deepest concerns seemed to be with what cannot be discussed meaningfully, all that "we must pass over in silence" (74). Take, for example, his extremely nonpositivistic assertion, "It is clear that ethics cannot be put into words. Ethics is transcendental. (Ethics and aesthetics are one and the same)" (71). Oddly enough, his later, nonformalist work appears far less mystical. By allowing a larger world of human experience and interaction to enter his philosophy, he seems to have lost the need for something that completely transcends that philosophy.

In any event, while Wittgenstein's early work was important in the development of formalism, his later work was crucial in the development of the nonformalist alternative. Early in the *Philosophical Investigations,* Wittgenstein wrote that "For a *large* class of cases—though not for all—in which we employ the word 'meaning' it can be defined thus: the meaning of a word is its use in the language" (20e). What is important about Wittgenstein's work is that he does not assume that "use" is a transparent concept. He sets out to examine what use is. One can read the bulk of the *Philosophical Investigations* as a study of just this problem.

Wittgenstein introduces several concepts in order to clarify and develop this concept of use. One of the most important is that of a "language game." This is a somewhat vague, but nonetheless suggestive, notion. The idea is that language may be thought of as comparable to a board game or even a sporting contest: It is, specifically, a form of personal interaction governed by a set of socially defined rules. Note what a difference this analogy makes to the way we think about language (in contrast with conceiving of language in terms of logic and set theory). Language becomes social and communicative in the first place, rational and referential only secondarily. (Though, it is still rational and referential; the concerns of the formalists are rendered secondary, not eliminated.)

This is clearer as we press Wittgenstein's analogy. Take chess. Words are like the chess pieces; the rules of language (including semantics and syntax) are comparable to the ways in which we are allowed to use the pieces (a bishop can move diagonally, a rook horizontally or vertically). But neither the pieces nor the rules have any function outside of actual games in which they are employed in specific moves made by specific players, with each move a response to all previous moves and to the situation resulting from all those previous moves. Clearly, the meaning of a move—say, knight to king's bishop 3—is its use in such a game, not the formal rule that the knight is permitted to move two squares in one direction then one at a right angle. (The analogy could be developed more accurately by noting various standard moves, their place in various standard openings, defenses, and so forth; however, the general point should be clear enough without this elaboration.)

Moreover, just as there are different sorts of game, there are different sorts of language game. An oral exam is one sort of language game, a religious ceremony another—picking someone up in a bar, being stopped for speeding, requesting a telephone number from Information, are all language games as well. Each has specific purposes, moves governed by social rules, and so on. To understand a language is, for Wittgenstein, not a matter of, say, recognizing truth conditions, but of being able to play a variety of language games. One of Wittgenstein's favorite examples of a language game concerns a builder and his/her assistant. The builder shouts, "Board!" and the assistant brings a board, or "Brick!" and the assistant brings a brick. One might also think of a surgeon saying, "Scalpel!" or "Suction!" or "Sponge!" Wittgenstein's point is that, in each case, understanding the utterance is a matter of knowing what to do in the language game. And this means knowing not only what to say, but what action to undertake, if that is what is required. It is not a matter of conceiving the class concept and the extension of "board" or "scalpel," but of handing over a certain object in a certain way.

The notion of a language game, however, is inadequate in and of itself. Though Wittgenstein does not put it this way, I suppose one could create a voice-sensitive machine that would transmit a scalpel at the right moment. But we would not say that the surgery-assistance machine was thereby understanding the language or even playing the language game. For language games are part of something larger. This is what Wittgenstein calls a "form of life" (a concept that is, in my view, widely misunderstood). A form of life is simply our socially determined existence, everything we do as a function of being in a particular society. The interaction between a man and a woman in a singles bar constitutes a language game (with specific conventions, purposes, and so forth) only insofar as it fits into an entire form of life that includes everything from dating (contrast a society in which marriages are arranged by parents) to a structure of physical space that gives bars a certain function, everything from the variety of ways we dress to the physical proximity in which we speak. "Can I buy you a drink?" does not have any simple meaning on its own. It has meaning only in a particular language game (picking someone up, having a business lunch, congratulating a Ph.D. student after a successful dissertation defense). And that language game itself has significance and confers meaning only due to its place in the encompassing form of life.

The same could be said for "Do you know how fast you were going?" spoken by a police officer. It is part of a specific language game—that of giving/receiving a speeding ticket. But that language game too has meaning only in the context of a larger form of life that includes driving, the actions and operations of a police force, and so on. Again, a language game cannot be understood in isolation from a form of life any more than an utterance can be understood in isolation from a language game.

I take this to be the central point of Wittgenstein's famous argument against the possibility of a "private language." It is commonly thought that Wittgenstein did not believe meaning could be idiolectal, that he insisted meaning must have a social existence. In other words, he is usually taken to be claiming that meaning can be presumed constant only if it is communally defined. This is clearly a variation on the common Romantic and Idealist notion that the world can be presumed to have fixed existence only if it is defined by a community. We have encountered this view in such writers as Schelling, Husserl, and Fish. In each case, it is highly problematic.

In any event, whether Wittgenstein held to this communal view or not, it does not seem to be the main implication of the private language argument, or at least not what is most important or valuable about that argument. Rather, the crucial idea seems to be that the entire function of a language is bound up with a social form of life. Removed from a social form of life, language has no function. Indeed, Wittgenstein indicated this pretty straightforwardly, when he wrote that "to imagine a language means to imagine a form of life" (8e; compare the claim of *On Certainty* that statements of doubt or certainty have no point outside of a [social] language game [see, for example, 5, 76, 88, 89]).

The most obvious value of Wittgenstein's thought for literary theorists is in criticizing theories of language—primarily textualist theories such as New Criticism and deconstruction—that isolate language from the particular situations of language games and the larger practices and attitudes that define forms of life. However, it could also prove useful to consider poetry or fiction or film or literary criticism or literary theory or popular reviewing as a language game—a series of interactive moves, following social conventions, aimed toward specific purposes—and to consider how that language game fits into our form of life. We often think of literary criticism in terms of validity or plausibility—in terms of truth conditions, though few humanists would put it this way. But literary criticism does constitute a language game in Wittgenstein's sense, or, rather, a set of language games: a New Critical language game, a deconstructive language game, a phenomenological language game. And these operate within a form of life that includes teaching classes, publishing, going to conferences, drawing a paycheck, applying for promotion.

Other distinctions drawn by Wittgenstein may prove valuable to literary study as well. For example, Wittgenstein argued that the extension of a term in ordinary language is not determined by a single class concept, but rather by a set of overlapping criteria that pick out a certain "family resemblance" in the objects. Thus, there is no single property held in common by all games, he argues. But there are a number of distinct similarities that link some games with other games (tennis is similar to chess in one way, to "catch" in another), so that each member is linked into the network. Games are, thus, similar to one another in the way that members of a family are similar: Jim and Sally have the same nose, Sally and Biff the same color hair, and so on. This notion may be of use in understanding literary movements, genres, periods, or other problematic categories of literary study. Instead of seeking a single criterion that defines, for example, the essence of Romanticism, we might be better advised to seek a cluster of concepts that sketch out the family resemblance among various forms of Romanticism.

Perhaps equally valuable are the ideas of Wittgenstein's student Elizabeth Anscombe. Focusing in particular on the notion of intention, Anscombe has brilliantly discussed a number of topics of central interest to literary theorists. For example, Anscombe has emphasized that every action is intended only "under a construal." There are infinitely many ways in which a given action may be described. But when I act, I intend or understand my action only under some limited number of descriptions. In other words, I construe it in a certain way. Suppose I am chopping wood. I may intend to make firewood or to build up some muscle or to make enough noise to awaken a sleeping house guest or to create a lot of sawdust or to improve the view from my window or to engage in the destruction of living things. In fact, I probably intend one or two of these; the others are unintended consequences of my action. To take a literary example, what is most perhaps striking about Othello's final speech is that he reveals his construal of the murder. He does not construe it as the murder of a particular individual, Desdemona, or of his wife or even of a woman whose honor had been unfairly questioned; he construes it as the murder of a Venetian. And he construes his suicide not as suicide, not as the death of this particular person, Othello, not even as the execution of a man who killed his wife, but as the execution of someone who is not European and who has killed a European. Clearly, the construal of an action—in literature or in life—can be as important as the performance of that action.

Anscombe also distinguishes between a mental cause and a motive for an action. A motive is one's self-conscious reason for doing something. A mental cause is a situation or event or series of events that drives one to act in a certain way. Suppose I get up and start pacing swiftly around the room, and you ask, "Why are you doing that?" If I say, "I want to look like Wittgenstein, who had a reputation for doing things like this," then we are dealing with a motive. However, if I say, "I don't know. I suppose the band music coming in the window got me stirred up," then we are dealing with a mental cause. This too is an extremely valuable distinction for literary study. For example, we might infer that revenge was the motive for Othello's murder, but a complex of racial conflicts was its mental cause.

Related to this, Anscombe distinguishes between the object of an emotion and the cause of an emotion. The object is, of course, the person or thing that the emotion concerns. The cause is what gives rise to the emotion. This distinction allows us to formulate and consider a series of interesting questions: What is the cause of Othello's love of Desdemona and of Desdemona's love of Othello? For example, what specific construals of the object of love are relevant to its cause in these cases? What factors are causally relevant outside of the object (as construed in a particular way)? How does this relate to the cause of Othello's subsequent hatred of Desdemona? Who is the object and what is the cause of Iago's hatred, or jealousy?

While Wittgenstein and Anscombe were working at Cambridge, another group of nonformalist philosophers was working at Oxford. This group included such theorists as Peter Strawson, Paul Grice, and John Austin. Strawson referred to this group by the name "theorists of communication-intention." He defined their project in the following terms: "first, present and elucidate a primitive concept of *communication* (or communication-intention) in terms that do not presuppose the concept of *linguistic meaning;* then show that the latter concept can be, and is to be, explained in terms of the former" (521). The "fundamental concept" in such a theory "is that of a speaker's, or, generally, an utterer's, *meaning something by* an audience-directed utterance on a particular occasion" (521).

This best describes Paul Grice's project, for Grice has set out to define word meaning and sentence meaning as functions of speaker's meaning—where "speaker's meaning" is (roughly) the speaker's intent to get a listener to understand some specific thing by a specific utterance. One can see immediately how this project shares with Wittgenstein's analyses a conception of meaning as located in the real world of practical activity. Indeed, we could use Wittgenstein's example to illustrate Grice's point. When the builder shouts, "Plank!" what is important for Grice is not the autonomous or textualist meaning of the word "plank" (if there is such a thing), but rather the speaker's aim of getting the assistant to understand that he/she should now bring a plank. Indeed, depending upon the circumstances, the builder may not want a plank at all. Perhaps, he/she has just taken the plank delivered by the assistant and thrown it away, shouting "Plank!" and thereby indicating that a plank is precisely what he/she does not want. Under other circumstances, the builder might be indicating that the assistant should bring the next thing set out on the plank or something made by Plank Bros., Inc., or the item that looks like a plank.

In Grice's view, every speaker has a certain "repertoire" of communicative techniques. These are formed on the basis of a wide range of social interactions of the sort discussed by Wittgenstein. In interacting with people, from childhood onward, we build up this repertoire, learning ways in which we can get other people to understand what we intend— for example, we learn to say "plank" when we wish to refer to a certain sort of object, "slab" when we wish to refer to something else, "Please bring the plank" when we wish to request a certain sort of action, and so on. In this view, then, the "meanings" of words and sentences are not autonomous entities, but derivatives of techniques commonly used by speakers to communicate their intents. In other words, as with Russell, uses, or techniques of communication, are primary; "meanings" are a sort of by-product or distillation or abstraction from these uses or techniques.

As part of this communicative and intentional conception of meaning, Grice sets out his four maxims of "conversational implicature." As Grice points out, very little of what we infer about an utterer's intent is the result of implication in the strict logical sense. Indeed, if we based our inferences purely on logical implication, we would understand very little of what people say to us. Thus we must rely on inferences guided by something other than logical implication. Grice calls this "conversational implicature."

The maxims isolated by Grice are directed to speakers but could easily be rephrased to address listeners. In fact, it is precisely because they are assumed by listeners that speakers can use them. Grice sees all four maxims as following from the general "cooperative principle" of conversation—the principle that speakers and listeners should speak in such a way as to further the purposes of the conversation. The four maxims are

1. Maxim of Quality: "Try to make your contribution one that is true," or, more specifically, do not make claims that you believe to be false or for which you lack adequate evidence. For example, if someone says, "Clinton is seriously ill," I assume he/she has some evidence for this. I feel that I have been seriously misled if I ask where he/she heard this and am told, "Oh, I didn't hear anything; it just occurred to me."

2. Maxim of Relevance: "Be relevant." We assume that speakers' comments are relevant to a topic under discussion, though there is, of course, no narrowly logical reason for this. Grice is widely misunderstood. Reading the preceding sentence, you no doubt assumed that I meant that Grice

is widely misunderstood about the maxim of relevance. Suppose I then add, this is because he stutters badly. You then see that I have suddenly changed topic without notifying you. I am no longer speaking about Grice's theories, but about the audibility of his oral speech. Thus I am violating the second maxim.

The second maxim is particularly crucial in our understanding of literature, for we assume the relevance of a wide range of properties and patterns that may, at first glance, seem irrelevant. Take Ezra Pound's poem "In a Station of the Metro," which consists of these lines: "The apparition of these faces in the crowd; / Petals on a wet, black bough." The poem works as a poem only if we assume the relevance of the title to the lines and vice versa. On the other hand, this is not an ideal example, for, in fact, we assume a much higher degree of relevance in literature than this example indicates. This case barely goes beyond ordinary conversational assumptions of relevance, while in literary interpretation, we assume the relevance of, for instance, widely dispersed image patterns. We assume that repeated images of, say, fire or of the seasons or plants and birds are relevant to the larger structure and meaning of the work. In short, we extend the maxim of relevance as far as we can; we assume "maximal" relevance (see Kiparsky 196 n. 7).

3. Maxim of Quantity: "Make your contribution as informative as required and only that informative." This is really an extension of the maxim of relevance. It states that we should give all and only the information relevant to understanding the topic at hand. If I tell you a story about how a bright job candidate was rejected by the hiring committee, in order to indicate that the committee was prejudiced, I need to tell you that the candidate was black and that all the committee members were white. Otherwise, you won't understand the point of the story. On the other hand, if I tell you that this candidate was born in Kansas, I am giving too much information; this is irrelevant.

4. Maxim of Manner: "Be brief, orderly, clear, and unambiguous in your phrasing." Perhaps the most obvious applicability of this maxim is to literary theory itself. It should come as no surprise that much literary theory violates the maxim of manner. It is often verbose, meandering, opaque, and ambiguous. However, readers favorably inclined toward such writings tend to assume that it does follow the cooperative principle and thus that it is as brief, orderly, clear, and unambiguous as possible. This gives rise to a sense of profundity—especially when the maxims of quantity and quality are also not followed. We assume that Lacan or Derrida has evidence for his claims, that he has given us adequate information to under-

stand these claims. Our lack of understanding, then, encourages in us a sense that we are inadequate to the task of interpretation, that the work is "above our heads." To a great extent, the mystique of currently prestigious literary theories rests on their authors' refusal to follow the cooperative principle consistently. This is not to say that they never follow it. In fact, they follow it most of the time. But they stop following it at certain key points. A thoroughgoing Gricean analysis of a range of literary theories, and the reception of these theories, would no doubt be a valuable project.

As Grice emphasizes, however, a speaker may violate maxims in a way that is not misleading. Specifically, he/she may "flout" a maxim. To flout a maxim is to violate it blatantly, in such a way as to make it obvious that one is violating the maxim and thus to "implicate" that there must be an unspoken reason for this violation. Consider a letter of recommendation for a college teaching position that says only, "Mr. Smith has been a student in our program for sixteen years. In all that time, he has never committed a parking violation. In addition, he is unfailingly well groomed." In saying nothing about the student's capabilities as a scholar and teacher, and in treating matters that have little importance for college teaching, this recommendation blatantly violates or flouts the principles of quantity and relevance. We conclude that it carries the "implicature" that Mr. Smith has no genuine academic qualities. The notion of flouting has considerable relevance to literary study, as we shall discuss below in connection with Mary Louise Pratt's theories.

It may be argued that our use and interpretation of Grice's maxims is merely a specification of an ordinary interpretive procedure of choosing the simplest hypothesis consistent with the data. Indeed, they are not an entirely accurate specification of this general procedure. We always follow principles of simplicity (within our capacities), but we do not always follow Grice's maxims. In other words, sometimes Grice's maxims conflict with simplicity evaluations, and in cases of conflict we choose simplicity. For example, it is usually simplest to assume that a speaker intends his/her comments to be relevant to a topic under discussion. On the other hand, it is sometimes simplest to assume that his/her comments are not relevant—if, for example, a sensitive topic has come up and we suspect that the speaker wants to avoid that topic, or if the speaker is someone notorious for going off on tangents; in these cases, we do not assume that the maxim of relevance is being followed.

Despite this, Grice's articulation of these four maxims is of great practical value. It specifies and thus renders salient the most common consequences of following simplicity criteria in interpretation. It thereby allows us to examine these consequences in greater detail and to understand them more fully. Another, perhaps even more influential strain of communication-intention theory is that of speech-act theory. First formulated by John Austin, then developed by John Searle and others, speech-act theory further extends the idea that meaning is best understood in relation to the functions of language in social interaction. Specifically, Austin points out that the vast majority of semantic theory focuses on assertions of fact: "The cat is on the mat," "Clinton is the President," and so on. However, we do many things with language besides assert. We order, persuade, promise, convince, inquire; we inaugurate, enact (a law), baptize, consecrate, and so on. While Russell and others made reference to the various uses of language beyond asserting, it was not until Austin's *How To Do Things With Words* that these other uses of language were systematically investigated.

Austin began by defining "speech acts" as actions performed by the use of language and "performatives" as the verbs that can be used to perform these acts. In contrast, "constatives" are verbs that can only describe and not perform. Baptizing, for example, or marrying or promising, is a verbal act that does not name a situation, but creates it; "baptize" and "promise" can function as performative verbs. "I pronounce you husband and wife" does not describe an act of marriage, but constitutes that act; the same holds for "I baptize you 'Biff'" or "I promise to be there at 7:30." In connection with this, Austin drew several distinctions. First of all, he distinguished between direct and indirect speech acts. Direct speech acts are speech acts in which the act is named explicitly by the use of the appropriate performative verb: "I *promise* to be there at 7:30" or "I *baptize* you 'Biff'." An indirect speech act, in contrast, does not use the appropriate performative verb; either it does not name the act ("I'll be there at 7:30," said as a promise) or it names the act wrongly ("I promise to be there at 7:30," said not as a promise, but as a threat).

The performative force of an utterance—its function as promising, baptizing, threatening, whether direct or indirect—Austin calls the "illocutionary force" of the utterance. More exactly, he contrasts locutions, illocutions, and perlocutions. A locution is simply whatever is said (including its linguistically specified meanings, referents, and so forth)—for example, "Be there at 7:30," with "be" in the imperative mood, "there" referring to a contextually defined place, "7:30" referring to a point in a particular time sequence, and so on. The illocution is the performative force of the utterance; for the preceding example, we would paraphrase the illocution as, for example, *he urged me to be there at 7:30*. The perlocution adds the effect of the utterance. In the case just cited, we might paraphrase the "perlocutionary effect" as, *he convinced me to be there at 7:30*—for convincing, unlike urging, implies a specific effect.

Just as an assertion has truth conditions, other illocutions have "satisfaction conditions." There are conditions under which a promise is fulfilled, an order carried out, and so on. In other words, for an assertion to be true, a promise to be fulfilled, an order to be carried out, certain conditions must obtain. In addition, Austin argued, for an assertion or a promise or an order to be *made* at all, certain conditions must obtain. Any speech act may be "infelicitous." For a speech act to be made successfully, it must fulfill certain "felicity conditions."

As to felicity conditions, consider the following examples. Suppose I am joking with some friends and say, "I now pronounce you husband and wife." I have not, in fact, married them. My speech act is infelicitous. Suppose I am in a play and deliver the line "I promise to kill the evil Don Fernando." I have not, in fact, promised to kill anyone. Suppose a student turns in yet another excellent paper, and I say, "You'd better watch out; another essay like this and I might just give you an 'A' in this course." I have not threatened the student. The first speech act fails because, among other things, I must have a certain institutional authority for my words to have the appropriate illocutionary force. Part of the felicity conditions for marrying people concerns the institutional position of the speaker. The second speech act fails because the words are uttered in a context where they are not used by the speaker, but in effect quoted from a text. And it is a general felicity condition that the speaker use the words of the locution and not merely quote them. The third fails because it is part of the felicity conditions for a threat that the action threatened be undesirable.

Austin further distinguishes between infelicities in which the speech act does not occur ("misfires," he calls them) and those in which it occurs, but is uttered insincerely ("abuses"). The preceding examples all concern misfires. Again, if I utter, "I promise," in a play, no act of promising has occurred, and this utterance is infelicitous precisely because no act of promising has occurred. In contrast, imagine that, in an ordinary conversation, I say "I promise to do such-and-such," but I say this with no intention of actually doing such-and-such. In this case, an act of promising has occurred, but it too is infelicitous, in this case because it is an abuse of promising (due to my insincerity).

There are many ways in which the speech-act theory can be applied to the study of literature. Some of these have been explored by Mary Louise Pratt, Stanley Fish, and others. For example, Pratt has developed a broad theory of literature, arguing that literature is itself a particular sort of speech act. Specifically, Pratt begins by arguing that the Russian formalists were mistaken in thinking that literary language is qualitatively different from ordinary language. In Pratt's view, literary speech follows the same general principles as ordinary speech. Most importantly, it follows the general principles isolated by Austin, Grice, and others—though literary speech instantiates these principles in a specific way that makes it literary (rather than, say, contractual).

More exactly, literature, according to Pratt, is an instance of a "display text," which is to say, a discourse presented because it is "tellable," that is, "unusual, contrary to expectations, or otherwise problematic." As Pratt explains, "In making an assertion whose relevance is tellability, a speaker is not only reporting but also verbally *displaying* a state of affairs, inviting his addressee(s) to join him in contemplating it, evaluating it, and responding to it" (136). As Pratt points out, this is not uniquely literary. Indeed, much of our ordinary conversational speech consists in display texts of precisely this sort (for example, amusing anecdotes). (In fact, Pratt is very close to Jakobson's view of poetry as message-emphasizing.) In connection with this, she stresses that literary narratives follow the general principles of conversational implicature—as well as the general principles of conversational storytelling, as analyzed by William Labov. At the same time, however, Pratt notes that many literary texts flout Grice's maxims, self-consciously deviating from standard structures.

Pratt goes on to explain that, when a literary work overtly violates a Gricean maxim, we assume that the cooperative principle is still in effect and that the author has not merely failed in his/her attempt at communication. For these reasons, we go on to interpret the work. For example, if an author seems to give us more information than is necessary for understanding, we do not assume that he/she is simply prolix (has failed to follow the maxim of quantity). Rather, we assume that the "extra" details are open to interpretation. If we read that "Othello turned and looked into Desdemona's blue eyes," we would assume that the "extraneous" word "blue" is open to interpretation. In fact, in the preceding pages, many of our analyses of *Othello* rest directly on this sort of assumption.

Pratt's argument is thoughtful and rigorous, and in my view provides us with many insights into the nature of literature, its relation to ordinary discourse, and so on. Unfortunately, as far as I have been able to ascertain, it has not really been taken up and extended by other thinkers. One can imagine many ways in which Pratt's insights could be extended. For example, it could be valuable to examine how Gricean maxims, as well as felicity conditions for speech acts, speech acts themselves, and so forth, are employed or flouted in different types of literature. Consider the mystery novel. It clearly depends in part on a systematic manipulation of the maxim of quantity. Specifically, it involves the withholding of some information ("who done it") until the end of the narrative. It also involves the providing of interpretable "excess" information ("clues"), as well as genuinely excess information ("false clues"), and so on. Postmodern works may typically involve the flouting of all maxims in such a way that each interpretation of one act of flouting contradicts interpretations of other acts, so that the reader cannot determine what precisely is true or false, relevant or irrelevant. A study of this sort (already hinted at in some of Pratt's analyses) might prove very valuable in the study of at least some genres, periods, movements—even in the works of single authors, who may have their own typical "strategies" for flouting Grice's maxims.

As to practical criticism, however, the most obvious way to use these theories is to examine the use of speech acts in a work of literature and the felicity or infelicity of these acts. Considering *Othello* in these terms leads to some unexpected insights into the play. If we look at patterns in the use of speech acts, some of what we find is quite predictable. For example, we discover that Iago's speech is filled with (duplicitous) acts of advice. However, when we look at Othello's speech, we find something much more interesting. Let us briefly consider two speech acts: questioning (that is, requesting information) and ordering. Othello has the authority to give orders. Giving orders is, in fact, central to his position as general of the Venetian forces. However, Othello is far less prone to order than he is to question. And when he does order, it is most often to put an end to conflict, and to begin a process of questioning. For example, when assaulted by Brabantio, he orders his followers to refrain from violence, then asks Brabantio where he might go to answer Brabantio's accusations. When Brabantio answers, "To prison," Othello does not order or threaten, but asks further questions (1.2.80–89). Similarly, when Cassio and Montano fight, Othello enters and asks, "What is the matter here?" He then orders them to stop fighting, asks three questions, again orders them to stop, orders silence, asks another question, then asks five more questions in the course of dialogue.

What does all this tell us? As to Othello, it provides further evidence that he is far from the impetuous, overly passionate character some critics have believed him to be. In fact, he is a man of reflection, not passion, a man of mind, not heart. He is deeply and systematically concerned to acquire knowledge before acting—though once he feels that he has acquired knowledge, he acts decisively, as one would expect from a general (and a surgeon).

Moreover, Othello's questioning indicates the thematic importance of questioning for the play as a whole. It is in many ways a play about the uncertainty and manipulability of knowledge, or what one takes to be knowledge. Indeed, the intensity of questioning in the play directly parallels the emotional intensity of the plot, as it mirrors the increasing confusion of the characters. The first two acts have only one question for every eleven lines. In the third act, this jumps to one question for every six lines; in the fourth act, to one question for every four lines; it trails off slightly in the final act (where the questions are, in effect, finally answered) with one question for every five lines. The frequency and intensity of this speech act thus follow a classic dramatic structure of increasing tension leading to resolution or partial resolution. Or, rather, they help to create that structure. And they help to thematize the tragic impossibility of knowing—especially, in this case, knowing someone else's mind, even a spouse's or a (supposed) friend's.

### Contemporary Linguistic Theory: Idiolect and Universals

In 1957, Noam Chomsky revolutionized linguistics. His book *Syntactic Structures* is widely held to have demonstrated the inadequacy of previous linguistic theories and the need for the formulation of a new approach to linguistic study. We have already discussed briefly his transformational conception of linguistic structure. Here, I will concentrate on some other concepts of Chomskyan linguistics, particularly the notion of universals—a notion that Chomsky shares with a range of linguists, from Roman Jakobson to Joseph Greenberg. Before going on to this, however, it is important to lay out some of the basic principles of Chomskyan linguistic theory.

After "transformations," the best known technical concepts articulated by Chomsky are those of "competence" and "performance." The distinction between competence and performance is frequently assimilated to the Saussurean distinction between langue and parole. However, this is a false parallel. And it is false in ways that are directly relevant to contemporary literary theory. As we have seen, many of the most influential modern critical theories assume that language is in some sense independent of speakers, that it is, one might say, "autonomous." For example, one way of construing deconstruction is as a method for understanding the systematic discrepancy between a speaker's intent and the meaning of the (autonomous) language he/she is using (see, for example, de Man 11). In deconstruction and related theories, this concept of an autonomous language is based primarily on de Saussure's idea of langue as a system independent of individual speakers.

However, for Chomsky, there is no such thing as langue, and more generally there is no such thing as autonomous language. Performance is, indeed, comparable to parole. Performance is simply what one says—with all of its errors, incompleteness, and so on. However, competence is not langue. It is, rather, what is sometimes called "idiolect." It is the set of rules that exist only in a given individual's mind and that guide his/her linguistic performance.

Admittedly, the rules of different speakers in one community will largely overlap. My rules and your rules will be substantially the same. That is why Chomsky refers to this as "competence." These internal or mental rules have been acquired through interaction with others and thus allow one to function in society. They are not a "private language," in the sense of an idiosyncratic set of rules that do not bear on social relations. On the other hand, they are not entirely identical from person to person. (Think, for example, of the different shades of meaning that words have for different speakers.) Most importantly, they do not have any existence independent of these speakers. They are solely and entirely mental entities. One consequence of this is that there is no such thing as the meaning of a word as such. There is only the meaning in my idiolect or in your idiolect or in someone else's idiolect. There is, of course, the meaning that is most widely shared by members of a given community, but, again, that meaning does not exist separately from those speakers. It is not part of any system distinct from the systems of those idiolects.

Chomsky phrases this issue slightly differently in his more recent work. There he contrasts "I-language" and "E-language." I-language or "internalized language" is idiolect. E-language or "externalized language" is langue or some other version of autonomous language. According to Chomsky—and most other theoretical linguists writing today—there is no such thing as E-language. There is only I-language. Correlatively, there is no such thing as "English" or "French" or "Hindi" or "Chinese." When we seem to be referring to E-language, we are merely abstracting from a variety of I-languages. We are merely referring to what a set of I-languages has in common. Saying "In English, plurals are formed by . . . " or "In Chinese, the meaning of . . . is . . ." is, in effect, a sort of shorthand.

Chomsky has offered powerful arguments for this view and they have been widely accepted within linguistics. However, they are virtually unknown to literary theorists, who tend to assume unself-reflectively that there is something along the lines of langue, some sort of autonomous language (even if they would not refer to it in precisely this manner). It is arguable that little current literary theory would survive, were Chomsky's arguments even taken into consideration.

In some ways, Chomsky's theories individualize and isolate speakers from one another. They cut speakers off from any unifying langue, in effect giving them each their own language. But, again, it is not a private language. Speakers work to accommodate their internalized principles to those of other members of their community. And they succeed—not perfectly, of course, but quite well. In large part, Chomsky argues, this success is due to the fact that our linguistic inclinations are so similar. Indeed, putatively different languages share a remarkable range of principles. Relative to their similarities, their differences are superficial. According to Chomsky, it is these shared principles that allow the child to achieve competence and, thus, allow linguistic communication. These shared principles are called "universals" (not only by Chomsky, but also by such non-Chomskyan theorists as Joseph Greenberg who have been influential in the study of cross-cultural linguistic invariance). This entire set of principles is called "universal grammar" and is, according to Chomsky, part of our genetic endowment. In this way, Chomsky does not isolate speakers from one another at all. Rather, he posits a profound link among all speakers. Thus, the difference between Chomsky and de Saussure, in this regard, is that de Saussure links speakers together at the level of national language, whereas Chomsky, denying the existence of national languages per se, links speakers together at the level of shared humanity.

To clarify the linguistic point, we need to introduce another distinction drawn by Chomsky, that between "descriptive adequacy" and "explanatory adequacy." This is a distinction that applies primarily to linguistic theory, but has implications for literary study as well. A grammar is descriptively adequate if it has described the competence of a speaker. And this is true only if it is "generative"—only if it consists in a system of rules that can generate all and only the (grammatical) utterances that a speaker could produce, along with a correct structural description of each of those utterances. In other words, the generative grammar must be able to produce such a sentence as "Bob Dole is an automaton fabricated by Martian robotics hobbyists" (even though this sentence may never have been uttered, had I not written it just now). And it must count "hobbyist" as a noun, not an adverb; it must make the sentence mean that Bob Dole is an automaton, and so forth, not that my desk lamp is red, and so on.

Chomsky seeks to achieve descriptive adequacy through the formulation of a generative grammar that is also transformational. For this reason, people frequently confuse the notion of a generative grammar with that of a transformational grammar. However, the concepts are distinct.

A theory has explanatory adequacy if it gives an account of how such a generative grammar is acquired, how competence comes about. Chomsky seeks to achieve explanatory adequacy by positing universal grammar as a set of specifically linguistic principles that are innate to all humans. (This is called "the innateness hypothesis.") One might also seek to achieve explanatory adequacy by reference to more general cognitive structures, and without positing any innate structures that are specifically linguistic.

These views have several consequences for literary theory. First of all, the existence of linguistic universals seems to indicate that there will be universal patterns across a wide range of cultural phenomena—including literature. The broad and detailed human commonality of language isolated by Chomsky, Greenberg, and others, gives us reason to seek a similarly broad and detailed human commonality in literature. Secondly, in pursuing the study of literary universals, we should seek to achieve descriptive adequacy in our formulation of literary principles. We should not only identify isolated universal patterns, we should also seek to articulate the complex of principles that define or "generate" these patterns. In other words, we should set as our ideal the formulation of a "generative poetics" (though not necessarily, or even probably, a transformational poetics—one serious mistake of literary theorists who have tried to apply Chomsky's theories to literature).

Finally, we should seek to achieve explanatory adequacy by giving an account of the genesis of the principles of generative poetics and thus of the literary universals they define. There are several ways in which we might do this. We may simply follow Chomsky's lead and posit an innate "module" for literature, an inborn universal poetics comparable to universal grammar. We might also make literary universals parasitic on linguistic universals. In other words, we might argue that literary universals simply result from universal grammar. This is the way in which Paul Kiparsky treats literary universals. Finally, we might explain literary universals by reference to more general cognitive structures, of the sort discussed by cognitive scientists, for example. This is my own view.

Before going on to some examples of literary universals, it is important to point out that there are several varieties of universals (for further discussion, see 15–22 and 30–35 of Comrie). First of all, universals may be absolute—for example, they may apply to all literatures at all times. But they need not be. And even absolute universals need not apply to all works. For example, it is almost certainly a universal that all literatures have literary forms structured by sound patterns. However, this is not to say that all works of literature are structured by sound patterns. For example, English has metrical poetry, and thus satisfies this universal claim; however, not all works of English literature are metrical poetry. Moreover, there are plenty of universals that do not apply to all bodies of literature. Specifically, there are "statistical" universals and "typological" universals. Statistical universals are patterns that hold across most, but not necessarily all, bodies of literature. Typological universals are universals that hold only for certain types of literature. For example, there seem to be a number of universals that apply to written literature, but not to oral literature (and vice versa). Thus these universals would be typological.

Another important distinction is that between "formal" and "substantive" universals (see Chomsky, *Aspects* 27–30). Formal universals concern abstract principles; substantive universals concern elements or constituents. This is a relative distinction, not an absolute one. But it is important in practice. Take the following assertion: "In literatures written in places with appropriate seasons, there is a frequent association of spring with love and winter with death." If true (as it probably is), this states a (typological) substantive universal. In contrast, consider the following: "All literatures frequently link some natural, cyclical phenomenon with the cycle of human life." If true (as it probably is), this states an (absolute) formal universal.

Finally, we should note an important methodological consideration. We have isolated a literary universal only if we have found it present in a range of unrelated traditions. If the traditions are historically related, then we may be dealing with a common ancestor or with influence, not with a true universal. Thus, for example, the postcolonial literatures of Africa, India, Europe, and so on, have no special relevance to the discernment of a universal. Rather, it is the precolonial African, Indian, Chinese, Japanese, European, and other traditions that are important.

The study of literary universals is primarily a part of the theory of literature and is likely to have fewer consequences for the theory and practice of interpretation. Again, in interpretation we are concerned with what differentiates one work from another. In the theory of literature, we are concerned with what similarities link them together. The study of literary universals is relevant primarily to our broad understanding of literature—and ultimately to our broad understanding of the human mind. (This is not to say that the study of universals never has interpretive consequences; see, for example, Lalita Pandit, "Patriarchy," for a detailed literary interpretation that relies on and extends universal principles).

There are many likely candidates for literary universal, most more formal than substantive. For example, all the following devices are found in the classical literatures of Greece, India, China, Japan, and the Middle East: plot circularity (such as beginning and ending in the same type of location or with the same sort of action or event), foreshadowing, structural and verbal parallelism, patterning of images, metaphors, alliteration, assonance. One might say that these are all part of the "repertoire of techniques" available to writers in creating literary works. Related to this, all or almost all traditions appear to have genres, recurrent patterns or structures of literary composition, including short nonnarrative verse (lyric) and short prose fiction (tale). There are also universals that are more substantive. As already mentioned, love is commonly linked with spring or some appropriate equivalent and death with winter. The separation and reunion of lovers is one standard plot across written traditions. Written traditions appear to share certain motifs, such as that of mistaken identity; certain character types, such as the bumpkin—as well as the hero, heroine, and villain; and certain themes, such as the conflict between desire and duty.

Sometimes a number of features cluster together to form a universal pattern of surprising complexity and detail. For example, all dramatic traditions (European, Indian, Chinese, Japanese, and so on) have a form of romantic tragicomedy. Moreover, this genre is usually prominent within a tradition. The plot of romantic tragicomedy centers around a man and a woman who fall in love, but their love in some way conflicts with society, often because they are from different social groups, but sometimes because of some specific fault or error on the part of one or the other. As a result of this conflict, the lovers are separated. The initial romance is most often associated with spring, or sometimes mild summer or autumn, with images of flowers in bloom and birds singing, or, sometimes images of harvest—in any case, the initial romance is linked with images of natural beauty, life, and fertility. The separation is represented in images of freezing winter or scorching summer, thus natural barrenness, and is presented as a sort of death. It is linked with darkness as well and frequently involves severe illness, and even apparent death. The lovers are ultimately reunited, again in spring, with appropriate imagery of birth or rebirth—often including cure from illness or even a miraculous resurrection. The final reunion often involves a spiritual element absent from the original union. In addition, these plays usually begin and end in the same place or the same sort of place (often a garden or some other place of natural fertility). Note that this is only an outline of some common principles of romantic tragicomedy, found in the dramatic traditions of Europe, India, China, Japan, and so on (as well as the story literatures of other regions). It does not come close to descriptive adequacy—much less explanatory adequacy—but does give some idea of just how extensive literary universals can be. (As this particular case suggests, there are clear precedents for this sort of study prior to Chomsky—most obviously the work of Northrop Frye. However, Frye drew almost entirely upon a single tradition. In consequence, he cannot be said to have isolated literary universals, but only to have suggested areas for research. For that, however, his work is extremely valuable.)

To gain a better understanding of both descriptive and explanatory adequacy, it is worth looking in more detail at one particular universal: poetic line length. All traditions have verse. This is an absolute universal. In other words, all traditions have some form of literature that is organized by what we call "lines," units defined not by syntactic or semantic completion, but by a certain number of occurrences of some syllabic property. More exactly, lines are determined by a simple count of syllables or by a count of a particular sort of syllable (stressed syllables, in English meter). Note that this is an important and surprising fact. Standard poetic lines could just as easily be defined by number of speech sounds or by number of diphthongs or by number of words. They are not.

How, then, do we explain this phenomenon? As we have already mentioned, Kiparsky seeks to achieve explanatory adequacy for universal poetics by deriving literary universals from universal grammar. For example, he argues that formal rules of poetry do not (standardly) make reference to any entity that does not figure in universal grammar. Simplifying somewhat, Kiparsky's analysis is roughly the following: All ordinary language is organized into periodized rhythmic sequences. The rules governing these sequences in everyday speech involve reference to syllable stress and to units composed of stressed and unstressed syllables. For this reason, periodic rhythmic sequences in verse are organized by reference to the same entities, the same properties and structures—syllable stress and units composed of stressed and unstressed syllables. (Kiparsky argues that this is true even in literatures in which it does not at first seem to be the case; see 194.) Rhythm in ordinary speech is never defined by, for example, number of speech sounds or number of diphthongs, nor is any other linguistic organization defined in these terms. Knowing this fact about universal grammar, we can understand the parallel fact in universal poetics.

An alternative to Kiparsky's theory would be to view both the linguistic and the poetic principles as manifesting broader cognitive/perceptual principles. In other words, in this view (which I favor), universals of poetic rhythm do not derive from a specifically linguistic endowment. Rather, our cognitive/perceptual makeup sensitizes us to rhythm and periodicity in certain ways, allowing us to perceive certain sorts of rhythm and not others, rendering some rhythmic patterns more salient than others. It is these cognitive/perceptual propensities that manifest themselves in linguistic principles concerning rhythm and in literary principles concerning rhythm. In other words, universal grammar and universal poetics are closely related, not because the latter is, so to speak, parasitic on the former, but rather because both are based on the more encompassing principles of human cognition and perception.

In any event, Kiparsky's theory clearly leaves a number of matters unexplained. And many of these could be profitably considered in relation to general principles of cognition and perception. For instance, although the precise versification systems of different languages vary widely, most have a standard line length that, however defined, almost invariably includes between five and nine words. English pentameter tends to center around ten syllables and seven words, for example. Chinese, in comparison, has standard line lengths of five and seven syllables; but, since it is a monosyllabic language, these lines contain five and seven words respectively. The major exceptions to this rule seem to be found in highly morphologically complex languages. For example, the standard line lengths of Mwindo or Dinka include fewer than five words. But in these cases, the words contain a much larger number of morphemes. This indicates that in speaking of words, we may not yet have achieved descriptive adequacy. It may be necessary for us to rephrase our universal principle here in terms of number of morphemes, perhaps morphemes of a certain type ("inflectional" morphemes, such as those marking subject/verb agreement, may not count).

In any event, we have a good explanation available to us for this phenomenon, however formulated—though this explanation too is inadequately specified in terms of whether it applies to words, morphemes, or something else. Specifically, contemporary cognitive science posits three types of memory. The first is perceptual memory, which retains sensory data very briefly (see Johnson-Laird 146). The second is long-term memory. This has two components, one for skills (for example, remembering how to ride a bicycle or do arithmetic), the other for "dictionary" or "encyclopedia" knowledge (for example, remembering that Jefferson City is the capital of Missouri) and personal experiences (for example, what happened yesterday). (I will refer to these as *skill memory* and *representational memory*, respectively. The latter term should not be taken to imply any commitment to "representational" theories of language or mind, such as those of Chomsky and Fodor.)

The final type of memory is "working memory." This has a fairly limited capacity and includes only items actively under one's consideration. More exactly, it involves the "rehearsal" of short "representational" strings, often as intermediate stages in larger cognitive processes. For our purposes, these strings are most importantly linguistic, though they may also involve spatial or other schemas. For example, suppose you are lost somewhere in a town with which you are broadly familiar. Combining linguistic and spatial structures, you might "keep in mind"—or rehearse in working memory—the turns you have taken thus far (so you can retrace your route). Simultaneously, you may be trying to "get your bearings" or solve the larger problem by locating yourself relative to some landmark stored in long-term representational memory and related to skills used in getting to a desired location (skills stored in long-term skill memory, including all the skills necessary to drive a car). Unfortunately, the structure of rehearsal memory has not been tested in connection with morphemes or morphologically complex languages. However, it has been tested in terms of words in morphologically simpler languages and, as it turns out, our rehearsal memory tends to "chunk" linguistic units into sequences of between five and nine words.

This leads to the following hypothesis. Again, every poetic tradition develops a method for determining poetic lines. This method is always a matter of counting syllables of some sort. Whatever method one uses, however, the resulting lines must be rehearsable in working memory. Thus they must be between five and nine words long (or, perhaps, they must have a certain number of morphemes, which very often works out to between five and nine words, at least in morphologically less complex languages such as English—or perhaps there is yet another organizing principle for working memory with this consequence). There are probably two reasons for this. One is practical and concerns recitation. Whether a poem is being composed extempore, in performance in an oral society, or has been memorized, the most memorable and recitable unit will be a unit that is rehearsable in working memory. More importantly, as Abhinavagupta argued, when we experience a literary work of art, we savor it, we "taste" it again and again; we do not skim through a poem to get the information, but linger over it. Lingering over a poem is, in part, a matter of rehearsing its lines—even as we are reading them and rereading them. Thus, to be most effective, the length of the poetic line should be appropriate to the capacity of our working memory—for rehearsal is a crucial part of aesthetic savoring and such rehearsal is performed in working memory. (For a further discussion of these issues, see my "Literary Universals" and citations.)

## Cognitive Science

This discussion of working memory and poetic line length leads us directly to cognitive science. The task of cognitive science is to understand the human mind—its faculties, capacities, processes, and so on. In seeking this understanding, cognitive scientists frequently employ the computer as a model for the mind and as one means of specifying and testing theories about the mind. One can already see the influence of a computing analogy in the account of memory just given. Perceptual memory is parallel to the screen of a monitor. Working memory is a small version of random-access memory (with a text component and a graphics component). And long-term memory is what is stored on disk—knowledge/experience falling under the category of "document files" and skill falling under the category of "programs." As to testing theories, this is primarily a matter of working to be as specific and detailed as possible, with the constant aim of advancing artificial intelligence. In the past, much psychology has been perniciously vague. It has often relied on intuitive concepts which are difficult to specify or explain. Cognitive scientists seek to avoid pernicious vagueness by specifying theories in terms of explicit, programmable computational procedures or algorithms. A theory is certainly not perniciously vague if it can be represented in a finite number of steps that can be executed by a computer.

Within this general framework, cognitive science is a vast field which is only now beginning to have influence in literary theory. I cannot give anything like an overview of this field. Rather, I shall focus on a few of the most obvious points of connection between the concerns of cognitive science and literary theory. (Unfortunately, this means that I will pass over some very worthwhile work in the field. To supplement the current account, I refer the reader to Hernadi, Spolsky, and Hobbs.)

First of all, we should distinguish three sorts of cognitive structure: "schemas," "prototypes," and what I shall call "exempla." (I should note here that the terminology of cognitive science is not entirely fixed even with respect to schemas, prototypes, and "models" [to which we shall turn below]. My use of these terms is broadly in keeping with that of cognitive scientists, but I am specifying the definitions of these terms as I will be using them. Readers who take up texts in cognitive science should not assume that these terms will be used in precisely my senses.) Put very simply, schemas are structures of abstract or general knowledge and skill that are specified or "filled in" in particular circumstances. A standard example of a schema (sometimes called a "script" in this context) is ordering a meal in a restaurant. We follow a series of steps that can, for the most part, be formalized in a computer program. We enter. We check for clues as to whether we seat ourselves or wait to be seated. Such clues range from explicit signs ("Please Wait To Be Seated") to the presence or absence of table cloths. We go to the table, read the menu, order, and so on. This general schema is specified by circumstances in obvious ways. We enter different restaurants by different doors, sometimes by different types of doors—doors with knobs, swing doors, revolving doors, for each of which we have a "door opening" schema. We read different menus, order different foods, and so on.

Schemas are stored in long-term representational or skill memory, specifically in a sort of mental lexicon. Perhaps the first thing to note about work on the lexicon in cognitive science is that here too standard post-structural views are indirectly refuted. Most approaches to meaning in cognitive science are psychological and "practical" or functional in focus. They are certainly not autonomist. As Philip Johnson-Laird writes, "A theory that relates words to the world . . . willy-nilly relates words to one another, and renders superfluous those theories that carry out only the latter task" (334).

The lexicon is often taken to include "encyclopedia" information as well as dictionary information (that is, empirical as well as "definitional" information), and even personal, associative material. I will assume that all this information is indeed contained in a single cognitive component—the lexicon—but nothing in what I am saying rests on this assumption. Everyone agrees that encyclopedia and personal information are linked with definitional information, whether within a single component, or across distinct components. Take, for example, the word "father." I will assume that definitional material ("male progenitor"), empirical beliefs ("often primary wage earner in petit bourgeois families, though much less so than formerly"), and personal information (say, recollections having to do with my own father) are all contained in my lexical entry for "father." But even if they are contained in three separate components of long-term memory, they will be cross-indexed. In other words, items in the definitional component will be linked with parallel items in the encyclopedia and personal components. And this comes to much the same thing. (On the other hand, combining all three in one component eliminates the potential problem of strictly separating definition from empirical belief—a separation that is difficult to maintain, as Quine has shown.)

More exactly, lexical entries clearly include lists of properties definitionally or typically applied to the objects named by the term. In appropriate cases, they include lists of procedures as well. Thus "father" would include the properties "male" and "parent." For many people, it would also include "primary breadwinner," "in charge of discipline," and so on. "Entering a restaurant" would include "check for self-seating versus seating by host/hostess." Property and procedure lists are organized into hierarchized structures that define schemas. Prototypes are constituted by the "typical" properties linked to a schema. A man may have one arm or two, but the "prototypical" man has two arms. Or, to take a more complex example, it is often remarked that "bird" has a specific prototype in most people's minds. This prototype is pretty much that of a robin. When I write "bird," most of you first call to mind a creature rather like a robin—not like a chicken or an ostrich or even a sea gull. The creature you call to mind is a prototype stored in your lexical entry for "bird." Sometimes, schemas are thought of as the entire list of properties, and so on, including all alternative possibilities, hierarchically ordered. In this sense, schemas encompass prototypes. On the other hand, sometimes schemas are thought of as the definitional part only, the section of a lexical entry common to all alternatives, the necessary and sufficient conditions of the entry (if there are any). In this sense, the prototype encompasses the schema. Either way, the work of Eleanor Rosch and others has established that prototypes are far more important to our cognition than are schemas in either of these senses. Finally, exempla are merely instances of schemas, concrete particulars. My father, for example, is an exemplum of "father" and is noted as such in my lexical entry.

The information in a lexical entry is best conceived of as ordered into a "default hierarchy," and divided into various subcomponents. A default hierarchy is an order of properties, procedures, and so forth, within schemas and prototypes. The order is set up in such a way that, when interpreting, we assume that all the highest level properties apply unless we are given reason not to do so. Thus, again, when I say that there are birds lining up on my window sill, you assume I mean robinlike birds, not chickens or penguins. Moreover, you assume that these are "normal" robinlike birds, with two wings, a beak, two eyes, and so on. In other words, you unreflectively or automatically assume the prototype case, defined by the default properties of a schema.

On the other hand, these default hierarchies may be reordered according to context. If I live on the sea shore, far from trees and greenery, you may assume that I mean gulls or other sea birds (though you may also assume the standard, robinlike default). Or, to take a specific property rather than a prototype, our default assumption about birds is that they can fly. But, in an appropriate context, we may bypass this default. As far as I can tell, in my lexicon, there are two alternatives to the default: (a) flightless birds: penguin, and (b) incapacitated birds. In an appropriate context (the wing amputation ward of a bird hospital?), I may switch to either as the default option. And, of course, in ordinary circumstances I will discard the default for specific cases (as when speaking of an injured bird).

Models are schemas, prototypes, or exempla that we use to structure and understand different schemas, prototypes, and exempla. Typically, models for a given "target" are drawn from a distinct "domain"; they are drawn from outside the complex of lexical entries that are closely related to the target entry. A good example of modeling across domains may be found in cognitive science itself, when the schema of a computer is used as a model for the human mind. In this case, cognitive scientists use what we know about computers to structure what we know about the human mind and to suggest and organize further ways of studying the mind. For example, they take the various sorts of memory in a computer and then look at what we know about human memory. We know that people can remember certain things for short periods, other things for long periods; we know that they can remember a certain amount of information when organized in one way, less if organized in a second way, more if organized in a third way, and so on. They then try to systematize this information and posit mental structures based on structures in the computer (or, more exactly, in our lexical schema for computers). Thus they posit long-term memory as something very close to disk storage, but working memory as much more loosely analogous to random-access memory, and perceptual memory as vaguely suggestive of what is actually present on a monitor screen. In thinking of the human mind on the model of a computer, we are not specifying the schema or prototype (as we would if we were learning how to use a new computer). Rather, we are using the computer to generate a new conceptual organization—which then may itself be formulated in an abstract schema, as has occurred with the theory of memory just discussed. (There are clearly limits to this modeling. The mind is not a computer, and thus the extensive use of this model is likely to distort our understanding of the human mind in certain ways, whatever its general usefulness. It is important to stress this point as it is something cognitive researchers do not always recognize.)

As George Lakoff, Eva Kittay, and others have emphasized, modeling is aptly conceived of as a form of metaphor. Thus it is reasonable to say, for example, that cognitive scientists explore mind through the metaphor of the computer. Lakoff, Mark Johnson, Mark Turner, and others have stressed that there are many metaphors or complexes of metaphor that are socially widespread and that, unbeknownst to us, guide our thought and action concerning a broad range of topics. For example, Lakoff and Johnson point out that we tend to conceive of dispute on the model of war: We engage in a *battle* of wits in which you *attack* my *position* and I *defend* my *ground*, and so on. Turner argues that this metaphor is only one form of a more general metaphor, that of the mind as a body moving in space (118). We find this metaphor when someone says, for example, "After presenting the new evidence, I *moved on* to another *point*" or "I used to indulge in a lot of self-pity, but I'm trying to *get away from* that now."

One may wonder whether these are always models (that is, "live" metaphors), or something more like schemas (literalized from "dead" metaphors). In either case, it is valuable to isolate and understand them—in general speech, in works of literature, or in works of literary theory and criticism. Lakoff and Turner have explored the operation of common metaphors and systems of metaphor in literary works. But it is perhaps equally interesting to examine the use of such metaphors in literary criticism, the ways in which models and schemas guide argument and analysis. Years before the development of cognitive science, M. H. Abrams engaged in just such an examination, treating metaphors of organism in Romantic literary theory. Abrams revealed the degree to which such metaphors pervade these writings, and the degree to which they—and not the logic of the arguments—determine the conclusions of these theories.

As far as I am aware, no one has undertaken this sort of analysis of contemporary literary theory, though it would no doubt be extremely valuable. Many contemporary theories make extensive use of physical models for language, meaning, discourse, and so on. One predominant metaphor is that of determinate meaning as government. In this model, authorial meaning is assimilated to authoritarian rule; reader response is linked with democracy, and so on. This sort of model is frequently extended to the advocacy of "destabilizing" fixed (authoritarian) signification through the celebration of a (democratic) multiplicity of meanings, and so on. Such an extension, in turn, participates in the more general metaphor of social forms as works of architecture—government as a building, language as a "structure." Contemporary textualists often use this model in an unusual way, for they tend to see language and meaning not as having structure, but as breaking structure, not as constructing, but as deconstructing. On the other hand, contemporary textualists also tend to see interpretations as things we "construct" (like houses), not things we "uncover," say, or "infer."

Many of the conclusions of contemporary textualists seem to follow directly from their metaphors. Recognizing these metaphors and their functions allows us to evaluate these theories more astutely, and to debate them more productively. For example, many critics would assert that meaning is stable, and many others would assert that it is unstable. But some (including myself) would reject the architectural/governmental metaphor that forces this choice upon us. Such critics would insist that it makes little sense to speak of meaning in terms of either stability or instability (and even less sense to dismiss as authoritarian all theories that do not celebrate "democratic" instability—including those theories that reject the entire model as misleading). But until we recognize the use of this metaphor, we can neither accept nor reject it.

The notions of schema, prototype, exemplum, and model have many implications for literary theory outside of the study of metaphor. For example, in reading, we "access" some general schemas which we specify in the course of reading. These schemas range from poetic forms (sonnet, ballad, and so forth), to genre conventions (such as the separation and reunion of lovers in romantic tragicomedy), to character types, and so on. Indeed, literary works invariably and necessarily presuppose such schemas, whether they follow or "subvert" them. Various theories of reader response and reception—most obviously the work of Iser and Jauss—could be redeveloped in relation to such concepts.

We also invoke exempla in reading, usually for more specific characteristics. Suppose you have read one novel by an author, and begin to read a second. In reading the second novel, you are likely to keep the first tacitly in mind as a model exemplum for interpreting and evaluating events in the second novel. If the first novel is filled with irony, made clear only at the end, you will be more inclined to find irony in the second novel, right from the beginning. The same holds for reading in a genre or a period (suppose you have read one postmodern novel, and are embarking on a second). We still invoke exempla as models even when we have read more than one book by an author or in a genre or period. However, as instances accumulate, they will tend to contribute to the formation of schemas and prototypes, or to break down the category. In other words, suppose I read many postmodern novels. As I read them, I will either begin to form them into patterns or I will not. If I form them into patterns, these are likely to become more and more like schemas and prototypes. If I do not form them into patterns, I am likely to come to think of the category "postmodern" as a sort of catchall for which there are no useful general structures and for which exempla are not helpful as models.

At least as interesting, in my view, are the schemas, prototypes, and exempla employed by authors. These should be central to our understanding of phenomena ranging from genre to literary influence to the relation between biography and literature. Consider, for instance, genre. The genre of a work may be defined in a number of ways. It may be defined by a set of textual properties (as isolated by a theorist). It may be defined by the expectations of a reader. It may be defined by the marketing strategies of a publisher. But it may also be defined by the author's generic conception of the work. This conception is a matter of schemas and/or prototypes, insofar as the author has (tacitly) abstracted principles from earlier works in that genre, and a matter of exempla, insofar as the author (tacitly) uses specific works from that genre as models.

More exactly, we may see literary creation as a "multi-stage" process (in Johnson-Laird's term [258]) in which the author writes, evaluates, rewrites, reevaluates, and so on, implicitly using schemas, prototypes, and exempla to guide each stage. Thus an author might (unself-consciously) develop an initial structure for a work on the basis of schemas and prototypes, subsequently revising that work by tacit comparison with successful exempla. (Actually, schemas, prototypes, and exempla enter at each stage; I divide them in this way simply for ease and clarity of exposition.)

Consider, for example, an author who wishes to write a story based on a romantic involvement in his/her life. He/she cannot represent all aspects, elements, details, of the romance—this would produce a work that was chaotic, tedious, and literally infinite. He/she needs to "cut and cast," as the Chinese theorists would say (see Liu 179). In drafting this story, then, this author will draw on some structure, such as the prototypical structure of romantic tragicomedy, that involves a painful separation of the lovers due to a conflict with society, particular sorts of associated imagery, and so on. This is not to say that he/she will self-consciously set out to use this structure. That is, of course, possible. But it is more likely that he/she has internalized this prototype by reading many romantic tragicomedies and that it will serve to guide his/her unself-conscious selection, alteration, and organization of details from his/her experience. Out of the infinite elements that went to constitute the real romance, the author will choose those that fit the prototype. Moreover, he/she will change the facts to fit the structure, perhaps exaggerating the conflict with society (if that was not a significant element), intensifying or prolonging the separation (if it was brief), linking the entire romance with appropriate imagery of nature, and so on.

Having sketched out a story implicitly based on this prototype, the author might then evaluate this initial product (or first draft) in part by tacitly comparing it with exempla from precursors—perhaps paradigm cases of romantic tragicomedy. Certain culminating phrases, variations in imagery, narrative sequences from precursors stand out for the author as prime cases of successful art. As the new author writes and rewrites, he/she strives to achieve similar effects. He/she judges his/her success (for example, in phrasing) by tacit reference to these exempla, which function, therefore, as models. The author will consider the work finished when he/she feels that it produces the same sort of effect as that produced by the (implicit) models/exempla. (Note that this cannot be done by mere repetition of the precursor, for a derivative work—a work that we perceive as simply repeating the principles of the precursor—does not produce the same effect as the precursor's work.)

Note that influence can be understood in precisely the same terms as genre. The difference is merely that the schemas, prototypes, and exempla are drawn from a single precursor. In writing an epic, I will draw on a broad generic schema of the epic (having 12 or 24 books, beginning in medias res); a prototype structure that includes standard narrative conflicts, character types, and so on; and exempla of such conflicts, character types, and so forth, drawn from Homer, Vyāsa, Milton, Walcott, or whomever. Insofar as I am influenced by Milton, however, I may in varying degrees draw all three—schemas, prototypes, and exempla—from Milton's works. Or, rather, in studying Milton's influence on an author, I focus only on those schemas, prototypes, and exempla drawn initially or primarily from Milton.

It is difficult to give a brief example of either sort. Even the analysis of influence usually requires extensive knowledge of at least two writers, for we must have a sense not only of their relation to one another, but of their generative poetics. However, to illustrate the general point briefly, we might consider two strikingly opposed passages in Agha Shahid Ali's "From Another Desert." The first is a derivative passage, instantiating structures from T. S. Eliot (about whom Ali wrote his dissertation). Ali is describing the complete loss of hope suffered by Majnoon. Literally, Majnoon has lost hope of being reunited with his beloved. Metaphorically, he has lost hope of achieving the ideal of India/Kashmir.

At the opening of the poem, Ali places Majnoon in a desert. He creates the image almost entirely out of Eliot's repeated—prototypical—image of a spiritual wasteland. This wasteland too is a desert; it is marked by proliferation of bones, wind, dry grass, the beating of wings, stone, broken stone in particular, broken icons, deserted buildings. In Eliot, we find this sort of thing most obviously in "The Waste Land," which begins with repeated references to rock, "dry stone," "broken images," and so on. Eliot's poem goes on to present a deserted chapel and makes repeated reference to wind in hollow places. The same complex of images recurs in "The Hollow Men" and "Ash Wednesday," which also includes a striking image of flightless wings beating in the empty air.

In the opening section of "From Another Desert," Ali takes up these images directly. He begins with "a strange spring," reminiscent of Eliot's well-known reference to the cruelty of April in "The Waste Land." He goes on to picture a place filled with bones, wind in deserted places, and beating wings. In the second section, he continues the use of Eliot, with references to "broken stone" and to a deserted place of worship. Following some further references to broken fragments, he proceeds to speak of "memory/at my doorstep" recalling the references to memory and forgetfulness at the beginning of "The Waste Land."

In these opening sections of this poem, then, Ali can be said to have transferred and respecified Eliot's structure of the spiritual wasteland. Indeed, he is employing prototypical details more or less directly from Eliot, using Eliot's standard images, and varying them only slightly in the context of the poem—for example, speaking of "gods" rather than "God" and giving these gods vermilion marks (thus shifting from Eliot's Christianity to Hinduism). His use of personification is a specification of a schema from Eliot as well. For example, when he refers to the wind *hearing* its own *restlessness,* Ali uses the sort of personalizing adjective of which Eliot was fond, as indicated in his characterization of April as cruel and snow as forgetful (though in Eliot, these are ironic and they are conceits, whereas in Ali they tend to be nonironic or predictable).

But later in the poem, Ali takes up two precursors and draws from them not only broad schemas, which he specifies more uniquely, but also more detailed exempla which he does not repeat, but which he uses to rethink his own experiences and the traditional story he is retelling. The first schema comes from the poetry of Faiz (which Ali translated). As we saw in

"Spring Comes," discussed in chapter 1, Faiz drew a parallel in some of his poetry between romantic love and love of one's country. Ali takes over this very general schema. But, at the same time, he uses the exempla of Faiz's poems as models to reconsider and reconceptualize his relation to his native Kashmir and his sense of a personal loss of India. Moreover, he employs these exempla to evaluate the aesthetic effect produced by his portrayal of this relation and loss.

This is not all. Ali simultaneously draws on the Romantic/Miltonic image of Satan as a brave rebel against religious oppression. This model allows him to reconceptualize his relation to the militant Islamic elements that have arisen in Kashmir in recent years ("the police of God," as he puts it toward the end of the poem). Perhaps most interestingly, he uses the exemplum of Satan and Satan's loss of Heaven to guide his depiction of the separated lovers (by guiding his choice of scenes, adjectives, etc.), to render salient certain aspects of his own exile from Kashmir, and so on. In other words, in thinking of himself in relation to Kashmir on the model of Satan in relation to Heaven, Ali begins to see himself and his exile in a certain way. Certain aspects of that exile become more evident and more significant, while others fade into the background. Aspects of his exile take on a different tone than they would have, had he used other models. Moreover, Ali is not speaking directly of himself here. He is creating a literary voice, though one based in some ways on his own experiences. When altering aspects of his own life or extending the characterization in a fictional direction, the model of Satan guides Ali in choosing among alternatives, drawing his attention to certain things, and certain aspects of things, and away from others, filling in details in particular ways, suggesting certain sorts of parallelism in structure or certain causal sequences, and so on. (Note how this is quite different from taking a schema or prototype and reinstantiating it, as Ali did with Eliot's desert at the beginning of this poem.)

One noteworthy example of this may be found in Ali's portrayal of Majnoon's misery in prison. Here, he tacitly relies on the famous scene in book 2 of *Paradise Lost* where Satan, in Hell, realizes his loss of Heaven and of God's presence and therefore weeps "Tears such as angels weep" (1.620). This scene seems to have guided Ali in conceiving of Majnoon's loss as sublimely superhuman and in portraying Majnoon himself as of almost Satanic size—pounding the earth, causing even a sort of eclipse; indeed, by the suggestion of the word "eclipse," Ali almost makes the prison into a Hell-like "darkness visible," as in Milton's poem (see *Paradise Lost* 1.63).

This second passage, then, involves a complex use of personal history, politics, and various cognitive structures drawn from precursor literary works. It is based on a very different relation to precursors from the simple repetition and respecification of Eliot's schemas and prototypes found in the opening of the poem.

In sum, genre, influence, and related literary phenomena are not mysteries. We can at least begin to explain them in terms of schemas, prototypes, and exempla, used within their lexical category ("literally") or as models ("metaphorically"), integrated with long-term skill memory and drawing on long-term representational memory as selected and organized by those schemas, prototypes, and so on.

Thus far, we have been considering literary topics that are almost solely cognitive—aptly, since the theory in question is cognitive science. However, cognitive science is equally valuable in considering affective aspects of literature. Indeed, it seems to fit particularly well with the rasadhvani theory of Abhinavagupta, as already suggested in chapter 1. In order to understand why this might be the case, we need to return to the structure and operation of the lexicon, specifically the retrieval or accessing of information from the lexicon.

To access information from the lexicon is to bring it to mind. When we access such information, we do not typically access an entire lexical entry with all its defaults and alternatives to schemas, with all encyclopedia information, personal memories, and so on. However, unaccessed information does not remain in mere latent storage, as it was before we accessed part of the entry. Rather, it is activated or "primed," which is to say, made ready for direct access, without the usual lexical search. (A "lexical search" is an automatic, nonconscious "scanning" of the internal lexicon in order to identify and activate a relevant item. For example, in reading the last sentence, you had to perform a lexical search to identify and activate the item "automatic." Clearly this is very swift process, as are all such automatic cognitive procedures.)

More exactly, cognitive scientists distinguish between (1) items to which we are attending directly or that we are holding in working memory, (2) items that are activated or primed and thus are immediately available for access without lexical search, and (3) other items of long-term memory that are more or less distantly accessible through lexical search. Beyond accessing various elements in a lexical entry (attending to them directly or bringing them into working memory), we prime the rest of the entry and its "semantic field." In other words, we activate related entries through a sort of lexical cross-indexing, usually by reference to a superordinate term.

For example, "Tuesday" is part of a semantic field with all other days of the week. One could imagine the entry for "Tuesday" containing some sort of instruction like "See 'day of the week'," with "day of the week" listing all seven days. Thus, accessing (part of) the lexical entry for "Tuesday" primes these other days. It places the entire semantic field, so to speak, at the ready.

In ordinary interactions (as in an invitation to dinner or directions to a home), our interpretations make as shallow and as narrow a use as possible of lexical entries and semantic fields. In any interpretation, we necessarily activate large areas of the lexicon. We call up lexical entries that may have many hierarchized schemas, prototypes, and exempla, as well as much associated personal material. We prime the semantic fields in which each term is placed. But we discard whatever is unnecessary. We do not access further schemas or models after we have found one that "fits." The superfluous lexical entries and semantic fields fade.

But this does not seem to be true in aesthetic experience. If Abhinavagupta was correct (and I think he was), then we would expect aesthetic "savoring" to differ from ordinary reading at least in that activation of lexical entries and semantic fields would be both deeper and more sustained. Rather than discarding unnecessary information, we would retain and even extend this information in a primed, but unaccessed, state.

First of all, we would expect that activation would extend further into our lexical entries, particularly into the personal memory component. Specifically, in reading a literary work, we adopt an appropriate attitude, an aesthetic attitude or a "rasadhvani attitude" (in Amaladass's phrase). To approach a work in this attitude is to approach it as art, as a potential source of aesthetic experience, rather than as a source of, say, information. In this attitude, we do not tightly constrain our associations—which is to say, the priming and accessing of entries. Rather, as Wittgenstein put it, "A poet's words can pierce us. And that is . . . connected with the way in which . . . we let our thoughts roam up and down in the familiar surroundings of the words" (*Zettel* 28e). In other words, it is connected with the way we prime, and even access, a wider range of lexical elements.

Secondly, in literary response, we retain primed elements more consistently than in nonliterary discourse. Specifically, in the rasadhvani attitude, we "savor" the work (as Abhinavagupta stressed) and in doing so we repeatedly prime lexical entries, thereby sustaining the primed elements. Some of these elements are almost continually primed, either directly or through cross-indexing of entries. These repeatedly primed elements correspond closely to what the Sanskrit theorists referred to as "dhvani," suggestion.

Finally, the elements primed in literary response are not necessarily or even primarily semantic, or encyclopedic. They are also affective. For example, in reading a romantic tragicomedy, a reader's personal memories of love, separation, and reunion are likely to be continually primed in the course of the work. These memories carry with them various emotions—love, obviously, as well as sorrow (linked with separation) and joy (linked with reunion). As these memories are not actually accessed during reading, the reader would not experience the full emotion associated with them. However, the feelings associated with repeatedly primed memories affect the reader. To use the Sanskrit distinction, one could say that they appear as rasa rather than as bhāva, sentiment rather than emotion. In other words, just as Abhinavagupta maintained, the feeling of rasa would result from dhvani by way of memory traces, in part via savoring, with the entire process now reunderstood in terms of an expanded, cross-indexed lexicon, lexical priming, and circulation of short lexical strings in rehearsal memory.

Thus, extending and rearticulating the ideas of Ānandavardhana and Abhinavagupta, we seem to have formulated a plausible account of aesthetic experience in terms of well-established principles of cognitive science. Literary theorists would be inclined to stop with this. But at this point a further issue arises for any cognitive scientist: How can we test this hypothesis? Where can we gather data as to whether or not it is valid? Cognitive science is an empirical discipline and thus any cognitive hypothesis about literature should lead ultimately to some sort of empirical evaluation. In other words, it should be fully integrated with empirical poetics. Though empirical poetics fairly clearly falls outside the field of philosophical literary theory, it is valuable to consider it briefly, for three reasons. First of all, it provides a useful transition to the philosophy of science. Secondly, a number of prominent Anglo-American philosophers, such as Willard Quine, have in recent years urged that parts of philosophy be tied more strongly to parts of empirical science, indicating that the traditional dichotomy between philosophy and science may no longer be absolutely binding. Finally, and most importantly, a discussion of empirical poetics will help to indicate some of the limitations of a nonempirical, "purely" philosophical approach to literary study, or anything else.

### Empirical Poetics

Our revised version of Abhinavagupta is a useful place to begin our discussion of empirical study of literature. There are, in fact, numerous difficulties with testing the preceding hypothesis. Perhaps the most important is that, in order to test it, we need to be able to establish when someone is reading in the rasadhvani attitude. Indeed, we have to establish that this is itself a well-defined concept, open to observation or inference. (Introspection probably won't do; it is notoriously unreliable.) This task is already daunting and points to some of the problems that face the empirical study of literature.

Nonetheless, it might seem that ordinary reading of literary and nonliterary works could provide some relevant evidence. Here, a second problem arises. How do we test depth and breadth of activation? The standard methods used to study priming rely on word-recognition tasks, which are not easily adaptable to the sustained reading of literary texts. Focusing on what they call "personal resonance," two psychologists, Uffe Seilman and Steen Larsen, designed an experiment that is relevant here. I will discuss this specific study before turning to the more general issues of empirical study of literature.

Seilman and Larsen hypothesized that reading literature involves a greater degree of personal recollection (that is, greater accessing of personal material) than does reading nonliterary prose. In order to test this hypothesis, they gave ten psychology students a short literary text and ten a short expository text. The expository text concerned "socio-political problems of population growth" (171), while the literary text concerned a man's encounter with a cripple. Seilman and Larsen asked the students to mark any "remindings" (memories) that occurred to them during reading, afterward dividing these recollections into those in which the student was a passive recipient and those in which he/she was active. Their assumption was that "active participant" recollections are more deeply personal than "passive recipient" recollections. They discovered that the literary text elicited far more active participant recollections. They concluded that literary texts involve more deeply personal recollection.

The problems with this study are symptomatic of the problems with the empirical study of literature generally. Some of these problems have to do with literature. For example, it is a relatively new field for empirical investigation and thus there are few established principles or practices. More importantly, it is highly complex and thus involves many variables—for example, variables in readers' attitudes when reading, variables that are both very important and very difficult to isolate and control, as just noted. Other problems are common to all controlled experimentation of this sort. For example, the whole situation is obviously extremely artificial, not only because the subjects had to mark remindings when they occurred, but, more importantly, because this task drew their attention to such remindings, made them constantly expect and recurrently reflect on remindings. This is clearly not a normal part of reading, in or out of the rasadhvani attitude.

On the other hand, many of the problems with this study result from its particular design. It is simply methodologically lax, as a great deal of work in the empirical study of literature tends to be. Let us assume for the moment that there are no problems with the attitude of the test subjects, that they are approaching the literature aesthetically and the nonliterature pragmatically (with a concern for information). (In fact, this is rather unlikely, given the artificial testing situation, but leave that aside for the moment.) Even given this, the researchers have not considered the degree to which remindings might be a function of the topic rather than the literary quality of the passages. In addition, they have not adequately justified their assumption that active versus passive is the appropriate axis along which to differentiate the personal and the impersonal (or the more deeply personal and the less deeply personal). Finally, it is unclear that the experimental subjects form an appropriately random sample—for instance, as psychology students, they may have been aware of the hypotheses that this study was designed to test. (Some of these problems have been dealt with in subsequent studies.)

All of these methodological problems are reducible to one: The authors do not adequately consider alternative hypotheses. Scientific method could be considered, at bottom, a method for generating and evaluating explanatory hypotheses. There is a widespread view—common since Romanticism—that scientific method has something to do with being objective, not having feelings, or not being concerned with the social or political results of one's research. This is nonsense. Scientific method has nothing to do with one's feelings or social goals or personal morals. Scientific method is indifferent with respect to whether one is like Mr. Spock or Counselor Troi or Gandhi or Lord Byron. Rather, scientific method is a method for formulating and judging explanatory principles based upon systematic observation and simplicity considerations. More exactly, scientific method is based upon producing many hypotheses and adjudicating their relative merits. To evaluate a set of hypotheses is to determine which hypothesis accounts for the most data most elegantly (that is, with the fewest principles and posits). (In practice, this construal of scientific method is fairly standard. In theory, however, it is somewhat controversial. We shall discuss some of the theoretical issues in the next chapter.)

Since the number of plausible hypotheses for any given set of data can be enormous, scientists seek to eliminate as many as possible through specific procedures of investigation. Consider the following three (closely related) procedures, all, in effect, consequences of the imperative to generate and evaluate alternative explanatory hypotheses: the use of random samples, the calculation of statistical significance, and the control of other variables (that is, variables other than those that are controlled by the use of random samples and statistical significance). These three procedures clearly overlap. I offer them not as a theoretically rigorous analysis of methodology, but as important practical principles that illustrate the sorts of procedures that must be followed if we are to arrive at reasonably plausible hypotheses.

For any given set of data, one explanatory hypothesis regarding any apparent pattern in the data is that the sample studied is not representative of the larger population from which it is drawn. Suppose I have decided that natural hair color varies with sex. (I choose an obviously false hypothesis as it illustrates the point more clearly.) I would test this hypothesis by taking a number of women and a number of men and comparing their hair. As we all know, I should find that there is no correlation between sex and natural hair color. But there are many ways in which this study could go awry. Suppose, for example, that I take a group of Norwegian women and a group of Italian men. I will seem to find that women tend to have blonde hair while men tend to have black hair. But this is only because my sample was unrepresentative. And this was because it was not random relative to the population that I was judging—I was judging humans and I did not take a random sample of humans.

Suppose that I now redo my study, this time choosing my subjects genuinely at random. But, having spent so much time on the first study, I decide to save time by considering only four people, two men and two women. As it happens, one man and one woman have brown hair; the remaining woman has black hair and the remaining man is blonde. I conclude that blondness is male and black hairedness female. But this pattern remains open to the initial interpretation: The sample is not representative. It was chosen at random, but it still may not reflect the actual proportions of hair color by sex in the populace at large. This is where statistical analysis comes in. A calculation of statistical significance will tell us how confident we can be about the representativeness of our sample. In this case, it would show that we can have very little confidence indeed.

Recognizing this second problem, I now extend my study so that the results are highly statistically significant. Suppose now that I have looked at the hair of hundreds of men and women and found that, say, fewer men than women have blonde hair and more have black hair. I hypothesize that black hair is somewhat masculine and blonde hair somewhat feminine. But then someone else hypothesizes that women are more likely to dye their hair blonde and men are more likely to dye their (gray) hair black. This is a hypothesis that I should have eliminated from the beginning by checking only natural hair color. Hair dying, then, is an "uncontrolled variable" in my study. By the way, I cannot necessarily solve this new problem simply by asking people: "Is that your natural hair color?" Though many researchers adopt this interview method, it is pretty unreliable—more unreliable, the more serious or consequential the question. For a wide range of questions, people are inclined to lie. And in more complex cases, when they do not lie, they are often mistaken, even about their own practices and habits.

These may seem to be entirely unrealistic examples. And, of course, in one sense, they are. No one is likely to claim that hair color varies by sex. However, the same sorts of methodological errors illustrated in these cases are to be found in a great deal of empirical research on literature—though usually these errors are less obvious because the conclusions of the research are not so self-evidently implausible. It is easy to pick out methodological flaws in studies we know to be mistaken. The very same flaws remain concealed in work that leads to intuitively plausible conclusions.

For example, in one study, David Bleich claimed to find that "objectivity . . . is much more provisional" for women than for men (265). Many readers will find the conclusion of his study plausible and therefore will not question the methodology. However, the study is no more methodologically rigorous than any of my fictional examples. For example, Bleich included only four men in the study—and Bleich himself was one of these four men. Moreover, all the other subjects, male and female, were Bleich's students. Thus the sample population was too small, and, even if it were not, the most obvious explanation for the students' responses is that they were shaped and guided by the instructor's (Bleich's) expectations and responses during the class. And this does not even touch on the issue of the degree to which Bleich's summary of the data is misleading. (For discussion, see my "Some Prolegomena.")

In sum, though the methodological standards will no doubt be raised as the field develops and draws more researchers from both literature and experimental psychology, a great deal of past and current work in the field fails to use random samples, fails to calculate for statistical significance, fails to control for other variables—in short, it fails to generate and eliminate alternative hypotheses. It is important to consider the empirical bases of our hypotheses about literature, especially those in the theory of literature. Thus it is important to see that appropriate, methodologically rigorous research is pursued. As Robert de Beaugrande has written, "the rising eminence of 'literary theory' has not led so far in any direct line to empirical studies. Instead, claims about the writing and reading of literature are typically advanced by sheer magisterial assertion, and the lack of agreement among theorists is seized upon as an occasion for renewing the tribal warfare formerly fought out over competing interpretations of particular literary works or of historical and biographical data. Only empirical studies can resolve this state of affairs by freeing these claims from their absolute dependence on the personal eloquence or effrontery of the individual theorists and by providing progressively more reliable and intersubjective grounds for preferring any set of claims over any other" (10).

As I have been emphasizing, we must always be critical of the results of any empirical research, scrutinizing its methodology and considering alternative hypotheses. But this does not mean that we should ignore or dismiss empirical study. Quite the contrary. It means that we should develop empirical study, rendering it more thorough, extensive, rigorous. We cannot ignore the empirical import of our theories—whether Marxist, feminist, phenomenological, Aristotelian, rasadhvanic, or whatever. In doing literary theory, including philosophical literary theory, we make claims about the world, about society, about the human mind. In making these claims, we should not rely on a priori reasoning, illustrated by an occasional example (not chosen at random, not statistically significant, and so on). Unfortunately, literary theorists too often do just this.

# 7

## Literary Meta-theory and the Philosophy of Science

The philosophy of science is one of the most rigorous and consequential areas of philosophy today. It is also an area that has enormous potential value for the understanding and evaluation of literary theory. The work of writers such as Popper and Kuhn has had a significant impact in this area. But other philosophers of science have been largely ignored in literary study. This chapter begins with positivist philosophy of science, turns to Popper, Kuhn, and the related writings of Lakatos, then concludes with a consideration of some more recent work—the anarchist theory of Feyerabend and the new movement of realism, including work by Putnam, Van Fraassen, and Bhaskar.

Theoretical reflection on premises and procedures can be reapplied at any level. In other words, we may engage in theoretical reflection about the structure, interpretation, or evaluation of literature, thereby producing "literary theory." But we may also engage in theoretical reflection about literary theory. We may reflect on its principles, purposes, types. Such a theoretical examination of theory is called "meta-theory" and it is an important component of theoretical study in literature, as it is in a number of other fields. More exactly, meta-theory (like literary theory per se) may be descriptive or normative. It may set out to describe the features common to literary theories in general or to those of a certain type—their common goals or structures—just as the theory of literature sets out to describe features common to literary works in general or to works of a certain type. In addition, it may seek to establish principles to guide the evaluation and revision of literary theories.

For the most part, descriptive meta-theories recapitulate lower-level theories—Marxist, psychoanalytic, cognitivist, and so on. Thus a Marxist descriptive meta-theory might trace the links between dominant critical schools in various periods and the political and economic conditions in which these theories rose to dominance. A cognitivist account would seek to isolate the operation of various types of inferential strategy, cognitive structure, and so forth, which are characteristic of all literary theory, or which differentiate schools of literary theory. An outstanding example of cognitivist meta-theory—addressing film theory, in this case, rather than literary theory—may be found in David Bordwell's *Making Meaning*, which isolates a range of detailed cognitive procedures common to even the most seemingly diverse film theories.

On the other hand, there are more narrowly "inductivist" approaches to descriptive meta-theory. These seek to isolate forms of literary theory without recourse to any extensively developed prior theory (such as Marxism or cognitive science). For example, Earl Miner has sought to categorize theories by reference to their assumption of a "paradigmatic" genre (e.g., for Aristotle, drama is the paradigmatic genre). He then goes on to argue that a theorist's choice of a paradigmatic genre has a wide range of consequences for how that theory will develop. Specifically, in Miner's view, theories focusing on drama will tend to emphasize mimesis, while theories based on lyric poetry will emphasize expression. (Miner sees the former as Western and the latter as Eastern. Both specific contentions are implausible, in my view.) The broad organizational principles set out in the introduction are of this general sort as well.

Despite the great intrinsic interest and intellectual value of descriptive meta-theory, normative meta-theory is, perhaps, the more urgent pursuit—at least for anyone who wishes to engage in literary theorization him/herself. For to engage in literary theorization, one must have a way of adjudicating rival hypotheses, deciding between different theories and between different versions of the same theory—or deciding not to decide. One has to have a way of choosing to pursue theory A rather than theory B, or of determining that a particular version of theory A (say, A″) is superior to another version of that theory (say A′), or of concluding that, at the moment, theories C and D are both very promising and thus should both be pursued without preference being given to one or the other. Normative meta-theory is the systematic study of just these sorts of problems. However, normative meta-theory has hardly developed at all as an autonomous field. Rather, it has been almost entirely parasitic on the related, but far more highly developed, field of philosophy of science. Thus, in this final chapter, I shall concentrate on the philosophy of science and its implications for normative meta-theory.

The normative portion of the philosophy of science sets out to define principles by which we can productively generate and evaluate theories.

As the aim of this generation and evaluation is most often understood as a matter of advancing knowledge, normative philosophy of science has typically begun with the epistemological issue of what we can know and how we can know it. Clearly, we do not know abstract theoretical entities directly. We do not know directly that the substance in this cup has a particular chemical structure, or that this story has such-and-such a theme. Is there anything, then, that we do know directly? One standard answer to this question is that we know what we experience. And what we experience is usually understood to be what we perceive "immediately"—that there is an odorless, clear liquid in the glass, that the words on page 1 of the story are "Once upon a time," and so on. The logical positivists referred to reports of such perceptions as "observation statements" or "protocol sentences." One can see theories, then, as abstractions and inferences from sets of protocol sentences. From our various observations of water—its properties, behavior in different circumstances, interaction with other substances—we infer that water has a particular, unobservable microstructure. From our various observations of a text, we infer that it has a particular, unobservable thematic structure. We adjudicate theories by choosing the ones consistent with protocol sentences over those that are inconsistent with protocol sentences. Thus, the chemical theory that says that water should be green and smell like fresh bread is inferior to the chemical theory that says that water should be clear and odorless; the interpretation of Othello as rash and overly passionate is inferior to an interpretation of him as generally rational and reflective, due to the fact the former is inconsistent with several of our observation sentences concerning the text (for example, our observation that Othello responds calmly when attacked by Brabantio).

While few people would deny that this is correct up to a certain point, it clearly does not fully resolve our meta-theoretical issues. Positivists themselves raised two problems with this scenario. First of all, as Otto Neurath (one of the most important Vienna positivists) noted, protocol sentences are themselves revisable. In other words, we do not absolutely know protocol sentences to be true. We may feel (subjectively) certain that they are true. But they can always turn out to be wrong. This is the case not only for the Cartesian reason that we might have dreamt or hallucinated them, but also, and more importantly, because protocol sentences are not presuppositionless; when our presuppositions change, our protocol sentences may change. Thus, we may find that a certain liquid appears colorless in ordinary, diffuse roomlight, but in brighter, focused light it does have a greenish tint; in formulating our initial observation statement, we had tacitly presupposed that our lighting was adequate (or, more broadly, we had tacitly presupposed that there were no hidden variables). An initial observation statement that Othello is rash turns out to have been mistaken when we reexamine the text; this initial observation statement was in fact an induction based on scenes of passion that we tacitly presupposed to be typical.

Indeed, the problem goes deeper still. Our observation statements are, as Willard Quine would later put it, "theory-laden" (see, for example, *Theories* 25). In consequence, different theories will actually lead to different observation statements. A structuralist theory about a poem will be corroborated by observation statements concerning homologies (for example, parallel structures across stanzas), but these do not count as observation statements for other theorists; a formalist theory will be corroborated by observation statements about semantic relations among parallel words (e.g., participles or rhymes), a Fishean theory (of temporal reading experience) will be corroborated by observation statements about the way poetic line breaks interrupt syntactic units, and so on.

Beyond this epistemological problem, this common view of evaluation provides no real methodological principles. For example, it assumes some sort of Baconian induction of generalizations from protocol sentences. However, simple induction combined with the laws of logic seems to count way too much as confirmatory for an hypothesis. In Carl Hempel's famous example (see chapter 1 of Hempel), every nonblack nonraven should, in this view, count as evidence for the theory that all ravens are black. For example, "This table is green" should count as a confirmatory protocol sentence for the theory that all ravens are black. (To make this more intuitively plausible, I should note that "For all x, if x is not black, x is not a raven"—a proposition obviously supported by "This object is green, and it is a table"—is logically equivalent to "For all x, if x is a raven, x is black.") Moreover, even without this problem, it should be clear that no generalization can ever be definitively proven, no matter how many positive instances we have. Even ten or one hundred or one thousand black ravens do not *prove* that all ravens are black.

Some positivists sought to resolve such problems by recourse to probability theory (see, for example, Carnap, "Testability" 32). By appealing to statistical significance, margins of confidence, and other notions from statistics—all of which seek to render precise the likelihood of a certain state of affairs—they sought to eliminate both sets of problems. First of all, protocol sentences could be reunderstood as highly probable, but not certain. For example, it may be very highly probable that what I judge to be a clear liquid is in fact a clear liquid. In this way, theoretical abstractions can rest pretty firmly on protocol sentences, even though these are not absolutely certain. Similarly, we can adjudicate theories on the degree to which they are probable, and the determination of probability will define relevant confirmatory instances. A green table will not increase the probability that all ravens are black; a black raven might increase that probability, but will not make it absolute.

The main problem with this approach is that it is not entirely clear how one can calculate the probability of the truth of protocol sentences without assuming the certainty of other protocol sentences—but *all* of them must be probabilistic. Specifically, in this view, probability estimates would be generalizations from a range of cases where protocol sentences had been asserted, then investigated, finally being "proven" true or false. Put very crudely: I see one object and judge it to be a clear liquid, and upon investigation it turns out to be a clear liquid; I repeat this ninety-nine more times, and get it wrong only once, giving a .99 probability to my protocol sentence, "That is a clear liquid." This is all well and good, except that the final probabilistic assessments of the protocol sentences under consideration necessarily rely on other uninvestigated protocol sentences. In order to determine whether my initial protocol sentence ("That is a clear liquid") is true, we have to rely on another protocol to the same effect ("that liquid really is clear"). But this merely pushes the problem back to the second protocol sentence.

On the other hand, the probability theorists were no doubt correct to point out that knowledge need not be deterministic or absolute; it can equally be probabilistic. Moreover, it is clear that probability considerations are crucial to methodological issues of induction. And, though it may seem entirely unrelated to literary study, probability theory is (or should be) important to a number of issues in the theory of literature. For example, broad generalizations concerning gender difference should be derived not from isolated observation statements ("Woolf's style in this passage indicates that women tend to adopt a more fluid sentence structure than men"), but on statistical correlations (for instance, "70 percent of the women writers studied employed such-and-such a technique, whereas only 40 percent of the men did so"—or, what is more likely, "though anecdotal accounts led us to expect that more men would employ this technique, larger-scale studies reveal no statistically significant correlations with gender when other variables are held constant"). (For a discussion of this issue, see Hogan, "Some Prolegomena.")

In his extremely influential *The Logic of Scientific Discovery* (first published in 1934), Karl Popper adopted a very different approach. Addressing the methodological problem, Popper argued that theory evaluation should focus not on the verification of theories, but on their *falsification*. Specifically, when evaluating theories, we should not set out to find evidence that supports the theory. Rather, we should set out to find evidence that undermines the theory. We should not try to prove a theory, but to disprove it. And this, Popper tells us, is something we can do. Millions of black ravens do not prove "All ravens are black." However, a single white raven disproves it.

Or, so it might seem. In fact, Popper's falsification criterion does not ultimately solve the problems we have been discussing. Most importantly, it is irrelevant to the epistemological problem, as Popper acknowledges. Popper himself emphasizes that there are no genuine protocol sentences— that is, there are no evidentially absolute observations (see 95–98). Again, it is not merely that we sometimes make mistakes ("Oh, I thought that liquid was colorless, but now I see that it has a green tint"). The problem is, rather, that our observations are not and cannot be presuppositionless, that they are, in Quine's phrase, theory laden. But to acknowledge this, it would seem, is to undermine falsificationism as a definitive method for evaluating theories. We cannot simply dismiss a "falsified" theory if that falsification may always be overturned. And clearly the falsification can always be overturned if the observation sentences on which it is based can always be overturned. Thus falsification ends up in the same leaky boat as verification.

Put differently, we prefer a theory that is highly "corroborated." This is a technical concept introduced by Popper to refer to theories that have withstood many difficult tests, designed to produce falsification. When a theory has been subjected to many such tests but nonetheless remains consistent with all observation sentences, it may be considered highly corroborated, though not of course verified. The problem, however, is that those observation sentences are themselves open to reversal or falsification, and that reversal might lead to the falsification of corroborated theories and the corroboration of falsified theories. This is even more obvious in literary study than elsewhere. One interpretation of Othello will be corroborated on the basis of such observation statements as "Othello is rash," but then falsified when we recognize that the latter is a theoretical claim, and substitute for it such observation statements as "Othello responds calmly and rationally to Iago's initial provocations," "Othello responds calmly and rationally to Brabantio's assault and accusations," "Othello responds calmly and rationally to Cassio's brawling," and so on. More seriously, one hypothesis will be corroborated on the basis of structuralist observation statements, another on the basis of formalist observation statements, a third on the basis of Fishean observation statements, and so on.

A closely related problem is that, not only may observation statements be reversed, theories may be revised. As the French philosopher of science Pierre Duhem emphasized, and as Willard Quine stressed more recently, a theory may be rewritten to accommodate any data whatsoever. Often this can be done by subtle adjustments at various points in the theory. But, at the very least, a theorist can always rely on ad hoc qualifications. Faced with an experiment that contradicts a particular chemical theory, a theorist might simply say, "Compounds behave in such-and-such ways, *except in the presently unknown special circumstances that prevail in this particular experiment.*" Consider a theory of Othello that claims that he is rash and overly passionate. This theory can be made consistent with the data of the play by ad hoc means; situations where Othello does not act rashly may be dismissed by qualifying the theory in the following way: "Othello is rash and overly passionate, though he sometimes manages to contain his passion." It may also be revised in more subtle, less clearly ad hoc ways—for example, "Othello has overly strong passions. However, he has learned to curb these passions in public. Thus we only see the 'true,' passionate Othello in more private or domestic settings."

In principle, structuralism or deconstruction or any other theory may be revised locally or in ad hoc ways in order to accommodate literary works that may initially seem to contradict those theories. On the other hand, the relation between literary works and literary theories is rarely formulated in such a way as to really allow any contradictory observation statements that would necessitate such revision. In other words, it is difficult to say just what sort of literary work would even appear to contradict structuralism, or deconstruction, or phenomenology, or psychoanalysis.

The revisability of observations and of theories—including their revision from deterministic to probabilistic (falsificationism is clearly aimed at deterministic theories)—seems, then, to pose insuperable problems for Popperian falsificationism as a solution to our epistemological and methodological problems. (Duhem's solution to these two problems is the use of a further criterion, simplicity, in the evaluation of theories; we shall return to this alternative below.) There is, however, another way in which one can interpret Popper's prescriptions—as primarily ethical. Popper insists that it is the duty of a scientist to formulate his/her views as lucidly as possible, explicitly drawing out their implications, and seeking ruthlessly to falsify them. In other words, theorists should not obscure the claims of their theories in the hope of avoiding dispute. And they should not set out to prove their theories, seeking and broadcasting a large number of (usually trivial) pseudo-confirmations. Rather, they should set out to falsify their theories, seeking and broadcasting instances where those theories fail. With some qualifications, this seems an eminently reasonable view. It is difficult to see how we can have genuine intellectual progress based on obscurantism and self-interest. The relevance of these views to literary theory in particular should be obvious. (It is worth mentioning here that Umberto Eco is one theorist who has tried to use Popper's views to combat relativism in literary theory; however, Eco errs, I believe, in trying to employ falsification as an epistemological/methodological principle, rather than as an ethical principle.)

Along with Popper, the most broadly influential philosopher of science—and certainly the most influential in the humanities—has been Thomas Kuhn. Kuhn's work develops not out of logical positivism (as does Popper's), but out of the history of science, and it has placed history of science at the center of much subsequent philosophy of science. Moreover, in doing this, Kuhn has developed and extended the epistemological and methodological problems we have been discussing. Specifically, Kuhn argues that, when we look at the history of science, we see that the evaluation of theories does not proceed by any neat method of verification or falsification. Rather, theorists shift from one theory to another for complex reasons, which may be rational and defensible, but are not by any means absolute, definitive, or even wholly self-conscious.

More exactly, Kuhn argues that a science develops in the following manner. First of all, any systematic study (of plants, of the stars and planets, of literature, of the human mind) begins in a sort of chaos of competing views. In this first phase (which Kuhn calls "pre-paradigmatic"), theorists have to build theories, so to speak, from the ground up. They write books that lay out and defend basic principles, develop their various consequences, and so on. Some of these theories will be taken up by smaller or larger groups; others will not. This is the stage of physical optics until Newton, chemistry until Boyle and Boerhaave, and so on (15). It is the current stage of literary theory.

In those fields that become sciences (for example, physics and chemistry, but not literary theory, at least thus far), one theory becomes dominant, so that its basic premises can be presupposed by all those working in the field. When this occurs, a discipline has entered the "paradigmatic" phase. During this phase, scientists in the field (say, chemistry) simply accept a wide range of (shared) theoretical presuppositions and proceed in their work on the basis of these presuppositions. This has a number of specific consequences. For example, the presuppositions of the field come to be presented dogmatically in school textbooks; practicing scientists write articles more often than books because they no longer need to develop the foundations of their theories.

Kuhn refers to this phase as "paradigmatic," because it is defined by a "paradigm." Paradigm is perhaps the most famous concept in Kuhn's work. Unfortunately, it is rather vague in Kuhn's initial formulation (as Kuhn himself later admitted). However, there are two basic senses in which Kuhn uses the term. First of all, a paradigm is a set of theoretical and related presuppositions—for example, that the earth is part of a heliocentric system, rather than a geocentric system, that planetary motion is the result of gravitation, and so forth, in Newtonian astronomy. It is, in the terminology of the preceding chapter, a sort of schema. Secondly, a paradigm is a specific case or set of related cases—in other words, an exemplum or a prototype—used as a model to guide how one thinks about scientific problems (problems in chemistry, say). For instance, as Kuhn emphasizes, scientific education involves a great deal of practical work—problem solving and experimentation in laboratories—the point of which is to train students to think about scientific problems in a certain way. Once one has learned how to solve one chemistry problem or how to perform one chemistry experiment (often a repetition, in simplified form, of some historically important experiment), one can use this as a model for solving subsequent problems or performing subsequent experiments. Paradigmatic science presupposes not only explicitly formulated theoretical principles, but tacit conformity to certain (paradigmatic) models of thought and action.

Once a paradigm has been established, Kuhn tells us, most scientists practice what he calls "normal science." Normal science is a form of "puzzle solving" (see Kuhn chapter 4). Specifically, normal science is the fairly mundane extension of the standard or paradigmatic theory in new domains (for example, the extension of Chomskyan transformational grammar to another language or language family, or to a new property of a previously studied language), and the local, limited revision of that theory in light of such extensions (for example, the slight alteration of some putative syntactic universal in light of work on a previously unstudied language). As Kuhn points out, the popular idea of scientific research is highly romantic. It envisions the scientist as formulating wildly new, innovative ideas, making bold new discoveries, and so on. But almost all scientific research is far from innovative; it is, in fact, very conformist and highly resistant to novelty. It is not even a matter of verification or falsification. It is, again, a matter of extension and limited reformulation. This is not to say that science is never innovative. It is. But only rarely. Kuhn refers to such innovative science as "revolutionary." (Romanticism has not entirely passed over the philosophy of science.)

Before turning to revolutionary science, however, it is worth dwelling for a moment on normal science in connection with our guiding epistemological dilemmas. The first thing to point out is that, within normal science, epistemological problems arise, but in a more limited and less theoretically troublesome form. Specifically, within normal science, there is no question of large theoretical differences in observation statements. There is, of course, always the possibility of observational error, of concealed variables, and so on. Observation statements remain revisable. But the more crucial theoretical problem—that of the theory-ladenness of observation—is solved, because it is not a problem for those who share a theory. There may be disputes among deconstructionists on how to interpret *Othello*. However, all the observation statements at issue are deconstructive observation statements. There is no issue of phenomenological observation statements, psychoanalytic observation statements, and so on. Moreover, while normal scientists still face the problem of evaluating different versions of a theory, they no longer face the problem of evaluating different theories. Again, they share a theory. Thus the more serious versions of both problems (that concerning alternative observation statements and that concerning alternative explanations for observation statements) are eliminated as practical issues within normal science.

The second thing to remark about normal science is that it is to be found not only within paradigmatic-phase disciplines, but also within preparadigmatic-phase schools—as the preceding reference to deconstruction indicates. In other words, even when an entire discipline has not adopted a single paradigm, advocates of any one of the (preparadigmatic) competing theories will for the most part behave in the manner of normal scientists. Thus, even though literary theory is clearly preparadigmatic, Kuhn's notion of normal science may be applied to the various schools of literary theory. (Stanley Fish's notion of interpretive communities involves a parallel idea; this is not surprising, as Fish's later work draws on Kuhn.) "Normal" deconstruction, for example, primarily involves the extension of deconstruction to literary texts that were previously undeconstructed, or to aspects of literary texts that were passed over in previous deconstructions. It may also involve some minor revision or extension of deconstructive theoretical principles. Such revision is relatively uncommon in literary theory. Again, literary theories are usually not formulated with such precision as to define what would count as exceptions or falsifications or recalcitrant observations. Thus they don't typically encounter exceptions, falsifications, or recalcitrant observations. Thus they don't typically require reformulation.

It may prove valuable to study schools of literary theory further in relation to Kuhn's theory of normal science. For example, beyond pointing out the shared theoretical presuppositions, the application of standardized principles to new objects, the occasional, highly localized revision of principles, one might look at the establishment of paradigmatic exempla and their operation in literary education. A course in deconstruction fairly clearly serves to train students in the deconstructive paradigm, practical interpretations serving the same sort of purpose as laboratory work in the natural sciences; in this context, it would be worth considering the degree to which, say, Derrida's deconstruction of Rousseau operates as a paradigmatic exemplum, how it works into practical deconstructive training, and so on.

Revolutionary science is science that initiates and advances a "paradigm shift," a move from one dominant paradigm to another. Specifically, as normal science proceeds, scientists will continually come upon phenomena that cannot be dealt with adequately in the paradigmatic theory. The theory will become burdened by ad hoc qualifications, and will prove increasingly problematic in its extension to new fields. During this period of "crisis," some theorists will propose a new theory, designed in part to deal with the problems that plague the paradigmatic theory. Eventually, scientists will shift their allegiance to the new theory, making it paradigmatic, or the new theory will die out due to the revivification of the initial, paradigmatic theory (or due to the success of yet a third alternative). For instance, relativity theory came to replace Newtonian theory after a period of crisis in Newtonian physics. (The idea of paradigm shifts has been influential in literary theory and criticism, though it is usually used somewhat loosely. For example, Houston Baker's treatment of the different phases of black literary theory draws on this aspect of Kuhn's work.)

The theoretical problem with such shifts, as explained by Kuhn, is that they are not and cannot be the result of strict methodological decisions. When a new theory replaces an older theory, the older theory has not been falsified, and the newer theory has not been verified. Indeed, the two theories, Kuhn tells us, are ultimately "incommensurable." They cannot be strictly compared with respect to the data—because the data are not, or are not fully, independent of the theories. In short, Kuhn's account partially solves our epistemological and methodological problems within a paradigm or within a theory, but it repeats and perhaps even exacerbates these problems across paradigms or across theories. When applied to literary theory, it allows, for example, deconstructionists a way of debating the value of a particular deconstructive literary interpretation, or the relative plausibility of two formulations of deconstructive theory. But it does not seem to allow us any way of evaluating the relative merits of, for example, deconstructive and cognitivist views of language.

On the other hand, Kuhn himself is insistent that paradigm shifts are not irrational or arbitrary. They are, rather, the result of ordinary evaluative principles (such as Duhemian simplicity; see, for example, 199). But it is not entirely clear that Kuhn has formulated his theory in such a way as to allow for this sort of rational, if nondefinitive, cross-paradigmatic evaluation. For it would seem that any application of evaluative principles would have to presuppose some constancy across paradigms, thus *some* sort of commensurability—of the theories with one another and with methodological principles. Moreover, Kuhn seems to view methodological principles as transcending the paradigms—a view with which I am in sympathy, but which is not clearly coherent with Kuhn's theoretical principles. (It is always important to distinguish between the strict implications of a theory and what a theorist claims about a theory.)

Imre Lakatos sought to preserve the insights of both Kuhn and Popper in a theory of "research programmes," which would more fully rationalize paradigm shifts, and thus provide a clearer criterion for the evaluation of competing theories. Lakatos's first point is that we need to evaluate not isolated theories, but rather ongoing programs of research in which theories have been set forth, tested, revised, retested, and so on. In my view, this is an enormous advance over previous discussions, especially given the implications that Lakatos draws from this reformulation. Suppose we are considering two isolated theories, A and B. Theory A has been developed and redeveloped by some of the best minds of the past three decades. Theory B is very new; while it has accounted for some unusual phenomena, it is not nearly as well-developed as theory A. According to Lakatos, we should not merely evaluate the current state of the two theories—in which case, theory A will probably win, by most standard criteria. (After all, a new theory is usually set forth in a preliminary form that cannot possibly account for the wide range of phenomena to which a better established theory has already been applied.) Rather, we should consider instead the trajectory of each research program. In other words, we should seek to judge not the current accomplishments of the two theories, but their potential, their promise. Usually we cannot come to any decision on this score when a new theory is introduced. However, by recognizing that the new theory has not yet been allowed to develop—by evaluating it as a research program, rather than as a final theory—we will be led to defer judgment; we will not dismiss the new theory as inadequate, but will wait to see how it develops as a research program.

Consider, for example, cancer research. Chemical and radiation therapies, designed to kill the cancer, have been extensively developed. When Linus Pauling proposed the investigation of vitamin therapies (to aid the body as a whole, rather than to kill the cancer per se), his ideas were to a large extent dismissed. If one judges theories alone, then this is perfectly reasonable. Pauling's views were very tentative and had little empirical support. However, if one adopts Lakatos's views, then the dismissal of Pauling's ideas was not rational at all. One could say the same thing about literary theories. Cognitive science is not at all coherent with poststructuralism (the dominant body of theory today, though it could not be called paradigmatic in the strict sense). In terms of literary study, poststructuralism is well-developed and cognitive science is not. Thus in comparing them as theories of literature, it would be very easy to dismiss cognitive science as inadequate. However, judged not as a finished theory of literature, but rather as a research program, cognitive science appears quite promising (a point widely recognized since I first wrote this paragraph).

Of course, this alone does not solve our methodological (not to mention epistemological) problems. We may have a rough intuitive sense of what sorts of research programs have promise and what sorts do not. But the whole point of doing theory and of formulating methodology is that we do not have to rely on our rough intuitive sense of things. Of course, one could always say that we have to fall back on unreflective presuppositions at some point, and that Lakatos has at least focused our intuitions on research programs rather than on theories. But Lakatos does, in fact, go further. Specifically, Lakatos sees a shift in paradigms—or, rather, in research programs—in roughly Kuhnian terms. He recognizes that as a research program develops, it will encounter problems, "anomalies" as Kuhn calls them. The problems will force the theorists to reformulate the theory. According to Lakatos, this reformulation can be done in one of two ways. It can be ad hoc or not ad hoc. In order not to be ad hoc, a reformulation of a theory must have testable content beyond the anomaly. More simply, it must give an explanation for the anomaly and that explanation must be testable by reference to other phenomena.

Suppose, for example, that we are investigating the theory that certain vitamin therapies can inhibit the spread of cancer. We meet with some early successes, but then we find several cases where the vitamin therapy seems to have no effect. We may dismiss these as exceptions ("It won't work in every case") or claim that the data are inaccurate ("Perhaps the initial scan missed part of the cancer") or otherwise adopt an ad hoc principle that has no real theoretical consequences. On the other hand, we may avoid such ad hoc approaches and formulate some general principle, for example, that vitamin therapy works only on certain types of cancer, or that it works only when the vitamins are assimilated in a certain manner (slow, constant intravenous drip vs. periodic oral megadoses), or that one manner of assimilation is effective for one cancer while a different manner of assimilation is effective for another. In each of these cases, the proposed account has testable consequences. The same holds for literature. Consider again the person who wishes to claim that Othello is rash. He/she may simply dismiss Othello's response to Brabantio as an exception ("Sometimes his rashness doesn't come out"). Or he/she may formulate a more general, explanatory principle—for example, that Othello has learned to curb his rashness in public, but that in private his true nature appears. The former response is ad hoc in Lakatos's sense; the latter is not.

Any given research program will involve some ad hoc qualifications. However, in periods of Kuhnian crisis, theorists come to rely increasingly on ad hoc formulations, and when they formulate more general principles to account for anomalies, they find that these more general principles fail, leading to further anomalies. In Popperian terms, their initial and reformulated generalizations are repeatedly falsified, and repeatedly salvaged only by ad hoc devices. Lakatos refers to this as a "degenerating" research program. During such a period of degeneration, an alternative theory may arise. Though it will not be as well developed as the (degenerating) paradigm theory, this alternative theory may show considerable success in accounting for new phenomena. In other words, the new theory will not initially explain as broad a range of phenomena as the paradigm theory. However, it may show considerable success in expansion to new areas. For example, it may successfully account for apparent anomalies through non–ad hoc reformulations. It may, in Lakatos's term, show itself to be a "progressive" rather than a "degenerating" program. As the paradigmatic theory continues to degenerate and the rival theory continues to progress, scientists will gradually come to adopt the new theory on the basis of its potential as a research program, until the older paradigm theory is discarded and replaced by the newer theory.

This does go some way toward solving the practical or methodological part of our epistemological problem—how to adjudicate between rival theories. However, Paul Feyerabend has argued in *Against Method* that Lakatos makes a serious error in believing that degenerating research programs will necessarily continue to degenerate, or that progressive programs will continue to progress. Moreover, Feyerabend argues, theoretical shifts often have far less to do with any sort of methodological considerations than Lakatos or even Kuhn believes. Consider Galileo. According to Feyerabend, Galileo succeeded in developing and promulgating heliocentrism primarily because he wrote in the vernacular (rather than in Latin), was clever and successfully manipulative in his use of rhetoric, and so on, not because his work was part of a progressive research program. These two claims lead Feyerabend to conclude that we should allow, indeed encourage, a wide range of theories, *not* a single paradigm. Moreover, according to Feyerabend, successful scientists do not necessarily observe rigorous methodological constraints in their research. For example, he argues that much of Galileo's work was based on implausible assumptions about the probative value of telescopic observation. Because of developments such as this, Feyerabend concludes that our only methodological principle should be "anything goes."

In my view, Feyerabend misrepresents Galileo, making his procedures appear far more irrational than they were. Thus, I do not believe that he has made a serious case "against method," as he contends. However, he does not, I think, exaggerate the influence of extraneous factors on the acceptance of Galileo's theories, and the degree to which theories generally achieve predominance for intellectually irrelevant reasons. He is also probably correct to assert—in a separate argument—that, at least in certain cases, we are more likely to improve one theory if there are active alternatives with which it may be contrasted. For both reasons, his advocacy of pluralism seems very reasonable. On the other hand, Kuhn would argue against such pluralism on the ground that it ends up diverting theorists' attention from the development of theories—from research programs—locking them into fruitless debates about fundamental principles, much as in literary theory today. This too seems reasonable. (In my view, Feyerabend's view is finally preferable, for reasons to which we shall turn below.) In any event, Feyerabend's criticisms of Lakatos call into question Lakatos's solution to our broader methodological problem concerning what and how we can know. Moreover, neither really addresses our basic epistemological problem.

Disturbed by the apparent relativism of such writers as Kuhn and

Feyerabend, a number of more recent philosophers of science have come to advocate various forms of "realism." Though all have sought to differentiate their brand of realism from "naive realism" (a commonsense view that the world is out there and we can more or less just look and see how it is), they have also maintained that there is indeed a real world, that scientific method can lead us to an understanding of that world, and that scientific research and theorization do indeed progress. Hilary Putnam, Bas van Fraassen, Roy Bhaskar, and others have been part of this "realist backlash," as Mary Hesse calls it (37).

Putnam is probably the best known of this group. For many years, he has defended a version of realism. Recently, he has moved away from what he calls "metaphysical realism" (the doctrine that there is a single, definite reality independent of our theories) and adopted what he calls "internal realism," a doctrine that affirms reality, but at the same time allows various incompatible theories to be true. Many of Putnam's readers have been uncertain as to whether or not this is a coherent option, evidently standing halfway between full-fledged realism and full-fledged theory-relativism. Consider, for example, the ambiguity of such statements as "truth is not (unique) correspondence" or "there [may] be correspondence between objects and (what we take to be) incompatible theories" (73–74). It is hard to say how these parenthetical qualifications are to be taken. Is truth correspondence, but not unique correspondence? Or is truth not correspondence at all, and thus necessarily not unique correspondence? If it is correspondence, but not unique correspondence, what does that mean? Elsewhere, Putnam says that reality is *"to some extent shaped by our concepts"* (54)—to some extent shaped? Does he mean that our concepts to some extent "give shape" to reality in the sense of selecting some elements and relations for emphasis, while downplaying or ignoring others? Or does he mean that we in part create reality through our concepts, shape it as we would shape a lump of clay?

Some of Putnam's claims are more straightforward. For example, Putnam has indicated that there is genuine progress in the formulas and equations of science, but not necessarily in the metaphysical interpretations of those formulas and equations. This is certainly a plausible view. However, one wonders if this leads to internal realism, or is even consistent with internal realism. For example, are we to assume that the formulas are always internal to the same theory? If not, how are they comparable? If they are not comparable, how can there be progress?

Bas van Fraassen agrees with Putnam that the language of science does not directly represent the world. But he does not speak of theories as "shaping" the world, nor does he refer to his realism as "internal." For van Fraassen, a theory articulates a model, which itself only partially represents the world. As a result, what we can say about the world at any given time is constrained and guided by the model. Nonetheless, not all knowledge is relative. There is a level of experience that is universal and that provides a basis for knowledge—and for ontological realism as well. Van Fraassen uses the following (rather ethnocentric) example to illustrate: "Suppose I show a tennis ball to a Philippine Stone Age man. There is no doubt he sees it; he picks it up and plays with it, we cannot deny that he sees the tennis ball. Yet he does not see it *as* a tennis ball, nor sees *that* it is a tennis ball. He can't 'read' it like that because he does not have the concept of a tennis game." Van Fraassen concludes, "I refuse to give up the robust realism in which the primitive and I see the same thing, both incontestably see the tennis ball" (219).

Of course, one still has to explain what precisely is shared across cultures, what it means for all of us to "see the tennis ball." This is more a question for cognitive and perceptual psychology than for the philosophy of science. However, insofar as the delimitation of (van Fraassenian or other) universalism is based upon scientific investigation, it cannot solve the epistemological problems we have been considering. The epistemological problems are, after all, at the base of every such scientific investigation. (In relation to van Fraassen's anecdote, it is worth mentioning that one particularly admirable feature of Feyerabend's writing is his recognition that there is highly sophisticated scientific knowledge in a wide range of putatively "primitive" cultures and that their characterization as "primitive" is a result of European misrepresentation.)

One of the most uncompromising realists is Roy Bhaskar, a Marxist writer who is as concerned with transforming society as he is with understanding quantum theory. (It is perhaps worth noting that Putnam was a socialist during his "metaphysical realist" phase, and that Bertrand Russell, also a socialist, disputed logical positivism at precisely those points where it appeared to lead to relativism. Writers who are deeply aware of the massive suffering caused by capitalism, imperialism, and so forth, are unlikely to find congenial the idea that reality is somehow a product of our theories.) Bhaskar insists "that the ultimate objects of scientific inquiry exist and act . . . quite independently of scientists and their activity" (12). He argues persuasively (as have other theorists, such as Davidson, and Earman) that Kuhn's claim of trans-paradigmatic incommensurability is a non sequitur—as indicated by the fact that we can distinguish the two paradigms, discuss their differences, and so on. Moreover, he argues that a great deal of philosophy of science has gone astray in drawing ontological conclusions from epistemological premises—concluding, for example, that the world is in some sense defined by theories because our knowledge of the world is in some sense defined by theories. On the other hand, he acknowledges the importance of Feyerabend's arguments, stressing, for example, that science is not always progressive, that it has periods of decline and even retrogression.

Bhaskar's views seem quite plausible. And they are admirably oriented toward political action. (For this reason, some politically active literary theorists and meta-theorists, such as Christopher Norris, have found his work useful.) However, they do not really address the epistemological problems with which we began. Nor, indeed, do other realist views. Bhaskar has responded well to some extensions of these problems, especially those of Kuhn and Feyerabend, and he has carefully outlined a realist ontology that is separate from positivist epistemology. But he has more or less set aside the dilemmas that in part gave rise to positivism and subsequent developments initially.

I should like to conclude, then, with a brief outline of my own view, a view that tries to take account of the degree to which the various positions in this debate have value.

First of all, I am a realist in that I believe that the world is as it is, independent of any theory. However, I am not an essentialist. I believe that objects are individuated only by intention. Thus there are many different ways in which the world can be divided up and organized in thought, many different ways in which we can conceptualize the world, and thus many different conceptual structures in which statements can be formulated. Consider, for example, the color spectrum. There does not seem to be any predetermined "correct" way of dividing the color spectrum. We can divide it any way we like. For example, we can discriminate many shades of blue but count red, orange, and yellow as one color. It is only once we have divided the color spectrum that our assertions about color ("This table is green") can have any meaning. And it is only once our assertions have meaning that they can be true or false. In other words, the truth or falsity of an assertion is "internal" to an organization of the world that is conventional—or, more accurately, the truth or falsity of an assertion is necessarily in part a function of the meaning of the assertion (as Davidson stressed) and that meaning is not a function of objective essences, but of human decision. In this way, my view is, perhaps, closer to Putnam's internal realism than to metaphysical realism. (Though perhaps Putnam does not intend anything of the sort; it is, again, difficult to tell.) On the other hand, once a meaningful assertion has been made, its truth or falsity is dependent only on the world. As Davidson might say, at that point it is as (metaphysically) absolute as one could imagine or desire.

Now, it seems clear that, while the world may in principle be organized or conceptualized in infinitely many ways (which would thus form the basis for infinitely many theories), human beings are designed to organize the world in relatively fixed ways. Though there are certainly differences in the way different societies organize the color spectrum, the differences are highly constrained. In fact, they are confined to a small number of options, presumably due to human biology. This means that a "stipulative realist" ontology (according to which the world is real, but the way it is organized is entirely a matter of implicit or explicit human stipulation) poses no particular problem for the "robust realism" sought by Van Fraassen. This robust realism—or, more accurately, robust universalism—is guaranteed by human physiology.

But, again, robust universalism does not put an end to our dilemma. If we add a hierarchical conception of theory formation to what we have said thus far, however, we seem have the beginnings of a solution to our epistemological problems. Specifically, we often conceive of a theory as a single, homogeneous structure through which we conceptualize the world. In fact, theories are internally hierarchized, and they are embedded in larger, hierarchized structures that define various sorts of presupposition, and so on. Indeed, when we refer to something as a "theory," we isolate some part of this hierarchical structure, somewhat arbitrarily. Consider, for example, the theory of quarks. Quarks are posited as constituents of protons, neutrons, and related particles, thus as part of a theory of subatomic particles. That theory is, in turn, a subtheory of atomic theory, itself a subtheory of physics. Physics is itself embedded in more encompassing theories, through which we can regress, until we reach the level of beliefs about ordinary objects. The same holds for literary theories. For example, Derrida's idea that logocentric hierarchies are necessarily self-undermining is located in a hierarchy of theories and presupposes (among other things) a Saussurean conception of meaning as a function of difference and deferral.

The fact that theories are always components of hierarchized systems of beliefs, or of subordinate and superordinate theories, is enormously important. For one thing, it indicates that, in any case where incompatible theoretical alternatives are at issue, it is always possible in principle to retreat to some level of presupposition, higher in this structural hierarchy (or more basic in the hierarchy, depending on which way one uses the metaphor). Disputes about quarks may be rationally discussed by retreat to the level of protons and neutrons (which may themselves be discussed by retreat to the level of atoms); disputes about certain aspects of deconstruction may be rationally discussed by retreat to Saussurean semantics. (Actually the situation is more complicated than this, but the general point should be clear.) Scientists of different paradigms or literary theorists from different schools are not prevented from engaging in productive debate due to the (putative) incommensurability of their views. Rather, they can always have recourse to some level of presupposition—in the final instance, a level of tacit conceptual stipulation, determined by human biology. Put differently, there are no such things as fully distinct paradigms, in the strict sense, for all paradigms share presuppositions at some level, at least at the level of the universal principles of human perception and cognition.

None of this means that disputes between theorists are open to definitive resolution. They are not. No theoretical dispute can be fully decided, for reasons we have discussed in connection with Duhem, Quine, Kuhn, and others. On the other hand, they can be discussed and analyzed rationally. Or, rather, they can be discussed and analyzed rationally, if we allow ourselves a small number of methodological principles. Specifically, I isolate three adjudicative criteria: discriminatory empirical data (thus data that are not equally suited to or compatible with all competing theories, and have usually been sought for just that reason), logical coherence, and simplicity.

We have already discussed discriminatory empirical data and logical coherence (in the preceding chapter). However, simplicity is a somewhat unusual notion, and thus bears elaboration, especially considering its extremely important role in the evaluation of rival theories. First of all, simplicity is not (as is sometimes thought) a property of theories considered in isolation. We cannot say that a theory is, in and of itself, simple or not simple. Rather, simplicity is a relation between two or more theories and a body of data. Given two theories, A and B, we say that theory A is simpler than theory B if it accounts for (roughly) the same data with fewer theoretical principles, posits, and so on, or if it accounts for more data with (roughly) the same number of theoretical principles, and so on. Obviously there are complications here relating to how we count principles, posits, and so forth, whether we are considering finished theories or research programs (and thus theoretical promise), and so on. However, we can leave those aside for present purposes. The contrast between a theory with many ad hoc qualifications (in Lakatos's sense) and a theory covering similar data but with few ad hoc qualifications provides a relatively clear case; the latter is simpler than the former and preferable on precisely those grounds. Most often, a paradigm shift occurs, not because an earlier research program has been unable to accommodate new data (it can always accommodate them through ad hoc qualifications) and not because the new theory explains more data (it usually has not yet had a chance to do so). Rather, a paradigm shift occurs because researchers come to feel that the newer theory shows greater promise of explaining as many or more types of observations and doing so more simply (at least without the ad hoc qualifications that plague the older theory). For example, though far from perfect in its early formulations, heliocentrism promised the eventual elimination of the vastly complex systems of epicycles required by Ptolemaic astronomy and thus appeared preferable to Ptolemaic astronomy in part on those grounds, which is to say, on grounds of simplicity.

Since there is considerable confusion over the issue, it is worth noting that a simplicity criterion for the evaluation of theories has nothing to do with assuming that the world is simple or that human psychology is simple—or that literary texts are simple, in the case of literary interpretation. Indeed, in some cases, an assumption that the world is "simple" directly contradicts the simplicity criterion in the evaluation of theories. For example, the world is in some sense simpler if there are no unobservable constituents of matter (such as atoms). But a theory that tries to account for all the experimental data—or even ordinary experiential data—without reference to unobservable constituents must involve wild complexity in principles, primarily via ad hoc qualifications. Similarly, human psychology is in some sense simpler if nothing whatsoever is nonconscious. But we cannot even explain the most elementary principles of speech if we make this assumption. Thus, to preserve a "simple" world, we would have to adopt a theory of vast complexity, and reject far simpler alternatives. This is particularly important to emphasize as literary critics seem to get nervous as soon as someone mentions "simplicity," worrying that the theorist in question is out to deny the richness of literary texts, reducing them to some bare, univocal theme. In fact, nothing could be farther from the case.

But this is not to say that simplicity criteria do not bear on the adjudication of literary interpretations. They are, in fact, central to such adjudication. Moreover, examining a case of this sort will allow us to see that simplicity is not merely a matter of the presence or absence of ad hoc qualifications. Consider once more the theory that Othello is overly passionate. Again, we can imagine two versions of this theory. One merely dismisses his moments of calm as unexplained exceptions. The other accounts for them by saying that Othello represses his rashness in public. The latter is clearly preferable to the former in being non–ad hoc. But what about the relation between this theory and the view that Othello is not rash, but is driven to violence by his beliefs about Desdemona in the context of his experience of racism. Neither of these theories has ad hoc qualifications. Nonetheless, we can, I believe, decide between them—on the basis of simplicity considerations.

First of all, note that both theories will have to give Othello's beliefs about Desdemona a causal role in the murder (even if Othello is rash, it is his beliefs about Desdemona that bring out this rashness and thus cause him to murder her). Moreover, both theories acknowledge that these beliefs are not adequate to account for the murder—after all, not everyone murders a spouse he/she believes to be unfaithful. Thus each theory must add another causal factor beyond the belief about infidelity. One theory hypothesizes that Othello is rash or overly passionate. The other hypothesizes that he feels Desdemona's betrayal is part of a more general racism of Venetian society, a racism that alienates him from society and from himself. Thus far, each account posits two distinct causal factors. However, the rashness hypothesis is inconsistent with some scenes in the play, and thus must add a third causal hypothesis—that Othello suppresses his rashness in public. This makes the racism interpretation simpler, in involving fewer explanatory principles, and thus preferable.

It is important to stress that simplicity criteria apply not only to abstract or highly developed theories. They apply equally to observation statements. Like everything else, observation statements are always open to dispute. However, we assume that, in ordinary circumstances, ordinary sorts of observation are what they appear to be. And we are justified in assuming this, because it is most consistent with our simplicity criteria. If comparable observations have almost never turned out to be mistaken, then it is simplest to assume that the current observation is not mistaken. If I seem to see a clear liquid, then I assume that I do see a clear liquid, for this is the simplest assumption. (Unless, of course, the circumstances are such that I have found myself to be mistaken about comparable judgments—for example, if I am in a house of optical illusions.) Note that this is a version of the statistical approach mentioned above. However, the statistical approach accomplishes its purpose only with the addition of simplicity criteria, for simplicity criteria are what allow us to assume (as the simplest hypothesis) that the apparent frequency of correct perception is the real frequency of correct perception. Simplicity criteria do not eliminate the possibility that we are mistaken, but allow us to assume, in certain circumstances, that we are not mistaken unless we find reason to believe otherwise. They place the burden of proof on the skeptic rather than on the observer or statistician, which eliminates the theoretical problem with the statistical approach.

Thus we seem to have found a solution to both our epistemological and methodological problems. But this solution rests on our acceptance of simplicity criteria (along with principles of logic) and leads to a further question: How can simplicity criteria be justified? In my view, they cannot—if we mean, "How can they be demonstrated?" However, that is not a problem, because, though they cannot be proven, they also cannot be denied. There is just no other principle that we can invoke consistently as an adjudicative criterion. Any other candidate—for example, "choose whichever theory is most politically expedient"—cannot be applied without presupposing simplicity criteria operating at another level. To say that theory A is more politically expedient than theory B, we have to invoke a range of observations and interpretations that themselves rest on simplicity evaluations. After all, no matter how politically inexpedient theory B might seem, we can always salvage the interpretation that B is highly expedient merely by making our interpretation of the data more complex (for example, by claiming that almost all of the politically inexpedient observations are the result of hallucination). Given this possibility—which, again, is always present—the theory that A is more expedient may be judged superior to the theory that B is more expedient only on the basis of simplicity criteria.

In short, simplicity criteria—and the laws of logic—are necessary to systematic thought. Without them, we would not be able to make even the most straightforward observations. Simplicity criteria and the laws of logic have the status of Kant's transcendental and regulative principles. Indeed, in the *Critique of Judgement,* Kant already noted that the "maxims" of reason "bid us always avoid as far as possible unnecessary multiplication of principles" (193). In a sense, we just have no choice in the matter.

And yet, none of this is to say that physics, literary theory, or any other discipline genuinely and systematically follows these principles in evaluating theories. The skepticism expressed by Feyerabend seems fully justified when we turn from principle to practice. Indeed, in the last three decades, there has been a great deal of research on reasoning as actually practiced in the sciences. The picture is grim. While intellectual criteria may play some role in the evaluation of theories, various economic and cognitive biases appear to be far more central. As to the former, research is bound up with economy at every level. This is most obvious in the natural sciences, which are closely linked with industry, and in the social sciences, which are frequently linked with government as well as business. But even in the humanities, there are strong personal and professional interests that skew evaluation.

As an illustration of this in the physical sciences, consider a case reported by Machlup: "a young medical researcher in the last year of his probationary period . . . had discovered toxic qualities of a drug distributed by a company which was supporting his university with generous research grants. Should he publish the report on his findings? Would he risk nonrenewal of his appointment if his publication angered the donor and the chairman of his department? As it was, or as I was told, the young man decided to publish and he lost his post" (337). Thus this researcher's future work was cut short, and other research along the same lines was concretely discouraged, at least for untenured faculty at that particular institution—and this was clearly for economic, not scientific, reasons. Sadly, this does not appear to be an isolated case.

Evaluation of theories is further distorted by various cognitive biases, most obviously "confirmation bias," the universal tendency to seek out and to recognize evidence supporting strongly held beliefs, while failing to seek or even to recognize evidence contradicting those beliefs. In everyday life, we act in precisely the opposite of the way advocated by Popper; we unreflectively seek to "verify" our beliefs, and to avoid falsifying them. To do this, we ignore disconfirming evidence, or, when this is impossible, we distort disconfirming evidence so that it appears confirmatory. There are particularly striking cases of this in sexism and racism. For example, for many people, no amount of evidence will indicate that women and men are equally rational. Apparent counterexamples to the stereotype of female irrationality are twisted into conformity, sometimes by complete denial ("She was just hysterical," said of a woman vehemently, but logically, arguing her point), sometimes by a more subtle reinterpretation ("Did you see how hard she was trying to seem logical?"), sometimes by reexplanation ("She's some sort of super-logical freak—probably has a lot of male hormones"). Other cognitive biases include overestimating the predictive or other importance of salient examples (thus we tend to estimate the value of a type of car on the basis of our own experience of one car of that type, and not on the basis of far more reliable statistical studies— "Sure, statistics tell you a Toyota is reliable, but the one I had . . .; I'd never buy one of those again!"). (For an overview of cognitive biases, see Nisbett and Ross.)

It is disturbing enough that most of our everyday interactions and evaluations are twisted by such systematic cognitive errors. However, it turns out that a great deal of evaluation in the sciences is biased in precisely the same ways. Mahoney and Kimper surveyed a range of scientists and discovered that most of them appear to believe that their task is confirming standard scientific beliefs; indeed, over half of the scientists surveyed did not even see falsification as a valid form of scientific inference (see Mahoney 162). David Faust has catalogued a wide range of cognitive biases common in science, demonstrating that there is very little difference between professional scientists and laypeople on this score. It seems likely that, if anything, the situation is worse in literary theory. At least in science, some theories have practical consequences that are too obvious to ignore (the airplane will either fly or it won't). In literary theory, there do not appear to be any parallel cases of straightforward practical success or failure. In other words, there seems to be little if anything in literary study that would serve to curb these biases.

An excellent example of cognitive bias may be found in Michael Mahoney's well-known study of publication prejudices. Mahoney wrote two versions of an experiment in psychology. In the first version, the experiment "confirmed" standard views. In the second version, Mahoney repeated the design, methodology, and so on, from the first version, but he switched the data tables so that the experiment "falsified" standard views. He found that the first version was much more likely to be accepted for publication than was the second version, even though the experiment was presented identically and even though disconfirmatory findings should have been of far greater scientific interest than confirmatory findings. This and related studies indicate fairly clearly that professional standards of evaluation, as represented by publication decisions, exhibit a strong confirmatory bias. Moreover, this confirmatory bias is almost certainly tied up with the economic and professional interests of "experts" in the field, who usually have a considerable economic stake in the continued acceptance of dominant views.

Along the same lines, we might consider the effect of institutional prestige on research publication. Peters and Ceci took manuscripts that were written by authors at high-prestige institutions and had been published in professional journals. Peters and Ceci changed the names and affiliations of the authors, substituting low-prestige institutions. They then resubmitted the articles for publication. Only 8 percent of the editors recognized the resubmission. Of those that were not recognized, 89 percent were rejected, often on the grounds that they suffered "serious methodological flaws"

(187). In short, institutional prestige of the author (or supposed author) virtually determined the fate of the article. High prestige meant publication; low prestige meant rejection—for the very same piece of work. This may be largely a cognitive matter (based on confirmatory bias with respect to institutional prestige). But it is not at all irrelevant to economic concerns, for, the higher the prestige of a university, the closer its ties with industry, the greater its tendency to draw its students and faculty from higher economic strata, and so on (for discussion, see Hogan, "Teaching").

In sum, definitive or absolute evaluation of theories is not possible. However, rigorous, rational evaluation, based on observation, logic, and simplicity, is entirely possible in principle. In order to engage in this sort of evaluation, we should try to extend the explanatory capacity of theories with minimum complication, presumably by continually comparing alternatives (following Feyerabend's advice), and by looking in particular for areas in which the theory, or the current version of the theory, may be falsified and redeveloped (Popper's advice), in the context of an ongoing research program (as discussed by Lakatos).

However, in practice, the evaluation of theories is economically and cognitively, socially and individually, biased. Moreover, we have no reason to exempt ourselves from the universal human tendencies that result in this bias. This leaves us in a quandary. In evaluating theories for ourselves, and in discussing the evaluation of theories, we should strive to be methodologically strict and highly critical (with the qualifications noted by Lakatos). But since our evaluations are likely to be twisted by a range of prejudices, they cannot be considered in any way definitive. At the very least, these evaluations cannot be invoked as justification for harming people's lives, for placing limits on their "flourishing" (in Martha Nussbaum's term)—as they are routinely in all intellectual disciplines (for example, in publication decisions and, still more obviously, in tenure decisions).

The solution to this problem is, I believe, not a matter of scientific method, but of politics and institutional structure. In order to diminish the dangers posed by our inevitable biases, we should set up our institutions in such a way as to drastically constrain the effects of our evaluations, permitting and even fostering a wide range of incompatible intellectual pursuits. In other words, our individual judgments should be highly rigoristic; but the political structures in which we make these judgments should be anarchistic. Put differently, no theory should be suppressed (thus left unpublished), but all should be rigorously criticized—especially those that have achieved prominence.

# Appendix

## I Dream It Is Afternoon When I Return to Delhi

AGHA SHAHID ALI

At Purana Qila I am alone, waiting
for the bus to Daryaganj. I see it coming,
but my hands are empty.
"Jump on, jump on," someone shouts,
"I've saved this change for you
for years. Look!"
A hand opens, full of silver rupees.
"Jump on, jump on." The voice doesn't stop.
There's no one I know. A policeman,
handcuffs silvering in his hands,
asks for my ticket.

I jump off the running bus,
sweat pouring from my hair.
I run past the Doll Museum, past
headlines on the Times of India
building, PRISONERS BLINDED IN A BIHAR JAIL,
HARIJAN VILLAGES BURNED BY LANDLORDS.
Panting, I stop in Daryaganj,
outside Golcha Cinema.

Sunil is there, lighting
a cigarette, smiling. I say,
"It must be ten years, you haven't changed,
it was your voice on the bus!"
He says, "The film is about to begin,
I've bought an extra ticket for you,"
and we rush inside:

Anarkali is being led away,
her earrings lying on the marble floor.
Any moment she'll be buried alive.

"But this is the end," I turn
toward Sunil. He is nowhere.
The usher taps my shoulder, says
my ticket is ten years old.

Once again my hands are empty.
I am waiting, alone, at Purana Qila.
Bus after empty bus is not stopping.
Suddenly, beggar women with children
are everywhere, offering
me money, weeping for me.

# Bibliography

Abhinavagupta. *Locana*. Ingalls.

Abrahams, Peter. *Mine Boy*. London: Heinemann, 1946.

Adams, Hazard. *Critical Theory Since Plato*. Rev. ed. New York: Harcourt Brace Jovanovich, 1992.

Al-Fārābī. "Canons of the Art of Poetry." Cantarino.

Ali, Agha Shahid. *The Beloved Witness: Selected Poems*. New Delhi: Viking, 1992.

Al-Jurjānī. "From *Kitāb Asrār al-Balāgha*." Cantarino.

Al-Qarṭajannī. "From *Minhāj al-bulaghā' wa-sirāj al-udabā'*." Cantarino.

Althusser, Louis. "Ideology and Ideological State Apparatuses (Notes towards an Investigation)." *Lenin and Philosophy and Other Essays*. Trans. Ben Brewster. New York: Monthly Review Press, 1971.

Amin, Samir. *Eurocentrism*. Trans. Russell Moore. New York: Monthly Review Press, 1989.

Ānandavardhana. *Dhvanyaloka*. Ingalls.

Anscombe, G. E. M. *Intention*. 2nd ed. Ithaca, N.Y.: Cornell University Press, 1957.

———. "On the Grammar of 'Enjoy'." *Metaphysics and the Philosophy of Mind*. Vol. 2 of *Collected Philosophical Papers*. Minneapolis: University of Minnesota Press, 1981.

Aristotle. *Nicomachean Ethics*. Trans. W. D. Ross. *Introduction to Aristotle*. Ed. Richard McKeon. New York: Modern Library, 1947.

———. *Poetics*. *Aristotle's Theory of Poetry and Fine Art with a Critical Text and Translation of the Poetics*. Ed. and trans. S. H. Butcher. 4th ed. New York: Dover, 1951.

Austin, J. L. *How to Do Things with Words*. Ed. J. O. Urmson and Marina Sbisa. 2nd ed. Cambridge, Mass.: Harvard University Press, 1975.

Ayer, A. J. *Language, Truth, and Logic*. New York: Dover, 1952.

Badawi, M. M. *Early Arabic Drama*. Cambridge: Cambridge University Press, 1988.

Baker, Houston. "Generational Shifts and the Recent Criticism of Afro-American Literature." Richter.

Bakhtin, M. M. *The Dialogic Imagination: Four Essays*. Ed. Michael Holquist. Trans. Caryl Emerson and Michael Holquist. Austin: University of Texas Press, 1981.

Balibar, Étienne, and Immanuel Wallerstein. *Race, Nation, Class: Ambiguous Identities*. Trans. of Balibar by Chris Turner. New York: Verso, 1991.

Baudrillard, Jean. *L'Échange symbolique et la mort* [*Symbolic Exchange and Death*]. Paris: Gallimard, 1976.

———. *La guerre du Golfe n'a pas eu lieu* [*The Gulf War Did Not Take (or Have) Place*]. Mayenne, France: Éditions Galilee, 1991.

———. *The Transparency of Evil: Essays on Extreme Phenomena*. Trans. James Benedict. New York: Verso, 1993.

Bennett, Tony. *Outside Literature*. New York: Routledge, 1990.

Bhaskar, Roy. *Reclaiming Reality: A Critical Introduction to Contemporary Philosophy*. New York: Verso, 1989.

Bleich, David. "Gender Interests in Reading and Language." *Gender and Reading: Essays on Readers, Texts, and Contexts*. Ed. Elizabeth A. Flynn and Patrocinio P. Schweickart. Baltimore, Md.: Johns Hopkins University Press, 1986.

Bordwell, David. *Making Meaning: Inference and Rhetoric in the Interpretation of Cinema*. Cambridge, Mass.: Harvard University Press, 1989.

Boudon, Raymond. *The Analysis of Ideology*. Trans. Malcolm Slater. Chicago: University of Chicago Press, 1989.

Bourdieu, Pierre. *Distinction: A Social Critique of the Judgement of Taste*. Trans. Richard Nice. Cambridge, Mass.: Harvard University Press, 1984.

———. *The Field of Cultural Production: Essays on Art and Literature*. Ed. Randal Johnson. New York: Columbia University Press, 1993.

———. *The Rules of Art: Genesis and Structure of the Literary Field*. Trans. Susan Emanuel. Stanford, Calif.: Stanford University Press, 1996.

Breisach, Ernest. *Historiography: Ancient, Medieval, and Modern*. Chicago: University of Chicago Press, 1983.

Burke, Edmund. *A Philosophical Enquiry into the Origin of Our Ideas of the Sublime and Beautiful*. Ed. J. T. Boulton. New York: Columbia University Press, 1958.

Butler, Judith. *Gender Trouble: Feminism and the Subversion of Identity*. New York: Routledge, 1990.

Cameron, Deborah. *Feminism and Linguistic Theory*. 2nd ed. New York: St. Martin's, 1992.

Cantarino, Vicente. *Arabic Poetics in the Golden Age: Selection of Texts Accompanied by a Preliminary Study*. Leiden, Netherlands: E. J. Brill, 1975.

Carnap, Rudolf. *The Logical Structure of the World and Pseudoproblems in Philosophy*. Trans. Rolf A. George. Berkeley: University of California Press, 1967.

———. "Testability and Meaning." *Theories and Observation in Science*. Ed. Richard Grandy. Englewood Cliffs, N.J.: Prentice-Hall, 1973.

Chomsky, Noam. *Aspects of the Theory of Syntax*. Cambridge, Mass.: MIT Press, 1965.

———. *Knowledge of Language: Its Nature, Origin, and Use*. New York: Praeger, 1986.

Cixous, Hélène. "The Laugh of the Medusa." Marks and de Courtivron.

———. "Sorties." Cixous and Clément.

Cixous, Hélène, and Catherine Clément. *The Newly Born Woman*. Minneapolis: University of Minnesota Press, 1986.

Clark Bekederemo, J. P. "Death of a Lady." *The Heinemann Book of African Poetry in English.* Ed. Adewale Maja-Pearce. Oxford: Heinemann, 1990. 65.

Coleridge, Samuel Taylor. *Biographia Literaria. Selected Poetry and Prose of Coleridge.* Ed. Donald Stauffer. New York: Random House, 1951.

———. *On the Principles of Genial Criticism Concerning the Fine Arts.* Vol. 2 of *Biographia Literaria By S. T. Coleridge Edited with His Aesthetical Essays.* Ed. J. Shawcross. London: Oxford University Press, 1907.

Comrie, Bernard. *Language Universals and Linguistic Typology: Syntax and Morphology.* Chicago: University of Chicago Press, 1981.

Culler, Jonathan. *Structuralist Poetics: Structuralism, Linguistics, and the Study of Literature.* Ithaca, N.Y.: Cornell University Press, 1975.

Dahiyat, Ismail, ed. and trans. *Avicenna's Commentary on the Poetics of Aristotle.* Leiden, Netherlands: E. J. Brill, 1974.

Daniélou, Alain. *The Myths and Gods of India.* Rochester, Vt.: Inner Traditions International, 1991.

Dasenbrock, Reed Way. "Do We Write the Text We Read?" Dasenbrock, *Literary Theory.*

———, ed. *Literary Theory After Davidson.* University Park: Pennsylvania State University Press, 1993.

Davidson, Donald. *Inquiries into Truth and Interpretation.* Oxford: Clarendon, 1984.

———. "Locating Literary Language." Dasenbrock, *Literary Theory.*

de Beaugrande, Robert. "Toward the Empirical Study of Literature: A Synoptic Sketch of a New 'Society'." *Poetics* 18 (1989): 7–27.

de Beauvoir, Simone. "From an Interview." Marks and de Courtivron.

———. *The Second Sex.* Ed. and trans. H. M. Parshley. New York: Random House, 1953.

de Lauretis, Teresa. *Technologies of Gender: Essays on Theory, Film, and Fiction.* Bloomington: Indiana University Press, 1987.

de Man, Paul. *Blindness and Insight: Essays in the Rhetoric of Contemporary Criticism.* 2nd ed. Minneapolis, Minn.: University of Minnesota Press, 1983.

de Saussure, Ferdinand. *Course in General Linguistics.* Trans. Wade Baskin. New York: McGraw-Hill, 1959.

de Stael, Madame. *De la littérature considerée dans ses rapports avec les institutions sociales* [*On Literature Considered in Its Relations with Social Institutions*]. Ed. Paul van Tieghm. Vol. 1. Geneva, Switzerland: Librarie Droz, 1959.

———. *De L'Allemagne* [*On Germany*]. 2 vols. Paris: Garnier-Flammarion, 1968.

Dewey, John. *Art as Experience.* New York: Capricorn Books, 1958.

———. "Introduction to Jagadish Chandra Chatterji's *India's Outlook on Life*." *1931–1932.* Vol. 6 of *John Dewey: The Later Works, 1925–1953.* Ed. Jo Ann Boydston. Textual ed. Anne Sharpe. Carbondale and Edwardsville: Southern Illinois University Press, 1985.

Dhanaṃjaya. *The Daśarūpa: A Treatise on Hindu Dramaturgy.* Trans. George C. O. Haas. New York: AMS, 1965.

Didion, Joan. "New York: Sentimental Journeys." *New York Review of Books* 17 January 1991: 45–56.

Dreyfus, Hubert, and Paul Rabinow. *Michel Foucault: Beyond Structuralism and Hermeneutics*. 2nd ed. Chicago: University of Chicago Press, 1983.

Eagleton, Terry. *Ideology: An Introduction*. London: Verso, 1991.

Earman, John. "Carnap, Kuhn, and the Philosophy of Scientific Methodology." *World Changes: Thomas Kuhn and the Nature of Science*. Ed. Paul Horwich. Cambridge, Mass.: MIT Press, 1993.

Eco, Umberto. *The Limits of Interpretation*. Bloomington: Indiana University Press, 1990.

Elders, Fons, ed. *Reflexive Water: The Basic Concerns of Mankind*. London: Souvenir, 1974.

Eliot, T. S. *Collected Poems: 1909–1962*. New York: Harcourt, Brace and World, 1970.

———. "The Metaphysical Poets." *Selected Essays: 1917–1932*. New York: Harcourt, Brace, 1932.

Ellmann, Richard. *James Joyce*. 2nd ed. New York: Oxford University Press, 1982.

Elster, Jon. "Belief, Bias, and Ideology." *Ideology*. Ed. Terry Eagleton. London: Longman, 1994.

Epstein, Cynthia Fuchs. *Deceptive Distinctions: Sex, Gender, and the Social Order*. New Haven, Conn.: Yale University Press; New York: Russell Sage Foundation, 1988.

Faiz, Faiz Ahmed. "Spring Comes." *The True Subject: Selected Poems of Faiz Ahmed Faiz*. Trans. Naomi Lazard. Princeton, N.J.: Princeton University Press, 1988.

Faludi, Susan. *Backlash: The Undeclared War Against American Women*. New York: Crown, 1991.

Fanon, Frantz. *Black Skin, White Masks*. Trans. Charles Lam Markmann. New York: Grove, 1967.

Faust, David. *The Limits of Scientific Reasoning*. Minneapolis: University of Minnesota Press, 1984.

Fausto-Sterling, Anne. *Myths of Gender: Biological Theories about Women and Men*. New York: Basic Books, 1985.

Feyerabend, Paul. *Against Method: Outline of an Anarchistic Theory of Knowledge*. London: Verso, 1975.

Fichte, J. G. *The Science of Knowledge*. Ed. and trans. Peter Heath and John Lachs. Cambridge: Cambridge University Press, 1982.

Fish, Stanley. *Is There a Text in This Class? The Authority of Interpretive Communities*. Cambridge, Mass.: Harvard University Press, 1980.

Foucault, Michel. *The Archaeology of Knowledge and The Discourse on Language*. Trans. A. M. Sheridan Smith. New York: Harper and Row, 1972.

———. "The Confession of the Flesh." Foucault, *Power/Knowledge*.

———. *Discipline and Punish: The Birth of the Prison*. Trans. Alan Sheridan. New York: Vintage Books, 1979.

———. *Madness and Civilization: A History of Insanity in the Age of Reason.* Trans. Richard Howard. New York: Vintage Books, 1973.

———. *The Order of Things: An Archaeology of the Human Sciences.* New York: Vintage Books, 1973.

———. *Power/Knowledge: Selected Interviews and Other Writings, 1972–1977.* Ed. Colin Gordon. Trans. C. Gordon, L. Marshall, J. Mepham, and K. Soper. New York: Pantheon, 1980.

Frege, Gottlob. *Translations from the Philosophical Writings of Gottlob Frege.* Ed. Peter Geach and Max Black. 3rd ed. Totowa, N.J.: Rowman and Littlefield, 1980.

Frye, Northrop. *Anatomy of Criticism: Four Essays.* Princeton, N.J.: Princeton University Press, 1957.

Gadamer, Hans-Georg. *Truth and Method.* 2nd ed. Trans. Joel Weinsheimer and Donald Marshall. New York: Crossroad, 1989.

———. "The Universality of the Hermeneutical Problem." *Philosophical Hermeneutics.* Trans. and ed. David Linge. Berkeley: University of California Press, 1976.

Garraty, John, and Peter Gay, eds. *The Columbia History of the World.* New York: Harper and Row, 1981.

Geach, Peter, and Max Black. "Glossary." Frege.

Geertz, Clifford. *The Interpretation of Cultures: Selected Essays.* New York: Basic Books, 1973.

Gerow, Edwin. *Indian Poetics.* Wiesbaden: Otto Harrassowitz, 1977.

Geuss, Raymond. *The Idea of a Critical Theory: Habermas and the Frankfurt School.* New York: Cambridge University Press, 1981.

Gilligan, Carol. *In a Different Voice: Psychological Theory and Women's Development.* Cambridge, Mass.: Harvard University Press, 1982.

Goodman, Nelson. *Ways of Worldmaking.* Indianapolis, Ind.: Hackett, 1978.

Gorman, David. "Davidson and Dummett on Language and Interpretation." Dasenbrock, *Literary Theory.*

Graff, Gerald. "Co-Optation." Veeser.

Greenblatt, Stephen. "Introduction to *The Power of Forms in the English Renaissance.*" Richter.

———. *Shakespearean Negotiations: The Circulation of Social Energy in Renaissance England.* Berkeley: University of California Press, 1988.

Greimas, A.-J. *Structural Semantics: An Attempt at a Method.* Trans. D. McDowell, R. Schleifer, and A. Velie. Lincoln: University of Nebraska Press, 1983.

Grice, Paul. *Studies in the Way of Words.* Cambridge, Mass.: Harvard University Press, 1989.

Guérin, Daniel. *Anarchism.* New York: Monthly Review Press, 1970.

Habermas, Jürgen. *On the Logic of the Social Sciences.* Trans. Shierry Weber Nicholsen and Jerry A. Stark. Cambridge, Mass.: MIT Press, 1989.

Haggerty, George E., and Bonnie Zimmerman, eds. *Professions of Desire: Lesbian and Gay Studies in Literature.* New York: Modern Language Association of America, 1995.

Halasz, Laszlo. "Emotional Effect and Reminding in Literary Processing." *Poetics* 20 (1991): 247–72.

Halhed, Nathaniel. "'The Translator's Preface' to *A Code of Gentoo Laws.*" *The British Discovery of Hinduism in the Eighteenth Century.* Ed. P. J. Marshall. Cambridge: Cambridge University Press, 1970.

Haraway, Donna J. "A Cyborg Manifesto: Science, Technology, and Socialist-Feminism in the Late Twentieth Century." *Simians, Cyborgs, and Women: The Reinvention of Nature.* New York: Routledge, 1991.

Hauser, Arnold. *The Social History of Art.* 4 vols. Trans. Stanley Godman. New York: Vintage Books, 1985.

Hegel, G. W. F. *Aesthetics: Lectures on Fine Art.* Vol. 1. Trans. T. M. Knox. Oxford: Clarendon, 1975.

———. *Hegel's Phenomenology of Spirit.* Trans. A. V. Miller. Oxford: Oxford University Press, 1977.

———. *Hegel's Philosophy of Mind, Being Part Three of the Encyclopaedia of the Philosophical Sciences (1830).* Trans. William Wallace. *Zusaetze* trans. A. V. Miller. Oxford: Clarendon, 1971.

Heidegger, Martin. *Being and Time.* Trans. John Macquarrie and Edward Robinson. New York: Harper and Row, 1962.

———. "The Origin of the Work of Art." *Poetry, Language, Thought.* Trans. Albert Hofstadter. New York: Harper and Row, 1971.

Hempel, Carl. *Aspects of Scientific Explanation and Other Essays in the Philosophy of Science.* New York: Free Press, 1965.

Hernadi, Paul. *Cultural Transactions: Nature, Self, Society.* Ithaca, N.Y.: Cornell University Press, 1995.

Hesse, Mary. "Texts Without Types and Lumps Without Laws." *New Literary History* 17.1 (1985): 31–48.

Hiatt, Mary. *Style and the 'Scribbling Women': An Empirical Analysis of Nineteenth-Century American Fiction.* Westport, Conn.: Greenwood Press, 1993.

———. *The Way Women Write.* New York: Teachers College Press, 1977.

Hirsch, E. D., Jr. *The Aims of Interpretation.* Chicago: University of Chicago Press, 1976.

Hobbs, Jerry. *Literature and Cognition.* Menlo Park, Calif.: Center for the Study of Language and Information, 1990.

Hogan, Patrick Colm. *Joyce, Milton, and the Theory of Influence.* Gainesville: University of Florida Press, 1995.

———. "Literary Universals." *Poetics Today* 18.2 (Summer 1997): 223–49.

———. "Meaning and Hegel: A Psycho-Linguistic Critique of Philosophical Beginning." *Southern Journal of Philosophy* 18.1 (1980): 51–61.

———. *On Interpretation: Meaning and Inference in Law, Psychoanalysis, and Literature.* Athens: University of Georgia Press, 1995.

———. "Paternalism, Ideology, and Ideological Critique: Teaching *Cry, the Beloved Country.*" *College Literature* 19.3/20.1 (October 1992/February 1993): 206–9.

———. *The Politics of Interpretation: Ideology, Professionalism, and the Study of Literature.* New York: Oxford University Press, 1990.

———. "The Possibility of Aesthetics." *British Journal of Aesthetics* 34.4 (1994): 337–49.

———. "Reading for Ethos: Literary Study and Moral Thought." *Journal of Aesthetic Education* 27.3 (Fall 1993): 23–34.

———. "Some Prolegomena to the Study of Literary Difference." *Poetics* 22 (1994): 243–61.

———. "Teaching and Research as Economic Problems." *Education and Society* 11 (1993): 15–25.

Hogan, Patrick Colm, and Lalita Pandit, eds. *Criticism and Lacan: Essays and Dialogue on Language, Structure, and the Unconscious.* Athens: University of Georgia Press, 1990.

———, eds. *Literary India: Comparative Studies in Aesthetics, Colonialism, and Culture.* Albany: State University of New York Press, 1995.

Horkheimer, Max, and Theodor Adorno. *Dialectic of Enlightenment.* Trans. John Cumming. New York: Continuum, 1986.

Hume, David. "Of the Standard of Taste." Adams.

Husserl, Edmund. *Cartesian Meditations: An Introduction to Phenomenology.* Trans. Dorion Cairns. The Hague, Netherlands: Martinus Nijhoff, 1973.

———. *Ideas Pertaining to a Pure Phenomenology and to a Phenomenological Philosophy.* Trans. F. Kersten. Bk. 1. The Hague, Netherlands: Martinus Nijhoff, 1983.

Ibn Rushd (Averroes). *Averroes' Commentary on Plato's Republic.* Ed. and trans. E. I. J. Rosenthal. Cambridge: Cambridge University Press, 1966.

———. *Averroes' Middle Commentary on Aristotle's Poetics.* Trans. and ed. Charles Butterworth. Princeton, N.J.: Princeton University Press, 1986.

Ibn Sīnā (Avicenna). *Avicenna's Commentary on the Poetics of Aristotle.* Dahiyat.

Iftikhar-Ul-Awwal. "State of Indigenous Industries." *Economic History.* Vol. 2 of *History of Bangladesh: 1704–1971.* Ed. Sirajul Islam. Dhaka, Bangladesh: Asiatic Society of Bangladesh, 1992.

Ingalls, Daniel, ed. *The Dhvanyaloka of Ānandavardhana with the Locana of Abhinavagupta.* Trans. Daniel Ingalls, Jeffrey Masson, and M. V. Patwardhan. Cambridge, Mass.: Harvard University Press, 1990.

Ingarden, Roman. *The Cognition of the Literary Work of Art.* Trans. Ruth Ann Crowley and Kenneth R. Olson. Evanston, Ill.: Northwestern University Press, 1973.

———. *The Literary Work of Art: An Investigation on the Borderlines of Ontology, Logic, and the Theory of Literature.* Trans. George Grabowicz. Evanston, Ill.: Northwestern University Press, 1973.

Irigaray, Luce. *This Sex Which Is Not One*. Trans. Catherine Porter. Ithaca, N.Y.: Cornell University Press, 1985.

Iser, Wolfgang. *The Implied Reader: Patterns of Communication in Prose Fiction from Bunyan to Beckett*. Baltimore, Md.: Johns Hopkins University Press, 1974.

Jakobson, Roman. *Language in Literature*. Ed. Krystyna Pomorska and Stephen Rudy. Cambridge, Mass.: Belknap Press, 1987.

James, Joy. "Media Convictions, Fair-Trial Activism, and the Central Park Case." *Z Magazine* (February 1992): 33–37.

James, William. *Pragmatism: A New Name for Some Old Ways of Thinking*. New York: Longmans, Green, 1931.

Jameson, Fredric. *The Political Unconscious: Narrative as a Socially Symbolic Act*. Ithaca, N.Y.: Cornell University Press, 1981.

———. *Postmodernism, or the Cultural Logic of Late Capitalism*. Durham, N.C.: Duke University Press, 1991.

Janko, Richard. *Aristotle on Comedy: Towards a Reconstruction of Poetics II*. Berkeley: University of California Press, 1984.

Jauss, Hans Robert. *Toward an Aesthetic of Reception*. Trans. Timothy Bahti. Minneapolis: University of Minnesota Press, 1982.

Jenkins, Richard. *Pierre Bourdieu*. New York: Routledge, 1992.

*Jerusalem Bible*. Ed. Alexander Jones et al. Garden City, N.Y.: Doubleday, 1966.

Jhally, Sut, Justin Lewis, and Michael Morgan. "The Gulf War: A Study of the Media, Public Opinion, and Public Knowledge." *Propaganda Review* 8 (Fall 1991).

Johnson, Randal. "*Editor's Introduction:* Pierre Bourdieu on Art, Literature and Culture." Bourdieu, *The Field of Cultural Production*.

Johnson-Laird, Philip N. *The Computer and the Mind: An Introduction to Cognitive Science*. Cambridge, Mass.: Harvard University Press, 1988.

Jones, Sir William. "On the Gods of Greece, Italy, and India." Richardson.

———. "On the Mystical Poetry of the Persians and Hindus." Richardson.

Kant, Immanuel. *Critique of Judgement*. Trans. J. H. Bernard. New York: Hafner Press, 1951.

———. *Critique of Pure Reason*. Trans. Norman Kemp Smith. New York: St. Martin's, 1929.

Kavanagh, Patrick. "Memory of My Father." *Collected Poems*. New York: W. W. Norton, 1964.

Keats, John. Letter to George and Thomas Keats. Richter.

Kiparsky, Paul. "On Theory and Interpretation." *The Linguistics of Writing: Arguments Between Language and Literature*. Ed. Nigel Fabb, Derek Attridge, Alan Durant, and Colin MacCabe. New York: Methuen, 1987.

Kittay, Eva Feder. *Metaphor: Its Cognitive Force and Linguistic Structure*. Oxford: Clarendon, 1987.

Klemenz-Belgardt, Edith. "American Research on Response to Literature: The Empirical Studies." *Poetics* 10 (1981): 357–80.

Knapp, Steven, and Walter Benn Michaels. "Against Theory." *Against Theory: Literary Studies and the New Pragmatism.* Ed. W. J. T. Mitchell. Chicago: University of Chicago Press, 1985.

*Koran.* Trans. N. J. Dawood. 5th ed. New York: Penguin Books, 1990.

Kripke, Saul. *Naming and Necessity.* Cambridge, Mass.: Harvard University Press, 1980.

Kropotkin, Peter. *Kropotkin's Revolutionary Pamphlets: A Collection of Writings by Peter Kropotkin.* Ed. Roger N. Baldwin. New York: Dover, 1970.

Kuhn, Thomas. *The Structure of Scientific Revolutions.* 2nd ed. Chicago: University of Chicago Press, 1970.

Kuntaka. *The Vakrokti-Jivita of Kuntaka.* Ed. and trans. K. Krishnamoorthy. Dharwad, India: Karnatak University, 1977.

Labov, William. "The Transformation of Experience in Narrative Syntax." *Language in the Inner City: Studies in the Black English Vernacular.* Philadelphia: University of Pennsylvania Press, 1972.

Lakatos, Imre. "Falsification and the Methodology of Scientific Research Programmes." *Criticism and the Growth of Knowledge.* Ed. Imre Lakatos and Alan Musgrave. Cambridge: Cambridge University Press, 1970.

Lakoff, George, and Mark Johnson. *Metaphors We Live By.* Chicago: University of Chicago Press, 1980.

Lakoff, George, and Mark Turner. *More than Cool Reason: A Field Guide to Poetic Metaphor.* Chicago: University of Chicago Press, 1989.

Lal, P., ed. and trans. *Great Sanskrit Plays in Modern Translation.* New York: New Directions, 1964.

Larsen, Steen, Janos Laszlo, and Uffe Seilman. "Across Time and Place: Cultural-Historical Knowledge and Personal Experience in Appreciation of Literature." *Empirical Studies of Literature.* Ed. E. Ibsch, D. Schram, and G. Steen. Amsterdam, Netherlands: Rodopi, 1991.

Lenin, V. I. *The State and Revolution.* Ed. and trans. Robert Service. London: Penguin Books, 1992.

Lentricchia, Frank. *Ariel and the Police: Michel Foucault, William James, Wallace Stevens.* Madison: University of Wisconsin Press, 1988.

Lévi-Strauss, Claude. *The Raw and the Cooked.* Vol. 1 of *Introduction to the Science of Mythology.* Trans. John and Doreen Weightman. New York: Harper Colophon, 1969.

Lewis, David. *Counterfactuals.* Cambridge, Mass.: Harvard University Press, 1973.

Liddell, H. G., and R. Scott. *Greek-English Lexicon.* Abridged ed. Oxford: Clarendon, 1982.

Liu Hsieh. *The Literary Mind and the Carving of Dragons.* Trans. Vincent Yu-chung Shih. New York: Columbia University Press, 1959.

Livingston, Paisley. "Writing Action: Davidson, Rationality, and Literary Research." Dasenbrock, *Literary Theory.*

Lukács, Georg. *Essays on Realism.* Ed. Rodney Livingstone. Trans. David Fernbach. Cambridge, Mass.: MIT Press, 1981.

———. "Reification and the Consciousness of the Proletariat." *History and Class Consciousness: Studies in Marxist Dialectics.* Trans. Rodney Livingstone. Cambridge, Mass.: MIT Press, 1971.

Luxemburg, Rosa. *Selected Political Writings of Rosa Luxemburg.* Ed. Dick Howard. New York: Monthly Review Press, 1971.

Lyotard, Jean François. *The Postmodern Condition: A Report on Knowledge.* Trans. Geoff Bennington and Brian Massumi. Minneapolis: University of Minnesota Press, 1984.

Machlup, Fritz. "In Defense of Academic Tenure." *Academic Freedom and Tenure: A Handbook of the American Association of University Professors.* Ed. Louis Joughin. Madison: University of Wisconsin Press, 1969.

Maclean, Ian. *The Renaissance Notion of Woman: A Study in the Fortunes of Scholasticism and Medical Science in European Intellectual Life.* Cambridge: Cambridge University Press, 1980.

Mahoney, Michael. "Publication Prejudices: An Experimental Study of Confirmatory Bias in the Peer Review System." *Cognitive Therapy and Research* 1 (1977): 161–75.

Marcuse, Herbert. *One-Dimensional Man: Studies in the Ideology of Advanced Industrial Society.* Boston, Mass.: Beacon Press, 1964.

Marks, Elaine, and de Courtivron, Isabelle, eds. *New French Feminisms.* New York: Schocken, 1980.

Marx, Karl. *A Critical Analysis of Capitalist Production.* Vol. 1 of *Capital.* Ed. Frederick Engels. New York: International Publishers, 1974.

———. *The Economic and Philosophic Manuscripts of 1844.* Ed. Dirk J. Struik. Trans. Martin Milligan. New York: International Publishers, 1964.

———. "Theses on Feuerbach." *The Marx-Engels Reader.* 2nd ed. Ed. Robert Tucker. New York: W. W. Norton, 1978.

Merleau-Ponty, Maurice. "Eye and Mind." Trans. Carleton Dallery. *The Primacy of Perception and Other Essays on Phenomenological Psychology, the Philosophy of Art, History, and Politics.* Ed. James Edie. Evanston, Ill.: Northwestern University Press, 1964.

Mill, John Stuart. *On Liberty. Essential Works of John Stuart Mill.* Ed. Max Lerner. New York: Bantam Books, 1965.

Milton, John. *Complete Poems and Major Prose.* Ed. Merritt Y. Hughes. Indianapolis, Ind.: Bobbs-Merrill, 1957.

Miner, Earl. *Comparative Poetics: An Intercultural Essay on Theories of Literature.* Princeton, N.J.: Princeton University Press, 1990.

Monier-Williams, Monier. *A Sanskrit-English Dictionary.* Delhi, India: Motilal Banarsidass, 1986.

Monk, Ray. *Ludwig Wittgenstein: The Duty of Genius.* New York: Free Press, 1990.

Montrose, Louis. "Professing the Renaissance: The Poetics and Politics of Culture." Veeser.

Morris, Charles. "Pragmatism and Logical Empiricism." Schilpp.

Mukarovsky, Jan. "Standard Language and Poetic Language." Richter.

Nagel, Thomas. "Moral Luck." *Mortal Questions.* Cambridge: Cambridge University Press, 1979.

Nandy, Ashis. *The Intimate Enemy: Loss and Recovery of Self Under Colonialism.* Delhi, India: Oxford University Press, 1983.

Nettl, J. P. *Rosa Luxemburg.* Abriged ed. Oxford: Oxford University Press, 1969.

Ngugi wa Thiong'o. *Decolonising the Mind: The Politics of Language in African Literature.* London: James Currey, 1986.

Nietzsche, Friedrich. *The Birth of Tragedy.* In *Basic Writings of Nietzsche.* Ed. and trans. Walter Kaufmann. New York: Modern Library, 1968.

Nisbett, Richard, and Lee Ross. *Human Inference: Strategies and Shortcomings of Social Judgment.* Englewood Cliffs, N.J.: Prentice-Hall, 1980.

Norris, Christopher. *Uncritical Theory: Postmodernism, Intellectuals, and the Gulf War.* Amherst: University of Massachusetts Press, 1992.

Nussbaum, Martha. *Love's Knowledge: Essays on Philosophy and Literature.* New York: Oxford University Press, 1990.

Ong, Walter J., S.J. "The Jinnee in the Well Wrought Urn." *The Barbarian Within and Other Fugitive Essays and Studies.* New York: Macmillan, 1972.

———. *Orality and Literacy: The Technologizing of the Word.* London: Methuen, 1982.

Orgel, Stephen. "Teaching the Postmodern Renaissance." Haggerty and Zimmerman.

Oxfam America. *In a World of Abundance, Why Hunger?* New York: Oxfam America, 1991. (Reprinted on HungerNet, 1995.)

Pandit, B. N., ed. and trans. *Essence of the Exact Reality or Paramarthasara of Abhinavagupta.* New Delhi, India: Munshiram Manoharlal, 1991.

Pandit, Lalita. "Caste, Race, and Nation: History and Dialectic in Rabindranath Tagore's *Gora.*" Hogan and Pandit, *Literary India.*

———. "Patriarchy and Paranoia: Imaginary Infidelity in *Uttararamacarita* and *The Winter's Tale.*" Hogan and Pandit, *Literary India.*

Pannekoek, Anton. *Lenin as Philosopher.* New York: Breakout Press, 1975.

Parekh, Bhikhu. *Marx's Theory of Ideology.* Baltimore, Md.: Johns Hopkins University Press, 1982.

Paton, Alan. *Cry, the Beloved Country.* New York: Collier Books, 1987.

Pavel, Thomas. *Fictional Worlds.* Cambridge, Mass.: Harvard University Press, 1986.

Peters, Douglas, and Stephen Ceci. "Peer-review practices of psychological journals: The fate of published articles, submitted again." *Behavioral and Brain Sciences* 5.2 (1982): 187–95.

Plato. "Ion." Adams.

———. *The Republic*. Vol. 4 of *The Dialogues of Plato*. Trans. Benjamin Jowett. Ed. R. M. Hare and D. A. Russell. London: Sphere Books, 1970.

Popper, Karl. *The Logic of Scientific Discovery*. New York: Harper and Row, 1968.

Poulet, Georges. "Phenomenology of Reading." Adams.

Pratt, Mary Louise. *Toward a Speech Act Theory of Literary Discourse*. Bloomington: Indiana University Press, 1977.

Putnam, Hilary. *Reason, Truth, and History*. Cambridge: Cambridge University Press, 1981.

*Questiones Féministes*. "Variations on Common Themes." Marks and de Courtivron.

Quine, Willard Van Orman. *Theories and Things*. Cambridge, Mass.: Harvard University Press, 1981.

———. "Two Dogmas of Empiricism." *From a Logical Point of View: Logico-Philosophical Essays*. 2nd ed. New York: Harper and Row, 1961.

———. *The Ways of Paradox and Other Essays*. Rev. ed. Cambridge: Harvard University Press, 1976.

———. *Word and Object*. Cambridge, Mass.: MIT Press, 1960.

Rapaport, Herman. *Heidegger and Derrida: Reflections on Time and Language*. Lincoln: University of Nebraska Press, 1989.

Richardson, Robert D. *The Works of Sir William Jones*. Vol. 2. New York: Garland, 1984.

Richter, David, ed. *The Critical Tradition: Classic Texts and Contemporary Trends*. New York: St. Martin's, 1989.

Ricoeur, Paul. *Freud and Philosophy: An Essay on Interpretation*. Trans. Denis Savage. New Haven, Conn.: Yale University Press, 1977.

Rorty, Richard. "Texts and Lumps." Vol. 1 of *Objectivity, Relativism, and Truth: Philosophical Papers*. New York: Cambridge University Press, 1991.

Rowbotham, S. "What's in a Name?" *Z Magazine* (May 1991).

Russell, Bertrand. *Human Knowledge: Its Scope and Limits*. New York: Simon and Schuster, 1967.

———. *Logic and Knowledge: Essays, 1901–1950*. Ed. Robert Marsh. New York: G. P. Putnam's Sons, 1971.

———. *Principles of Mathematics*. New York: W. W. Norton, n.d.

Said, Edward. *Culture and Imperialism*. New York: Alfred Knopf, 1993.

Sartre, Jean-Paul. *Being and Nothingness*. Trans. Hazel Barnes. New York: Washington Square, 1966.

Schelling, F. W. J. *Schellings Werke*. Vol. 2. Ed. Manfred Schroter. Munich: Beck, 1927–28.

———. *System of Transcendental Idealism (1800)*. Trans. Peter Heath. Charlottesville: University Press of Virginia, 1978.

Schiller, Friedrich. *On the Aesthetic Education of Man in a Series of Letters*. Trans. Reginald Snell. London: Routledge and Kegan Paul, 1954.

Schilpp, Paul Arthur, ed. *The Philosophy of Rudolf Carnap*. La Salle, Ill.: Open Court, 1963.

Scholes, Robert. *Textual Power: Literary Theory and the Teaching of English*. New Haven, Conn.: Yale University Press, 1985.

Schor, Juliet. *The Overworked American: The Unexpected Decline of Leisure*. New York: Basic Books, 1991.

Schwab, Raymond. *The Oriental Renaissance: Europe's Rediscovery of India and the East, 1680–1880*. Trans. Gene Patterson-Black and Victor Reinking. New York: Columbia University Press, 1984.

Searle, John R. *Speech Acts: An Essay in the Philosophy of Language*. Cambridge: Cambridge University Press, 1969.

Sedlar, Jean. *India and the Greek World: A Study in the Transmission of Culture*. Totowa, N.J.: Rowman and Littlefield, 1980.

Seilman, Uffe, and Steen Larsen. "Personal Resonance to Literature: A Study of Remindings while Reading." *Poetics* 18 (1989): 165–77.

Shakespeare, William. *The Tragedy of Othello The Moor of Venice*. Ed. Alvin Kernan. New York: Signet, 1986.

Shelley, Percy Bysshe. "A Defense of Poetry." Adams.

Shklovsky, Victor. "Art as Technique." Richter.

Showalter, Elaine. "Feminist Criticism in the Wilderness." *Writing and Sexual Difference*. Ed. Elizabeth Abel. Chicago: University of Chicago Press, 1982.

Spiegelberg, Herbert. *The Phenomenological Movement: A Historical Introduction*. 3rd ed. The Hague, Netherlands: Martinus Nijhoff, 1982.

Spivak, Gayatri Chakravorty. *In Other Worlds: Essays in Cultural Politics*. New York: Routledge, 1987.

Spolsky, Ellen. *Gaps in Nature: Literary Interpretation and the Modular Mind*. Albany: State University of New York Press, 1993.

Strawson, P. F. "Meaning and Truth." *Philosophy As It Is*. Ed. Ted Honderich and Myles Burnyeat. New York: Penguin Books, 1979.

Taylor, Gabriele. "Love." *Philosophy As It Is*. Ed. Ted Honderich and Myles Burnyeat. New York: Penguin Books, 1979.

Taylor, Gary. *Cultural Selection*. New York: Basic Books, 1996.

Van Fraassen, Bas C. "The World We Speak Of, and the Language We Live In." *Philosophie et Culture: Actes du XVIIe Congrès Mondial de Philosophie (Montréal 1983)*. Ed. Venant Cauchy. Vol. 1. Montréal: Édition du Beffroi/Éditions Montmorency, 1986.

Veeser, H. Aram, ed. *The New Historicism*. New York: Routledge, 1989.

Wartofsky, Marx. *Feuerbach*. Cambridge: Cambridge University Press, 1977.

Wellek, René. *A History of Modern Criticism, 1750–1950*. Vol. 2. Cambridge: Cambridge University Press, 1981.

Whorf, Benjamin Lee. *Language, Thought, and Reality: Selected Writings of Benjamin Lee Whorf*. Ed. John B. Carroll. Cambridge, Mass.: MIT Press, 1956.

Wiesner, Merry. "Women's Defense of Their Public Role." *Women in the Middle*

*Ages and the Renaissance: Literary and Historical Perspectives*. Ed. Mary Beth Rose. Syracuse, N.Y.: Syracuse University Press, 1986.

Williams, Raymond. "Base and Superstructure in Marxist Cultural Theory." *Problems in Materialism and Culture: Selected Essays*. New York: Verso, 1980.

Wimsatt, W. K., and Monroe Beardsley. "The Affective Fallacy." Adams.

———. "The Intentional Fallacy." Adams.

Wittgenstein, Ludwig. *On Certainty*. Ed. G. E. M. Anscombe and G. H. von Wright. Trans. Denis Paul and G. E. M. Anscombe. New York: Harper and Row, 1972.

———. *Philosophical Investigations*. 3rd Ed. Trans. G. E. M. Anscombe. New York: Macmillan Publishing, 1958.

———. *Tractatus Logico-Philosophicus*. Trans. D. F. Pears and B. F. McGuinness. London: Routledge and Kegan Paul, 1961.

———. *Zettel*. Ed. G. E. M. Anscombe and G. H. von Wright. Trans. Denis Paul and G. E. M. Anscombe. Oxford: Basil Blackwell, 1967.

# Index

Abhinavagupta, 5, 13, 35–37, 39–42, 49, 74, 115, 156, 157, 294, 305–8
Abrahams, Peter, 161, 162
Absorption (Dewey), 155
Absurdity (Sartre), 127
Actual world, 269–72
Ad hoc qualifications, 319, 323, 325, 326, 332–34
Adorno, Theodor, 69, 118, 216
Aesthetical ideas (Kant), 61, 82
Aesthetic disinterest, 58, 60, 67
Aesthetic distance (Jauss), 142, 143
Aesthetic education, 66, 67, 78, 155, 215
Aesthetic theory (definition), 1–3
Affective fallacy, 144
Affective theory (definition), 3
Alaṃkāra, 27, 32, 33, 35, 36
Al-Fārābī, 5, 27, 31
Ali, Agha Shahid, 9, 96, 218, 221, 252, 302–4
Alienation, 78, 84, 205
Al-Jurjānī, 31
Al-Qarṭajannī, 30
American dream, 212
Amin, Samir, 94
Analysis (Foucault), 182
Analytic philosophy, 4, 7, 118, 253, 255, 260, 261, 264, 269
Ānandavardhana, 5, 13, 35–40, 307
Anarchism, 93, 171, 313
Anarkali, 222, 243, 252
Androcentrism, 249, 250
Anglo-American linguistic theory, 253, 286–95. See also Cognitive science
Anglo-American philosophy of language, 253–86; and logical formalism, 253–73; and meaning in use, 253, 273–86
Angst, 123, 124
Anscombe, Elizabeth, 7, 253, 254, 259, 277, 278
Antifoundationalism, 53
Antithesis (dialectic), 72–74, 79, 81, 90
Antiuniversalism, 103
Anubhāvas. See Consequents
'Apithana, 23
Apollonian, 63, 85–87
A posteriori knowledge, 258
Apparatus, 187, 188
Appropriation (Greenblatt), 192
A priori knowledge, 49, 53, 258, 312
Aristocracy, 95, 97, 98, 101, 102
Aristophanes, 26
Aristotelians, 29, 43, 135
Aristotle, 4, 5, 13, 16–31, 41–44, 61, 78, 131, 272, 314
Asiatic mode of production, 94
Associations, 37–40, 42, 47, 115, 147, 296, 306
Ātman, 33, 36
Austin, J. L., 7, 114, 118, 253, 254, 278, 282, 283
Authenticity (Heidegger), 122–25, 130, 131
Authoritative discourse, 186, 187, 223, 224, 226–29
Authority, rules of (Foucault), 185, 186
Automatization of language, 222, 223
Avant-garde art, 58, 200, 214–16
Averroes. See Ibn Rushd
Avicenna. See Ibn Sīnā
Ayer, A. J., 253, 254, 260, 261

Bacchic, 84, 85

Baconian, 7

Bad faith, 201, 203, 204

Baker, Houston, 323

Bakhtin, M. M., 7, 63, 123, 219, 223–29

Balibar, Étienne, 100, 102

Base. *See* Economic base

Base/superstructure model, 91

Baudelaire, Charles, 221

Baudrillard, Jean, 6, 158, 205, 206, 208–11, 217

Beardsley, Monroe, 144, 147

Beauty, 2, 13, 30, 36, 37, 44, 47–51, 54–63, 66–68, 70, 85–87, 89, 104, 122, 215, 262, 291

Bedeutung (Habermas), 136, 137

Being (Heidegger), 118, 121–25, 130, 132; originary unconcealedness of, 122, 129–32, 247

Being-for-itself, 126–29

Being-in-itself, 126–29

Being-in-the-world, 119–26, 128, 129, 131, 132, 136, 152, 250

Being-towards-death, 123–25

Being-with Others, 120, 125

Bennett, Tony, 89

Bentham, Jeremy, 183

*Bhagavad Gita*, 73, 74

Bhāmaha, 33

Bharata-muni, 33, 34, 39

Bhaskar, Roy, 7, 313, 328–30

*Bhāvas*, 34

Bias. *See* Evaluation

Biblical interpretation, 133

Bi-implication. *See* Logical connectives

Binary opposition, 235, 244, 250, 251

Blame, 29, 30

Bleich, David, 311

Bloom, Leopold, 142

Booby, Lady, 141

Boole, George, 254

Bordwell, David, 314

Boudon, Raymond, 159

Bourdieu, Pierre, 6, 158, 179, 191, 196–204

Bourgeoisie, 92, 96–98, 101–3, 163, 199, 200, 202, 203, 209, 212, 215, 296

Bracketing, 108, 109

Brentano, Franz, 109

Burke, Edmund, 5, 43–49, 56, 65

Butcher, S. H., 18, 23

Butler, Judith, 179

Cameron, Deborah, 168, 175

Canon, literary, 178

Cantarino, Vicente, 27

Capital, circuit of, 99, 100

Capitalism, 138, 150–52, 159, 160, 163, 200–202, 204, 213, 216, 217, 329; contradictions of, 98, 100, 101; industrial, 90, 91, 94–97; mercantile, 97, 102

Capitalists, 92, 95–97, 100, 206

Carceral system, 183

Care (Heidegger), 119–24

Carnap, Rudolph, 254, 269, 316

Carnival (Bakhtin), 227, 228

Cassio, 25, 189, 285, 318

Categories of the understanding (Kant), 52, 53

Categorization (Foucault), 181, 184

Catharsis, 18, 19, 24, 27, 41, 42

Ceci, Stephen, 337

Central Park jogger, 174

Change of fortune (Aristotle), 23. *See also* Reversal

Channel (Jakobson), 220

Character (Aristotle), 19, 20

Chatterji, Jagadish, 157

China, 27, 291, 292

Chomsky, Noam, 7, 173, 197, 217, 239, 250, 253, 286–90, 294. *See also* Anglo-American linguistic theory; Transformational grammar

City, 97

Cixous, Hélène, 175, 176

Clark Bekederemo, J. P., 144

Class concept, 90, 94

Classical art (Hegel), 82, 83, 85, 86
Class struggle, 90, 94
Code (Jakobson), 220
Cognitive science, 7, 225, 253, 293–308, 313, 314, 324, 325; computer analogy in, 295, 296, 298, 299
Cognitive theory (definition), 3
Coleridge, Samuel Taylor, 5, 43, 63, 66, 68–70, 77
Colonialism, 62, 102, 103, 169, 170, 174
Combinative axis. See Syntagmatic axis
Comedy, 19, 20, 26, 29, 40, 84, 85, 102, 207, 291, 292, 300–302, 306, 307
Comic mask, 26
Commodities (Marx), 92, 96–98, 199, 205, 210, 211
Commodity stage (Baudrillard), 210
Common sense. See Common sensibility
Common sensibility, 54, 59
Communication-intention, 273, 278, 279, 282
Communicative action, 136, 138–40
Communicative situation (Jakobson), 220
Communism, 90–95, 98, 104, 171, 210; left-wing, 93; primitive/pre-accumulative, 94, 95; statist, 92, 93
Competence (Chomsky), 286–89
Complication (Aristotle), 24
Comrie, Bernard, 289
Concepts (Kant), 52, 53, 55–57, 59, 61
Conceptual scheme, 264–66
Concretization, 116, 117, 140, 141
Confirmation bias. See Evaluation
Consciousness raising, 206, 209
Consecration (Bourdieu), 200, 201
Consequents (Sanskrit aesthetics), 34, 35
Consistency. See Logical consistency
Constable, John, 267
Constatives, 282
Constitution (Husserl), 109–15, 117, 118, 120, 143, 145, 244–46
Construal, 277, 278
Constructivism, 179

Consumerism, 211, 212, 216
Context (Jakobson), 220–22
Controlled distancing (Habermas), 139
Conversational implicature, 279, 284. See also Maxims of conversational implicature
Cooperative principle, 279–81, 284
Co-optation, 205, 215–17
Copyright, 103
Corneille, Pierre, 4
Cornwall, 195
Corroboration, 318
Counterfactuals, 269–71
Counterparts, 270
Countryside, 95–97
Creativity, 19, 65, 141
Culler, Jonathan, ix
Cult (Hegel), 84, 85
Cultural capital, 200, 202
Cultural field. See Field (of culture)
Cultural identity, 177–79
Cultural Poetics, 190, 196
Culture: bourgeois, 200, 202; elite, 199–202; popular, 199–203
Culture study, 6, 196
Cyberneticization, 206, 208
Cyborg, 213, 214

Dahiyat, Ismail, 28, 29
Dasein, 119, 121, 123–26, 130, 152
Dasenbrock, Reed Way, 269
Davidson, Donald, 7, 253, 254, 261, 262, 266–70, 329–31
Death. See Being-towards-death
Death instinct, 63
De Beaugrande, Robert, 312
De Beauvoir, Simone, 107, 128, 129, 167, 173, 179
Deconstruction, 5, 7, 63, 108, 175, 177, 190, 214, 219, 223, 225, 235, 244–52, 276, 286, 287, 319, 322–24, 332
Deconstructive reversal, 248, 252
Defacement, 30

Defamiliarization, 142
Default hierarchy, 297
Deferral, 244–46, 249, 250, 252
Definite description, 259, 260
Definition, 259, 261, 263, 264, 296, 297
De Lauretis, Teresa, 179
Delinquency, 183
De Man, Paul, 287
Democracy, 98, 103, 160, 299
Demonic possession, 185, 194
Demystification, 103
Denotation, 35
Denouement, 24
Derealization, 208
De Santillan, Diego Abad, 93
De Saussure, Ferdinand, 7, 219, 229, 287, 288
Descartes, René, 113, 260
Descriptive adequacy, 288, 289, 292, 293
Desdemona, 21, 25, 37, 38, 40, 87, 102, 103, 124, 125, 128, 135, 140, 145, 187, 189, 195, 199, 228, 229, 237–39, 277, 278, 284, 334
Design (Aristotle), 22
De Stael, Germaine (Madame), 5, 43, 66, 78, 79
Destruction (Heidegger), 247
Determinants (Sanskrit aesthetics), 34, 35
Dewey, John, 6, 107, 118, 149, 152–57
*Dhvani* (suggestion), 5, 27, 32, 33, 35–39, 42, 192, 307; attitude, 39; *alaṃkāradhvani* 35, 36; *rasadhvani*, 35–38, 74, 156, 157, 305, 306, 308, 309; *vastudhvani*, 35, 36
Diachronic, 230, 231
Dialectical materialism, 89–91
Dialectics, 79, 80, 82–84, 88–91, 94, 217
Dialogism, 219, 225, 226, 228, 229
Didion, Joan, 174
*Differance*, 190, 245–49, 252
Difference (Saussure, Derrida), 224, 233–35, 244–50, 252
Differences, system of, 233–35, 244–50
Dionysian, 63, 85–87
Discipline (Foucault), 182, 185–87, 190, 193

Disclosure (Heidegger), 122, 129, 132
Disconfirmation. *See* Falsification
Discourse (Foucault), 180, 184–88, 190, 191, 193
Discourse of authority. *See* Authoritative discourse
Discriminatory empirical data, 332
Discursive formation (Foucault), 185, 187, 193
Disinterest. *See* Aesthetic disinterest
Display text, 284
Dissociation of sensibility, 67
Distribution, relations of, 92
Dogmatism (Fichte), 71
Doings (Dewey), 152, 153
Domain (cognitive science), 298
Dreyfus, Hubert, 186, 187
Duhem, Pierre, 319, 332

Earman, John, 329
Eco, Umberto, 178, 271, 320
Economic base, 88, 89, 91, 93
Economic class, 90–96, 98–101, 104
Economic superstructure, 91
Economism, 90
*Écriture féminine*, 176
Ego (Sartre), 127, 128
Eidetic reduction, 110, 111, 246, 247
E-language, 287
Eliot, T. S., 67, 302–5
Ellmann, Richard, 159
Elster, Jon, 166
Embellishment, 30
Emotion: cause of, 278; discharge of (Dewey), 155; expression of, 65; object of, 278
Empirical poetics, 7, 253, 307–12
*Énoncé. See* Statement
Entailment. *See* Logical connectives (implication)
Epic, 13, 26, 84, 101, 302; Bakhtin on, 223, 225–29
Episteme, 185–87, 191; Classical, 180–82,

184; Modern, 180–83, 185; Renaissance, 180, 181, 184, 185, 187

Epistemology, 43, 51, 68, 330

Epoché, 108

Epstein, Cynthia Fuchs, 175

Equipment (Heidegger), 120, 121, 124

Eros, 63

Error. See Flaw

Essences, 110, 111, 117, 120, 246, 277

Ethical/political theory (definition), 1, 3

Ethics, 24, 25, 50, 51, 261, 273

Ethnocentrism, 213

Eulogy, 29

Evaluation, 2, 7; and confirmation bias, 336–38; and economic bias, 335–38; and institutional prestige, 337, 338

Exempla, 295, 297, 298, 300–306, 323

Existentialism, 6, 107, 108, 118–29

Experience (Dewey), 150, 152–57; completeness of, 153, 155; incoherence of, 153, 154; mechanical quality of, 153–55

Experiential propositions (Ayer), 261

Experiential theory (definition), 3

Explanatory adequacy, 288, 289, 292

Expressivism, 63

Extension, 259, 260, 263, 266, 267, 275, 276, 280, 300

Faculties of the mind (Kant), 51, 54, 55, 59, 61, 62, 66

Faiz, Faiz Ahmed, 36–38, 303, 304

Fallenness (Heidegger), 125

False consciousness, 206

Falsification, 318, 320, 322, 323, 326, 337, 338; ethics of, 319, 320

Falsity, 258, 263, 330, 331; and logic, 255, 256

Faludi, Susan, 179

Fancy, 45, 68

Fanon, Frantz, 127

Fascism, 125

Faulkner, William, 91

Faust, David, 337

Fausto-Sterling, Anne, 168, 174, 175

Fear, 16, 18, 19, 23–25, 30, 40, 42, 48, 61, 131

Felicity conditions, 283, 285

Feminism, 6, 158, 167–79, 213, 236, 262; basic, 169–71, 173, 174, 178; of cultural identity, 177, 179; egalitarian, 172, 173; empirical, 174, 175; of gender difference, 169, 176; of human diversity, 176, 179; of justice, 173, 174, 178; minimal, 171; reflective, 174, 175; separatist, 171–73; of solidarity, 173, 174, 178; standard, 169, 171; supremacist, 173; utopian, 171, 173, 178

Feminist critique, 178

Fetishism (Marx), 98, 99, 205

Feudalism, 92, 94, 97

Feyerabend, Paul, 313, 327–30, 335, 338

Fichte, J. G., 5, 43, 53, 68, 71–75, 77, 79, 80, 83, 85, 88, 89, 113, 126, 127

Field (Bourdieu), 196–202; autonomous, 196, 197, 199, 202, 314; heteronomous, 197, 202; of culture, 199, 201, 202

Fielding, Henry, 141

Fish, Stanley, 107, 144–46, 240, 269, 276, 283, 322

Five-stage theory, 93

Flaw, 17, 19, 24–26

Flourishing (Nussbaum), 238

Fodor, Jerry, 294

Foregrounding, 221, 223

Foreknowing, 129–31, 133

For-itself. See Being-for-itself

Formalism. See Anglo-American philosophy of language; Russian formalism

Form drive, 66, 85

Form of life, 275, 276

Foucault, Michel, 7, 93, 118, 158, 173, 177, 179–93

Foundationalism, 53

Fractal stage (Baudrillard), 211

Frailty. See Flaw

Frame of reference, 266

Freedom, 123, 124, 126, 127, 129, 169
Frege, Gottlob, 254, 259
Freud, Sigmund, 2, 47, 63, 132
Frye, Northrop, 4, 145, 240, 292
Fusion of horizons, 134, 135

Gadamer, Hans-Georg, 6, 107, 118, 129,
    131–36, 138, 142, 229
Gaps (Iser), 141
Garraty, John, 91, 101
Gay, Peter, 91, 101
Geertz, Clifford, 193
Gender, 169, 174–76, 179, 214, 311, 317
Generative grammar, 288, 289
Generative poetics, 289, 302
Genius, 59, 60, 76, 77
Genre, 28, 142, 143, 225, 227, 271, 291, 300–
    302, 305; paradigmatic, 314
German Idealism, 53, 68, 71–85, 88, 111,
    122, 139, 158
Gerow, Edwin, 33
Geuss, Raymond, 159
Gilligan, Carol, 176
Goldman, Emma, 93
Goldman, Lucien, 229
Goodman, Nelson, 266, 267
Good Samaritan, parable of, 32
Graff, Gerald, 216
Grammar, 197, 262, 292, 293; internalized,
    287, 288; transformational, 289, 321
Greenberg, Joseph, 286, 288, 289
Greenblatt, Stephen, 158, 190–96, 228
Greimas, A. J., 219, 235, 236, 239
Grice, Paul, 7, 253, 254, 278–81, 284, 285
Guérin, Daniel, 93
Gulf War, 160, 208, 209

Habermas, Jürgen, 6, 107, 129, 136–40
Habitual criminality, 183
Habituation, habitualization, 54, 55, 59, 73,
    154, 220, 223
Habitus, 196–99
Halhed, Nathaniel, 73

Hamlet, 127
Haraway, Donna, 158, 213, 214
Harsnett, Samuel, 194
Hauser, Arnold, 97, 101
Hegel, G.W.F., 5, 14, 43, 66, 69, 73, 77–89
Heidegger, Martin, 6, 77, 107, 108, 118–27,
    129–32, 134, 136, 140, 152, 244, 247, 250,
    273
Hempel, Carl, 316
Hermeneutic application, 133, 135
Hermeneutic circle, 129–31, 135
Hermeneutic interpretation, 133, 135
Hermeneutics, 6, 9, 107, 108, 118, 129–42,
    193, 244, 247, 267; of revelation,
    suspicion, 8, 164
Hermeneutic understanding, 133, 135
Hernadi, Paul, 295
Hesse, Mary, 328
Heteroglossia, 214, 226–29
Heterosexism, 213
Hiatt, Mary, 175, 179
Hierarchization of theories, 331
Hinduism, 41, 73, 74, 77, 85, 303
Hirsch, E. D., 107, 131, 146, 147
Historically effected consciousness, 134, 135
Historical materialism, 5, 6, 43, 88–104, 162
Historicism, 6, 66, 78, 79, 89, 142, 158, 175,
    179, 190, 192, 193, 195, 196, 202
Historicity, 116, 190
Historiography, 22, 79, 177
Hobbs, Jerry, 295
Holistic science, 264, 265
Homology, 165, 202, 203, 236, 238, 239, 243,
    250
Horace, 4
Horizons, 109–12, 134, 135, 142, 143, 145;
    of expectation, 112, 143
Horkheimer, Max, 69, 118, 216
Human (definition of), 64–67, 70
Humanities, 27, 64, 65, 320, 336
Hume, David, 4, 5, 43, 44, 49–51, 56
Husserl, Edmund, 6, 107–14, 118, 132, 140,
    141, 145, 244–46, 248, 260, 276

Hypostatization, 121, 128, 268, 281, 289, 294, 307–12, 314, 316, 319, 334

Hypotheses, 4, 8, 260, 268, 281, 289, 294, 307–12, 314, 316, 319, 334; generation of, 310, 312

Ibn Rushd, 5, 27–30

Ibn Sīnā, 5, 13, 27, 28, 30, 31

Idea (Plato), 14, 15, 18, 88

Idealism, 5, 6, 43, 52–54, 65, 68–74, 76, 77, 79, 88–91, 111, 122, 127, 139, 145, 149, 158, 184, 250, 276

Ideas of reason, 53, 61, 62

Ideology, 6, 93, 102, 103, 138, 150, 158–67, 172, 175, 209; capitalist, 159; critique of, 158, 163–67, 178, 179; epistemic component, 159, 160, 162, 163; functional component, 159, 162–67; genetic component, 159, 166, 167; telic component, 159, 161–63

Idiolect, 275, 286, 287

Idle talk (Heidegger), 123, 129

Iftikhar-Ul-Awwal, 96

Illocution (Austin), 282

Imagination, 39, 44–46, 48, 50, 52, 54, 55, 59–61, 65, 66, 68–70, 141, 156, 162; productive, 73

Imaginative assent. See Takhayyul

Imaginative creation. See Takhyīl

Imaginative variation, 110, 111, 120, 246

Imitation, 13, 15–20, 27, 29, 30, 31, 44–46, 60, 65, 192, 271, 314

Implication. See Logical connectives

Implicature. See Conversational implicature

In-itself. See Being-in-itself

Inauthenticity (Heidegger), 123, 125

Incommensurability, 329, 332

Indic literary theory. See Literary theory (South Asian)

Individualism, 41, 101

Induction, 316, 317

Inductivism, 314

Influence, 290, 301, 302, 305

Ingalls, Daniel, 35

Ingarden, Roman, 6, 107, 114–18, 140, 141

Innateness hypothesis, 289

Innovation, 33, 49, 131, 150, 216

Inspiration. See Poetic inspiration

Instantiation, 257, 284

Institutions, 172, 178, 180–83, 185, 186, 188, 194

Instrumental view of literature, 13, 16

Intellect (Fichte), 66–68, 72, 75, 77

Intending subject, 109

Intention, 263, 264, 277. See also Communication-intention; Intentionalism

Intentional correlates, 115

Intentionalism, 107, 140, 145–49, 269

Intentional object, 109–11, 113

Internally persuasive discourse, 224, 225, 228

Interpretation, 1, 2; Foucault on, 181, 182, 184, 185, 188, 191; in logic, 257–59; validity in, 7, 8, 148

Interpretive community, 145, 146

Introspection, 197, 308

Irigaray, Luce, 167, 168, 174, 175, 179

Irreality, 208

Iser, Wolfgang, 107, 114, 141–43, 300

Isotopy, 236, 237

Jakobson, Roman, 7, 219–21, 284, 286

James, Joy, 174

James, William, 107, 149–52

Jameson, Fredric, 6, 158, 173, 207, 208, 210, 216–28

Janko, Richard, 26

Jauss, Hans Robert, 107, 114, 141–43, 229, 300

Jenkins, Richard, 204

Jhally, Sut, 160

Johnson, Mark, 299

Johnson, Randal, 197

Johnson-Laird, Philip, 293, 296, 301

Jones, William, 55, 59, 74, 77

Joyce, James, 91, 142, 159, 267
Judgment: Burke on, 44, 46–48; Kant on, 51, 53, 55–58, 60

Kant, Immanuel, 4–6, 43, 44, 51–63, 65–67, 69, 71, 75, 82, 83, 126, 158, 206, 207, 215, 258, 268, 335
Karma, 42
*Karuṇarasa*. See Pathos; *Rasa*
Kavanagh, Patrick, 42
Keats, John, 70, 73, 77
*King Lear*, 193, 194
Kiparsky, Paul, 280, 289, 292, 293
Kittay, Eva, 299
Knapp, Stephen, 107, 147, 148
Konstanz School, 141
Kripke, Saul, 254, 269
Kristeva, Julia, 168
Kropotkin, Peter, 93
Kuhn, Thomas, 7, 313, 320–27, 329, 330, 332
Kuntaka, 33

Labor, 92, 93, 104
Labov, William, 22, 284
Lacan, Jacques, 118, 127, 177, 229, 244, 280
Lakatos, Imre, 7, 313, 324–27, 332, 338
Lakoff, George, 299
Lal, P., 34
Landlords, 92, 252
Language: autonomous, 3; ornamentation of, 19, 20, 26, 27, 30, 32; poetic, 220–23; private, 275, 276, 287, 288. *See also Langue*; Philosophy of language
Language game, 274–76
*Langue*, 230, 231, 286–88
Larsen, Steen, 308
Laughter, 47, 227, 228
Law (Renaissance), 187, 195
Laws of beauty (Marx), 89, 104
Legal interpretation, 133
Legitimation principles, 200, 201
Lenin, V. I., 93

Lentricchia, Frank, 151
Lévi-Strauss, Claude, 219, 221, 229, 235, 239–41
Lewis, David, 272
Lewis, Justin, 160
Lexical access, 40, 300, 305–8
Lexical activation, 79, 305, 306, 308
Lexical priming, 40, 42, 305–8
Lexical search, 305
Liddel, H. G., 23
Limbaugh, Rush, 215
Line length. *See* Poetic line length
Literariness, 220
Literary realism, 214
Literary theory: Arabic, 26–32; definition, 1; descriptive, 1, 2; linguistic, 3; mentalistic, 3; normative, 1, 2; social, 3; South Asian, 32–42
Liu Hsieh, 301
Livingston, Paisley, 269
Locution (Austin), 282, 283
Logic, 253–64, 268, 269, 272–74, 279, 299, 315, 316, 317, 320, 329, 332, 335, 336, 338
Logical atomism, 7
Logical connectives: bi-implication, 256; conjunction, 256, 257; disjunction, 257; implication, 255, 256, 258, 260, 279
Logical consistency, 260
Logical positivism, 7, 253, 254, 260–64, 272, 273, 315, 316, 320, 329, 330
Logocentrism, 63, 248–51, 331
Longinus, 63
Lukács, Georg, 90, 91, 98
Luxemburg, Rosa, 93
Lyotard, Jean François, 6, 158, 212–17

Machlup, Fritz, 336
Maclean, Ian, 187, 195
*Mahākāvya*, 32
Mahoney, Michael, 337
Majnoon, 303, 304
Mandel, Ernst, 216

Manifold of intuition. *See* Sensible manifold

Mannerism, 102

Manner of poetry, 16, 19, 20

Marcus, Ruth, 269

Marcuse, Herbert, 206, 209

Marriage practices, 101–3, 127, 186, 187, 192, 196, 199, 212, 215, 282

Marx, Karl, 4, 6, 78, 88–104, 150, 152, 156, 158, 205

Master narratives, 212–16

Materialism, 5, 6, 43, 88–91, 162

Maxims of conversational implicature, 184, 185; flouting of, 281, 285; manner, 280; quality, 279, 280; quantity, 280, 281, 284, 285; relevance, 279–81, 284

Maxims of reason, 35

*Māyā*, 74, 85, 86

Meaning, 1; family resemblance view of, 276, 277; primary, 35–37; secondary, 35–37; speaker's (Grice), 278, 279, 281; stipulation of, 263; and use, 273, 274; varieties of, 263; verifiability criterion for, 261

Medium of poetry (Aristotle), 19

Memory, 303, 305–7; long-term, 294; perceptual, 293, 295, 298; representational, 293, 294, 296, 305; skill, 293–96, 305; working, 294, 295, 298, 305

Memory traces (Abhinavagupta), 39, 40, 42, 307

Mental cause (Anscombe), 277, 278

Mental lexicon, 269, 298, 305–7

Mercy, 30–32, 84

Merleau-Ponty, Maurice, 108, 118

Message (Jakobson), 220, 221, 225

Metanarratives, 212

Metaphor, 33, 35, 36, 91, 132, 192, 213, 252, 299, 300, 332

Metaphysics of presence, 246–50, 252

Metatheory, 5, 7, 313, 314

Metonymy, 35, 192

Michaels, Walter Benn, 107, 147, 148

Micro-hierarchization, 162

Mill, John Stuart, 9

Milton, John, 64, 70, 223, 302, 304

Mimesis. *See* Imitation

Mind-body problem, 80

Miner, Earl, 163, 314

Modal logic, 269

Modal operators, 269

Models (cognitive science), 295, 298–302, 304–6, 321, 329

Modernism, 58, 63, 90, 91, 158, 204, 212, 214, 216, 218

Moleschott, 88

Money, 92, 94, 95, 99, 197, 203, 210, 211, 218, 222, 241–43

Monier-Williams, Monier, 34

Monk, Ray, 273

Monologism, 226–29

Montrose, Louis, 158, 190, 191, 196

Morgan, Michael, 160

Motive (Anscombe), 277, 278

Muḥammad, 27

Mukarovsky, Jan, 222, 223

Multeity in unity (Coleridge), 68

Multi-stage process, 301

Museumization, 152, 156

Music, 18, 19, 55, 57, 59, 85, 86, 206, 215

Mystification, 103

Myth, 228, 239, 240

Names (Kripke), 259

Narrative knowledge (Lyotard), 212

Narrative voice, 16

National character (de Stael), 78

Natural attitude (Husserl), 108, 130

Naturalism, 90, 91

Natural stage (Baudrillard), 210

Nazism, 125

Necessary conditions, 40, 256, 260, 297

Necessity, 267, 269; in plot, 18, 21–23, 42, 272; retrospective, 23

Negative capability, 73, 77, 213

Neoclassicism, 48, 51, 56, 60, 63

Neurath, Otto, 315
New Comedy, 84
New Criticism, 36, 63, 146, 148, 202, 223, 224, 276
New Historicism, 6, 179, 190, 196
*Nicomachaen Ethics,* 24, 25
Nietzsche, Friedrich, 4, 5, 63, 66, 77, 85–87, 158
Nisbett, Richard, 139, 336
Noema, 109–14, 117. *See also* Intentional object
Noesis, 109, 111, 114, 144, 146
Nomological sciences, 136
Noncontradiction, law of, 54, 258
Normal science, 321–23
Normative theories (definition), 1, 2
Norris, Christopher, 208, 209, 330
Nothingness (Sartre), 126, 128
Noumenon, 52, 53, 59, 61, 62, 65, 68, 71, 72, 74–76, 81, 113, 207, 208, 246, 248
Novel, 223, 225–28
Novelistic, 225–28
Nussbaum, Martha, 50, 338

Object of poetry (Aristotle), 19, 20, 23
Observation, 315–19, 322, 327, 334, 338; theory ladenness of, 315, 318
Observation sentences, 261
Odysseus, 142
One-dimensionality (Marcuse), 209
Ong, Walter J., 107, 148
Oral speech, 249–52
Orature, 94
Ordinary language philosophy, 7, 253, 254, 257, 259, 263, 273, 276, 284, 292
Organicism, 176, 230
Originalism, 131
Originality, 60, 78
Originary unconcealedness of being. *See* Being
*Othello*: and Anscombe, 277, 278; and Aristotle, 24–26; and Bakhtin, 228, 229; and Bourdieu, 198, 199; and Burke, 47;

and concretization, 116; and Dewey, 155; and Foucault 187, 189; and Gadamer, 135; and Greimas, 237–39; and Grice, 284; and Habermas, 140; and Heidegger, 122, 124, 125; and Hirsch, 147; and historical materialism, 102, 103; and interpretive particularity, 2; and New Historicism, 195; and Nietzsche, 86, 87; and *rasadhvani,* 37, 38, 40, 41; and revelatory hermeneutics, 164; and Sartre, 128; and Schelling, 76; and speech acts, 285, 286; and theory evaluation, 315, 316, 318, 319, 322, 326, 333, 334
Other (Sartre), 127, 128
Ownership, relations of, 92, 93

Pandit, B. N., 74
Pandit, Lalita, 291
Pannekoek, Anton, 93
Panopticon, 183
Paradigm (Kuhn), 153, 321–24, 326, 327, 333
Paradigmatic alternatives, 233
Paradigmatic axis, 232, 235
Paradigmatic science, 320–26
Paradigm set, 235
Paradigm shift, 323, 333
Parekh, Bhikhu, 159
*Parole,* 230, 231, 286, 287
Passions (Burke), 47, 48
Pathos, 23, 38
Paton, Alan, 164–66
Patronage, 95, 101
Pauling, Linus, 325
Pavel, Thomas, 271
Peace, 42
Peirce, Charles Sanders, 149
Perception, 244–46, 248, 249; Dewey on, 154–56
Performance (Chomsky), 286, 287
Performatives, 282
Performativity (Lyotard), 213–16

Periodicity, 293
*Peripeteia*, 23. *See also* Reversal
Perlocution (Austin), 282
Personal resonance (Seilman and Larsen), 308
Peters, Douglas, 337
Phallocentrism, 249–51
*Phaulos*, 18
Phenomenological reduction, 108, 110, 244
Phenomenology, 5, 6, 107–18, 125, 130, 142–44, 146, 149, 158, 177, 206, 244–46, 319
Philosophical aesthetics, 5, 43–63
Philosophical realism: epistemology and ontology in, 329–31; internal, 328–30; metaphysical, 328–31; models and, 329; stipulative, 330, 331
Philosophy: of experience, 6, 107; of language, 5, 7, 219, 253, 254, 273; of mind, 5; of science, 5, 7, 8, 146, 307, 313–38
Phonocentrism, 249–51
Phonological features, 234, 235
Phonology, 230, 232, 234, 235, 239
Physicalism, 88–91
Piaget, Jean, 229
Picasso, Pablo, 58
Piety, 30, 31, 61, 62, 227
Pity, 16, 18, 19, 23, 24, 30, 48, 78, 131, 299
Plato, 4, 5, 13–19, 27, 29–31, 43, 48, 63, 70, 131
Play drive, 66, 73
Plot, 17, 39, 42, 84, 102, 144, 169, 189, 241, 242, 268, 272, 286, 291; beginning (Aristotle), 21, 22; completeness (Aristotle), 19–21; end (Aristotle), 20–24, 26; magnitude (Aristotle), 19, 20, 22; middle (Aristotle), 21, 22; and normalcy, 21; seriousness (Aristotle), 19, 20, 22; wholeness (Aristotle), 21. *See also* Necessity
Plural (English), 197, 220, 230, 239, 241, 287
Poetic craft, 13, 17

Poetic inspiration, 13, 17, 70
Poetic language. *See* Language
Poetic line length, 292, 293, 295
Poetry: vs. business, 64, 65, 67; and deceit, 27, 28; vs. history, 22, 64; humanizing effect of, 65, 69, 70; manner of, 16, 19, 20; medium of (Aristotle), 19; object of (Aristotle), 19, 20, 23; vs. philosophy, 22, 64; vs. science, 64, 65, 67, 86
Police corruption, 183
Political philosophy, 5, 87
Popper, Karl, 7, 313, 318–20, 324, 336, 338
Possibility, 269, 272, 275
Possible worlds, 253, 254, 269–72; accessibility of, 270–72; and literary realism, 271; and plot structure, 272; proximity of, 270–72, 275
Postmodern condition, 204–6, 212, 214, 217, 218
Postmodernism, 63, 204–18; culture of, 204, 205, 214–16, 218; literature of, 204, 214; theory of, 6, 204–6, 208, 217
Poulet, Georges, 114, 143, 144, 146
Power (Foucault), 177, 179–91, 193
Practical-sensuous activity, 153
Pragmatism, 6, 107, 147–57
Prague School, 220, 222
Praise, 28–30, 49, 51, 201
Pratt, Mary Louise, 7, 147, 281, 283–85
Prejudice (Gadamer), 131, 133, 134
Pre-paradigmatic science, 320, 322
Presence at hand (Heidegger), 120–22, 124, 125, 129, 131
Primal instituting, 110
Priming. *See* Lexical priming
Probability theory, 316, 317
Problematics, 160–63, 165, 166
Production: large-scale, 165, 200; means of, 92, 94, 104; relations of, 92, 93, 100; restricted, 199–201
—mode of, 91–97; dominant, 91, 92, 94, 97; emergent, 92, 94, 97; residual, 92
Production of knowledge (Foucault), 180

Productive intuition, 76, 77
Profit, 91, 92, 95, 96, 98–100, 201
Proletariat, 202
Propp, Vladimir, 4, 240
Protention, 109, 111, 117, 245
Protestantism, 101
Protocol sentences, 315–18
Prototypes, 83, 295, 297, 298, 300–302, 304–6, 321
Pseudo-entities, 262
Psychoanalysis, 34, 108, 132, 145, 167, 176, 177, 203, 250, 313, 319, 322
Publication, 103, 164, 189, 251, 336–38
Purchase (Greenblatt), 192
Purgation. See Catharsis
Putnam, Hilary, 313, 328, 330

Questions (Gadamer), 133, 135
Quine, W. V. O., 7, 253, 254, 264–67, 297, 307, 316, 318, 319, 332
Qur'ān, 27–29, 31

Rabinow, Paul, 186, 187
Racism, 3, 25, 26, 41, 47, 103, 116, 122, 125, 135, 163, 169–71, 173, 174, 198, 334, 336
Rama legends, 157
Random samples, 310, 312
Rapaport, Herman, 247
Rasa, 5, 27, 32–35, 37–42, 60, 307; ancillary, 34–37; pathos, 38, 41; peace, 42; primary, 34–37
Rasadhvani. See Dhvani
Reactions (James), 150
Reader response theory, 107, 140, 144–46, 152, 263, 299, 300
Readiness to hand (Heidegger), 120, 121, 124
Realism. See Literary realism; Philosophical realism
Reason (Kant), 51, 53, 54, 61, 62
Receiver (Jakobson), 220, 245
Reception aesthetics, 140–44
Recognition, 23, 24; Dewey on, 154, 155

Reduction. See Phenomenological reduction; Eidetic reduction
Referent, 210, 259, 260
Reflection, 54, 61, 63, 72, 85
Reformation, 101
Regulative principles (Kant), 65, 335
Reification, 98, 121
Representation (Foucault), 182, 184
Repression, repressive coercion, 159
Research program, 13, 14, 29, 30; anomalies in, 325, 326; degenerating, 326, 327; progressive, 326, 327, 330
Resemblance (Foucault), 181, 182, 184, 185
Resistance (Dewey), 153–55
Retention, 109, 111, 117
Retrospective necessity, 23
Revealed religion (Hegel), 81, 83, 85
Reversal, 23, 24, 29
Revolutionary science, 322, 323
Rg Veda, 73
Rhetoric, 29–31, 150, 327
Rhythm (Aristotle), 18–20
Ricoeur, Paul, 8, 118, 132, 138, 164
Romantic art (Hegel), 83, 85
Romantic dualism, 63
Romanticism, 5, 43, 44, 48, 60, 62, 63–88, 154–56, 206, 249, 277, 322
Romantic tragicomedy, 291, 292, 300–302, 306, 307
Rorty, Richard, 149, 152
Rosch, Eleanor, 297
Ross, Lee, 139, 336
Rowbotham, S., 168
Rudraṭa, 33
Russell, Bertrand, 253, 254, 259–62, 273, 279, 282, 329
Russian formalism, 7, 219, 220, 284
Ryle, Gilbert, 118

Sahṛdaya, 38–40
Śaivism, 74
Śāntarasa. See Peace; Rasa

Śānti, 42
Sapir, Edward, 267
Sartre, Jean-Paul, 6, 107, 108, 118, 123, 126–28, 203, 245
Satan, 64, 103, 304
Satire, 29, 227
Satisfaction conditions, 283
Scene of suffering, 23, 24
Schelling, F. W. J., 5, 43, 66, 68, 73–77, 79, 83, 88, 112, 113, 145, 276
Schemas, 294–306, 321
Schiller, Friedrich, 2, 43, 63, 67, 70, 73, 78, 85, 87, 156, 176, 215, 220
Scholes, Robert, 146
Schwab, Raymond, 74
Science (Foucault), 180, 182, 183, 185, 187
Scott, R., 23
Script (cognitive science), 296
Searle, John, 7, 253, 254, 282
Seilman, Uffe, 308
Self-positing, 74, 75, 82
Semantic analysis, 261
Semantic field, 305, 306
Seme: contextual, 235–39; definitional, 235–37
Semic nucleus, 235
Sender (Jakobson), 220, 245
Sensations (James), 150
Sense. See Sinn
Sense drive, 66, 85
Sensibility, 44–46, 48, 52, 54, 55, 59, 62, 65–67, 78; training of, 67, 155. See also Aesthetic educaton
Sensible intuition. See Sensible manifold
Sensible manifold (Kant), 51, 66, 72, 75, 207
Sensitivity (of senses), 45, 47, 49, 64, 67
Sentiment. See Rasa
Set, 254, 258, 259, 263, 274
Set theory, 254, 258, 274
Sexism, 28, 128, 172, 175, 236, 251, 336
Shakespeare, William, 9, 47, 76, 78, 83,

87, 101–4, 135, 143, 147, 189, 191–95, 198, 225, 228, 229, 237, 241. See also Othello
Shelley, Percy Bysshe, 5, 43, 66, 69, 70
Shklovsky, Victor, 220, 223
Showalter, Elaine, 168, 178, 179
Sidney, Philip, 4, 31, 32, 64, 65, 152, 200
Sign, 231, 232, 235, 250
Significance (Hirsch), 146, 147
Signified, 231, 232, 235, 245–49, 251
Signifier, 121, 231, 232
Simplicity, 268, 281, 309, 319, 324, 332–35, 338
Simpson, O. J., 122
Simulacrum, 208, 209
Simulation, 192, 210, 211
Sinn (Habermas), 136, 137
Situatedness (Sartre), 127
Śiva, 74
Slave economy, 94
Social philosophy, 78, 166
Social theories (definition), 3
Socrates, 14, 26, 86, 87, 269
Solicitude (Heidegger), 120
Sonnets (Shakespeare), 143
Sophos, 18
South Africa, 116, 117, 162, 164, 165
Space, 51, 52, 68, 115, 120, 125, 152
Spanda, 74
Spectacle: Aristotle on, 16, 20; Foucault on, 181
Speech. See Parole
Speech acts, 254, 282–86
Spiegelberg, Herbert, 108, 152
Spirit (Hegel), 79–85
Spivak, Gayatri, 175, 179
Spolsky, Ellen, 295
Spoudaios, 18–20
State, 93, 100–102, 180
Statement (Foucault), 186
Statism, 92, 93
Statistical significance, 310, 312, 316
Stereotypes, 135, 175, 336

Stipulation. *See* Meaning; Philosophical realism

Strata of a literary work (Ingarden): object, 114, 115, 116; phonic, 114, 115; schematized/aspectual, 114, 117; semantic, 114, 115

Strawson, Peter, 254, 278

Structuralism, 5, 7, 69, 89, 179–81, 185, 186, 193, 219–21, 229–44, 247, 250, 316, 319, 325

Structural stage (Baudrillard), 210, 211

Subjective purposiveness (Kant), 65, 113, 207

Subjectivism, 52, 53

Sublimity, 2, 44, 47, 48, 51, 60–63, 82, 83, 85–87, 215

Substitutive axis. *See* Paradigmatic axis

Sufficient conditions, 40, 256, 260, 297

*Suggestion.* See *Dhvani*

Superstructure. *See* Economic superstructure

Surplus wealth, 94

Surprise, 23

Surveillance, 183

Symbolic acquisition (Greenblatt), 192, 193

Symbolic art (Hegel), 82, 83

Symbolic capital, 200–202, 204

Synchronic, 230, 231

Syntagmatic axis, 232, 233, 235

Synthesis (of dialectic), 72–74, 79, 81, 82, 86, 90

*Takhayyul,* 31

*Takhyīl,* 30, 31, 77, 192

Tarski, Alfred, 261

Taste, 33, 39, 44, 45, 47, 49–51, 55–58, 79, 240, 294; judgments of, 55, 56, 58, 60; laws of, 56; moral or religious belief and, 50; rules of, 49, 51

Tautology, 260, 261

Taylor, Gary, 103

Teleology, 78, 206

Tellability, 284

Temporal expectations (Fish), 144

Temporality, 115–17, 144

Tenants, 92

Tenure, 157, 189, 190, 203, 204

Themistius, 29

Theories: and dogma, 8; fecundity of, 7; heuristic or instrumental value of, 7, 9; and holism, 264, 265; as incitements to reflection, 7, 8; validity of, 7, 8

Theory. *See* Literary theory

Theory of interpretation (definition), 1, 2

Theory of literature (definition), 1, 2

"Theses on Feuerbach," 152

Thesis (dialectic), 44, 72, 81

Thing-in-itself. *See* Noumenon

Thought (Aristotle), 20

Three unities. *See* Unities

Thrownness (Heidegger), 123, 127

Time, 51, 52, 68

Trade unions, 91

Tradition: Dewey on, 157; Gadamer on, 133–35; Habermas on, 136, 138, 140; Heidegger on, 118, 130, 132

Tragedy, 17–20, 22, 24, 26, 28, 29, 34, 78, 84–87, 128, 140, 228

Transcendental ego, 111

Transcendental intersubjectivity, 112, 113

Transcendental principles (Kant), 54, 268

Transcendental signified, 245–49, 251

Transcendental subjectivity, 111–13, 117

Transformation, 239–41

Transformational grammar, 289, 321

Transformational poetics, 289

Transformation sets, 240, 241

Translation, indeterminacy of, 265, 267

Tributary economy, 97

Truth, 255–58, 261–64, 266, 268, 269, 274, 276, 283, 317, 328, 330, 331; analytic, 258, 261, 264, 265; a posteriori, 252; a priori, 258; empirical, 258, 261; in Heidegger, 122, 129–32; and logic, 255–58, 260, 261

Truth conditions, 261, 262, 269, 274, 276, 283

Truth value, 257

Turner, Mark, 299
Tying-up. *See* Complication

*Umwelt*, 112, 113, 140, 206, 209
Unconscious, 2, 4, 75–77, 79, 87, 149, 173, 183, 263
Undergoings (Dewey), 152, 153
Understanding: Fichte on, 73; Kant on, 51, 52, 54, 55, 57, 58, 61–63, 66, 69, 77
Unified sensibility, 78
Unities, 51, 59, 69, 141
Universal grammar, 288, 289, 292, 293
Universalism, 102, 103, 329, 331
Universals, 22, 89, 286, 288–93; absolute, 289, 290, 292; formal, 290, 291; statistical, 290; substantive, 290, 291; typological, 290
Untying. *See* Denouement

*Vakrokti*, 33
Value: exchange, 211, 216, 218; sign, 210; surplus, 99, 100; use, 96, 99, 210
Vamana, 33
Van Fraassen, Bas, 313, 328, 329, 331
Van Gogh, Vincent, 122
Variables: control of, 273, 309, 310, 312; in logic, 257, 258; in research, 308, 316, 317, 322
Vastudhvani. See *Dhvani.*
Vedas, 73, 157
Veeser, H. Aram, 190

Velasquez, Diego Rodriguez de Silva y, 193
Verifiability. *See* Meaning
Verification, 318, 320, 322
Vibhāvas. *See* Determinants
Virtue, 15, 29–31, 126, 141
Voice (Bakhtin), 224–27
Voluntarism, 90

Wallerstein, Immanuel, 100, 102
Wartofsky, Marx, 88
Wavering (Fichte), 73, 74
Wellek, René, 114
Whitehead, Alfred North, 254
Whorf, Benjamin Lee, 267
Wiesner, Merry, 195
Wilkins, Charles, 73
Williams, Raymond, 92
Wimsatt, William, 144, 147
Wittgenstein, Ludwig, 7, 118, 253, 254, 273–79, 306
Woolf, Virginia, 91, 317
Wordsworth, William, 70, 73
Workers, 92, 97, 100, 101, 104, 159, 162–64, 182, 206; councils of, 93
World lines, 271; bifurcation of, 270
World making, 266
World versions, 266
Worldview, 138–40
Writing (Derrida), 249–52

Zola, Émile, 90
Zone of contact, 225

Patrick Colm Hogan is professor of English and comparative literature at the University of Connecticut. He is the author of *The Politics of Interpretation: Ideology, Professionalism, and the Study of Literature* (1990), *Joyce, Milton, and the Theory of Influence* (UPF, 1995), *On Interpretation: Meaning and Inference in Law, Psychoanalysis, and Literature* (1996), and *Colonialism and Cultural Identity: Crises of Tradition in the Anglophone Literatures of India, Africa, and the Caribbean* (2000).